Daniel R. Hittleman

Queens College, City University of New York

DEVELOPMENTAL READING, K–8

Teaching from a Whole-Language Perspective

Third Edition

MERRILL PUBLISHING COMPANY
A Bell & Howell Information Company
Columbus   Toronto   London   Melbourne

Published by Merrill Publishing Company
A Bell & Howell Information Company
Columbus, Ohio 43216

This book was set in Palatino.

Administrative Editor: Jeff Johnston
Production Coordinator: Carol Driver
Cover Designer: Cathy Watterson

Photo credits: Ben Chandler/Merrill, p. 26; Alan Cliburn, pp. 70, 74, 108; Paul
Conklin/Merrill, p. 346; Kevin Fitzsimons/Merrill, p. 7; Jean Greenwald/Merrill, pp. 3,
113, 129, 258, 262, 291; Mary Hagler/Merrill, p. 295; Carol G. Hittleman, p. 79; Lloyd
Lemmerman/Merrill, p. 172; McNeilia/Merrill, p. 193; Merrill Publishing Company, pp.
235, 275, 387; David S. Strickler/Strix Pix, pp. 21, 28, 36, 88, 122, 165, 221, 267, 304,
375, 433

Acknowledgments for excerpts in chapter 8: *A Spy in Old West Point* by Anne Emery;
Misty of Chincoteague by Marguerite Henry; *Noise in the Night* by Anne Alexander;
Tonka, the Cave Boy by Ross Hutchins; and "The Thing from Ennis Rock" by Thomas
F. Monteleone in *More Science Fiction Tales* (ed. Roger Elwood) used by permission of
the publisher, Rand McNally & Company.

Library of Congress Catalog Card Number: 87-62716
International Standard Book Number: 0-675-20871-8
Printed in the United States of America
1   2   3   4   5   6   7   8   9—92   91   90   89   88

Preface

This text gives preservice, inservice, and teachers-in-training a theoretical framework of the reading process, along with instructional strategies consistent with that perspective. It is intended for introductory courses in the methodology of reading instruction for the elementary and intermediate grades.

This book's position frames reading as a transactional process involving all aspects of language and thinking. The explanation of this process relies on my own insights as well as those of scholars, investigators, and other practitioners in the fields of whole-language learning and psycholinguistics. I presented only a single interpretation of the reading process because I believe it provides a consistent, logical, and natural picture of reading and how students become literate.

THE THIRD EDITION

When the first edition of *Developmental Reading* appeared, the instructional strategies based on the ideas of psycho- and sociolinguists were not widespread, and many educators considered them the esoteric thoughts of researchers. By the time the second edition appeared, socio- and psycholinguistic concepts were more familiar; reading practitioners were recognizing the importance of integrating the learning and teaching of reading and writing (composing). Now these ideas are appearing with greater regularity in professional journals and conferences, and they are being translated into instructional procedures in both teaching materials and in state education reading and language arts curricula.

In this edition, the current thinking of reading researchers and scholars as well as my experiences with guiding students in attaining literacy are revised, reorganized, and expanded. You will see how the development of students' reading comprehension strategies is enhanced when the teacher integrates reading and writing instruction and is mindful of the social context of literacy learning. Reading is not separated from all language learning nor from the environment of learning. The change in the subtitle—substituting *whole-language* for *psycholinguistics*—reflects this thinking. As in the previous editions, instructional strategies are presented as suggestions. The text's users are encouraged to make independent instructional decisions and to collaborate with their students and colleagues in learning about literacy.

ORGANIZATION AND CONTENT

The chapters in this text contain a broad overview of the nature and extent of reading programs in kindergarten through eighth grade. Chapter 1 contains a definition of reading and a review of society's general needs for and use of reading and writing. Chapter 2 presents evidence of the validity of the whole-language perspective in the form of whole-language models of reading as well as my own model of the act of reading. Chapter 3 contains a discussion about developing literacy readiness at any level for any type of reading material. In Chapters 4 and 5, strategies for guiding students' understanding of an author's text structure are developed; the concepts of teacher-guided student comprehension and student self-guided reading are contrasted. Chapter 6 presents a discussion of strategies for extending vocabulary and recognizing words in context. Chapter 7 has strategies for understanding content-area texts. In Chapter 8, authors' literary techniques are presented and suggestions are offered for developing students' literature appreciation and reading. Chapter 9 aims to identify some students' special needs and to provide suggestions for adapting learning strategies from previous chapters to those needs. In Chapters 10 and 11, the ideas of analytical teaching and student assessment with informal and formal tests are examined. Chapter 12 presents ideas for organizing school and classroom reading instruction; in previous editions these ideas were in other chapters. Chapter 13 contains the theoretical information about language, thinking, and children's learning upon which the whole-language perspective is based. These ideas expand those introduced in Chapter 2 about reading as a transaction.

ACKNOWLEDGMENTS

I am indebted to my friends and colleagues in the field and to the students at Queens College who have freely shared their ideas with me through personal communications and professional writings. As is always the case, I assume full responsibility for the interpretation and final form those ideas take in this text.

For their insightful comments and suggestions about portions of the revised manuscript through formal reviews and to me personally, I wish to thank Patricia L. Anders, University of Arizona; David Bloome, University of Michigan; Sally Lipa, SUNY, Geneseo; Thomas Potter, Cal State, Northridge; and Eileen Tway, Miami University. In addition, the ideas given me by Richard Allington, Diane DeFord, Kenneth S. Goodman, Walter J. Moore, P. David Pearson, and Esther Schatz, who commented during the preparation of previous editions, still remain a vital part of this edition.

I am indebted to Beverly Kolz, former Administrative Editor at Merrill Publishing Company, for her encouragement to proceed with this revision, and I gratefully appreciate the support and assistance of Jeffrey W. Johnston, Administrative Editor, and the editorial associates at Merrill during its preparation and production. I especially thank Naura Gillespie for her efforts in coordinating the early production of the book and Carol Driver for her care in editing the manuscript.

With affection, I acknowledge H. Alan Robinson's continued personal support and professional influence. He is an outstanding teacher, a respected colleague, and most important, a dear friend. Although Carol Hittleman has not formally collaborated with me in preparing this edition, she greatly affects my thinking and contributes to my professional growth. Throughout the text, there are many ideas which I know originate with her, but they are now so much a part of my thinking that I cannot single them out. With love, I dedicate this book to Carol for her love, understanding, and support.

D. R. H.

Contents

CHAPTER 11
Principles of Analytical Teaching through Standardized Tests 363

CHAPTER 12
Organizing for Reading Instruction 381

CHAPTER 13
Human Communication and the Development of Thinking and Language 397

Organizer

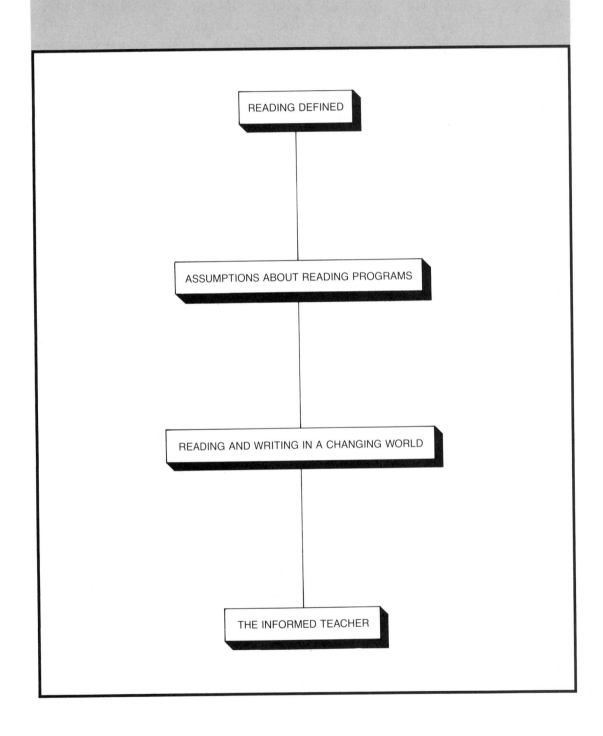

READING DEFINED

ASSUMPTIONS ABOUT READING PROGRAMS

READING AND WRITING IN A CHANGING WORLD

THE INFORMED TEACHER

CHAPTER 1

Literacy in Today's Society

Focus Questions

- How do reading and writing fit into a world in which ideas are increasingly being transmitted through multimedia devices?
- How can reading programs be made relevant for the literacy demands of today's society?
- How can the classroom teacher remain current in literacy theory and practice?

Reading and writing are acts of communication, and as such share character-istics with other modes of communication. These various ways of communi-cating provide many alternatives for gaining information and communicating with others. Educating students means helping them develop skills and strat-egies for choosing the best mode of communication at any given time.

READING DEFINED

The reading process differs from the teaching/learning situation in which the reading process develops. Reading is a thinking, linguistic, and cultural/social process that is interrelated with and supportive of the other communication processes—listening, speaking, and writing. Throughout this text, interrelat-ing the teaching/learning of reading with listening, speaking, and writing is called **whole-language instruction.**

Reading entails both reconstructing an author's message and constructing one's own meaning using the print on a page. A reader's reconstruction of the ideas and information intended by an author is somewhat like a listener's re-construction of ideas from a speaker's combinations of sounds. The reader, like the listener, may create meanings that are different from those intended by the author. What a reader understands from the reconstructed and constructed meanings depends on the reader's prior knowledge, prior experiences, and his or her maturity and proficiency in using language in various social contexts.

Learning to read develops from a person's ability to understand and use both oral and written language in social situations; the ability to understand written language is an extension of the ability to communicate orally. Learning to read requires an understanding of the daily social functions of oral and writ-ten language. Learning to read requires a knowledge of the structure of oral and written language. Learning to read requires the application of thinking strategies to ideas communicated in written form. Therefore, school programs for developing reading skills need to cultivate students' cognitive learning pro-cesses, oral language proficiency, and use of language in social contexts.

Rosenblatt (1978) calls reading a "transaction," an "ongoing process in which the elements or factors are . . . aspects of a total situation, each condi-tioned by and conditioning the other" (p. 17). In other words, a **transaction** is an exchange among the reader, the text, and the reading situation. Changes in all three elements result from this exchange. It is more than just an interaction, a term sometimes used synonymously by many whole-language reading edu-

cators. It is a change in the reader and the reader's ideas and feelings about what is read.

A transaction in reading involves several factors, some of which are not inherent in the text or the reader. These factors include:

the purposes for which something is being read,
the types and formats of the material being read,
the situations and contexts in which the reading occurs,
the means by which understanding is determined or measured, and
the reader's skills, abilities, and experiences.

Within this framework, there is no assumption that an author's intended meaning automatically becomes the reader's reconstructed meaning. Considering the five factors of a reading transaction, such a direct correspondence is inconceivable. In Chapter 2 these factors are explained within a model of the reading act. Chapter 13 includes a detailed discussion of the psychological, sociological, and linguistic theories supporting a whole-language definition of reading.

The approach teachers take toward reading affects the way an instructional program is structured. It is difficult to simply answer the question, "How can

I teach reading?" Instead, teachers should ask new questions: "How can I best promote the learning of reading?" "What activities foster cognitive development?" "What materials most effectively support reading instruction?" "What strategies do students need to become independent readers?" "What kind of classroom environment promotes reading transactions?" The major portion of this text is devoted to providing some answers to these questions. The teaching and learning of reading are presented in light of ideas about the whole-language nature of reading. The environment of the classroom, the methodology of the teacher, the materials used, the strategies presented, and the amount and effectiveness of reading practice are all part of reading instruction. These elements transact/interact as children develop the ability to read.

ASSUMPTIONS ABOUT READING PROGRAMS

A few basic assumptions about reading programs underlie the recommended strategies for efficient and productive development of the reading process in students. These are:

All language activities have improved communication as their prime goal. Reading is learned only through the attempt to communicate with and through written language.

Knowing how to read and write will help people function within the demands of society.

Reading, one of the language arts, is integral to the other language arts. Instruction in composing messages accompanies instruction in reading messages. By creating their own oral and written texts, students gain insight into how to reconstruct the intended meaning of others. The language arts should be taught as a unit, not as separate subjects.

Instruction directed toward developing the reading process is planned and purposeful, involves students in direct experiences of using reading and writing strategies in meaningful situations, and allows students to assume some of the responsibility for their learning.

Reading and writing are learned within the context of all subject areas, not as separate skill subjects.

READING AND WRITING IN A CHANGING WORLD

Reading and writing are important in the complex society of today. These forms of literacy are needed for improving people's understanding of government, expanding their understanding of contemporary conditions that conflict with others' rights and responsibilities, and accepting their obligation to participate in social and political discussions. Reading, moreover, is one of the most

flexible means of communication. The receiver of the written message is in almost full control of the communicative situation. The author's intended sequence can be followed or not, and the communication begins and ends at the reader's will. The reader can find other sources to verify meanings or find additional sources with differing ideas. The rate at which ideas are processed and how many ideas are processed can be adjusted. No other communication medium allows this much flexibility. Even visual communication does not give the viewer total control, because pictures have one basic shortcoming in relation to written ideas: Not all statements can be turned into images, especially when the ideas are concepts and not actions (Gombrich, 1974).

There are certainly limitations in using the print medium to convey ideas, and surely many ideas can be conveyed in ways other than through print. The existence of alternative modes of communication, however, does not decrease the need for reading and writing in our society. For example, consider the growing use of word processors in businesses and homes. As a result, educators and students must develop varied ways of relating to technology and print (McCorduck, 1985; Suhor, 1984).

Society cannot retard or stop the explosion of knowledge, nor can it usurp the freedom of the press. Instead, its responsibility lies in teaching students to discriminate between what is worthwhile and what is not. The concern should not be whether reading and writing should be taught, but what is being taught about communicating. Are students taught to question and analyze the information they receive regardless of its source? Are they literate no matter in what form they encounter language?

These questions have particular importance in light of the studies done by the National Assessment of Educational Progress of the reading ability of 9-, 13-, and 17-year-olds for the 1979–80 and 1983–84 academic years. The NAEP concluded that although American school children learn to read a wide range of materials better than they did in 1970, the majority do not develop adequate thinking skills or the ability to interpret what they read beyond a superficial level (Fiske, 1981; NAEP, 1985).

Teachers, then, should not be caught up in the controversy of whether reading is outmoded and irrelevant, but should be concerned with helping to develop citizens who can select the most advantageous means for learning at a particular time, at a particular place, and for a particular subject. Values and knowledge are in constant flux. No one can ever be sure what the world over the "edge of history" will be like (Thompson, 1972). Students, however, will be shortchanged if educational practices are not adjusted so that they can explore life fully and learn to make choices from their available experiences (Bell, 1974). If students are not given the opportunity to learn to read, they will be forever limited in their range of choices and in their opportunities for personal satisfaction. Teachers need to develop new instructional techniques to meet the challenges of the future.

Education historians show that recurring arguments exist about the nature of literacy and its effects on society. The meaning society gives to literacy (knowing how to read and write) changes as the values of society change. An analysis of this change shows that literacy's different meanings result from the way people measure literacy; the function it plays in their lives; and from the significance it holds for strategy and tactics in research, public policy, school organization, and teaching practices. These changing meanings reflect changes in the understanding of the human capacity to understand and learn (Clifford, 1984; Iannaccone, 1984).

Within the last few years, members of English-speaking cultures have reexamined literacy and how schools should deal with this subject. The Bullock Report, done in Great Britain, examined all aspects of teaching reading, writing and speech, the practices of teacher training, and student evaluation (Bullock, 1975). The report included recommendations in support of integrating the teaching of reading and writing with other curriculum areas and teaching reading and writing in a whole-language perspective. In the United States, a study entitled *Becoming a Nation of Readers* contained twelve recommendations for parents, teachers, and school administrators for instructional practice (Anderson, Hiebert, Scott, & Wilkinson, 1985). Those that support the various recommendations in these reports seem to overlook the major methodological criticism: The authors do not provide adequate empirical support for their recommendations (Pikulski, 1976; Goodman, 1985; Botel, 1985; Grundin, 1985).

To be sure, the reports will not settle the critical attacks on the teaching of reading which arose in the late 1960s and early 1970s. Reading was characterized as irrelevant and even antisocial. Some critics contended that print was no longer this culture's dominant medium of communication, even though the schools acted as if it were (Postman, 1973). This polemic was reminiscent of McLuhan's argument (1964) that our information about the world now comes more through multimedia devices than through print alone. (However, note the following line from an advertisement: "Marshal McLuhan says the printed word is 'obsolete' and to prove it, he wrote fifteen books.")

During the later 1970s and early 1980s, reading instruction again came under attack, but from a different direction. This new attack, from the "back-to-basics" movement in American education, emphasized strict standards, the extensive use of phonics in reading instruction, and the teaching of reading at an early age (Heckinger, 1980; Maeroff, 1981). It has been the belief of back-to-basics advocates that adherence to these principles will overcome the problems they see in literacy teaching. A recent view of the literacy problem is that reading and writing are being threatened by a preoccupation with computers. However, the widespread enthusiasm about the potential of computers in homes and school may soon meet with certain countertrends as questions are being raised about the limited cognitive and social values of computer programs (Suhor, 1984).

Obviously, many people do not believe that reading will become an "art form" limited to an elitist group. There are those who feel that the back-to-basics movement merely disguises the indecision and confusion in American educational philosophy and in society's expectations of the public schools (Johnson, 1979). There can be no denying that how reading and writing are taught will remain a volatile political issue; however, reasons for this explosive polemic include misconceptions about the nature of reading and confusion over the differences between reading and the instruction of reading.

These preceding ideas are relevant to the world in which today's students must function and to a world that may be quite different by the time they are adults. As such, the program is part of the message: Not that what is done, or the substance of the program, is unimportant but that how the program is implemented has an effect on student learning. The acquisition of the reading process is an interaction among the student, the teacher, the instructional material, and the environment in which the learning occurs. "The ways in which

the child is taught to read have direct bearings on both his [or her] productivity as a reader and his [or her] aspirations about being a reader" (Jacobs, 1971, p. 465).

THE INFORMED TEACHER

To develop lifelong learners among their students, teachers must be lifelong learners. A growing body of knowledge to be explored exists in almost every subject area. Teachers should, of course, be knowledgeable about the world in which they live. They should also be familiar with the field of education. The purpose of this book is not to inform teachers about their world. This they must do on their own. Suffice it to say that teachers should not live their lives just as a teacher; to be well-rounded they should also have interests that go beyond their vocational training. As Thompson (1972) stated, if an individual "could not survive the subtraction of his job from his identity, then there wasn't really much to him in the first place" (p. 163).

To make instructional decisions, teachers need a theory about learning and literacy and a current knowledge of research, publications, and instructional practices related to that theory. This knowledge does not need to come solely from education. Many allied fields of study have their own specialized knowledge of and their own techniques for a whole-language study of reading and writing. Contributions to our knowledge of the reading process will continue to come from sociology, mass media and social class structure, social psychology, child development, cognitive and language development, linguistics, psycholinguistics, educational psychology, the media of instruction and behavior analysis, ophthalmology, and perception. The classroom teacher must decide what information is valid to his or her theory and is helpful for guiding learning in a relevant reading and writing program. Just as children should cultivate the art of critical acceptance of written communication, so must the classroom teacher. Everyone must learn to be wise consumers in the scholastic market.

As someone concerned with providing an educational program to foster the growth and development of the reading and writing processes, a teacher must also be a reader and writer. To develop literate students who are independent and self-reliant, who are comfortable with and proficient in handling printed material in various forms and from many sources and disciplines, who are able to search for alternatives to problems without dogmatically accepting a printed message just because it is printed, and who are aware that education does not occur only in the classroom, a teacher must also possess these traits. To develop the potential of their students, schools must be staffed with teachers who recognize their own qualities and who continually search to fulfill their own potential as informed teachers and members of society. As Jacobs (1971) asserted, "The essence of being human is to be in charge of one's life—to assume responsibility for oneself, to be willing to renew and remake oneself on the basis of evidence that renewal and remaking are essential to one's well-being as an individual" (p. 467).

DISCUSSION QUESTIONS AND ACTIVITIES

1. How would you explain to a group of parents why their children should learn to read? What characteristics of the school population would you have to consider when formulating your answers? After deciding how you would explain this issue, present it to someone else.

2. Give your reaction to the following statement by Robinson (1969).

    The saddest scene is to observe those teachers who work in the midst of a changed environment but don't recognize it—who go trying to do what they have learned and, in the face of failure, blame their failure on the learners. (p. 5)

3. Write about your reading and writing experiences in school or about a teacher associated with those experiences. Share these recollections with others who have written about their experiences.

4. Select an area of work (storekeeping, office work, nursing, etc.) and analyze the reading and writing demands related to that job. Which aspects of the job's literacy demands are specialized? Which are general, not requiring specialized knowledge or skills? What alternative modes of communicating (nonreading or writing) exist in that work area?

FURTHER READING

For each chapter in the book, annotated references are provided to extend the ideas of the chapter and to take the reader beyond the scope of this book. The following provide information about reading instruction and the influence of computers on society.

McCorduck, P. (1985). *The universal machine: Confessions of a technological optimist.* New York: McGraw-Hill.

Manning, J. C. (1985, November). What's needed now in reading instruction: The teacher as scholar and romanticist. *The Reading Teacher, 39,* 132–138.

Turkle, S. (1984). *The second self: Computers and the human spirit.* New York: Simon & Schuster.

Many professional organizations publish journals, books, and other materials that teachers find informative and useful. The following journals contain articles, comments from readers, news of recent materials or instructional and professional literature, summaries of research, advertisements for educational products, and information about the organizations.

The Reading Teacher and *The Journal of Reading.* The International Reading Association (IRA), 800 Barksdale Road, P.O. Box 8139, Newark, DE 19711

Language Arts. The National Council of Teachers of English (NCTE), 1111 Kenyon Road, Urbana, IL 61801

Reading Research and Instruction. The College Reading Association (CRA), c/o Norman A. Stahl, Treasurer and Business Manager, Box 872—University Plaza, Georgia State University, Atlanta, GA 30303

The following are other magazines pertaining to reading and language arts.

Childhood Education. Journal of the Association for Childhood Education International, 11141 Georgia Avenue, Suite 200, Wheaton, MD 20902

Computers, Reading and Language Arts. Modern Learning Publishers, Inc., 1308 East 38th Street, Oakland, CA 94602

Instructor. The Instructor Publications, Inc., P.O. Box 6099, Duluth, MN 55806

Teacher. CGM Professional Magazines, Inc., 22 West Putnam Avenue, Greenwich, CT 06830

The Elementary School Journal. The Elementary School Journal, University of Chicago Press, Journal Division, P. O. Box 37005, Chicago, IL 60637

Two references for general and research articles on reading, writing, and language arts and their related topics are the *Educational Index* and the *Current Index to Journals in Education.* These are monthly publications with semiannual and annual cumulations, indexes to periodicals, book reviews, government documents, conference proceedings, and yearbooks.

As an aid to educators in locating and using information about the American educational system, a national network of information clearinghouses, called the Educational Resources Information Center (ERIC), was established and is supported by the U. S. Department of Education. ERIC provides ready access to current research results and related information. The ERIC Clearinghouse on Reading and Communication Skills (ERIC/RCS) is one of the centers in the nationwide network. Its task is to organize, analyze, and make available products to people interested in the field of reading. It has produced a wide variety of resources, including state-of-the-art monographs (produced in conjunction with the IRA and the NCTE), interpretive monographs directed to special audiences, special bibliographies and reviews, broad subject bibliographies, basic references on reading, and bibliographies related to special ERIC collections.

Many of the ERIC documents are reproduced in hard copy, and all are available on microfilm. The ERIC materials are found in the educational/periodicals section of most college and university libraries and in the periodicals section of many public libraries. All resources of the ERIC systems are catalogued in the monthly journal *Resources in Education (RIE).*

For teachers that are interested in children's literature and its related aspects, the materials and newsletters of the Children's Book Council, 67 Irving Place, New York, NY, 10003, report on new publications, events for stimulating the use of books in the schools and libraries, information about authors and illustrators, free or inexpensive materials provided by commercial publishers, and suggestions for fostering the reading habit. Send them a large, stamped, self-addressed envelope to obtain more information.

Teachers wishing to be placed on mailing lists to receive catalogs and brochures can contact the publishers of instructional materials advertised in professional journals. Quite often publishers are willing to send teachers examination copies of instructional materials appropriate to their teaching situations.

Organizer

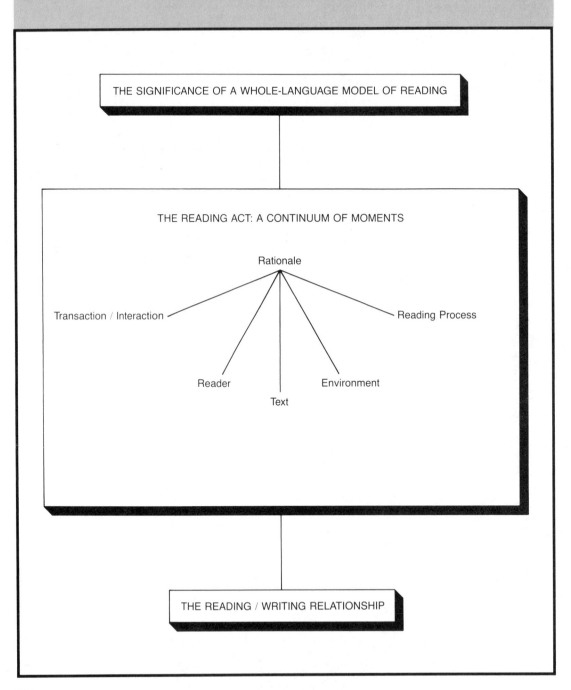

THE SIGNIFICANCE OF A WHOLE-LANGUAGE MODEL OF READING

THE READING ACT: A CONTINUUM OF MOMENTS

Rationale

Transaction / Interaction

Reading Process

Reader

Environment

Text

THE READING / WRITING RELATIONSHIP

The Nature of Reading

Focus Questions

- What factors are involved in any reading situation?
- What is the distinction between the reading act and the reading process?
- How is writing related to learning to read and reading?

Imagine three people who are selecting copies of the same book to read. The first, a high-school student, is buying the book to read for a required school report. The second, a corporate sales representative, is buying the book in an airport to read during a two-hour flight delay. The third person, a university professor, is choosing the book in a library for recreational reading. An onlooker watching these three people read might think the same activity is occurring. However, only the text remains constant. The readers' characteristics, their reading purposes, and their locales differ. Even the way they read the text differs. What results are three different acts of reading.

The process of reading is different from the act of reading. Every time someone reads a book, magazine, or newspaper, he or she is engaging in a reading act by undertaking the action, the doing, of reading. Life is filled with reading acts, and the purposes for reading may change with each act. The reading act, however, is not the reading process; the process of reading is only one aspect of the act of reading. The **reading act** includes the reading process and the complex transaction of reader, text, and environment. The **reading process** focuses on the linguistic, physiological, and psychological aspects of reading and their interaction in creating meaning from a text.

As mentioned in Chapter 1, reading is transactional: It is more than the interplay of inherent reader characteristics. Reading at any moment results from the transaction among sets of variables, including the reader's purpose(s) for reading, the types and structures of the reading material, the situations in which reading occurs, the way understanding is determined or measured (by the reader or by someone else), and the reader's characteristics.

From whole-language instruction in classrooms, students practice strategies that foster their awareness of those variables and procedures. Learning results from such an awareness.

Students and teachers should understand that

during reading, information is related to prior knowledge. This new information is integrated with that prior knowledge through elaboration techniques involving additional reading and writing tasks.

reading for one specific purpose or with attention to one specific feature or aspect of a text impedes readers' understanding of other features or aspects.

a reader's understanding is affected by his or her perception of the author's purpose(s) as well as the purpose(s) assigned for instruction.

14

different types of content, stylistic patterns, and organizational structures represent different levels of understanding for readers of different backgrounds, abilities, ages, and interests.

reading instruction's purpose is to develop independent readers who can apply several strategies to many types of textual material in different situations.

In this chapter the reading act and the reading process are examined. First, some ideas about the general significance of whole-language models of reading are offered with a brief history of their development. Then, a model of the reading act is presented to illustrate how the reading process operates during actual reading situations. Finally, the relationship between the acts of reading and writing are discussed to show that writing contributes to the development of students' reading skills and comprehension abilities. The model of the reading act supports the definition of reading in Chapter 1. Many of the principles of language and learning touched on in this chapter are developed more fully in Chapter 13. For expanded ideas of the rationale and procedures discussed here, see Chapter 13 or refer to the index for the location of specific subjects.

THE SIGNIFICANCE OF A WHOLE-LANGUAGE MODEL OF READING

To explain the nature of reading, educators have created models—theoretical frameworks designed to clarify what reading is. Even though models are based on supportable research, they are still hypotheses. Their usefulness depends on how clearly they explain reading behaviors. Each model is adequate only for describing a particular set of conditions, but not all conditions (Samuels & Kamil, 1984). Any model, useful as it is in understanding reading's nature, should not be considered complete. It must be modified or even discarded as new evidence accumulates. According to Geyer (1972), a model of reading should serve three general purposes:

1. It should explain the complex phenomenon of reading.
2. It should describe how the phenomenon of reading operates.
3. It should provide a basis for predicting changes that will occur in one aspect of reading when changes are made in other aspects.

Models with psycholinguistic, sociolinguistic, information processing, and whole-language perspectives are created from the insights of cognitive psychologists, and psycho- and sociolinguists. Using these models, many educators changed their interpretations of the nature of reading. Before the 1960s and 1970s, reading was modeled as an accumulation of discrete skills. Most of the attention of reading researchers was on the word, because reading was thought to begin with recognizing first a single word, then another, and so on (Guthrie, 1980).

By the late 1970s, researchers were investigating the cognitive processes of readers to explain how they understand, not what they do. Their studies revealed that readers are able to understand the structure of a story or to draw inferences from a passage when they undertake reading as a search for information and when they relate that information to their background knowledge. Only then are individual words on a page recognized and their particular meanings determined. These studies also showed that reading is a language process, a psychological process, a psycholinguistic process, a sociolinguistic process, and a physiological process. Investigators concluded that the research of cognitive psychologists, linguists, sociologists, and psycholinguists has direct implications for reading instruction (Ryan & Semmel, 1969; Raven & Slazer, 1971; Stauffer, 1971).

More recent models attempt to explain reading as a transaction/interaction. Whereas those who make discrete skills models try to explain only the specific skills involved in reading, those who formulate transaction/interaction models show not only the skills involved but also how readers use those skills and strategies interdependently. Researchers conclude that comprehension during reading is an elaborate process that depends on variables both within and outside words and sentences (Baker & Brown, 1984; Mason, 1984b; Pearson & Tierney, 1984; Pezdek, 1980; Linden & Wittrock, 1981). These researchers define comprehension as a constructive process. Readers create meaning from a transaction/interaction among some information, the context of the information, and the reader's existing knowledge schemata. Schemata are the ways concepts and generalizations are organized in our minds. The ideas readers construct from the transaction are used to complete a communication or to perform an action, such as completing an application or operating a new appliance. Students learn to comprehend written material through instruction about (1) recognizing the structures of text, (2) relating their knowledge and experiences to the author's ideas, (3) understanding how to control their learning, and (4) building personal associations (schemata) on those ideas.

THE READING ACT: A CONTINUUM OF MOMENTS

The reading act is a complex transaction/interaction of four sets of variables (see Figure 2–1). The result of the transaction is understanding and learning. The sets of variables composing the reading act are (1) the reader, (2) the text, (3) the environment and purpose(s) for reading, and (4) the reading process. These sets of variables interact with and influence one another. None of the sets exists in isolation—a reader deals with a text in a given environment for a stated or implied purpose; nevertheless, for convenience each set is discussed here separately before examining their transaction.

The model of the reading act is called a continuum of moments for two reasons. First, a reading act is not reducible to a single event or component; it is ongoing and causes change in the reader. The reader's approach to the next moment of reading is immediately changed as the result of understanding and

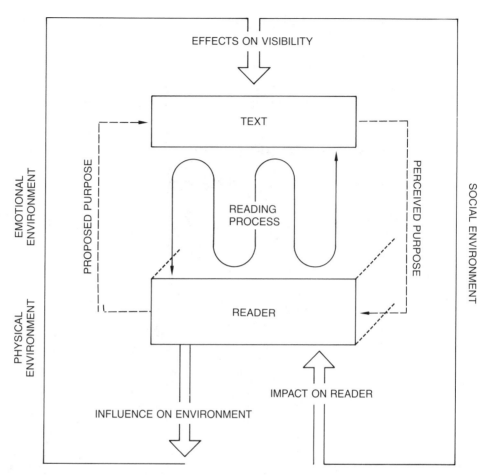

FIGURE 2–1
The Reading Act: A Continuum of Moments (Simplified)

learning from the previous moment. Second, the reading act can be studied only by examining what occurs at any one moment. There is no way to measure or determine the total, ongoing transaction among the variables. At any moment, an interaction of only one or two variables can be examined.

Although there is research revealing the existence and effect of one or two particular sets of variables, it may not be possible to study the totality of a reading act or the reading process. In physics and molecular biology, this principle is well documented and is recognized as a valid analytical assumption. Studying reading may be analogous to studying a human cell—analyzing its parts destroys its essence.

Nevertheless, it is possible to observe reading in action, describe the outcomes of a reading act, and speculate about the transaction. With regard to the three readers previously mentioned, each brings to the reading act different backgrounds and reading abilities and each is reading for different reasons in different environments. One could speculate about the three transactions with knowledge of the variables, such as what their previous experiences with reading have been, how much they know about the book's author and subject, how sensitive they are to reading in public, how closely the author's language patterns match their own, and why they picked the particular book.

The Rationale for the Continuum of Moments Model

The model of the reading act results from a synthesis and expansion of a few researchers' and educators' specific ideas and the ideas of scholars in education, cognitive psychology, language development, social psychology, sociology, sociolinguistics, linguistics, and text analysis. Specifically, the influences come from models of

1. learning from texts;
2. schema theory;
3. text structures and patterns;
4. the influence on behavior of one's perception of a communication's context;
5. reading as an interactive process;
6. the concept of intellect;
7. the concept of the moment of readability;
8. reading comprehension and readability;
9. the phases of reading before, during, and after the eye meets the page;
10. a transactional theory of literature, and the concept of the reader reading like a writer (Brown, 1981; Combs, 1958; Combs & Snygg, 1959; Goodman, 1969a, b; Graesser, 1981; Guilford, 1967; Hittleman, 1973; Kintsch, 1979; Pearson & Tierney, 1984; Robinson, 1978; Rosenblatt, 1978; Rumelhart, 1976).

These ideas are summarized in the following paragraphs.

Cognitive psychologists studying the structure of human memory conceive of thinking as a process in which the information an individual receives from the world is systematically organized. Both the manner in which the information is catalogued and the strategies of the process seem to depend on prior experiences and prior information. It seems that children develop a strategy for putting information into their long-term memory. This strategy is learned during interaction with older children and adults. By induction children realize that certain information in the world is ignored and other information is emphasized. For example, children can learn to distinguish among "school shoes, play shoes, and dress shoes" even when there are no nonphysical distinctions among them. Or, they can learn to distinguish between male and female red-bellied woodpeckers based on a subtle physical characteristic.

Language is conceived of by linguists and sociologists as a template or screen through which children learn to catalog the world. The language of a society or group contains the categories into which the events of the world are placed. When a language does not have a specific category for a particular event, distinction, or aspect of reality, one of two things may happen: The event or distinction is ignored totally; or it is placed into another category. In the second instance, two events, although observed by members of another group as different, may be perceived as being the same thing. This is another way of saying that unless two people share similar social and linguistic contexts, communication is not possible. For example, children who grow up with sail boating experiences begin to classify ropes as *lines, sheet lines, bow lines, guy lines, jibsheets, mainsheets,* and *pennants,* and they learn that *waterlines* and *bed sheets* do not belong in that set. To the many who have never sailed, a rope is a rope and a sheet belongs on a bed.

A distinction is usually made between a language's structure and its function. Structure refers to the language's form, or the way its sentences and paragraphs are spoken or written and how words indicate possible meanings. When grammar is studied, the structure of language is examined. Function refers to why language is used. Generally, English is considered to have five major functions of language as discussed in Chapter 13: controlling, sharing, informing, ritualizing, and imagining.

The concept of schema is important to a transactional definition of reading. **Schemata** are generalized descriptions both of the categories into which people place some of life's experiences and of the hierarchical arrangement into which they place other experiences. They are private theories about the nature of the world, its objects, and events, and they are evaluation guides of how well new information conforms to the old. Schemata are like scripts or little plays stored in people's memories. They allow people to know and understand activities that contain many ideas and ways of acting. Schemata are used to make predictions about unobserved or new events and as guides for action in both conventional and novel situations. In this way, *thinking* is the transaction/interaction among schemata, and *understanding* is realizing how new information conforms to or disagrees with previous knowledge.

For example, the script for an activity such as going to school may include sets of rules, actions, and dialogues for being students, teachers, and principals; information about using desks, pencils, books, and paper; procedures for how students learn and teachers teach; and routines for arriving at school, doing the morning activities, dividing the day into periods or subjects, and participating in lunch, recess, and dismissal.

There are six general categories of schemata. In a sense, these categories of schemata are an individual's long-term memory. Each category is a set of rules for organizing and using information. One governs the use and sequence of sounds, denotative word meanings, words in sentences, and the social functions of language. A second controls how statements, oral and written, are introduced, ordered, and interrelated in different kinds of literary forms. A third orders and sequences ways to deal with nonintentional events and social conditions (activities which a person does not initiate and events which he or she cannot control). A fourth organizes language depending on the user's goals, plans, and actions (intentional activities). A fifth controls how a person deals with the physical conditions of communication (the environment). A sixth organizes the different formality levels of language dealing with people, objects, and events.

These categories, or cognitive domains, are not discrete. They interact throughout the communication process and they control the formation of a message. They control both the sender's message and the receiver's perception and evaluation of the message. What is relevant to classroom learning is whether students receive messages as intended or whether they are hindered by some barrier or interference. Getting an author's message depends largely on shared knowledge and similar use of rules by students, teachers, and the author.

Effective classroom communication among teachers and students results from a classroom environment in which all share knowledge. Teachers, detecting differing social or cultural viewpoints that impede communication, should try to develop a common system of communication to reduce classroom misunderstandings and conflicts. Teachers need to be committed to understanding students and the content of instruction; learning occurs "only when the child is interacting with people in his environment and in cooperation with his peers" (Vygotsky, 1978, p. 90).

The Transaction/Interaction

Reading situations differ among students, even those who are reading in the same group for the same stated purpose. Classroom students have varying backgrounds and abilities, different levels of language maturity and qualities of experiences, and differences in their previous instruction.

For each reader the four sets of variables do not function individually. Each set has variables that transact with other variables in its own set and with those of the other sets. Although the three readers mentioned in the beginning of the chapter selected copies of the same book, they are engaged in three different acts of reading because their reader variables, environment variables, reading process variables, and purposes differ. (See Figure 2–2 for the reader variables, text variables, environment variables, and reading process variables.)

The transaction of reading is a continual interchange among the reader, the text, the environment, and the reading process. It is more than an interaction because any change in one variable set creates change(s) in the others. It is a continuous interchange in both a circular and spiraling manner. The flow lines in Figures 2–1 and 2–2 show the major directions of influence, but these flows vary in degree and influence throughout the continuum of moments. All variables may be at work at any time, or some might be temporarily suspended; however, each variable is never inactive.

The Reader

Every reader begins a reading act with cognitive, physical, and emotional energies. For example, a 10-year-old student, Sal, feels fidgety because he has been
sitting for over an hour doing worksheets at his desk. He generally likes read-

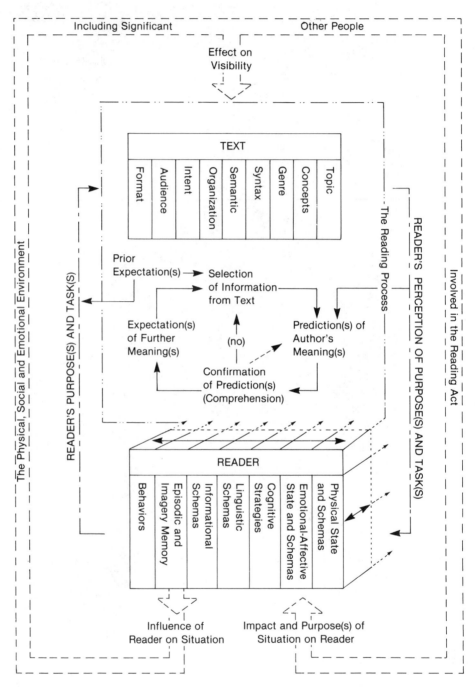

FIGURE 2-2
The Reading Act: A Continuum of Moments

ing, but at this moment he feels a little upset because his best friend chose not to sit next to him. When the teacher announces that the passage to be read is about bird migration, Sal remembers the bird house he tried but had trouble building at the last Cub Scout meeting and decides that he does not want to read about bird migration. Opening the book, he sees some charts and a graph, then he calls out, "This stuff is too hard," and drops the book on the floor.

The specific energies that are involved in the reading act are (1) physical condition and schemata, (2) affective–emotional state and schemata, (3) cognitive strategies, (4) linguistic schemata, (5) information schemata, (6) episodic and imagery memories, and (7) behaviors.

The reader has a **physical condition and schemata** for body control and use. A reader's health and maturity influence his or her response rate to life situations. Since thinking has a biological and chemical basis, variables such as the rate of nerve impulses, metabolism, chemical composition of the blood stream, muscular coordination, and degree of fatigue or stimulation all affect a reading act.

The **emotional state and schemata** consist of attitudes, general personality factors, and mood. These are not static but fluctuate daily and even throughout the day. They are the ways people react to and with various psychological conditions involving themselves and others.

The **cognitive schemata** are the individual's skills, strategies, and processes for thinking through a problem. The **linguistic schemata** are the individual's knowledge of language, language usage and function, forms, and vocabulary.

The **informational schemata** are all the ideas, facts, concepts, and generalizations that a person accumulates through life experiences and schooling.

In the **episodic memory**, thoughts are stored about dated events and the temporal–spatial relationships relating to those events.

Imagery memory contains representations, both concrete and referential, that are not stored in a verbal code. They are images, but they can be activated by associations from other schemata. For example, hearing the word *rose* or perceiving that flower's scent can cause someone to visualize a rose.

The **behaviors** are all the paralinguistic and nonverbal associations, actions, gestures, expressions, body postures, and use of space that have been acquired through socialization and acculturation. These behaviors are sometimes called *body language.*

Sal, the student previously mentioned, may be physically healthy and a developmentally normal 10-year-old, but his body might have been signaling a need for a nonsedentary activity. Sal's negative reaction to the passage about bird migration might have been influenced by memories of learning difficulties or frustrations with bird-related information, or he might have been disappointed about his friend's seating preference. By selecting the charts and graphs as an indication of the passage's difficulty, Sal could have been expressing a perception about his proficiency as a reader of graphic information. The way he expressed his reactions was an indication of his personality development and his understanding of the limitations imposed by the classroom environment.

During a reading act such as Sal's, the transaction causes changes in the reader through an expansion and modification of his or her schemata. The dotted lines extending from the reader in Figure 2–2 represent such changes. Sal can undergo change in his physical, emotional, cognitive, or linguistic states depending on how the teacher involves him in the lesson.

The Text

A text is a product of an author's, or a group of authors', cognitive and emotional energies—his or her schemata. These result in a text that (1) has a topic and subject, (2) contains concepts, (3) fits a genre, (4) uses standard syntax, (5) has organized information, (6) is semantically appropriated, and (7) is in a particular format.

An author writing for a specific purpose creates a text that reflects an awareness of and attention to these variables. The order in which the variables are discussed here is not necessarily the order in which an author addresses them. Research evidence shows that writing is transactional and recursive. As each variable set is considered, the others are influenced. An author may make revisions or modifications of one or more sets as a result of decisions made about any single set of variables.

The **topic and subject** are the broad area the author chooses and the specific focus the author takes. This includes the author's intent and the intended audience.

The **concepts** are ideas considered in terms of how they are spaced in the text (idea density) as well as the manner in which they are ordered. The author also considers how the concepts will be supported by illustrations and expanded explanations.

The concepts are related to another variable set, **genre**—the literary form selected for setting out ideas. Examples of genre include short story, exposition, and poem.

The author selects the **syntax** and **organization**, or specific sentences and paragraph forms, to best reach the intended audience. The meanings and relationships of words, or **semantics**, are also chosen in relation to the intent, audience, and topic.

Finally, when the text is published, it is placed in some **format**—size of type, color, quality of paper, binding, and size of page.

For example, an author preparing a science text might choose to write specifically about a barometer, which is part of the larger topic of weather and climatology. The author might decide to write about the barometer's construction or its use. The author might decide to use an informational literary form, and, thinking ahead to the audience (primary elementary students), he or she would decide what sentence and paragraph patterns to use. Then the author would select words accordingly, being sure to provide definitions and explanations of technical terms. When the final manuscript is sent to the publisher, it is accompanied by suggestions by the author for page layout and appropriate illustrations.

During reading, changes that might occur to the text are limited. There may be poor lighting affecting visibility, or there may be physical changes made by pulling pages from the text, duplicating it, altering the color presentations, or reprinting it on a different quality of paper. The reader may also cause some changes by underlining the text, writing in the margins, substituting vocabulary, or cross-referencing.

The Environment

The reading situation consists of three subenvironments: physical, social, and emotional. The **physical setting** is the location, time, and position of the reading act. For example, the reading might occur while sitting or standing, at a desk or on a bench, indoors or outdoors, in the morning or the evening. The temperature might be hot, cool, or moderate. There might be glaring lights and loud noises or semi-darkness and absolute quiet.

The **social setting** consists of other individuals or groups of individuals with whom the reader has contact during the reading act. Even when reading alone, a reader is part of a cultural/social context. Each social setting has a protocol and each individual involved in a setting has schemata, partial or complete, for that situation. For example, school classrooms have sets of rules governing how one is to read in the library corner or at one's desk. There are also rules for reading when using public transportation (such as folding a newspaper so that it will be contained in one's body field and reading silently rather than aloud), and reading as part of a public performance.

The **emotional climate** is the governing feeling of a situation, influenced by both the physical and social settings. The climate can be humorous, sorrowful, tense, or generally pleasant.

These environmental factors create demands on the reader—purposes for reading and specific or general tasks to be performed during or after the reading. For example, the social setting may demand oral reading with accuracy (without deviations from a transposition of print into sound) or for testing (seeking out specific information). These may be actual demands in that a teacher or peer gives the reader the goal, or they may be inferred in that the reader perceives a task or purpose different from that given in spoken or written directives. For example, a student may think the task is a test of oral accuracy even though the teacher has stated a different task—to determine the author's meaning. Or the reader may perceive that a text is to be read for enjoyment when it is intended to persuade the reader to engage in a particular behavior.

As part of the total context, the reader exerts an influence on the environment. If there is a dislike for the setting, an attempt is often made to change it—to move to another chair or location or to turn on a brighter light. There may be an attempt to read with friends and share information or a desire to read alone in a secluded location. The reader can also influence the emotional climate by releasing feelings of frustration that result from an interpretation of the purpose(s) for the reading act (as Sal did).

The Reading Process

The transaction between the reader and the text is a reconstructive and constructive process and constitutes the reading process. It is what occurs before, during, and after the reader perceives and evaluates the graphic imprint.

Educators commonly classify explanations of the reading process as bottom-up, top-down, or transactional/interactive. The bottom-up theory states that reading starts with some graphic input (print); it begins with the synthesis of letters into words, words into sentences, and so on until a large enough unit of language is perceived and the reader understands what the author has written.

Top-down explanations show reading as beginning with the reader's cognitive structures (schemata). In this view, the reader understands what is on the page only if the ideas are already present in his or her mind. Reading, from a top-down view, begins with the reader's prior understanding and proceeds to the reconstruction of the author's message. Whole words and entire sentences are the input, not individual letters.

The transactional/interactive explanation portrays the reader as drawing from both the top and the bottom while simultaneously monitoring whether understanding occurs. In general, the transactional and the top-down proponents have more in common than do either group with the bottom-up proponents. The ideas presented in this text are consonant with the transactional/interactive and top-down views.

The three readers mentioned at the chapter outset can be considered proficient readers. Whether the high-school student, the corporate sales representative, or the university professor satisfy their purposes for reading depends on their individual reading transactions. A whole-language explanation of their reading assumes each begins the reading act with expectations (Figure 2–2) built on prior experiences with reading. He or she selects information (sentences, whole words) from the text, forms other expectations, and predicts the author's possible meaning(s). The information each reader selects depends on the reader's proficiency—the proficient reader does not use all available printed information because that slows reading. As additional information is taken from the page, the reader determines how it fits in with his or her expectations and predictions. Reading in this way is a process of matching incoming information with already existing information (schemata) and with the reader's purposes (stated or inferred). If the predictions are confirmed (the author's meaning is reconstructed and new meaning is constructed), these ideas are stored in the reader's memory and other information from the text is selected.

If the reader does not confirm predictions or if additional information seems incongruous with reconstructed and constructed meanings, the reader will search the text for information to resolve the anomaly. This might mean rereading portions of the text or continuing reading, but holding confirmation of predictions (comprehension) in abeyance until other information is collected. The reason for a lack of confirmation may be the reader's (unformed, incomplete, or incorrect schemata) or the author's (text variables are confusing or too mature for the audience). When the inconsistency is resolved, the transaction continues.

In the chapters that follow, suggestions are given for building students' linguistic, cognitive, and social information base. Suggestions are also given for teaching students how to form predictions before reading, what information to select from a page during reading, how to confirm predictions so meanings are created, how to be aware of their own abilities to reconstruct authors' meanings, and what to do with the information after reading so learning is retained and extended.

THE RELATIONSHIP OF WRITING TO READING

A basic premise of this text is that students of all ages gain immeasurably in their reading proficiency if they compose their own text. In the first chapter, one of the assumptions about reading programs states that instruction in writing accompanies instruction in reading. By creating their own texts, students learn how to reconstruct the intended meaning of others.

The act of composing text allows students to learn how texts work. They learn how to organize information, how to present ideas clearly and without ambiguity, how to establish purposes for communicating, and how to address their writing to particular audiences. The current thinking and research on the integration of reading and writing programs support this conclusion.

From her study of beginning readers, Chomsky (1971) reports how beginners learned to read by creating their own spellings for familiar words. They became active participants in teaching themselves to read. Introducing children to writing their own words makes them aware that the messages created belong to them and have grown out of their own minds. Chomsky feels that a word is born from a young learner's creative efforts with language.

Elkind (1976) has been associated with the interpretation of Piagetian principles and the cognitive development of children. He indicates that ''comprehension, or the construction of meaning, is also helped by the child's own efforts at giving meaning (i.e., representing) his own experiences'' (p. 338). Elkind proposes that the more opportunities and experiences children have to

represent thoughts verbally, the better prepared they will be to interpret others' representations. Since reading and writing are reciprocal processes of meaning construction, "the more children write, the more they will get from reading" (Elkind, 1976, p. 338).

An extensive body of research reveals the strong interrelationship among the language skills of speaking, listening, reading, and writing (Lehr, 1981; Pearson & Tierney, 1984; Stotsky, 1984; Wilson, 1981). The evidence indicates that combining instruction in reading and writing leads to greater proficiency in both. It does not seem to matter whether reading or writing is presented first; each has a positive influence on the development of the other. Both structure meaning, and both develop as natural extensions of children's desire to communicate. As students have opportunities to experience the trials and satisfactions of structuring their own language (writing), they will be better prepared for interpreting the structuring of others'.

When students learn to write, they learn to "invent reading for themselves" (Guthrie, 1978, p. 966). This is true for students of all ages as they learn to compose different prose styles for various purposes and for many audiences. Teaching students how to write their own reading material results in better comprehension of material written by others (Maya, 1979).

In sum,

> students who write expressively are thinking on paper. They begin to *see* relationships, connections, and ideas which once were elusive and abstract. . . . Students who are able to organize their thinking on paper are in a better position to understand another writer's organization of ideas. This is what reading comprehension is all about and this is what makes expressive writing a powerful teaching tool for reading comprehension. When writing and reading are used together . . ., students soon become conscious of themselves as writers working through a process, then as readers working through the product of another writer's process. . . . Students as readers/writers grow in control of their thinking processes. They learn to think as the writer generating text; they learn to think as the reader making meaning from text; and this is what makes expressive writing a metacognitive activity. (Collins, 1985, p. 52)

DISCUSSION QUESTIONS AND ACTIVITIES

1. Prepare a short statement for a parents' newsletter interpreting the following statement by Cambourne (1981): "[Whole-language] research clearly shows that everything which has been claimed about comprehending spoken language also applies to the comprehension of written language" (p. 96).

2. Yetta Goodman encourages teachers to "kid watch." Try to observe students of different ages reading in all sorts of places, not just in classrooms. Talk to them about what they were doing after they have finished reading. How do their actions and comments show their underlying process of reading?

3. Select two reading passages on different topics which contain information not generally known by a particular group of students. Then:

   a. Ask the students to read the first passage. After they read, test their retention of the main idea and the major details of the passage (1) immediately after the reading, (2) one hour later, and (3) one day later. Determine the type of information not retained by the students (for example, main ideas or major details).

   b. Plan a lesson so that the type of information not retained in the first reading will be remembered after reading the second passage. Again, test the retention (1) immediately after the reading, (2) one hour later, and (3) one day later. Was there greater retention after the second reading?

4. Obtain definitions of reading from at least three other texts on reading instruction. How are they similar to or different from the one presented in this text?

5. The verb *to read* is defined in the dictionary as both a transitive and an intransitive verb. Explain the confusion that may arise between two speakers who are using different sets of definitions about reading.

FURTHER READING

The following two books by Frank Smith offer scholarly yet highly readable examinations of the whole-language principles of learning to read. They present in greater depth many of the principles underlying the reading act model presented in this chapter.

Smith, F. (1985). *Reading without nonsense* (2nd ed.). New York: Teachers College Press, Teachers College, Columbia University.

Smith, F. (1978). *Understanding reading* (2nd ed.). New York: Holt, Rinehart & Winston.

There are several books that contain a discussion of the way reading and writing codevelop in children. In the following, the authors relate their personal experiences in observing children develop as readers and writers.

Baghban, M. (1984). *Our daughter learns to read and write.* Newark, DE: International Reading Association.

Calkins, L. M. (1983). *Lessons from a child: On the teaching and learning of writing.* Exeter, NH: Hienemann.

Clay, M. M. (1979). *What did I write?* Exeter, NH: Hienemann.

Additional understanding of the composing process can be found in the following books. The first is a theoretical presentation of the composing process, and the second is a collection of interviews with authors of children's literature regarding their own feelings about writing.

Smith, F. (1982). *Writing and the writer.* New York: Holt, Rinehart & Winston.

Weiss, M. J. (Ed.). (1979). *From writers to students: The pleasures and pains of writing.* Newark, DE: International Reading Association.

Organizer

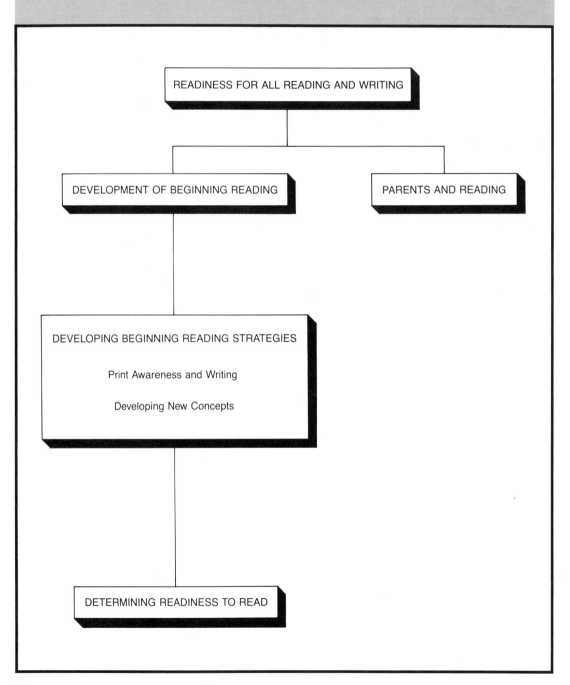

READINESS FOR ALL READING AND WRITING

DEVELOPMENT OF BEGINNING READING

PARENTS AND READING

DEVELOPING BEGINNING READING STRATEGIES

Print Awareness and Writing

Developing New Concepts

DETERMINING READINESS TO READ

Strategies for Developing Beginning Literacy

Focus Questions

- What does it mean to be ready to learn to read, and how does this concept relate to the idea of schemata?
- What factors affect students' beginning to read and write?
- What strategies must students use to be ready to receive formal reading instruction?
- How can students' beginning reading be assessed?

Making decisions about students' readiness for literacy is an ongoing concern of educators. Teachers wanting to know when students can receive formal reading instruction often ask, "When are children ready to have a book placed in their hands and to begin reading?" Professional texts and journals contain many checklists for identifying those students who are ready to read, and these checklists are accompanied by programs of readiness training. Using extensive and detailed checklists is a problem, however, because teachers begin to see readiness as a specific collection of subskills that have a demonstrable connection with the process of reading. This thinking also fosters the impression that readiness is a period of time or a specific program that must be completed before reading instruction can begin.

The aim of this chapter is not to present another checklist or to list specific skills required for learning to read. It is to present what it means to be ready to read and compose any type of material at any stage of development and at any age. Ideas about identifying general factors that affect readiness to use language in oral and printed form are presented, and these factors are related to the first stage of literacy—commonly called reading readiness. Although beginning reading and writing activities often occur in school at the kindergarten or first-grade levels, readiness activities precede all learning. Therefore, reading readiness, in the broad sense of the term, is the concern of all school teachers, regardless of the grade level they teach.

READINESS FOR ALL READING AND WRITING

In a Piagetian sense, readiness means possessing skills and abilities of a preceding stage of development. Or, simply, "development determines learning" (Elkind, 1974, p. 115). Every student in school, regardless of grade level, is ready to learn something about the reading process. What that something is should be selected and prepared in keeping with the student's abilities at the moment. The teacher's responsibility is to identify what the student is to learn and to determine whether the student has the necessary knowledge and strategies to learn what is expected.

All of a student's school experiences affect the manner in which any later school task is undertaken. Although no definitive developmental pattern of school tasks has been established, it seems logical that positive experiences, which develop a student's understanding of school routines, aid in learning. Students need preschool experiences with language-oriented activities, such as those in this chapter. Those without these experiences are less likely to begin learning to read and write with the same facility as those who understand what school is all about.

Cognitive and linguistic skills, psychomotor understanding (cultural body language, gestures, and movements), and emotional and social development—these constitute what is being called readiness. No sequence of skills is presented here because any such sequence would be arbitrary; no empirical evidence justifies the use of one hierarchy of skills over another. Indeed, little is known about what specific skills should be taught, and little is known about (1) the specific student characteristics required to master a given task, (2) the specific characteristics amenable to literacy training, and (3) the specific training procedures that can be used for children who lack the prerequisites for learning written language tasks (Blanton, 1972; Mason, 1984a).

Prereading and prewriting are discussed because evidence exists showing early preparation for literacy can be fostered. However, the evidence indicates only the broad kinds of activities with which children should have experiences, and it is these that are discussed.

Since reading is a thinking process, much of what constitutes readiness is the development of schemata and a predisposition for learning. Recent research indicates that preparation for literacy results more from specific social, linguistic, and cognitive experiences related to reading and writing than from general cognitive and perceptual–motor tasks (eye–hand coordination) (Bloome & Green, 1984; Mason, 1984a). Many children begin to learn how to read and write at a very early age through being read to; learning to identify and name letters and words; and learning to print, spell, and use print labels in their drawings (Mason, 1984a; Harste, Woodward, & Burke, 1984; Clay, 1986; Cannella, 1985). Three general types of experiences seem to foster young children's learning about reading and writing:

> (a) interaction with adults in speaking, listening, reading, and writing situations; (b) independent explorations of print, initially through pretend reading and "scribbling," and later through rereading familiar storybooks and composing messages with "invented spellings"; and (c) adult modeling of language and literacy (ECLDC/IRA, 1986, p. 823).

PARENTS AND READING

Teachers can and should involve parents in the development of their children's reading and writing strategies. Parents are their children's first teachers, and they can remain involved throughout their children's school education. Increasing evidence indicates that a child's literacy begins in the home. Readiness for and achievement in formal reading instruction is based on a child's experiences with print before reaching the classroom (Holbrook, 1985). Once children begin school, parents can reinforce classroom learning through language games and activities.

Parents contribute to their children's reading skills and leisure reading development in many ways (Greaney, 1986). Through verbal interactions they prepare children for written forms of literacy. Parents prepare children during oral discourse when they read or tell stories; they provide interest in reading; they provide access to print; and they stimulate their children's imaginations and help them to understand words long before the words are recognized in print. When parents, teachers, and children all participate in prereading and prewriting activities, the responsibility for learning is shared (Burke, 1985).

Teachers can describe to parents the skills and strategies being learned in the classroom and can also encourage them to reinforce and extend this learning through easy, fun activities that they and their children can share. These activities might include playing language games; watching television programs; participating in family trips and hobbies; and using books, games, and records. Teachers can decide how to distribute and use these materials and how to introduce these ideas to the parents. They may choose to do it at a back-to-school night, at a parents' meeting, through a class newsletter, at a workshop with a specific theme, or through a note home. As students begin to understand and use written communications, they are encouraged to invite their parents to be partners in their learning. The activities just mentioned are based on the ideas presented in this chapter with, of course, adjustments made for the student's age. The literacy development fostered by parents at home continues after their children enter school, and it is lifelong (Holbrook, 1985).

Figure 3–1 contains a sample parents' letter describing what the class is learning and what activities parents and children can do at home to support that learning. In this case, the students are organizing and classifying items. The parents' letter shares some ideas with parents that link school and home learning.

In the resource section at the end of this chapter and Chapter 11 there are other suggestions and lists of books that teachers can encourage parents and children to share.

DEVELOPMENT OF BEGINNING READING

The beginning reading program is one of creative problem solving (Lundsteen, 1974b). It is a program that develops and extends a child's ability to think. In Piagetian terms, the teacher causes some cognitive conflict (disequilibrium). The conflict, which is a challenge but not an excessive one, makes it possible to maintain motivation (McDonell, 1975).

Problem solving depends on careful and conscious acts by both the teacher and the student. Lundsteen (1974b) says that by using a variety of school problems full of unknowns, the teacher leads students to:

Clarify the problem. During the beginning of the problem-solving process, the teacher leads students to recall already known information relevant to the problem.

Generate a hypothesis. The teacher guides students in generating alternative ways of stating the problem. This helps students further clarify the problem.

Plan procedures. The students, with the teacher's guidance, attempt to determine various ways in which the question or hypothesis may be answered. The teacher helps students determine which of the plans seem more workable and leads them to attempt those first.

Evaluate results. The teacher leads students to examine the various results obtained by working through the procedures for solving the hypothesis. If the hypothesis cannot be verified, he or she guides students in how to deal with an unresolved problem. Plans for suspending judgments for future verification or rejection are developed.

Dear Parent:

During the next few weeks, your child will be instructed in reading and writing materials dealing with classifying and organizing. To classify and organize information, your child should

* understand that a variety of objects may have a common characteristic by which they can be grouped together: Wheels, coins, plates, and jar covers are all round.
* understand that certain objects are usually found in a particular place: A bed, a dresser, and a clothes closet are usually found in a bedroom.

The following activity can increase your child's ability in classifying and organizing:

Cut out pictures of different objects from magazines or newspapers. You might have pictures of animals, people, toys, foods, clothing, etc. Place the pictures on the table. Choose a category that a number of the pictures belong to. Place those pictures in a separate group. Have your child look at the pictures you have chosen and try to guess your category. For example, you might choose the category "soft" and then pick any pictures having a soft quality.

Let your child pick a mystery category and choose the pictures that belong. You guess the category.

Sincerely,

Your child's teacher

FIGURE 3–1
Parent Newsletter

The parent letter was developed by Carol G. Hittleman.

Readiness is the ability and desire to take risks (McDonell, 1975). With the teacher's guidance, students discover prediction strategies and develop schemata about written language forms for selecting, questioning, testing, and generalizing about the information in their world. This is how children learn their language in the first place—as a social interaction process (Thomas, 1985).

In helping to develop students' cognitive strategies, the teacher's task is to instruct them about their environment. The students' world is not only the classroom, but also their homes, stores, streets, playgrounds, and the people and language experiences they encounter. To help them cope with their environment, the teacher helps students focus attention on the immediate problem, realize how information is found and evaluated, and find alternatives for searching out and evaluating the obtained information (Mishler, 1972). Throughout, the importance of language is underscored. Special or important words relating to the environment are given attention and their roles in helping students think are identified.

The emphasis of beginning reading activities is on language development. "Children become familiar with written language by hearing the language of literature and other print within their environment, just as they learned oral language by listening to complex, but meaningful speech" (Cohn, 1981, p. 550). An important part of every school program is daily oral reading of printed messages, stories, and information by the teacher to students. Whenever possible, students should have a representation of what is being read. For example, students can have an individual copy for following the teacher's reading or an enlarged version of the story. In "Resources for the Teacher" are the names of publishers who produce sets of enlarged texts, or "big books," and multiple copies of various books for shared reading activities.

As stated before, children become familiar with written language by being involved in producing their own written and oral texts (Jaggar, Carrara, & Weiss, 1986). They become facile with written language as they fulfill their daily need to produce some form of communication for a variety of purposes and with a variety of audiences. Children are creators of responses who become literate by being encouraged to construct those responses through reading, talking, writing, and drawing. These activities require children to relate, link, remember, call up, relearn, monitor, and problem solve known information and real world events (Clay, 1986).

A program of readiness, then, prepares students to learn to read and write effectively and naturally when it is concerned with developing expectancies in both the oral and written language systems. In one's language system, the expectancies are both verbal and nonverbal. To review from Chapter 2, the expectancies for reading are

1. procedures for regulating the physical aspects of reading;
2. a language repertoire containing all rules and cues of spoken and written language; and
3. meanings, concepts, and schemata that have been acquired.

The development of a readiness to read, therefore, results from teachers giving students opportunities to store the knowledge, rules, and strategies for constructing and reconstructing meaning from language in their long-term memories. These are the schemata referred to in Chapters 2 and 13. In the following sections, instructional procedures for developing beginning reading and writing are presented.

DEVELOPING BEGINNING READING STRATEGIES

One previously cited misconception about readiness is that readiness must be acquired before reading can begin. This over-simplified belief is fostered when teachers believe reading readiness exists independently of the methods and materials used and the pace of instruction (Mayer, 1975). Students are made "ready" only if they are made ready for something; therefore, what a teacher assumes to be the literacy process determines what it is that constitutes readiness for reading and writing. The literacy readiness program cannot be considered apart from the available reading instruction (Durkin, 1968).

Since most beginning reading programs occur in elementary schools at kindergarten and first grade, the following discussion may seem to be concerned more with students of this age. Nevertheless, teachers need to be aware that these procedures are really *readiness for literacy procedures.* Any student, regardless of age or grade, without the strategies for using and producing oral and written language needs readiness development. Teachers can easily adapt these procedures for older students or for students with special needs (see Chapter 9).

The question often arises about whether kindergarten is the time for "formal" reading and writing activities. The question, in many instances, draws attention to the wrong aspect of readiness instruction. There is no doubt that a planned, systematic, language-oriented readiness program has more positive and lasting effects on later reading and writing achievement than does an incidental readiness program (Blanton, 1972; Mason, 1984a). This means that the teacher who intentionally fosters whole-language readiness activities provides a better foundation for reading and writing than does a teacher who haphazardly or infrequently promotes such activities.

In addition, a question about using formal or informal readiness activities many times refers to the use of a particular commercial program. The answer to such a question depends not so much on whether the materials are teacher-made or commercially produced but on the type of activities and the use made of the materials. There is no inherent wrong in commercial readiness materials if they are used wisely by teachers. Teachers need to know what authors and publishers claim about their readiness materials and what the materials actually teach. Research results indicate that both formal and incidental readiness programs that emphasize language development and experiences appear more successful than those that focus on narrow aspects of readiness (Blanton, 1972;

Mason, 1984a). In addition, it appears that language development "is neglected when children are placed in a regimented situation whereby all children merely follow directions" (Church, 1974, p. 364). Most important, readiness activities should be appropriate for the students' linguistic, social, emotional, and physical maturity.

Children learn to use language in social situations. Since the purpose of language is to communicate, there must be ample opportunity for social interactions with other children and with adults. The goal of a readiness program is to provide situations that foster cognitive, affective, psychomotor, and linguistic growth in using and producing written language. This is accomplished through experiences in which students act on the environment and in turn are affected by the environment. Linguistic factors are the common strand running through all the other factors; they provide for the students' internal manipulation of the environment, their thinking organization, their development and self-expression, and their interrelationship of thoughts and actions (Clay, 1986; Foerster, 1975a).

Print Awareness and Writing in Beginning Reading

The study of beginning readers and writers reveals that young children gain their knowledge of print and its functions developmentally. The stages of print awareness begin at about age two or three, and they continue through the child's first year of formal instruction (Chomsky, 1971; Clay, 1975, 1982). The growth period of children includes a wide span of understanding and schemata acquisitions. Students' understanding of print begins with their learning that a sign or a symbol is a means for delivering a message. For example, *cat* means an animal, and "the golden arches" means a place to eat. Then follows a complicated period of attempting to relate spoken messages to written ones. As children develop knowledge of the alphabet, they experiment with and invent words and sentences. Attempts to copy print and explore various combinations of letters and words (invented spelling; see Chapter 6) lead to greater understanding of what they know and the ability to classify that knowledge (comprehension monitoring; see Chapter 4). When directionality is understood, there may be a natural period of reversing or mirror imaging. Last, the child begins to develop a concept of spacing words and varying arrangements of information on a page.

After students gain an ability to produce written messages, their writing develops in stages that seem to have some theoretical basis in Piaget's stages of cognitive growth. The stages begin with an egocentric (here and now) form and progress to the inclusion of a hypothesizing and abstracting (there and then) form (Moffett, 1968; Britton et al., 1975). The stages do not represent ages but periods of acquiring facility in producing written language. In the first, **recording,** the student produces an eyewitness account or running commentary. (Spellings are standardized in the following examples.)

I have a shirt with a soccer ball. It has the colors green and yellow. The shirt is for soccer. (Jenny, Age 6)

In the second, **reporting,** the student provides a narrative or description of a particular series of events.

Making Salad.
Get the tomato.
Wash the tomato.
Cut the tomato.
Put it in the salad. (Jenny, Age 6)

In the third, **generalizing,** the student provides a more general narrative that detects and demonstrates patterns of repeated events, places, or characters.

Squeeky the mouse gets in the frigidaire.
I open the door for Squeeky.
Squeeky loves cheese.
He likes cheese every day. I open
the door. He sleeps
in the frigidaire.
Squeeky loves Jenny. (Jenny, Age 6)

In the last, **hypothesizing,** the student produces theories, deductions, and hypotheses backed up by logical arguments and idea development.

Sunglasses
I would like a pair of sunglasses so I can wear them in the car. The sun is always in my eyes. When I put the sun viser down it does not work because I am too short. Sunglasses is dark brown and the earpiece is black. My brother has a pair too. (Andrea, Age 9)

During the development of written language, students need to have chances to write. Opportunities to create texts should grow from a classroom context that helps students extend an effective control of their spoken language to include all sorts of written prose (Clay, 1982).

Strategies for Developing New Concepts

Concepts are acquired in three ways: (1) through direct experience, (2) through direct verbal explanation, and (3) through conceptual explanation (J. Smith, 1972).

In **direct experience,** something is learned without explicit verbalization. A student might observe the teacher performing some task and then, using the teacher's performance as a model, attempt to do the same task. Or the student, after several experiences of a situation, forms his or her own concept. Without associating that experience with a verbal label or description, however, it will remain locked in a student's imagery memory.

Direct verbal explanation takes the form of a definition (e.g., "This is a hammer") or the form of an explanation of how or why something functions:

> The water comes through the pipe at the top and falls into the little buckets. The buckets are now heavy so they move downwards. The falling buckets are attached to the wheel. The wheel turns as each bucket gets full, falls toward the river, empties into the river, and then rises up to be filled again.

With direct explanation, the situation is concrete; the situation is within the sight, sound, smell, or touch of the student. The success of a verbal explanation depends on the similar experiences of the speaker and hearer—the speaker and hearer assign the same meanings to the same words because they have had similar experiences.

However, in a **conceptual explanation** the verbal message and reality may not be directly connected. Conceptual explanation is abstract; the student must have long-term memories of other experiences to which the new experience can be related. Successful learning by conceptual explanation requires that the speaker and hearer share a total experience.

In the development of reading readiness with young students, the sequence of instruction should move from direct experience to direct verbal explanation to conceptual explanation. If teaching begins at the conceptual explanation level without a base of experience, learning is hindered. When a student is able to deal with an experience or concept abstractly (has developed a schemata), then the student is ready to speak, read, and write about that particular topic.

This last point is important. For every idea one can read about, there must be a readiness. No single general skill can account for an individual's ability to read. For example, a reader whose strategies are limited to dealing with the graphophonological cues in language cannot fully reconstruct an author's message. Therefore, materials for beginning reading contain experiences and concepts familiar to the reader. Chapter 4 contains strategies for formally introducing students to the reading process through the language experience approach. In this approach, emphasis is placed on activities that allow students to develop facility with the oral language system so that functioning in the written language system becomes an extension of it. Reading and writing should become as natural and easy as listening and speaking.

The following outlined readiness program has a variety of activities with differing purposes. Individual activities do not develop single skills, strategies, or schemata, and so there is no attempt to classify them as if they do. The classifications presented, therefore, should not be construed as hierarchical or absolute; they are tentative and heuristic—a means for initiating and stimulating investigation into the nature of readiness to use written language.

Activities for Developing Readiness

Cognitive Factors

Some teachers refer to cognitive factors as "comprehension skills." These cognitive factors represent the knowledge domains discussed in Chapters 2 and 13. They include specific information and the scripts for creating statements about that information in oral and written form. Many of the following activities may seem like play, but play is an integral part of preschool and kindergarten programs and is important to the development of the thinking process (Anastasiow, 1979).

Classifying and Patterning

- Show pictures or objects belonging to several general categories. Once the objects and the categories are learned, mix up the items of two or three categories and then have students sort them. Some classifications might be:

zoo	farm	street
ride on	ride in	jobs
wear	outdoors	indoors
eat	furniture	containers

- Provide a series of items. From additional items, many of which are not related to the items in the series, have students select an item or group of items that continues the series. *It is important to ask students why they selected an item. Sometimes they see a pattern that is not intended by the teacher, yet it is logical.* Some suggested series are given in Figure 3–2.

- After students understand how to detect patterns in a series, provide them with a matrix. Make the dimensions of the matrix represent two different series. After students discover how the matrix works, have them complete partial matrices. Two sample matrices are shown in Figures 3–3 and 3–4.

- Provide students with objects, or with pictures of objects and places, to show the relationships expressed by the prepositions of language: *in, on, under, over, behind*, etc. Have students create a statement that indicates the relationship between two or more objects. Or, have them place the objects in a relationship expressed by the teacher. For example, have students identify "The car is next to the tree," or direct them to put the block under the ruler.

  The procedure in the previous activity can also be carried out using the adverbial relationship *how*. For example, "The catsup comes slowly out of the bottle."

- Provide students with objects having different characteristics that can be identified using different senses. Have students classify the items according to the sense(s) they use to gain the most information about the item. This activity works well with items that share characteristics. For example, use items that look somewhat alike (sugar–salt), feel somewhat alike (sand–sugar), smell somewhat alike (flower–perfume), etc.

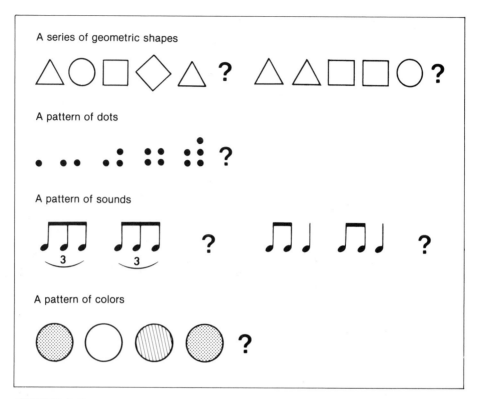

FIGURE 3–2
Patterns in Series

- Play samples of various sounds heard in the students' environment. Have them match the sound to the appropriate object or a realistic representation of the object. Have the sounds prerecorded so that home and street sounds are included.

  Also, have students compare sounds of objects placed in closed canisters, such as plastic film containers. Use objects such as seeds, pebbles, sand, flour, nails, money, or water. Have the students classify the sounds by intensity and by descriptive qualities—"clinky," "rattly," "swishy."

  The previous activities can be extended for other modalities: Have students taste or touch an object and attempt to name the object or match the taste or feel to the real object.

- Present students with a group of objects that have one or more characteristics in common. Ask them to indicate what the items have in common. This activity may be extended by using items that have one or more characteristics which are different. For young children, the characteristics must be observable. As students mature, more abstract qualities can be used to group the objects. For example, young children may be asked how several different kinds of blue objects are all the same. As they mature, the objects may be classified by function ("used in cooking"), or higher-

FIGURE 3–3
Classifying Actions

order quality ("all made of metal"). *It is important that teachers ask students what their reasons are for classifying distinguishing features.*

■ Provide students with a sequence of pictures that tell a story. Mix up the pictures and have students rearrange them to tell the story. As students gain facility in this task, provide them with a sequence of pictures but do not show them the completed story beforehand.

■ Present students with a problem. Have them generate as many solutions to the problem as possible and then test out each to determine which are workable. Alternative solutions do not always have to be workable. Allow students to determine whether a solution is workable or not after it has been tried.

■ Provide students with various illustrations of completed events. Have them indicate possible causes of the activity or incident. Give the situations to students pictorially

FIGURE 3-4
Classifying Shapes

or verbally. For example, show students a picture of the results of a storm, or tell them that a baseball player is being congratulated at home plate. Allow students to generate as many possible causes as they can.

Understanding

- Let students listen to a story. When the story is completed, ask them what the story was about. Discuss the details or major events of the story, the general plot, and the theme of the story. Students who have trouble remembering the events of a story can be guided in developing strategies for remembering. One such device is to allow students to make simple drawings as they listen to a story. Then in the retelling, they use their simple sketches as notes.

    To aid their memories, help students develop techniques for sequencing events. As they listen, have them apply sequence cues—first, second, third, etc.—to the events.

- Remembering is also developed through variations of the game "Concentration." This game is played by using a deck of playing cards that have paired items of the same shape, color, use, etc. The deck is dealt out face down in rows. When a student turns over two paired cards, he or she keeps them. Unsuccessful matches are turned face down again, and the next student takes a turn. Encourage students to develop "tricks" for remembering where the various cards are after they have been returned to play.

- To help students develop an understanding of plot, provide them with some sample story outlines. Have students try to match the story outline to stories they know or have heard. For example, ask students to name some of the more common fairy tales from outlines such as the following:

    A little girl takes some food to a sick relative.
    A girl finds an empty house and tries out the family's food and furniture.
    Three animals try to set up homes but run into trouble from another animal.

- To help students develop an understanding of theme, have them listen to stories, poems, plays, etc. which are all examples of a particular theme. Start with themes within students' experiences and to which they can relate. As they hear stories, encourage them to state the theme of the story and classify it with other known stories of the same theme. Some themes common to stories for young elementary students are:

  We cannot always do everything we want to do.
  Family and close friends can be of great help sometimes.
  Some people have different ways of doing things.
  We have different feelings when we are personally rejected or accepted.
  Things are not always what they appear to be.

- Provide students with opportunities to follow different types of directions. Begin with simple, one-step directions, then move to more complex directions. Allow students to discuss among themselves why certain directions are difficult to follow and others are easier. Let students suggest how directions are remembered over brief periods of time.

  This activity can be extended to an investigation of the ways people of all ages remember a set of directions. Have students question their parents, relatives, teachers, other students, and any other people they have contact with about ways they remember directions.

- Find examples of directions that are given pictorially or symbolically. Have students translate these directions into verbal directions. (Pictorial directions, for example, often accompany toys and games.) Have students write out directions for an activity of their own choosing.

- After students hear a story, have them listen to a musical version. For example, read or tell the story *Peter and the Wolf* or the *Sorcerer's Apprentice,* and then play a record of Prokofiev's "Peter and the Wolf" or Dukas's "Sorcerer's Apprentice." After students have become familiar with both the story and the music, have them narrate the story to the music.

  Extend this activity by having students create their own musical versions of well-known stories. Allow them to orchestrate a story by using rhythm instruments supplied by the school or that students make themselves. This activity works best with stories in which the number of characters is not too large and each character is repeated in the story at least twice.

- Have students listen to brief vignettes, but do not complete the stories—have them offer possible endings. This activity may also be done with a long story. At various points in the story, stop reading and ask students to suggest what might happen next. (See Chapter 4, "Developing Guided Reading–Thinking Lessons.")

- Read a story about some familiar activity that includes some incorrect information. After you have finished, have students identify the incorrect information. Be sure to tell them before reading the story what you will ask them.

Affective Factors
Activities devoted to the development of attitudes and interests are considered to foster readiness in affective factors. Included in this area are activities that

lead students to make generalizations about themselves both as individuals and as members of groups. Language is studied as a key to understanding social relationships (Mishler, 1972). The affective factors represent the schemata of roles, personalities, and objects; the scenarios for the spatial domain; and the goals, plans, and actions of the intentional conceptualization domain.

- Provide students with opportunities to differentiate themselves as physical bodies in space to develop a sense of their own bodies as well as a sense of themselves in relation to other individuals and objects. This may be accomplished by having students build columns of blocks that extend over their heads. Another possibility is to have students walk narrow mazes through walls of blocks, furniture, or other students without touching the boundaries of the path.

- Have students create family portraits through montages of photographs or drawings. Have them pay attention to the physical characteristics that distinguish one individual from another. Also ask students to identify how body parts change as people get older.

- Play games that require the identification of body parts and their relative positions in space. Use games such as "Simple Simon" and the dance movements accompanying songs such as "Looby Loo" and "Hokey Pokey."

- Read stories to students that deal with body parts and with individual characteristics (hair, skin, and eye color; shape of face; type of hair). Have students discuss what everyone has in common and how individuals differ.

- Play matching games in which students match a piece of clothing to the part of the body for which it is intended.

- Have students use thumb-, hand-, or footprints to create animal characters or abstract designs. Or have students lie down on large pieces of paper and have other students trace their outlines. Then have them draw in their facial features and clothing. Incorporate these drawings into a "me" book.

- Provide students with opportunities to express their feelings about themselves in different situations. These activities may be combined with stories about how other children and animals feel in different situations. Have students list words that relate to and evoke emotions. In the latter case, connotations of some common words can be explored. For instance, students can discuss what feelings are evoked by words like *bacon, bath, ice cream, vacation,* and *dentist.* (For additional suggestions, see Chapter 6.)

- Read different types of literature to students (see Chapter 8). Have them discuss the types of stories they prefer. Extend the discussion to include television programs and movies. Make students aware of the factors that affect their interests and preferences in such situations as choosing a program to watch, selecting a friend, buying a dessert in a restaurant, and picking an outfit to wear.

- Give students several different roles to act out. At first, choose roles that require them to portray the observable motions of a house builder, a baker, etc. Then have students act out situations in which they must show emotions such as fear, happiness, anger, sadness, and the like. You may choose to extend the role-playing to hypothetical situations. Use open-ended stories to enable students to explore answers to questions such as, "What could you do?" "What would you do?" "What should you do?"

- Have students survey adults and older children about their attitudes toward reading. Let the class as a whole classify the various feelings about reading and try to hypothesize why people feel differently about it.

- Have students express their feelings and attitudes through art. Have them examine various pictures or reproductions of artists' work grouped according to theme. Ask them to describe what characteristics in the pictures create different moods. Then have students create mood pictures by illustrating a story or a musical selection. Encourage them to experiment with realistic and abstract renditions of things, using color, size, and so forth to create different moods. Let other students try to explain what the pictures mean to them.

Psychomotor Factors

The activities included in this section are aimed at helping students understand that some body movements relate to the culture or group to which they belong and that other body movements relate to their own personalities (Foerster, 1975b). Cultural body movements are the conventional body movements that distinguish members of one culture from members of another. Individual body movements distinguish individuals of the same culture and are an expression of personality. These compose the paralinguistic aspect of language development.

- Using pantomime, have students communicate an idea to the class. Have them use facial expressions to convey feelings and gestures to convey an idea or mood. As a group, study the body language people use in different situations. Lead students to notice how most people who grew up in the same area use similar movements with individual variations.

- Play games such as "Who's the Leader?" Have everyone sit in a circle. Ask one student to leave the room and choose someone from the circle to be the leader. Allow the student who left the room to return. Have the leader initiate different actions or movements, without using any verbal communication, that the other students must follow. The student who was out of the room should then try to figure out who the leader is.

- Have students play "moving" games such as performing some task as if they were some other person or animal. Some suggested movements are being a baby, walking up or down the stairs, carrying a heavy load, eating something sticky, being bored, and finding a dollar. Encourage the other students to verbally express the idea or feeling being conveyed by the performer's movements.

    This activity may be expanded by having students move to different rhythms. You may also have them do various movements with another student or a group. Have students explain how doing something alone differs from doing it with others.

- Have students lead other blindfolded students around the room without using any verbal communication between them. Explain that they may only touch the blindfolded students' arms with one hand. Have students tell how it felt to be totally dependent on others.

- Watch a movie or television program without using the sound. Have students suggest from the body movements of the actors what ideas are being conveyed. Then allow students to watch the same program again but with the sound turned on. Have them discuss how their interpretations coincided with or differed from the intended meaning.

- Have students make up dances to musical selections that vary in tempo, rhythm, melody, sound, and pitch.

- Have students learn and act out the movements to songs such as "If You're Happy and You Know It." When they become familiar with the song, change *happy* to some other emotion or feeling. Then have students move other body parts and make appropriate facial expressions.

- Have students explore the various sounds it is possible to make with their bodies. For instance, have them make sounds such as a knock, slap, snap, tap, "raspberry," and so on.

- Have students learn and act out various work songs. When they understand the idea of work songs, they may want to create parodies of them to express their own "work" in school.

- Have students play any type of circle game in which the outcome of the game depends on being able to "read" the body movements of other students. Such games as dodgeball and "crows and cranes" are examples.

- Have students create artwork using materials of various textures. Then have them create mood stories that are "read" only by running their hands over the completed work. Have other students give their interpretations of the various stories.

- Have students explain to an imaginary space alien how certain physical activities are performed. During the explanation, do not allow students to use any physical motions. This can also be done by putting the explainer behind a screen. Have students explain to the alien how to use a telephone, how to tie a shoelace, and how to eat with a knife, fork, and spoon.

- Have students repeat various sentences that could be ambiguous except for the intonation and gestures that accompany different meanings. Sentences such as the following may be used: "That's great." "I like growing children." "I ate the whole thing."

- Blindfold students and seat them in the middle of the room. Have other students make sounds from different sides of the room. The students in the middle should indicate the directions from which the sounds came. Give them ample opportunity to develop eye-hand coordinations and spatial relations. An activity that fosters spatial orientations is building with blocks, especially making tall towers!

- Allow students to act out stories using puppets. Let them create their own character puppets and use them to perform. Puppets can be made easily and inexpensively from paper bags, fingers, fists, sticks, socks, toilet paper or paper towel tubes, and old tennis balls.

A variation of puppet plays are finger plays in which a story is dramatized with the hands. In finger plays no additional props or make-up are used. In this sense, finger plays resemble a kind of sign language.

Linguistic Factors

Linguistic factors permeate all the other factors involved in developing readiness. However, some activities relate to the nature of language itself. To develop linguistic factors, students must be able to identify and interpret the oral and written cues of language. Here the student learns how language works, what types of activities or situations may or may not promote effective communication, and the appropriateness of different kinds of language in different situations.

Since most reading material is prose and not conversation, reading readiness instruction moves from conversation to spoken prose before reading instruction is begun (McDonell, 1975). Part of each day should be devoted to reading aloud to students. Research supports this suggestion: A teacher's reading aloud daily is associated with a measurable increase in students' language ability (Cullinan, 1974). Stories read aloud to students help them draw inferences at a higher level than when they read the stories to themselves. They also provide models that students can use when writing their own stories. In addition, a special program in literature using daily oral reading by teachers has been shown to have a significant effect on students' reading and writing abilities.

Traditional readiness programs have often assumed that students hear words as units of sound within sentences. Traditional programs also assume that students recognize and understand the relationship between letters and their sounds or meanings. However, there is evidence that neither assumption is correct; instead, these abilities seem to be a function of experience and maturation (Sawyer, 1975). For children under five, the sentence is probably the basic psychological unit of meaning. The ability to analyze speech into units of single words does not begin to appear until after the ages of five or six (Sawyer, 1975; Downing & Oliver, 1973). For adults, the smallest unit of speech processes is the syllable. Chapter 6 contains a discussion about invented spellings and their relationship to reading readiness, beginning reading, writing, and word recognition. The following activities build on students' linguistic knowledge.

- Students may be introduced to the discussion and investigation of linguistic factors by asking "How can we communicate with others when they are not nearby?" This helps students recognize how newspapers, magazines, letters, and other written material preserve ideas for others to benefit by at a later time. Students also learn the function of records and films. Have them try to answer the question: "When is writing a better way of saving and communicating ideas than records or films?"

- Discuss the use of picture language and sign language. Have students create their own stories using only picture sequences. Then have them create symbols for some of their activities, feelings, and attitudes. Encourage students to write stories for one another using these symbols. Have students discuss what happens when someone uses a symbol the others do not know, or when some of the symbols devised are similar to other symbols and therefore seem ambiguous.

- Let students explore the advantages of the telephone, radio, and television for quickly bringing information to people. Discuss the use of the telephone for reporting a fire or accident. Guide students to an understanding of the techniques used for sending and receiving calls on the telephone. (The local telephone company's business office provides many services free to schools, including demonstration telephone kits, films, filmstrips, recordings, and sample telephone information materials.)

- Make a collection of words that have multiple meanings. Explore with students how they can discover what meaning a word has in a particular situation. Some words for this activity are *run, play, bank,* and *story.*

- Read riddles to students and allow them to solve them. Let students begin to write their own riddles. For those who do not catch on to the idea, point out how many riddles use words with multiple meanings.

- Read or tell students stories in which confusion occurs between two or more individuals because different meanings are applied to words. From these stories, let students explore some of the common idioms of our language. Have students draw pictures of the literal and intended meanings of the idioms to show how confusion may arise when one does not know the use of a particular idiom. For instance, read Peggy Parish's *Amelia Bedelia.* Then let students illustrate the literal and idiomatic meanings of: The principal laid down the law. We got on the bus. He took the bike path home.

- As an alternative to listening to the teacher, small groups of students or individuals can listen to recordings of a story in a classroom listening center. The recordings can be teacher-produced or made commercially. This activity works well when copies of the book are available for students to follow along. Be sure the recordings, whatever their source, clearly identify the page being read and allow enough time for students to peruse the illustrations.

- Using the basic kernel sentences beginning on page 413, provide students with oral and written models of how these sentences may be transformed or expanded. Let students make suggestions for transforming and expanding other sentences. Also, provide sentences which are transformations and expansions of kernel sentences and have students identify the kernel sentences and the embedded sentences. For instance, the activity could start with a sentence like "The player saw the ball." Have students use this sentence to create a question, a passive, a negative, and a sentence beginning with *there* or *it.* Then, a sentence such as "The funny clown rode on the brown horse" could be broken down into

The clown is funny.
The clown rode the horse.
The horse is brown.

This activity requires much repetition and modeling in oral and written form. The task is not easy for young students, and the teacher should not expect all students to gain facility in doing these tasks. Many will be able to find only a few sentence patterns, but some will be able to find many. If the teacher constantly asks, "Is there another way to say that?" and "Can we put those two ideas together?" or "Can we take those two ideas and say them separately?" then students will be alerted to the possibilities for dealing with the syntactic patterns of their language. As a result, they will develop an appreciation of the English language and increase in their ability to use language in general.

■ Read a sentence to students in which a word has been deleted (an oral cloze exercise). Have them generate words that could complete the sentence and ask them to explain how they selected the word they did. To those who have some difficulty, make the activity a multiple choice one—provide a correct response, a word that is the correct part of speech but semantically incorrect, and a word from another part of speech. Whenever students give the correct response, ask them how they selected that word.

■ Play word games in which students' answers are words that rhyme with the key words. You might use incomplete rhyming couplets such as,

> One fine day
> We went out to _____.

Or you might use rhyming adjective–noun combinations such as fat/cat, green/bean, mad/dad.

■ Have students begin to develop a sight vocabulary from various labels and signs that the teacher or students place around the classroom. In many instances, teachers can use single words to label things on bulletin boards as well as things such as doors and windows. However, it is a more natural lead-in to reading if these labels contain sentences. Instead of controlling students' vocabularies, the teacher could begin to use sentence patterns that are used in many first-grade readers (not preprimers, which often use artificial language). For instance, a bulletin board about community helpers could include captions for pictures that read "This is a fire fighter"; "This is a police officer"; "This is a postal worker." Classroom signs could say, "We go to Art at 9:30 a.m."; "Please close the closet door"; "The coat hooks are in the back of the room."

■ Introduce students to the alphabet through a discussion of how their names are spelled. They can become acquainted with the many alternative forms and shapes in which letters are drawn by creating montages of words from newspapers, advertisements, and signs. This provides practice in distinguishing letters when they have various forms.

cat milk TOOTHPASTE

■ Let students play games in which they describe letters to other students who cannot see them. Use only basic lowercase or uppercase manuscript letters. For example, one student might say, "I see a letter that has one long line going up and a circle on the left side of the line," and the other student answers, "*d*."

■ Have students begin to "read" calendars, maps, globes, thermometers, pictures, simple graphs, and the like. On many of these, symbols are used. After students have become familiar with the symbols, have them read the information to other students. Then allow students to try to make similar items. For instance, using some of the common symbols used on television weather programs, have them create weather maps. Other students can then interpret the maps.

■ Acquaint students with the different parts of a book. As a story is read to them, demonstrate techniques for the careful handling of the book. Identify the cover, title page with author and publisher, main text, and table of contents. Have them use these parts when creating their own books.

■ Sometimes communication among individuals is hindered because the speaker uses many pronouns. Young children will use pronouns so much that the referents of each may become ambiguous. As they engage in various oral activities, be alert to their use of ambiguous pronouns. Also, read or tell stories in which many pronouns have been substituted for the characters' names. Each time a pronoun is said, have students supply the name of the person to whom the pronoun refers.

■ Another type of substitution is the use of *this* and *does* for entire ideas, as in: "It is raining; because of this, we will not go to the beach"; "Sometimes Melissa does not help her mother, and sometimes she does." As sentences such as these are read to students, ask them to supply the words for which *this* and *does* are substitutes.

■ Create a "word of the day" display in which a new word is posted each day. To maintain students' interest, the words could be related to some upcoming school event or national holiday. The display could be changed seasonally—a tree with colored leaves in the fall, a snowman in the winter, children flying kites in the spring. Words can be printed on small signs that fit the decor of the display. A few minutes each day should be spent discussing the word and its meaning or meanings. During the day, students should be encouraged to use the word as many times as they can in "natural" situations. No word is too big to be learned; the length of a word in no way determines its appropriateness for students. The teacher should, however, take care to select words students can conceptualize. Words with high imagery are good.

■ Provide opportunities for students to become familiar with language's melodic qualities. Use echo activities in which they must repeat a sentence exactly as it is said by the teacher or another student. This "follow the speaker" activity can be used as an introduction to choral speaking. Beginning with short poems or rhymes that are easily memorized, interpret each reading differently by changing the rhythm, intonation, and accent given to the words and sentences. Then let students decide which interpretations they prefer. (In using choral speaking, the teacher is an active leader. The purpose is not to develop individual styles of interpretation but to develop a sense of several individuals working together to produce a group result. After students understand what leading and following mean in these activities, they can assume the leadership positions.)

DETERMINING READINESS TO READ

As stated previously, many teachers prefer a simple way to identify students who are ready to read. To accommodate them, test writers devise reading readiness tests that are supposed to discriminate between those who are ready to read and those who need additional readiness activities. There is strong evidence, however, that reading readiness tests cannot distinguish those who are ready nor are they so precise that they specify the areas in which a student needs additional instruction (Johnston, 1984; MacGinitie, 1969; Pikulski, 1974a; Rude, 1973; Sawyer, 1975; Vogel & McGrady, 1975).

First, *readiness* means different things to different people. Whatever one's definition of reading, there are some factors that make a student ready to read. The question with instructional implications is: What definition of readiness is consistent with what is known about children's language and thinking development? By using a definition of readiness consistent with one's definition of reading, the prerequisites for reading can then be determined. Any assessment of students' readiness to read considers the methods and materials that will be used to teach reading.

Second, reading readiness tests are predictive, not diagnostic. Since there is little agreement among authorities about what constitutes reading readiness skills, the tests were designed to predict which students would be successful on a reading achievement test after a period of instruction. The discussion of standardized tests in Chapter 11 points out how some achievement tests may not measure reading ability. In the same vein, what the readiness tests may be measuring is general potential for doing academic work.

In assessing readiness to read, then, the wrong questions have been asked (MacGinitie, 1969). Instead of asking, "Is the student ready to learn to read?", teachers should be asking, "What and how is the student ready to learn?"

The predictive value of any estimation of a student's readiness comes from the similarity of the tested task to the process of reading. Since reading is a complex transaction of cognitive, affective, psychomotor, and linguistic factors, "there appears to be no nice, clean way to identify children who are likely to encounter difficulty in reading" (Pikulski, 1974a).

Readiness assessments should instead grow out of classroom activities, and they should be based on a careful analysis of the task of beginning reading (Johnston, 1984). Using analytical teaching procedures (Chapter 10), the teacher assesses the student's cognitive and linguistic abilities and how these abilities are used in different situations.

Some formal instruments do exist for a teacher to use in determining what abilities students possess and what additional learning is needed. Two representative standardized instruments, which measure students' mastery of concepts considered necessary for achievement in the first year of school, are

> *Test of basic concepts—revised.* (1985). New York: The Psychological Corporation. Forms C and D. Intended level: Kindergarten and grades 1 and 2.
> *Bracken basic concept scale.* (1984). Columbus, OH: Merrill. Forms A and B. Intended level: Ages 2 1/2 to 8.

These tests are used to identify students with deficiencies in concepts common to various curriculum materials and to identify individual concepts for which particular students could profit from additional instruction. The manuals of instruction contain information for the teacher about using the tests for analytical purposes and include suggestions for instructional practices.

Another instrument is the *Concepts about print test* (Clay, 1972, 1979). With this test, teachers observe students at the beginning stages of reading and evaluate their concepts about (1) the orientation of books; (2) whether the message is carried by the print or the pictures; (3) the directionality of the print, the sequence of pages, and the directionality of words; (4) the relationship between printed language and oral language; and (5) words, letters, spacing, and punctuation.

This test is unique and significant in its contribution to the assessment of beginning reading and writing readiness. It does not predict students' behaviors; it contains "defined early reading tasks that are directly interpretable in terms of instruction" (Johnston, 1984). With it teachers analyze what students know about oral–written language relationships and how they use these schemata. The test is used to distinguish the knowledge that students possess after a year of formal instruction (Johns, 1980). The test does have a few limitations that teachers can overcome after gaining familiarity with it (Goodman, 1981). One limitation is that the test manual has norms of performance that were created using schoolchildren in New Zealand. These norms in other English-speaking countries need to be used with caution or disregarded. This should not be a problem because the test is a good informal means of assessing student behavior. A recent pilot project in the Columbus, Ohio, schools indicated modifications can be made and the program can be adapted to local programs.

The test books, *Sand* and *Stones*, contain subtests of upside down print and words, letters, and sentences out of order. These may be confusing to readers of all levels of proficiency. Teachers may wish to substitute other picture books for these test books and adapt the testing procedures. This alternative also provides sources of reading with more cultural relevance to students' situations. Any use of the test needs to be interpreted cautiously, since an "awareness of concepts about print may interact with the reading acquisition process so that it exists as both a consequence of what has occurred and as a cause of further progress in reading" (Johns, 1980).

To use the test, the following are needed:

Clay, M. M. (1985). *The early detection of reading difficulties* (3rd ed.). Exeter, NH: Heinemann.
Clay, M. M. (1972). *Concepts about print test: Sand.* Exeter, NH: Heinemann.
Clay, M. M. (1979). *Concepts about print test: Stones.* Exeter, NH: Heinemann.

Measures for research and evaluation in the English language arts (Fagan, Cooper, & Jensen, 1975—cited in Chapter 10, "Further Reading") can be used or adapted for assessment purposes. The sections on measures for assessing language development and listening should be helpful. In addition, some of the Resources for the Teacher in this chapter contain suggestions for assessing pupil proficiency in the cognitive, linguistic, psychomotor, and affective areas.

RESOURCES FOR THE TEACHER

A teacher starting the development of a reading readiness program is faced with the task of accumulating instructional materials. Readiness materials from a basal reading program often consist only of exercises in letter–sound relationships. In such cases, the teacher can supplement the program with activities and materials that provide a well-rounded program of readiness for reading and writing. The criteria given in Chapter 10 for appropriate instructional materials can guide teachers' selections.

The following resources can be used for creating a language-centered readiness program. The first group are commercial programs. If an entire readiness program is not available for instructional purposes, teachers can obtain one or more of the manuals as handbooks or guides.

Hunter-Grundin, E., & Grundin, H. U. *Language, literature, and literacy* (Levels 1 and 2). Louisville, KY: rdr, Ltd.

Language experiences in early childhood, Teacher's Resource Book. Chicago: Encyclopedia Britannica.

Ginn oral language development (GOLD), Teachers' Manual. Columbus, OH: Ginn.

The following series, introductions to reading and to the basic concepts needed for reading, develop young readers' strategies through thematic books.

Beginning to learn about. Milwaukee, WI: Raintree. (Themes: numbers, seasons, shapes, colors, sensory experiences, and communication)

Ready–Set–Look. Milwaukee, WI: Raintree. (Themes: all about me, animals, around the house, colors, trips)

The following books contain activities that can be used as experiences for fostering the development of reading and writing.

Brown, S. (1981). *Bubbles, rainbows & worms: Science experiments for pre-school children*. Mt. Rainier, MD: Gryphon House.

Redleaf, R. (1983). *Open the door, let's explore: Neighborhood field trips for young children*. St. Paul, MN: Toys 'n Things.

Rockwell, R. E., Sherwood, E. A., & Williams, R.A. (1983). *Hug a tree: And other things to do outdoors with young children*. Mt. Rainier, MD: Gryphon House.

The following texts contain suggestions for instructional activities.

Carin, A., & Sund, R. B. (1978). *Creative questioning and sensitive listening techniques: A self-concept approach* (2nd ed.). Columbus, OH: Merrill.

Glazer, S. M. (1980). *Getting ready to read: Creating readers from birth through six*. Englewood Cliffs, NJ: Prentice-Hall.

Moffett, J., & Wagner, B. J. (1983). *Student-centered language arts and reading, K–13: A handbook for teachers* (3rd ed.). Boston: Houghton Mifflin.

Norton, D. (1985). *Language arts activities for children* (2nd ed.). Columbus, OH: Merrill.

Rhodes, L. K. (1981). *Children's literature: Activities and ideas*. Denver: UCD School of Education.

Stewig, J. W. (1982). *Teaching language arts in early childhood*. New York: Holt, Rinehart & Winston.

Anthologies are useful when seeking stories and poems for listening and act-ing-out activities. Anthologies such as the following contain a variety of litera-ture in a convenient form.

Arbuthnot, M. H. (Revised by Z. Sutherland). (1976). *The Arbuthnot anthology of children's literature* (4th ed.). Glenview, IL: Scott Foresman.

Johnson, E., Sickels, E. R., Sayers, F. C., & Horowitz, C. (1977). *Anthology of chil-dren's literature* (5th ed.). Boston: Houghton Mifflin.

Lists of predictable and wordless story books are included in the following articles.

Abrahamson, R. F. (1981). An update on wordless picture books with an annotated bibliography. *The Reading Teacher, 33,* 417–421.

Bridge, C., Winograd, P. N., & Haley, D. (1983). Using predictable materials vs. preprimers to teach beginning sight words. *The Reading Teacher, 36,* 884–891.

Degler, L. S. (1979). Putting words into wordless books. *The Reading Teacher, 31,* 399–402.

Ellis, D. W., & Preston, F. W. (1984). Enhancing beginning reading using wordless picture books in a cross-age tutoring program. *The Reading Teacher, 37,* 692–699.

Jalongo, M. R., & Bromley, K. D. (1984). Developing linguistic competence through song picture books. *The Reading Teacher, 37,* 840–845.

Rhodes, L. K. (1981). I can read! Predictable books as resources for reading and writing instruction. *The Reading Teacher, 34,* 511–518.

Some publishers produce predictable books, big books for shared reading, and book–record sets. The following are representative of such materials.

Bill Martin's instant readers and *Bill Martin's big books.* New York, NY: Holt, Rinehart & Winston.

Predictable book collections (Levels 1–3); *Skill cassette programs* (Units I, II, III); and *Big books* (Levels 1–3). Jefferson City, MO: Scholastic.

Read-together (Sets A–C); *Read-together with cassettes* (Sets 1–3); *The big books of the read-together sets;* and *More big books.* San Diego, CA: Wright.

The following companies produce recordings and filmstrips for all curriculum areas. Teachers developing readiness programs will find them to be a good source of recordings of songs, games, children's literature, rhythmic activities, and of filmstrips and picture–study–story prints.

Educational Activities, Inc.
P. O. Box 392
Freeport, NY 11520
Educational Teaching Aids
159 West Kinzie Street
Chicago, IL 60619
Good Apple
Box 299
Plainview, NY 11803
Incentive Publications, Inc.
2400 Crestmore Road
Nashville, TN 37215

Raintree Publishing Group
205 West Highland Avenue
Milwaukee, WI 53203
Troll Associates
320 Route 17
Mahwah, NJ 07430

Teachers need resources for informing parents about home activities with children. The following short monographs, intended for distribution to parents, are available from the International Reading Association, P. O. Box 8139, Newark, DE 19711:

Chan, J. M. T. *Why read aloud to children?*
Brinnell, P. *How can I prepare my young child for reading?*
Glazer, S. M. *How can I help my child build positive attitudes toward reading?*
Ransbury, M. K. *How can I encourage my primary grade child to read?*
Rogers, N. *What is reading readiness?*
Rogers, N. *How can I help my child get ready to read?*
Rogers, N. *What books and records should I get for my preschooler?*

The IRA also provides Parent Brochures. Single copies are free upon request with a stamped, self-addressed envelope.

Your home is your child's first school.
You can encourage your child to read.
Good books make reading fun for your child.
Summer reading is important.
You can use television to stimulate your child's reading habits.

The following brochure contains suggestions for parents to encourage their children to write at home and to support a school writing program. It is available from the National Council of Teachers of English, 1111 Kenyon Road, Urbana, IL 61801.

How to help your child become a better writer. (1980). One to fourteen copies are free.

The following books are written for parents by noted reading authorities.

Butler, D., & Clay, M. (1982). *Reading begins at home.* Portsmouth, NH: Heinemann.
Goodman, K. (1986). *What's whole in whole language?* Portsmouth, NH: Heinemann.
Taylor, D., & Strickland, D. (1986). *Family storybook reading.* Portsmouth, NH: Heinemann.

A guide for teachers and parents that includes book lists is

Trelease, J. (1982). *The read-aloud handbook.* New York: Penguin.

A periodical for parents of young children is

Sesame Street parents newsletter. Children's Television Workshop, 1 Lincoln Plaza, New York, NY 10023.

Other materials for parents are listed in the following:

Rhodes, L. K., & Hill, M. W. (1985). Supporting reading in the home—naturally: Selected materials for parents. *The Reading Teacher, 39,* 619–623.

DISCUSSION QUESTIONS AND ACTIVITIES

1. Select a basal reading series and examine the teacher's manual for the readiness materials. In what ways do the activities foster the development of a readiness to read in light of a whole-language definition of reading? Is the aspect of readiness viewed as a broad, many-faceted process or as a limited, one-dimensional one? How are the teaching and learning of reading and writing integrated? (See the checklist in Chapter 10.)

2. Some kindergarten teachers in a particular school wish to implement a beginning reading program that consists primarily of a workbook purporting to teach the letters of the alphabet and their sounds. What advice would you offer these teachers to assist them in the development of a whole-language beginning reading program?

3. A parent of a first-grade student wants to know why the student's class plays so much each day. The parent is concerned that the students in this class will not learn to read as well as students in the other first-grade classes. The class, however, consists of a large number of immature students, and the "games" are activities of the type described in this chapter. How would you answer the parent?

4. How would you support Black's (1980) statement to teachers and parents who feel that uncorrected errors only lead to the reinforcement of bad habits?

   While young children are allowed by parents and preschool teachers to make "mistakes" when learning to talk, most teachers feel they must correct children's "mistakes" when learning to read . . . [even though] pointing out "mistakes" seems to do little in helping them develop communicative competency. (p. 509)

   How would you explain to parents the "errors" students make in learning to write (compose)?

5. Examine several reading readiness tests and their accompanying manuals. In your opinion, what items on each of the tests, although they may predict possible reading achievement, do not indicate the strategies used during the reading process?

6. Administer a series of informal language and cognitive tasks like those discussed in this chapter to a child in kindergarten or the beginning of first grade. (In developing these informal language and cognitive tasks, use the information in Chapters 2 and 13 about language structure and schemata.) Describe the student's behavior—apparent cognitive strategies, linguistic proficiency, psychomotor understandings, and emotional reactions—while undertaking the tasks.

FURTHER READING

Various issues of *Language Arts* are devoted to themes dealing with language development and reading and writing readiness. Many articles contain not only theoretical discussions but also suggestions for instructional activities. Of particular interest may be the following issues.

November/December 1983:	Reading
February 1984:	Talk
January 1985:	Making meaning, learning language
September 1985:	Learning through interaction
December 1985:	Home–school links.
December 1986:	The worlds of children

In addition to the Baghban, Calkins, and Clay books cited in the "Further Reading" section of Chapter 2, insights about young children's development of reading and writing can be gained from the following:

Butler, A., & Trubill, J. (1984). *Towards a reading–writing classroom.* Rozelle, Australia: Primary English Teaching Association.

Calkins, L. M. (1986). *The art of teaching writing.* Portsmouth, NH: Heinemann.

Geller, L. G. (1985). *Wordplay and language learning for children.* Urbana, IL: National Council for Teachers of English.

Harste, J., Woodward, V., & Burke, C. (1984). *Language stories & literacy lessons.* Portsmouth, NY: Heinemann.

Hunter-Grundin, E. (1979). *Literacy: A systematic start.* New York: Harper & Row.

Pflaum, S. (1986). *Development of language and reading in young children* (3rd ed.). Columbus, OH: Merrill.

Organizer

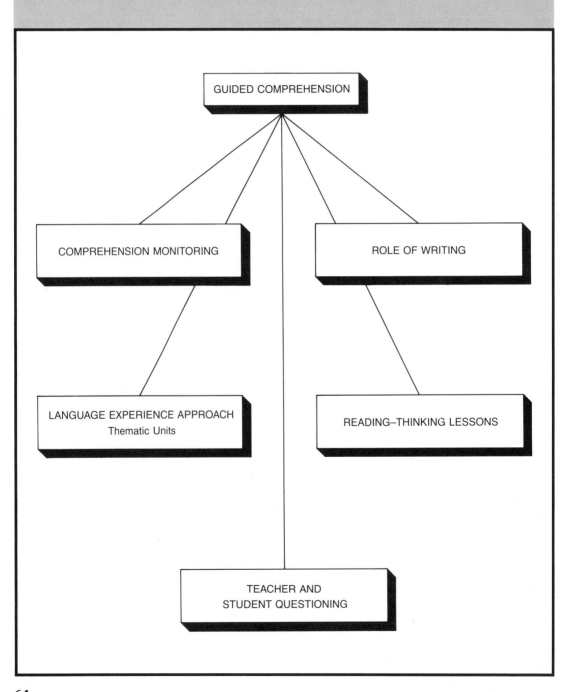

GUIDED COMPREHENSION

COMPREHENSION MONITORING

ROLE OF WRITING

LANGUAGE EXPERIENCE APPROACH
Thematic Units

READING–THINKING LESSONS

TEACHER AND
STUDENT QUESTIONING

CHAPTER 4

Strategies for Guided Comprehension

Focus Questions

- What is the distinction between guided reading and independent, self-guided reading?

- How can the language experience approach be used to introduce students to literacy?

- How can classroom instruction be organized by using thematic units?

- What are the procedures for developing a guided reading–thinking lesson?

- What different types of questions can be used to develop and extend students' understanding during guided reading?

In this text, a distinction is made between reading guided by the teacher and reading guided by students themselves. In guided reading, the teacher has the responsibility for directing students in reconstructing the author's message and in constructing their own meanings. Just as a guide leads an inexperienced naturalist to a bird site but leaves the actual photographing for the novice, the teacher structures a session so that students arrive at a point where they can recreate the author's thoughts and produce their own. In independent, self-guided reading, students take responsibility for initiating and completing a reading act. At such times, they are their own guides.

A reading program meets the needs of students when it provides both types of activities. The teacher should guide students' reading until they are mature enough for independent reading. Since students are always capable of some independent reading, both types of instruction are appropriate.

In this chapter, the focus is on strategies a teacher can use to navigate students through a reading selection. In succeeding chapters, the focus is on strategies that students can use to find their own way through a story. All chapters include writing strategies to help students understand printed messages.

THE NATURE OF READING COMPREHENSION AND COMPREHENSION MONITORING

When an author creates a message, communication with a reader or group of readers is initiated. The author has some intended audience in mind, although there can never be total assurance that the message will reach that particular audience. The author builds a message using his or her knowledge of 1) the subject area and topic to be discussed; 2) how much the intended audience is assumed to know about the subject area and the topic; 3) the style of language in which the message is to be written and the manner in which the ideas are to be organized; and 4) the assumed language maturity of the intended audience. Once the message is formed, the author presents it in printed paragraphs, sentences, and words. Whether the message is meaningful to the reader depends on factors within the reader and within the reading situation. Assuming the situation is conducive to reading, a message is meaningful when the reader's knowledge of the subject area and topic, the reader's language maturity, and the reader's familiarity with language styles (including the printed form of the message) are sufficiently developed to rebuild the author's message.

Traditionally, the process of dealing with an author's message has been called comprehension, which is thought by many to be a set of skills the reader must possess to understand the author. It has been assumed that these comprehension skills can be defined separately, developed sequentially, and applied generally to any and all reading situations (Harker, 1973a).

Traditional comprehension skills are identified as the abilities to grasp the main idea, understand stated and implied details, follow a sequence of events, make inferences, and understand vocabulary in context. Through the application of these skills, the reader is supposed to know what the author means. However, traditional comprehension skills do not refer directly to language but to how people classify information (Bormuth, 1969b); the skills themselves are just a manifestation of the inner cognitive processing of language (Harker, 1973a). These skills (getting the main idea, following a sequence, understanding details, etc.) are *products* of the comprehension process. They represent what is produced after comprehension has taken place (Simons, 1971). The traditional explanation of comprehension fails to (1) specify skills unique to reading and found in general mental processes and (2) distinguish between the how and the what of something that is comprehended.

Recent research on comprehension development indicates comprehension processes are mental operations (thinking) that occur while an individual is reading (Duffy & others, 1984; Flood, 1984; Guthrie, 1980; Harker, 1973a; Pearson, 1985; Spiro, Bruce, & Brewer, 1980). Research also suggests that comprehension is a multidimensional process involving the cognitive processing of language. From a whole-language viewpoint, "the features of language provide the information upon which the comprehension processes operate" (Bormuth, 1969b). These features of language are the syntactic, semantic, and knowledge domains discussed previously and in Chapter 13. They are represented in the interactive and transactional aspects of reading as shown in the model of the reading act (see Figure 2–2).

Reading strategies and reading skill are different (Duffy & Roehler, 1987). Strategies are plans readers use to reconstruct and construct messages. They are used flexibly in appropriate situations. Reading skill is proficiency in using these reading strategies. As students become aware of the strategies they know and use, they can keep track of their comprehension success.

When students are aware and oversee their own reading and writing, it is considered comprehension monitoring, or the use of metacognitive mechanisms (Baker & Brown, 1984). **Metacognition** is a person's awareness of what skills, strategies, and resources are needed to perform a task effectively as well as that person's ability to use self-regulatory mechanisms to ensure the successful completion of the task. Less-proficient or immature readers seem to have difficulty taking charge of their cognitive processes, and they seem less flexible and efficient than better readers in adapting their level of cognitive processing for reading and writing tasks. Although it is not possible to assign a causal relationship between a lack of metacognition and ineffective literacy, there is evidence that instruction aimed at initiating cognitive monitoring and developing self-regulatory mechanisms is desirable. These self-regulatory mechanisms (checking outcomes, planning next moves, evaluating effectiveness, testing and revising strategies for learning, and remediating difficulties) are discussed in this chapter and in Chapters 5 and 7.

THE LANGUAGE EXPERIENCE APPROACH

In using the language experience approach to reading, teachers develop students' reading proficiency through natural language processes. The language experience approach is predicated on the idea that

> reading can be most meaningfully taught when the reading materials accurately reflect the child's own experience as described by his language. The language of instruction then must be that which proceeds from the wealth of linguistic, conceptual, and perceptual experience of the child. A child is more likely to learn to read when the activities associated with the approach have functional relationships with his language, experience, needs and desires. (Cramer, 1971, p. 37)

A common misconception about the language experience approach is that it is an activity for the first grade. Nothing is further from the truth. The language experience approach to reading is a way to foster literacy in students of any age. Since the difficulty of the reading material is controlled by the learner's own language abilities, the language experience procedure is appropriate for any age, including high-school dropouts and adult basic-literacy learners (Hittleman, 1980).

Hall (1972, 1981) suggested the following:

- Beginning readers are users of language. A teacher should accept the student's language as a starting point. (The language of speakers with divergent dialects is discussed in Chapter 9.)
- Beginning readers should learn to view reading as a communication process.
- Beginning readers should understand the reading process as the conscious relating of print to oral language.
- Beginning readers should incorporate the learning of writing with the learning of reading.
- Beginning readers should learn to read meaningful language units. The minimum meaningful language unit is the sentence.
- Beginning readers should learn to read with materials written in their own language patterns.

Although the language experience approach to reading has been researched extensively, reviews of the literature show contrasting findings (Hall, 1978; Vilscek, 1968). These conflicting findings seem to be differences in how researchers defined *language experience*, selected their subjects, and designed and implemented the research itself. Although some unanswered methodological questions exist concerning the research, there is continued interest in the language experience approach as a means for guiding students to literacy. The research does substantiate the language experience approach as an effective way to teach reading and related communication skills. Specifically, students taught by the procedure produce satisfactory or superior results on achievement tests compared with students taught by other procedures. The approach provides learners with meaningful reading and writing vocabularies; it motivates students with special learning problems; and students' performances in writing are particularly impressive (Hall, 1978).

One complaint about the language experience approach, however, is that it offers too little structure to the teacher. So, although it is not a panacea and is not necessarily an easy program to implement, through the language experience approach the teacher can provide a rich experimental and activity-oriented program that uses the child's own language and provides for individualized instruction (Schwartz, 1975). One teacher discovered that the language experience approach can bring revelation to the teacher as well as the student (Gelb, 1975). When working with a ten-year-old nonreading child on a series of activities related to colors, the teacher decided to let the student become physically involved in mixing and creating colors. The teacher concluded:

> Finally the experience meant something to him. The words were felt because he was living them. That was the key to the whole problem: One must live the words to understand them. I felt I had read this 10 million times, but until this day, they had no meaning because I had not lived them either.

Implementing the Language Experience Approach

The most important idea to the language experience approach is that language communicates meaning. In using the approach, teachers should not attempt to separate strategy development from the process of thinking. (See Chapter 3, "Strategies for Developing New Concepts.") Stauffer and Pikulski (1974) suggest that the language experience approach includes planned and continuous activities such as

- individual- and group-dictated stories;
- individual student word banks of known words;
- creative writing situations;
- daily oral reading of prose and poetry by the teacher to the students;
- students' illustrations of dictated stories;
- student notebooks containing individual- and group-dictated stories;
- opportunities for working at learning stations;
- teacher-guided reading–thinking lessons; and
- records of students' progress.

Many opportunities can be structured into the school day:

The teacher can work with the whole class.   The teacher can read aloud to the class from some book or story related to a class activity, lead class discussions, show

a movie, introduce a new game, sing or perform rhythmic activities, and lead choral reading or speaking.

The teacher can work with small groups.   A teacher can follow up a large group lesson, take dictation, listen to students' oral reading, develop a reading strategy lesson, lead listening-development lessons, and guide the reading of a story.

The teacher can work with individuals.   A teacher can engage in many of the same activities carried out with the whole class or in small groups.

The teacher can work as a resource person.   A teacher can suggest ideas for students' creative writing or drawing, help them explore and think out an activity, assist those who need help, and act as a sounding board for their ideas.

The learning stations within a classroom can consist of library centers, writing resource centers, listening stations, viewing areas, art centers, and game corners. The number and structure of the learning stations depend on the facilities of the school as well as the ingenuity of the teacher. For example, a writing center can be established by placing a table in one part of the room and supplying it with some paper, writing instruments (pen, pencils, brush-point pens, crayons, possibly a typewriter or a microcomputer); resources for words such as picture dictionaries; and story motivators such as story beginnings, pictures, and comic strips with the words removed. A dictating center can be created by placing a tape recorder and some story starters together. At a later time, the teacher and the student can listen to the story. The teacher can write it out for the student, or in schools where they are available, educational assistants, aides, or volunteer parents can function as transcribers.

In using a language experience approach and in planning and selecting topics and activities, teachers should take into account students' experiences with words, their proficiency with English, and their experiences with authors' ideas. The activities from each of these three areas of student experiences should be simultaneous and continuous throughout the school year. There never should be a final feeling about learning. An air of things being a little unfinished is a great stimulus for further independent learning.

A language experience approach has listening, speaking, writing, and reading as its goals and is a broad communication-based approach to learning (Allen, 1976). The following is an outline of such a program.

Strand One: Experiencing communication emphasizes the employment of multiple media that are natural and normal ways of self-expression—talking, painting, singing, dancing, acting, writing.

1. Sharing ideas orally—talking about topics that are self-selected and of personal interest; telling or illustrating on a purely personal basis something that may or may not be related to classroom activities.
2. Visually portraying experiences—using art media and scrap material to explore combinations for the sheer pleasure of observing what happens; representing what one observes, imagines, or understandings in abstract as well as realistic forms; illustrating what someone else has thought and said in such ways that those ideas are internalized or interpreted (not copied); creating new schemes for ideas.
3. Dramatizing experience—creating and re-creating with voice and body movement the feelings and ideas of others as well as the roles that are impossible in real life; putting self in other's place; communicating without words through pantomime; interpreting facial expressions, gestures, posture, and tone of voice.
4. Responding rhythmically—using self-selected body movements to illustrate meanings from sounds of music, sounds of language, and personal feelings; moving to predetermined patterns with rhythmic accompaniment; illustrating meanings through body rhythm and dancing.

5. Discussing and conversing—talking about topics, as they arise, in ways that require more mature skills than oral sharing; interacting with what other people say and write by altering contributions to fit into discussions and conversations around a theme.

6. Exploring writing—learning and using in conversational situations such topics as letter recognition, letter names, letter formation, letter orientation; copying dictated stories on paper and on a chalkboard; writing of own ideas using appropriate forms of alphabet letters to represent sound of language; contacting, in a natural setting of writing, language characteristics such as capitalization, punctuation, standard spelling, sound–symbol relationships; observing the writing process when dictating.

7. Writing individual books—writing and publishing in many forms and for many purposes; editing and illustrating publications; using pupil-produced publications in the reading program.

Strand Two: Studying communication emphasizes an understanding of how language works for individuals, learning alternatives offered for natural speech patterns, understanding sound–symbol relationships, acquiring vocabularies of the form class words and of high-frequency structure words.

8. Recognizing high-frequency words—developing awareness that English contains many words and patterns common to all speakers and writers; mastering the words of highest frequency for sight-reading and correct spelling; using the high-frequency structure words of English in meaningful relationships to other words in sentences.

9. Exploring spelling—contacting and mastering regular and irregular phoneme-grapheme relationships during processes of writing and reading; making adaptations of personal pronunciation and standard spelling; using phonetic analysis when applicable; mastering frequently used words that defy phonetic analysis.

10. Extending vocabularies—increasing listening, speaking, reading, and writing vocabularies of words and word clusters that pattern in language, such as nouns, verbs, adjectives, and adverbs; adding new meanings to known words; recognizing and using known words in new and creative ways; creating new words for nonsense and fun talking and writing.

11. Studying style and form—profiting from listening to reading and studying well-written materials that reflect the ways in which authors express their feelings, observations, and imaginings in beautiful language; increasing sensitivity to varieties of styles and forms of expression; replicating artful forms of self-expression such as couplets, quatrains, cinquains, haiku, letters, and diaries; sensing the humor of passages; differentiating poetry from prose; expanding sentences with descriptive words and passages.

12. Studying language structure—pronouncing and understanding words through processes of analysis and synthesis; developing meanings by stringing language sounds into sentences and portions of sentences; using affixes to extend meanings of time and number; responding to rhyming and rhythm of language; recognizing the repetition of some syllables in many words; studying specific topics of structure such as use of prepositions, determiners, pronominal references, and subject–verb–object relationships.

13. Reading nonalphabetic symbols systems—responding to the meanings of symbols systems that are not represented by the alphabet, such as clocks, dials, maps, numerals, and graphs; responding to primary readings in the environment, such as weather, plants, human emotions, color, texture, size, shape, taste, and smell.

Strand Three: Relating communication of others to self emphasizes the influences of the language and ideas of many people on the personal language of learners as they browse and read many types of books, see and hear films, listen to records and tapes, listen to music, enjoy fine arts prints and photographs, handle sculpture and discuss it, and add to their personal repertoire of self-expression abilities.

14. Listening to and reading language of others—hearing and reading the language of many authors through stories and poems; responding naturally with new words and sentence patterns as illustrated by authors; comparing and contrasting personal ways of saying things with those of authors.

15. Comprehending what is read—understanding what is heard or read; following directions; reproducing the thought of a passage; reading for detail; reading for general significance; understanding words and their meanings in context.

16. Organizing ideas and information—using various methods of putting ideas from multiple sources into an overall concept that can be reported, such as picture painting, collage, montage, sculpture, making games, composing music, and construction; planning and producing stories with sequences of ideas, multiple characters, and settings; planning and writing poetry in predetermined patterns; classifying briefly the stated ideas of others.

17. Assimilating and integrating ideas—using listening and reading for specific purposes of a personal nature; extending personal meanings and using the new meanings in self-expression as a result of reading stories, viewing films, listening to recordings; talking about things like and not like what has happened; seeing and hearing experiences elaborated and extended in many ways.

18. Searching and researching multiple sources—finding information on topics of interest and on assignments by using interviews, ref-

erence books, tapes, films, filmstrips, observations, and other ways available when information is needed.

19. Evaluating communication of others—determining the validity and reliability of statements; sorting out and evaluating the real from the imaginary; sorting out assumptions from facts; recognizing an author's purpose and point of view; recognizing styles that include exaggeration, sarcasm, and humor.

20. Responding in personal ways—illustrating confidence and technical skill in responding to communicative efforts of others without duplicating them; performing personally as a result of influences from many sources without specific reference to the sources of those influences; reflecting humanistic qualities of an author, an artist, a teacher, a composer, an architect, a musician, a scientist, and any other contributor to society who is dependent on creative self-expression for survival. (Allen, 1976, pp. 6–10)

In summary, the language experience approach to reading gives students multisensory experiences in observing their world, listening to and reading about what others have observed, experiencing authorship themselves, and understanding various literary forms.

A specific language experience activity is a series of student experiences structured to lead students from a concrete experience to the verbalization of that experience. Then they are guided to the conceptualization of that experience and the skill of using story language and information. This approach with young students might be implemented in three phases spanning a few days.

Phase I: From Concrete Experience to Verbalization

- Describe a concrete experience as an attention-getter and conversation-starter. If possible, the experience should allow students to manipulate objects.
- Allow students to talk spontaneously about the experience.
- Using pertinent questions, guide students' attention to relevant features of the experience.
- Solicit from students some dictation about the experience. In small group settings, allow each student to contribute at least one sentence to the narrative account.
- Read the completed story to students.
- Have students make a drawing of or illustrate in some way a significant aspect of the experience. On the illustration, place a sentence from the dictation that corresponds to the student's representation.

Phase II: From Verbalization to Conceptualization

- Reread the story or narrative to students.
- Have students read the story as a group.
- Allow individual members of the group to read the story and offer additions or suggestions for revisions; discuss these suggestions with the entire group.
- Revise the story according to student preferences.
- Ask students to describe similar experiences they may have had.
- Connect the story to other student experiences by reading or having them read literature related to the story topic. After the material has been presented, allow them to peruse the literature individually.

Phase III: From Conceptualization to Skill Development

- Reproduce the story for each student. Have each one find in the story particular sentences, phrases, and words.
- Place all words from the dictated story that can be identified without teacher help into students' word banks.
- Give students a skills lesson based on language in the story that develops or extends their ability to read independently.

The following account illustrates how this approach was used successfully with three fourth-grade students who were having difficulty acquiring beginning reading strategies (Bercari, 1975). The result was the filmstrip illustrated in Figure 4–1.

The activity was initiated by reading and carrying out with pupils the instructions for making salt dough which was in a supermarket magazine. My aims in getting the girls to produce the filmstrip were to develop a sense of sequence, exercise their memories, develop written expression of their own experiences, and to give each girl a sense of accomplishment.

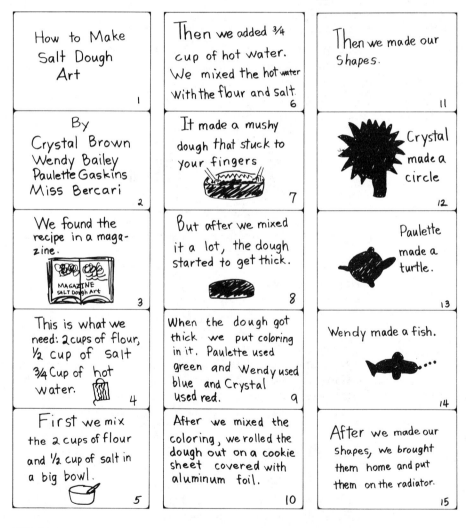

FIGURE 4–1
Language Experience Filmstrip

We developed the strip by: (a) writing individual stories on how we made the salt dough, (b) reading each other's stories and discussing what had been left out of all three, (c) taking the ideas from all three stories and making a master story following the sequence in which the project was carried out, (d) writing sequences on 5 × 7 inch papers for each frame, (e) illustrating those frames in which there was room with ideas that could be drawn, (f) doing a final editing of the story to see what had been left out, and including additional material and frames.

When the filmstrip came back from the processing lab, the girls discussed what colors should be added with permanent marking pens to the filmstrip.

Finally, the filmstrip was shown to the other pupils. The girls alternated in reading the frames on the filmstrip during the showing.

Individual and small-group dictations transcribed on class charts can be one of four types (Lee & Allen, 1963):

1. Personal language charts, which are the student's own dictation in written form.
2. Narrative charts, which are the record of a group's dictation.

3. Work charts, which represent the consensus of a class or small group on how something should be organized or directions for using class resources.
4. Skill charts, which are records of or instructions for carrying out strategies in one language area.

Teachers should model the composing process when developing experience charts: Charts should be drafted first, revised, edited, and then prepared for "publication." When preparing the final copies of charts for use in the classroom, teachers should follow certain principles:

Make the charts attractive. Be sure to letter them neatly and clearly. The final chart should be copied from a draft after the teacher and students have made their final editorial changes. Allow students to decorate the charts with planned illustrations.

Give the charts some measure of literary quality. Although most of the charts should retain students' own language, the imaginative and resourceful teacher can lead them, through modeling and guided questions, to emulate the literary forms with which they have become familiar from the teacher's daily readings.

Give consideration to phrasing. Especially with younger children, the lines should provide a maximum of language redundancy through helpful syntactic and semantic clues.

Compose the charts with consideration for the greatest legibility. Aside from well-drawn letters, the teacher should consider the spacing of the lines, margins, typographical clues such as numerals or symbols, color, and contrast between the color of the printing and the color of the paper.

Figure 4–2 shows examples of group and individual language experience charts.

Implementing a Thematic Unit

One way to organize the language experience approach to reading is using thematic units. In this organization, various student experiences are related to a theme, a problem, or an area of interest. The contents of these various areas are brought together in a series of lessons. The basic unit, called a resource unit, is developed beforehand by the teacher and is flexible enough to allow cooperative planning by the teacher and students. Flexibility allows changes to be made as classroom conditions change.

The selection of a theme depends on the cognitive and affective needs of the class members; the school's and community's resources; and the available instructional materials such as textbooks, records, audio-visual aids, maps, ref-

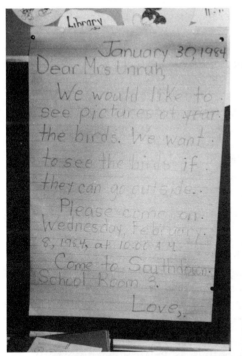

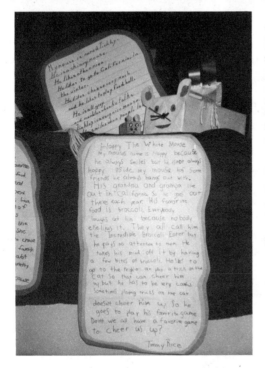

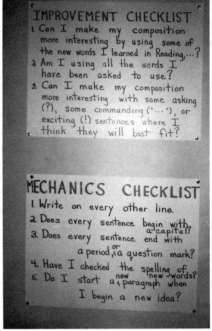

FIGURE 4–2
Language Experience Charts

erence books, resource persons, and library facilities. The themes may come from one content area or from students' interests.

The resource unit contains suggestions for activities, materials, and concepts to be learned. It details information for both the teacher and the students about activities, resources, and instructional plans, with specific reference to titles of books, films, and records and to materials that may be needed to carry out a project. The thematic unit is introduced to students through a stimulating activity that focuses attention on the topic—students are much more motivated when the teacher capitalizes on their natural curiosity.

There is no single pattern for constructing and organizing a resource unit— it can take the shape of an outline or a curriculum web. The teacher's instructional methods may vary depending upon the teaching objectives, students' needs, and the materials available. The more common teaching methods include whole-class group discussions, trips, dramatizations, audio-visual materials, and individual- and small-group research projects. The activities include speaking, listening, reading, and writing in a variety of modes.

The teacher's preparation may also vary according to students' abilities and needs, the opportunities in the school and community, and the time available. Teachers should allow time both for their preparation and for the students'. In developing a thematic unit or curriculum web, teachers should go through some preliminary steps by preparing answers to specific questions (Meyen, 1981). The Chapter 4 appendix has a sample resource unit and a curriculum web.

Rationale.   What are the reasons for teaching this particular unit at the present time? What contributions will the unit make to implementing your curriculum? State your rationale in a broad, descriptive statement.

Sub-units.   What are the possible related themes within the context of the unit topic on which lessons can be grouped? What lessons need to be developed to teach the content of these themes?

General objectives.   What general objectives (representing the major goals of the unit) will be developed through lessons? What sequence of objectives fits the pattern of the unit?

Core activities.   What activities can be used to teach information and skills related to each of the curriculum areas (arithmetic, social studies, science, health, etc.)?

Resources.   What resource materials and people for you and the students would be appropriate in teaching the unit?

Vocabulary and key concepts.   What words and concepts are crucial to students' learning and can easily be taught in the context of this unit?

STRATEGIES FOR GUIDING STUDENT COMPREHENSION

Basal reading series are used extensively in reading and language-arts classrooms. Each series has a teacher's manual or a guidebook which details lesson plans. For each story, teachers are given summaries, objectives, lists of materials, vocabulary, teaching strategies and activities, questions for directing silent and oral reading, specific skills, and enrichment activities. There is evidence, however, that these manuals and guidebooks do not help teachers develop the types of strategies that lead to effective, independent readers. Teachers' guides often have lessons that put undue emphasis on isolated aspects of language and lead learners to put value on bits and pieces of language. They also tend to discourage students from taking risks and introduce arbitrary sequences of skill. Most important, they often create artificial language passages and mar the use of literature by gearing it to irrelevant skill development (Goodman, 1986).

The teachers' manuals and guidebooks for five major basal reading series were examined to identify the procedures used to teach comprehension strategies (Durkin, 1981). For this examination, an important distinction was made between comprehension tasks that deal with the process of comprehending and those dealing with comprehension assessment. The manuals were examined for information and activities provided to teachers for (1) instructional purposes, (2) review purposes, (3) application purposes (transfer of learning), (4) practice purposes, and (5) prereading or preparation purposes.

The results of the study led to the following conclusions: First, there are many application and practice activities but little explicit instruction in comprehension strategies. Second, when instruction does exist, it does not link individual skill activities with direct applications to reading; they seem to exist totally for their own sake. Third, there is little attention to the schemata of writers and what writers do to help or hinder a reader's comprehension. Fourth, there is little help to either teachers or students in explaining what it means to answer a question and what strategies are used to answer different types of questions.

Another analysis of the questions in some basal series' manuals reveals that they are not consistent in their development (Beck & McKeown, 1981). Some questions seem to be adequate for developing comprehension, but others are not. The questions are not central to the comprehension of the story. Instead, they include tangential questions that may deal with the topic but not with the ideas in the specific story, a sequence of questions that violates the natural progression of the story ideas, and irrelevant questions that include trivial details and pointless inferences.

Basal readers themselves are convenient anthologies of stories and informational selections. There are teacher's manuals and guidebooks for some series that develop instructional activities based on whole-language principles like those activities presented in this text, and they are structured in ways that lead students to become independent thinkers and learners. Therefore, it is the teacher's responsibility to assess the appropriateness of the lesson plans in a basal series, and when they are found lacking, to develop lessons based on whole-language principles and models. The **guided reading lesson** is built on the premise that reading material communicates directly with the reader. "It is through pupils' actions upon material and their interaction with each other that sound intellectual reading skills and appropriate emotional dispositions are best acquired" (Stauffer, 1975, p. 33). The guided lesson is a procedure that can be used with almost any type of reading material.

Since reading is a thinking activity, the guided reading lesson is a guided thinking lesson, and can be adapted for use as such. Some authorities consider what is here called guided-reading to be critical reading. All reading, however, involves critical thinking.

Developing Guided Reading–Thinking Lessons

The three stages of the guided reading–thinking lesson are 1) the act of inquiry, 2) the processing of information, and 3) the validating of answers (Stauffer, 1975). During the lessons, both student and teacher have active roles (Burrows, Monson, & Stauffer, 1972).

Pupil Actions

> Predicting (setting purposes)
> Reading (processing ideas)
> Proving (testing answers)

Teacher Actions

> Activating thought (What do you think?)
> Agitating thought (Why do you think so?)
> Requiring evidence (Prove it!)

The strategies students learn through using guided reading–thinking lessons are (1) examining information, (2) hypothesizing, (3) finding proof, (4) suspending judgement, and (5) making decisions (Stauffer, 1975). These strategies are applied in four steps:

1. Predicting from title and picture clues;
2. Predicting from first-page clues;
3. Predicting from one or more subsequent pages; and
4. Predicting from the point just before the story climax.

The exact number of lines, paragraphs, or pages that a teacher expects the student to read will vary according to (1) students' cognitive maturity, (2) the amount of data they are capable of processing, (3) the type of information contained in the story, and (4) the purposes for reading the selection (Burrows et al., 1972).

For example, some teachers may find students need to read the story one paragraph at a time. In such cases students may have limited experience in either making predictions or processing the information. There may be so many concepts in the reading material that they strain students' memory. However, other teachers may find that the reading material is so familiar that students can process as a unit the information given on two, three, or more pages.

The guided reading–thinking lesson differs from the typical directed reading lesson advocated by many reading authorities and found in many basal readers. One major difference is that the responsibility for establishing a purpose for reading the story is shifted from the teacher to the students. Following the teacher's model lessons, students identify a purpose or set of purposes for reading the story based on what they perceive to be the author's purpose for writing the story.

Another difference is that all "new" words are not presented to students before reading the story. Only by meeting some unfamiliar words in the natural context of a story can students use their word recognition strategies. Teachers are often mistaken about how students should be prepared for reading. Teachers selectively present the new and unfamiliar words before reading a story and lead a discussion about their meaning and pronunciation. By doing this, teachers prevent students from learning through the application of their word recognition strategies. Also, what is new to one student may not be new to another. No basal series author, and few classroom teachers, can accurately predict those words that are unfamiliar to each student. Since the lesson is guided by the teacher, whenever a student fails to use word recognition strategies successfully, the teacher and the student together can explore why the word was not understood and how it may be processed in the future.

The lessons in Figures 4–3 and 4–4, one constructed around a story from a first-grade basal reader and the other from a fourth-grade reader, illustrate a teacher's beginning preparation for guided reading–thinking lessons.

During the reading–thinking lesson the teacher is able to guide students through the reading of a story and help them reconstruct the author's meaning and construct their own meanings. The guided reading–thinking lesson allows students to show their mastery of various reading strategies. When mastery is not evident, the teacher can help students while they read and think. The teacher should be alert to signs that students cannot apply their reading–thinking strategies to new situations or to particular types of material. The teacher must understand the reading tasks expected of students and the significance of students' behavior while performing these tasks. The analytical teacher observes students' application of various reading strategies during silent and oral reading. Based on these observations, follow-up lessons on specific strategies for making students independent readers can be planned and implemented.

Guided Reading–Thinking Lesson for "The Mouse and the Lion"

Story Theme: No one is too little to help.

Story Plot and Summary: A rather pompous lion catches a mouse. The little creature begs for mercy, appealing to the lion's common sense by pointing out that he, the mouse, would hardly be much of a meal. When the mouse is free, he expresses his gratitude, vowing to help the lion someday. The lion is amused by such a promise and laughs. But it is the mouse who has the last laugh when he rescues the lion from a trap by chewing through the binding ropes (Fay, Ross, & LaPray, 1974).

Guiding Questions:
1. Title and picture, first page of story
   Do you think this is a real story?
   Does the title give you any idea as to what may happen in the story?
   What do you think may happen?
2. First page
   What has happened?
   Do you have any idea from this part of the story as to what may happen next?
3. Second and third pages
   Were any of you correct in what you thought?
   If the lion was talking, what kind of voice would he have? What about the mouse?
   What do you now think the rest of the story will be about?
4. Fourth page
   Were any of you right? What do you now think will happen?
   Do you want to change your ideas about what will happen?
5. Fifth, sixth, and seventh pages
   Why did the author write this story? What message did he want to give you?
   Why couldn't any other animal help the lion?
   Were there any words you didn't know and couldn't figure out from the story?
   What information on the page let you understand the story without knowing what those words were?

FIGURE 4–3
Guided Reading–Thinking Lesson, Grade 1
Source: Fay, L., Ross, R. R., & LaPray, M. (1981). *The Rand McNally Reading Program, Level 6,* "Red Rock Ranch" (teachers ed.), Chicago: Riverside. Reproduced by permission of Riverside Publishing Company.

Analytical teaching is a process whereby the teacher continually adjusts the teaching pace and methods to meet students' learning needs. (See Chapter 10 for a detailed explanation of analytical teaching.) The guided reading–thinking lesson provides an opportunity for students to gain insights about monitoring their own reading and for the teacher to observe and assess them in actual reading situations.

Guided Reading–Thinking Lesson for "Miss Esta Maude's Secret"

Story Theme: Outward appearances do not necessarily indicate a person's true interests and personality. Even very staid and quiet people may secretly long for excitement in their lives.

Story Plot and Summary: Esta Maude Hay, a school teacher for twenty years, leads what the townspeople think is a pitifully dull and ordered life. Nobody knows that locked in Miss Esta Maude's barn is a powerful red racing car, with which she tinkers every night. On Friday nights, dressed in helmet and goggles, she speeds down the highway and often meets with adventure. She saves a stray flock of lambs, brings a sleepwalking boy home, and successfully races the stork to the hospital.

Central to the story is the contrast between Miss Esta Maude's outwardly quiet life and her secret love of speed. However, the car is not her only source of happiness. Miss Esta Maude enjoys teaching and likes to help people: the car merely adds a note of excitement and adventure to her life (Fay & Anderson, 1974).

Guiding Questions:
1. Title and pictures on first and second pages
   What do you think this story is about?
   What kinds of feelings do the pictures give you?
2. First and second pages
   What do you think now?
   What have you learned about Esta Maude?
   Are there any clues as to what her secret might be?
   Are there any words you could not figure out from the story?
   Was the word important to understanding the story?
3. Third and fourth pages
   Were you right about her secret?
   What have you learned about Esta Maude?
   Which description shows the "real" Miss Maude?
   What type of adventures might she have?
   Why wouldn't people know who she is while riding in the sports car?
4. Fifth, sixth and seventh pages
   Do you think people will ever find out about Esta Maude's secret?
   What might happen if many people started talking about a "stranger in a sports car"?
   What message did the author want to get across to the reader of this story?

FIGURE 4–4
Guided Reading–Thinking Lesson, Grade 4
Source: Fay, L. & Anderson, P. S. (1981). *The Rand McNally Reading Program, Level II,* "Twirling Parallels" (teachers ed.), Chicago: Riverside. Reproduced by permission of Riverside Publishing Company.

STRATEGIES FOR TEACHER AND STUDENT QUESTIONING

The thought-provoking questions of the guided reading–thinking lesson are only one type of question that generates students' thinking strategies. Teachers can tap different thought processes with questions requiring different cognitive operations. In this chapter are discussions of different question types, the source of answers, some positive and negative features of question types, and a procedure for developing students' question-generating strategies.

The following question types foster different thinking strategies (Torrence & Myers, 1972):

Recognition Questions

Multiple Choice

In the story, Chun Toy was allowed to

build the boat

paint the boat

row the boat

Matching

Match the character in the story with a word that describes the person

Li Lun	ashamed
Teng Lun	wise
Sun Ling	afraid

Analysis Questions

Interpretive

What did Sun Ling mean when he said, "There are other things than fishing?"

Comparison

In what ways was the kitten like the tiger?

Analysis of Series or Process

How do the animals and insects in the story get ready for winter?

Synthesis or Hypothesis-Formation Questions

Based on how Josie felt about her brother, what might you expect her to do?

Convergent Thinking or Redefinition Questions

Which solution offered by Pierre would be acceptable in our school?

Reprinted with special permission of King Features Syndicate.

Open-ended or Divergent Thinking Questions

What are some other ways Chun Toy might have helped his brothers as they worked on the boat?

Evaluation Questions

Judgmental
In this story, do you think the grasshoppers are thieves?

True–False
Is the following statement true or false? "Megan's actions in the story were more out of fear than out of love."

Provocative or Extension of Thinking
If an earthquake were to hit this school five minutes from now, what things would we do?

In addition to classifying questions by thinking processes, questions are classified by 1) the type of answer expected, and 2) the relationship between questions and responses.

The type of answer expected, or the product of the questions, is the particular information that teachers want from students. The information could be a concept definition, a generalization, or an application of a rule. In any case, if a question is asked that is different from the purpose given for reading, students will not accurately produce the product intended. For example, students may read a native American legend about the creation of corn. If they are told to focus attention on applying cause-and-effect relationships, a question directed at specific details or one asking students to compare that legend with a science article about agriculture requires them to produce information different from that of the original focus. Learning outcomes are related to the goals

given to readers and to the purposes set for their attention or action. Goals may fail when they imprecisely or indirectly define what it is students are to learn (Frase, 1977).

The relationship between questions and responses is the source of an answer's information. Three sources of information for questions have been identified (Pearson & Johnson, 1978): text-explicit, text-implicit, and script- or schema-implicit. Text-explicit information is found directly in the passage being read, but the relationship between and among information is unstated and must be supplied by the reader. Script-implicit information is that which must be supplied fully by the reader.

For a passage such as, "As Paul came into the apartment, Pee Wee flew from its cage and landed on his hand, unbalanced for a moment then righting itself. It opened its beak and gave out a tiny squawk for food," a text-explicit question might be "What did Pee Wee do when Paul entered the apartment?" A text-implicit question deals with information that requires a less obvious answer, but the source of the information is still in the passage. Such a question might be, "What type of a creature is Pee Wee?" To answer a script-implicit question, readers need to use information stored in their schemata, or scripts. Such a question might be "What will Paul feed Pee Wee?"

How teachers use questions affects how students learn to understand and monitor their own understanding. The types of questions teachers ask and the way they interpret student responses lead to impressions of student learning. Teachers, then, should be aware of the positive and negative features of the question patterns just discussed (Strange, 1980; Torrence & Myers, 1972).

Questions that focus on remembering may be of limited value because (a) no further learning is compelled, (b) answering the questions may be interpreted by students as either a punishment or a reward, and (c) the information received by students is only as accurate or complete as that given by the teacher.

Recognition questions are popular and can be used to identify incorrect thinking; however, they may foster unstructured guessing.

Analysis questions may have limited use if students do not have background information to make interpretations or comparisons. Too many of these questions can be tedious.

Synthesis questions are good because they lead students to discover generalizations, but they are limited because the responsibility to select the significant details lies with students. Therefore, students may never arrive at a generalization.

Convergent thinking questions require students to already know what would be "best" or "acceptable" in a given situation.

Open-ended or divergent thinking questions give students the chance to offer several responses. They may be of limited value for immature students or students with special needs who are unable to generate alternatives. Some students may also become upset or frustrated by questions that do not have a "right" answer.

Evaluation questions stimulate rational thinking, but they are limited to the degree that students a) have been given appropriate criteria for forming judgments, b) have had experience in decision making, and c) have the ability to extend their thinking.

Questions classified by the type of answer expected and by the relationship between the question and answer can result in miscomprehension. Students might not have a schema, or might have a naive or incomplete schema, about the topic. In this case, the questions implicit in the script will be missed. Sometimes when students have incomplete schemata, there are intrusions from other incomplete but related schemata. Students might then create far-fetched answers that result in changes of meaning. Or, the question might not be clearly or precisely stated and more than one schema or script can be an appropriate source for the answer.

Many of these limitations can be overcome. Throughout the school year, teachers can use a variety of questions to foster different thinking operations. Not all stories lend themselves to all types of questions; nevertheless, when possible a teacher can direct students through the question types using a variety of reading material.

Good instructional questions affirm the following guidelines:

- Do the questions tap more than a limited number of thought processes?
- Do the questions focus on information significant to the general plot and theme of the story?
- Do the questions imply that there is no "right" answer all the time, and do they allow for possible alternative responses?
- Do the questions require students to use a type of thinking for which they are cognitively ready?
- Do the questions challenge, but not frustrate, students so that information is obtained about how they perform in problem-solving situations?

WRITING AS A STRATEGY FOR COMPREHENSION

In this section the place of writing in the language experience approach is considered. As writers, students create texts for themselves and for others. Even first-grade students can share their work. In one school, first graders wrote books, stocked the shelves of their class libraries, and then invited parents, older students, and other members of the school community to use the library and share their books (Powers, 1981).

Students learn to read like authors by being authors. Experimental research reports show that students who use writing activities or exercises specifically to improve reading comprehension or information retention have better recall of material and improved reading achievement test scores (Stotsky, 1983). Reading and writing instruction are not substitutes for each other; nevertheless, teachers who seek to improve reading through writing activities may be most successful when they use writing exercises linked to the reading of student texts.

Students can compose their own stories using stories from their directed reading–thinking activities, independent reading, or those read aloud by the teacher as models. For example, young students can create alphabet books or picture books. Students can write sequels to their favorite stories or use popular characters in new settings and situations. Students can create new characters and put them into familiar plots and themes. Journals may be written from the point of view of familiar characters. Whatever its form, the writing can be individual or team (collaborative), and done by hand or at a computer terminal.

Writing has an important part in guided reading–thinking lessons. In establishing purposes and testing answers, students can use writing as a means for organizing and expressing their ideas. Many teachers and basal series authors assume that guided lessons will be done orally, but there is no valid reason why students must "think on their feet" all the time, and respond orally to a teacher's questions. Predictions and confirmations of those predictions often take time, and students who are asked to write out their responses have the opportunity to mull over, reexamine, and elaborate on their first responses and actively interact with the ideas and information of the reading passage.

Comprehension is also facilitated when students write out their own questions. (See Chapter 5 for a discussion of reciprocal teaching/questioning.) Using the teacher's questions as models, students can write questions for other students who are reading the same book or will read it at another time. The interaction among students as they respond to peers' questioning leads to a greater understanding of an author's organization, development of ideas, and themes. In addition, students gain insight into their own roles as the author's audience.

RESOURCES FOR THE TEACHER

Understandably, some teachers feel a limited background in children's literature and in resources for initiating student activities hinders them in implementing thematic units and a language experience approach to reading. Nevertheless, a teacher who is hesitant to create an original language-based program can use commercial materials to foster language experiences for reading and writing. The following are selected resources with brief notes about their contents.

Allen, R. V., & Allen, C. (1970). *Language experiences in reading: Teacher's resource guides, Levels I, II, III.* Chicago: Encyclopedia Britannica.

Each resource book contains five or six thematic units. Although the material is geared toward the primary grades, a creative teacher, using the formats of the units, can adjust the themes for use with older students.

In addition to three texts recommended in the further reading section, two important complements to the previous resource are:

Allen, R. V. (1976). *Language experiences in communication.* Boston: Houghton Mifflin.
Allen, R. V., & Allen, C. (1982). *Language experience activities* (3rd ed.). Boston: Houghton Mifflin.

The following kits contain detailed lesson plans, picture cards, story posters, recorded stories, puppets, and manipulative materials that can be used in language experience activities.

> *Peabody language development kits, Levels I, II, III* (Rev. ed.). (1981). Circle Pines, MN: American Guidance Service.

Several computer software programs available for Apple and IBM computers support language experience activities.

> *Bank Street Writer, III, School Edition.* Scholastic, Inc. (A word processing program for grades 2–12 which has a spelling checker and thesaurus)
> *Rainbow Keyboarding, Grades 2–3* and *Success with Typing, Grades 5–12.* Scholastic, Inc. (Programs for learning to type)
> *Crossword Magic: Mindscape.* (A program for creating crossword puzzles—mazes, clues, word lists, and answer key)
> *The Newsroom, Scholastic Edition.* Scholastic, Inc. (A program for writing, designing, and printing newspapers)
> *The Print Shop.* Broderbund. (A program for designing and printing greeting cards, invitations, letterheads, signs, and banners)

Teachers who wish to find existing publications of thematic units can refer to the following:

- State and city education departments and boards of education.
- Specialized groups and societies such as natural history and ecology societies, various associations of manufacturers and industrial groups, and historical and scientific societies.
- Major encyclopedia publishers, who often provide supplementary educational materials.
- Files in public libraries and in university curriculum centers.

The following annual publications contain offers of free materials for teachers. The information is listed by subject for easy reference.

> *Educator's Guide to Free Films, Educator's Guide to Free Filmstrips.* Randolph, WI: Educator's Program Service.

The following text is a guide for providing and coordinating educational activities that help young children develop self-confidence, individuality, and creative freedom. The book has a series of unit plans organized around major themes appropriate to young children.

> Taylor, B. J. (1974). *When I do, I learn.* Provo, UT: Brigham Young University.

Some basal reading series contain activities that integrate reading, writing, and spelling instruction and emphasize the development of comprehension strategies, and their stories and informational articles represent quality literature by award-winning authors of children's literature. The teachers' manuals have annotated lists of books relating to individual stories or unit themes for students to read or teachers to read to students. Table 10–3 contains critical questions that should be used in evaluating the appropriateness of a series for use in whole-language reading and writing programs.

The major publishers of these basal series are: The Economy Company (Oklahoma City, OK), Ginn and Company (Columbus, OH), D. C. Heath and Company (Lexington, MA), Holt, Rinehart and Winston (New York), Houghton Mifflin (Boston), Harcourt Brace Jovanovich, Publishers (Orlando, FL), Macmillan Publishing Company (Riverside, NJ), and Scott, Foresman and Company (Glenview, IL).

DISCUSSION QUESTIONS AND ACTIVITIES

1. Prepare a teacher's resource unit on a particular theme. Be sure the unit contains the age or grade level for which it is intended; the major skills that will be developed, stated in instructional objectives; the period of time the unit will cover; the particular experiences and activities in which the students will be engaged; the school and community resources that are available; and examples of the books, records, and films that will be available for the teacher and students.

2. Present an argument that either supports or refutes the following statement by Lohmann (1968):

   The teacher who is unfamiliar with the relationships in language, unfamiliar with concept development, and unfamiliar with ways to assess growth in language might find [the language experience] approach, in total, beyond her [or his] capacity to use. (p. 28)

3. Examine a basal reading series to see (a) how it presents a guided reading activity and (b) what types of questions it suggests for comprehension development. Are the lessons and questions constructed according to the guidelines presented in this chapter? Do the criticisms of Durkin (1981) and Beck and McKeown (1981) apply to the series you examined?

4. Select a story from a magazine or book and use it to create two sets of comprehension questions. The first should attempt to tap different thinking processes, and the second should be a combination of questions. If possible, try out these questions with a group of students. How do their responses give you insight into how well they understand the story?

   For students who are currently teaching:

5. Prepare a series of questions to initiate reciprocal teaching/questioning with a group of students. Carry out the lesson and evaluate its success. Plan a series of follow-up lessons to help students generate their own questions.

6. Select a story and prepare a guided reading–thinking lesson for a group of students. Use the lesson. In what ways did you have to modify your original plans because of the students' responses?

7. Create a language experience lesson and use it with two groups of students of different ages and grade levels. How did you have to modify the lesson to meet the cognitive, affective, and instructional needs of each group? How did the group's language performances differ?

8. Plan a series of lessons to initiate peer interaction groups. After introducing the technique and modeling the reading act, note what kinds of responses you get from the students. How would you modify your plans based on their responses?

FURTHER READING

The following give detailed instructions on how to use a language experience approach to reading.

Dunne, H. W. (1972). *The art of teaching reading: A language and self-concept approach.* Columbus, OH: Merrill.

Hall, M. A. (1981). *Teaching reading as a language experience* (3rd ed.). Columbus, OH: Merrill.

Mallon, B., & Berglund, R. (1984, May). The language experience approach to reading: Recurring questions and their answers. *The Reading Teacher, 37*(9), 867-871.

Veatch, J., Sawicki, F., Elliott, G., Barnette, E., & Blakey, J. (1973). *Key words to reading: The language experience approach begins.* Columbus, OH: Merrill.

Two books that contain syntheses of research about how students understand are

Flood, J. (Ed.). (1983). *Understanding reading comprehension: Cognition, language, and the structure of prose.* Newark, DE: International Reading Association.

Flood, J. (Ed.). (1984). *Promoting reading comprehension.* Newark, DE: International Reading Association.

Additional ideas about developing students' questioning strategies are in the following:

Christenbury, L., & Kelly, P. P. (1983). *Questioning: A path to critical thinking.* Urbana, IL: ERIC Clearinghouse on Reading and Communication Skills, National Institute of Education and National Council of Teachers of English.

Wixson, K. K. (1983, December). Questions about a text: What you ask about is what children learn. *The Reading Teacher, 37*(3), 287–293.

The following articles have additional insights about the process of comprehension monitoring.

Mier, M. (1984, April). Comprehension monitoring in the elementary classroom. *The Reading Teacher, 37*(8), 770–774.

Schmitt, M. C., & Baumann, J. F. (1986, October). How to incorporate comprehension monitoring strategies into basal reader instruction. *The Reading Teacher, 40*(1), 28–37.

Ways to promote students' writing as means for developing their comprehension strategies are offered in the following:

Boutwell, M. A. (1983, December). Reading and writing process: A reciprocal agreement. *Language Arts, 6,* 723–730.

Hains, M. (Ed.). (1982). *A two-way street: Reading to write/writing to read.* Urbana, IL: National Council of Teachers of English.

Hennings, D. G. (1982, January). A writing approach to reading comprehension— schema theory in action. *Language Arts, 59*(1), 8–17.

Tway, E. (1985). *Writing is reading: 26 ways to connect.* Urbana, IL: ERIC Clearinghouse on Reading and Communication Skills, National Institute of Education and National Council of Teachers of English.

CHAPTER 4 APPENDIX

Curriculum Web

Curriculum Web
Nature: The Park
A Curriculum Web of Possibilities
by Lisa Draluck

The park is Forest Park in Richmond Hills, Queens, New York City. We plan several hands-on experiences in the park for our second-grade class.

Bibliography of Books Mentioned in the Web

1. Baskin, Tobias — *Hosie's Aviary*
2. Batherman, Muriel — *Animals Live Here*
3. Brockman, Frank C. — *Trees of North America*
4. Bronson, Wilfred S. — *The Wonderful World of Ants*
5. Burroughs, John — *Wake Robin*
6. Carlisle, Norman and Madelyn — *The True Book of Maps*
7. Carrick, Carol — *The Empty Squirrel*
8. Conklin, Gladys — *I Like Beetles*
9. David, Eugene — *Spiders and How They Live*
10. Dixon, Dougal — *Geology—Rocks, Minerals and Fossils*
11. Farb, Peter — *The Story of Butterflies and Other Insects*
12. Freschet, Berniece — *The Web in the Grass*
13. Green, Norma B. — *Bears, Bees and Birch Trees*
14. Grimm and Humperdinck — *Hansel and Gretel*
15. Hogner, Dorothy Childs — *Water Beetles*
16. Lambert, David — *The Seasons*
17. Lane, Margaret — *The Spider*
18. Lionni, Leo — *Inch by Inch*
19. Lukešová, Milena — *Julian in the Autumn Woods*
20. McDermott, Gerald — *A Tale from the Congo: The Magic Tree*
21. Marcher, Marion W. — *Monarch Butterfly—Winging North and South*
22. Morris, Dean — *Read About Butterflies and Moths*
23. Oliver, John — *What We Find When We Look at Maps*
24. Overbeck, Cynthia — *The Butterfly Book*
25. Piers, Helen — *Grasshopper and Butterfly*
26. Rinkoff, Barbara — *A Map Is a Picture*
27. Sammis, Kathy — *The Beginning Knowledge Book of Butterflies*
28. Selsam, Millicent — *See Through the Forest*

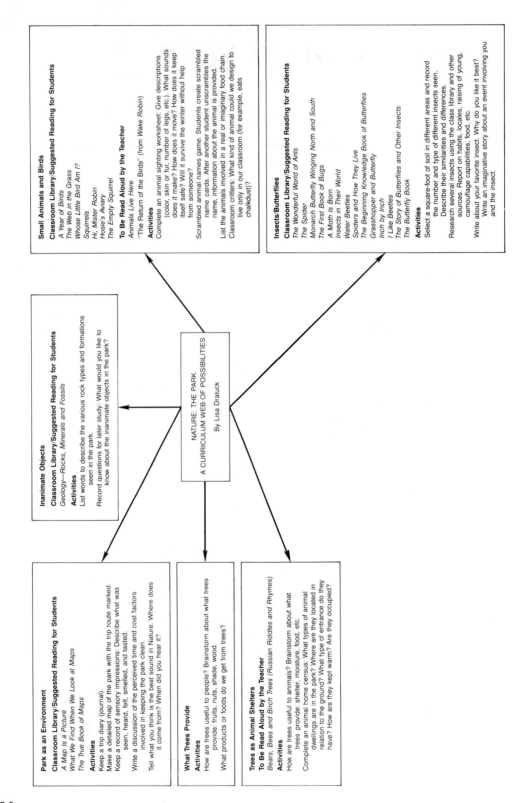

Small Animals and Birds

Classroom Library/Suggested Reading for Students
A Year of Birds
The Web in the Grass
Whose Little Bird Am I?
Squirrels
Hi, Mister Robin
Hosie's Aviary
The Empty Squirrel

To Be Read Aloud by the Teacher
Animals Live Here
"The Return of the Birds" (from *Wake Robin*)

Activities
Complete an animal sighting worksheet: Give descriptions (color, skin or fur, number of legs, etc.). What sounds does it make? How does it move? How does it keep itself safe? Will it survive the winter without help from someone?
Scrambled animal names game. Students create scrambled name cards. After another student unscrambles the name, information about the animal is provided.
List the animals involved in a real or imaginary food chain.
Classroom critters: What kind of animal could we design to live only in our classroom (for example, eats chalkdust)?

Insects/Butterflies

Classroom Library/Suggested Reading for Students
The Wonderful World of Ants
The Spider
Monarch Butterfly Winging North and South
The First Book of Bugs
A Moth Is Born
Insects in Their World
Water Beetles
Spiders and How They Live
The Beginning Knowledge Book of Butterflies
Grasshopper and Butterfly
Inch by Inch
I Like Beetles
The Story of Butterflies and Other Insects
The Butterfly Book

Activities
Select a square-foot of soil in different areas and record the number and type of different insects seen. Describe their similarities and differences.
Research several insects using the class library and other sources. Report on habits, locales, raising of young, camouflage capabilities, food, etc.
Write about your favorite insect. Why do you like it best? Write an imaginative story about an event involving you and the insect.

Inanimate Objects

Classroom Library/Suggested Reading for Students
Geology—Rocks, Minerals and Fossils

Activities
List words to describe the various rock types and formations seen in the park.
Record questions for later study: What would you like to know about the inanimate objects in the park?

NATURE: THE PARK
A CURRICULUM WEB OF POSSIBILITIES

By Lisa Draluck

Park as an Environment

Classroom Library/Suggested Reading for Students
A Map Is a Picture
What We Find When We Look at Maps
The True Book of Maps

Activities
Keep a trip diary (journal).
Make a detailed map of the park with the trip route marked.
Keep a record of sensory impressions: Describe what was seen, heard, felt, smelled, and tasted.
Write a discussion of the perceived time and cost factors involved in keeping the park clean.
Tell what you think is the best sound in Nature. Where does it come from? When did you hear it?

What Trees Provide

Activities
How are trees useful to people? Brainstorm about what trees provide: fruits, nuts, shade, wood.
What products or foods do we get from trees?

Trees as Animal Shelters

To Be Read Aloud by the Teacher
Bears, Bees and Birch Trees (Russian Riddles and Rhymes)

Activities
How are trees useful to animals? Brainstorm about what trees provide: shelter, moisture, food, etc.
Complete an animal home census: What types of animal dwellings are in the park? Where are they located in relation to the ground? What type of entrance do they have? How are they kept warm? Are they occupied?

96

29. Sewell, H.   *A Book of Myths*
30. Swain, SuZan N.   *Insects in Their World*
31. Testa, Fulvio   *Leaves*
32. Tresselt, Alvin   *Hi, Mister Robin*
33. Udry, Janice May   *A Tree Is Nice*
34. Walker, Barbara   *Nigerian Folk Tales: The Dancing Palm Tree*
35. Walker, Herbert B.   *A Moth Is Born*
36. Weisgard, Leonard   *Whose Little Bird Am I?*
37. Wildsmith, Brian   *Squirrels*
38. Williamson, Margaret   *The First Book of Bugs*
39. Wolff, Ashley   *A Year of Birds*

Teacher Resources

1. *A City Herbal;* Silverman, Maida; New York, Alfred A. Knopf; 1977.
2. *A Field Guide to Wildflowers;* Peterson, Roger Tory and McKenny, Margaret; Boston, Houghton Mifflin; 1968.
3. *Lights and Shadows: Space Relationships Through the Phenomena of Shadows—An Illustrated Teacher's Guide for Use in the Early Primary Grades.*
4. *Nature With Children of All Ages;* Sisson, Edith A; Massachusetts Audubon Society, Englewood Cliffs; Prentice-Hall.
5. *Outdoor Education "The Great Outdoors";* The University of the State of New York, The State Education Dept. Bureau of Elementary Curriculum Development, Albany, NY.
6. Queens College Center for Environmental Teaching and Research; Caumsett State Park, Huntington, New York, 11743.
7. *Spring Activities Flyer—Urban Park Rangers—*Queens; Published by The City of New York Parks and Recreation (offers workshops and walks/ideas).
8. *The Urban Environment—A Teacher's Guide Grades K–3*: Busch, Phyllis S.; J.G. Ferguson Company, Chicago, Illinois; 1975.

CHAPTER 4 APPENDIX

Resource Unit

COMMUNICATION MODULE—FIFTH GRADE

---

by Patricia Batine

I.	Introduction: What is communication?	2 weeks
II.	Nonverbal communication: gestures, body movements	1 week
III.	Speech and listening	1 week
IV.	Writing and reading	2 weeks

Introduction to Class. We will be working on a unit about communication. To communicate means to give information to another person or thing. The person who gives the information out is the sender or transmitter. Right now I am the transmitter. The person who gets the information is the receiver; you are the receiver. The sender and receiver are involved when any communication takes place; otherwise, the communication is not complete.

Let's look at some different ways to communicate. Suppose you are across the street and I want you to come to me. How many ways can I send this message to you?

Let's experiment and see whether some means of communication are more effective or easier than others. Everyone think of some pose you can make to get an idea across to the receiver (e.g., boxer's pose, salute).

1. Get pupils to pose. Does everyone understand the meaning?
2. Communicate another idea to a receiver by adding something to your pose. Can we still understand the message? Was it easier or harder?
3. Now communicate an idea through movement and voice. Do we understand the message? Is it easier or harder to understand now? Why?
4. Everyone write a paragraph about any subject. Read it to a small group of your classmates.
   a. Communicate the idea of the paragraph in one sentence.
   b. In one word.
   c. With one letter.
   d. Discuss which is easier to understand and why.

Teacher Activities for Module

Ideas for Pantomime

1. Playing with a yo-yo
2. Using a pencil sharpener
3. Playing with a mechanical toy
4. Being a sky diver
5. Being a skier going off a jump
6. Working a toaster
7. Using a can opener
8. Breaking open an egg
9. Using a tube of toothpaste
10. Filling a ball with air

Ideas for Listening

1. Pouring water
2. Bouncing ball
3. Turning eggbeater
4. Rubbing sandpaper
5. Crinkling cellophane
6. Hitting rhythm sticks
7. Hitting a triangle
8. Snapping an elastic
9. Letting air out of a balloon
10. Playing a music box

Commands

1. Stand close to a building, face the building, stretch to look at someone in a very high place.
2. Try to push a wall over without striking the wall.
3. Play with a bug in your hand.
4. Hang a picture on a wall.
5. Eat a peanut butter sandwich.
6. Slice a piece of cake.
7. Polish your shoes.
8. Have an itchy foot and you can't take off your shoe.
9. Get gum off your shoe.
10. Step on a thumbtack.

Communication Module

Objectives

1. You will be able to define *transmitter* and *receiver*.
2. You will be able to define *communication*.
3. You will be able to tell why people communicate.
4. You will be able to list at least five ways people can communicate.
5. You will be able to discuss ways that communication can take place without talking.
6. You will be able to tell the part that facial expressions play in communication.

7. You will understand the function of body movements or gestures used to communicate.
8. You will know what *language* is.
9. You will be able to tell what part listening plays in communication.
10. You will be able to explain the importance of intonation in oral language.
11. You will learn the different types of writing and some reasons for writing.
12. You should be able to explain:
    a. What *propaganda* is.
    b. Why propaganda is used.
13. You will learn some codes.
14. You will be able to tell how art can be used to communicate.
15. You will be able to tell how music can be used to communicate.
16. You will learn about different signals of meaning used only in writing.
17. You will be able to tell how "reading" is communicating.

Suggested Books:

Bueher, W. (1957). *Sending the word: The story of communications.* New York: Putnam Sons.

Bathelor, J. (1953). *Communication: From cave writing to television.* New York: Harcourt Brace Jovanovich.

McGough, E. (1974). *Your silent language.* New York: William Morrow. (Ill. by Tom Huffman.)

Lubell, W. & Lubell, C. (1972). *Pictures, signs and symbols.* New York: Parents' Magazine Press.

Wise, W. (1970). *From scrolls to satellites: The story of communication.* New York: Parents' Magazine Press. Pictures by Hans Zander.

Suggested Audio-visual Materials:

Filmstrips
Newspapers in the Classroom—A Series. Copley Productions.
Story of Communication Series. Eye Gate House.
Films
Communication—Let It Begin Now. Mountain States Telephone and Telegraph.
Signals for Survival. New York: McGraw-Hill Textfilm.

Requirements

1. You must do a minimum of five activities:
   a. One must be chosen from activities 1–4.
   b. One must be chosen from activities 5–8.
   c. One must be chosen from activities 9–11.
   d. Two must be chosen from activities 12–18.
2. You must listen to the presentation of five other pupils' activities.
   a. Submit a list of six things you learned from the presentations.

Activity Alternatives	**Reporting/Sharing Alternatives**

Activity Alternatives

1. Show what the jobs of the receiver and sender are.

2. Locate as many different definitions of *communication* as possible.

3. Research and discover five different reasons for communication.

4. Show five ways that people communicate.

5. Imagine that you were unable to talk for 24 hours.

6. Show the importance of facial expressions to speech.

7. You are a pantomime actor or actress.

8. Investigate the sign language of the deaf.

8a. Investigate the sign language of a referee or umpire for some sport.

9. You are to become a sound detective.

10. Investigate how gestures help a spoken message.

10a. Observe the different gestures used by people you meet for one day.

Reporting/Sharing Alternatives

Make a chart and set up a color code.

Create a transparency overlay.

Make a picture chart showing this information.
Make an outline showing this information.

Prepare a picture chart.

Prepare a list of all the ways you could communicate with others.

Make a list of the different emotions. What words describe the facial expressions of these feelings?
Find pictures of facial expressions showing different feelings.
Make a chart.

Pick an idea or role to act out.
This may be done with another pupil.

Make a presentation showing and explaining how these people communicate.

Give a demonstration of the signs and explain what they mean.

Listen to the "Sound Tape" and list the sounds you hear.
Tell a story to a group using only sounds to show the action and the characters.

Select a poem or story and read it orally to a group:
    First, without gestures.
    Then, with gestures.
Get the group's reaction to the two readings.

Make a list of all the gestures you saw people use. Explain how some of the same gestures were used differently.

Activity Alternatives	**Reporting/Sharing Alternatives**
11. You are a politician and want to know the importance of *intonation* in speech.	Find out what *intonation* is and what part it plays in communication. Read a speech (yours or someone else's): First, without intonation. Second, with intonation. Third, with a different one.
12. Compare how the same thing is written about in at least two different books or magazines.	Find a paragraph in either your science or social studies book. Look up the same topic in an encyclopedia. List how the styles of writing differ.
13. You are a government agent and your job is to research propaganda techniques.	Prepare a composition or a short talk telling what it is, and why it can be used to change people's thinking. Make a scrapbook with examples of the different types of propaganda.
14. You are a code expert.	Find out what you are called. Using *Codes to Captains* (1) Decode the Indian message on page 24, or the cowboy code. (2) Send messages using these codes. (3) Make up a code of your own using the rules on page 31.
15. Tell a story through art.	Using "circle symbol" characters, create two stories: One, familiar to the others. Two, not familiar to the others.
15a. You are an Indian cave artist.	On brown paper, draw a story of a tribal event.
16. Communicate through music.	Select music without words that gives you different ideas or feelings. See if these same ideas and feelings are communicated to others.
17. Investigate all the communication signals in writing other than letters and words.	Prepare a poster showing the different writing signals and explain what each communicates.
18. Investigate how there can be a breakdown in communication.	Read one of the following stories and discuss why there is a breakdown in communication. "Henny Penny" "40 Thieves" "Emperor's New Clothes" "Tale of Peter Rabbit" "Amelia Bedelia"

Keep a Record of your Work Here:

1. I have performed the following activities:
   a.
   b.
   c.
   d.
   e.

2. I have listened to the following OTHER activities:
   a.
   b.
   c.
   d.
   e.

3. I have learned:
   a.
   b.
   c.
   d.
   e.
   f.

Organizer

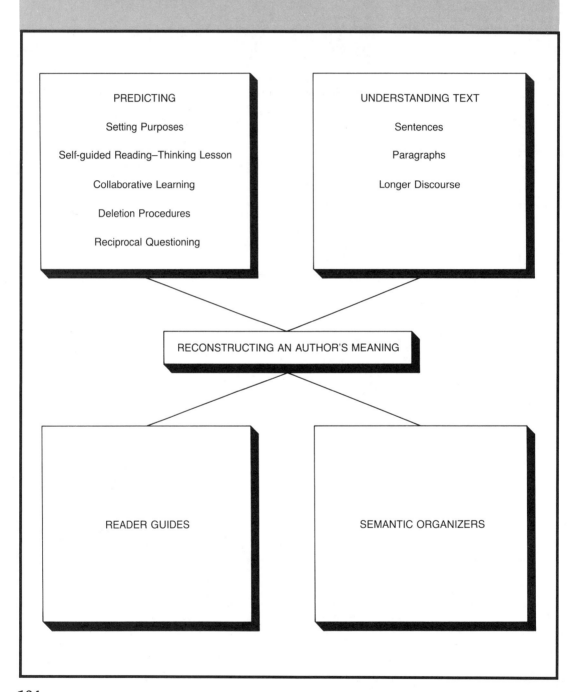

PREDICTING

Setting Purposes

Self-guided Reading–Thinking Lesson

Collaborative Learning

Deletion Procedures

Reciprocal Questioning

UNDERSTANDING TEXT

Sentences

Paragraphs

Longer Discourse

RECONSTRUCTING AN AUTHOR'S MEANING

READER GUIDES

SEMANTIC ORGANIZERS

CHAPTER
5

Strategies for Reconstructing and Constructing Meaning

Focus Questions

- What is the function of prediction strategies in understanding an author's message?
- What typical sentence and paragraph constructions do authors use?
- How can knowing the structures and functions of sentences and paragraphs increase one's understanding of an author's message?
- What are the steps in developing a reading strategy lesson?
- How does composing sentences and paragraphs aid students in reconstructing an author's messages?

In this chapter, strategies are presented to help students understand how authors create written messages and to let them develop strategies for self-monitoring their reading and writing. By analyzing various sentence, paragraph, and longer passage patterns and by constructing their own messages in sentences, paragraphs, and whole passages, students can become independent processors and self-monitors of language and information. (Chapter 7 contains additional ideas about reading and writing expository prose.)

The strategies presented for reconstructing an author's meaning and for constructing one's own messages are based on the following premises:

- Information is more easily gained when it is learned as a process and not as a collection of facts.
- Comprehension involves cognitive processing of language and language cues.
- Understanding oral language and oral language cues is preparatory to understanding written language and written language cues.
- Proficient readers monitor their reading through an awareness of the congruency between what the author intended and what they understand.

THE READER RECONSTRUCTS THE AUTHOR'S MESSAGE

Strategies to develop students' proficiencies as independent readers include: (1) techniques for fostering students' prediction strategies; (2) students' strategies for understanding sentences, paragraphs, and extended prose, and (3) students' strategies for answering questions that appear in instructional materials. Although the techniques and strategies are presented in this order, reading comprehension instruction uses information from all areas. For example, students predict effectively when they understand text organization patterns, and they question effectively as they gain security in predicting and confirming techniques.

Writing as a Strategy for Reconstructing Meaning

"Children learning the written form of language ought to be producing it as well as reading it" (Holt & Vacca, 1981, p. 939). In learning to understand how authors build meanings through sentence structures, paragraph structures, and longer organizational patterns, no greater insight is gained than when being an author oneself. Students' reading and writing comprehension development is made easier when they learn how a text is constructed and can relate their own knowledge and experience to building associations, abstractions, and inferences (Goodman, 1984; Linden & Wittrock, 1981; Pearson & Tierney, 1984). To do that, the teacher can have students generate summary sentences or paragraphs about stories and expand on some character, place, or event in the story. To expand on a character, students can write what happens to that person either the week before or the week after the story occurs, or write what happens when two characters meet in a different location at a different time.

Specific lessons to help students develop the ability to create sentences containing various sentence information or to write similar information in different ways provide them with insight into how ideas are transmitted in multiple forms. Teachers can do this by discussing how the ideas take on a new or different meaning in the transposed form. For example, students may take a paragraph describing an object and turn it into a dialogue between two people—one teaching the other about the object. The students' aim should be to make the dialogue informative yet natural. Or the emotions and emphasis shown by specific words can be rewritten to convey the same meaning through graphic cues: bold print, italics, or exclamations.

A thoughtful reader who is reading like a writer is a planner, a composer, an editor, and a monitor (Pearson & Tierney, 1984). As a planner, the reader predicts what the author will say, creates goals for reading, mobilizes his or her knowledge, and judges the author's believability. As a composer, the reader searches for coherence in the author's ideas by matching a working model (predicted meanings) with the actual text. As an editor, the reader revises the working model during reading. As a monitor, the reader decides whether the created meaning is suitable.

Writing activities place students in the position of thinking through the decisions authors make while allowing them to appreciate, as both sender and receiver, the total in-print communicative process. They learn that reading and writing are interrelated flexible processes that vary with purpose, audience, content, users' proficiency with language, and orthography (Goodman, 1984). Writing affects student learning because the more they manipulate in writing new material they have read, the better they will understand the material. In effect, what they write about they learn (Applebee, 1984). The techniques and strategies discussed in this chapter and based on the structures of language and the reading process as explained in Chapters 2 and 13 are learned simultaneously by students as reading and writing processes.

Prediction Strategies

Often teachers' attempts to encourage the development of prediction strategies are dismissed as encouragement to guess. The negative connotation of guessing is unfortunate. To some, the term implies a random attempt at discovering the correct answer. Yet guessing is an important strategy used throughout people's lives. When viewed as a proper activity, it is called hypothesizing or predicting. For example, individuals who estimate the outcome of economic or financial events rarely refer to their endeavors as guessing; instead, they refer to it as predicting based on the best available information.

In school, students are not encouraged to guess, but instead to test hypotheses or predict. Activities to direct their attention to information signals in written language can help them make accurate predictions about a word's meaning in context or a story's meaning as the author intended it.

Setting Purposes

An important aspect of prediction strategies is setting purposes. As stated previously, authors have specific purposes when they create messages; however, many readers undertake reading acts without a purpose. If they do have one, it is often not consistent with the author's. "When students are encouraged, indeed required, to set logical purposes for reading non-fiction and to make predictions when they are reading fiction, they soon discover that the ideas and sense of form of the author are frequently different from their own" (Cramer, 1970, p. 259). So, it is important for students to make predictions about and set purposes for any reading they undertake.

Predicting requires the use of prior knowledge relevant to the material being read (Smith, 1975b). Individual words have many possible meanings out of context, so a reader must first have some experience with the topic and its related vocabulary to predict a meaning consistent with the author's. Often the spelling of a word does not give clues to how it should be pronounced, so the reader must already know what the word should be. (More on this subject is found in Chapter 6.) Because the amount of visual information processed by the brain during reading is limited, the reader must have a knowledge base to associate with the author's ideas and to store them in his or her memory. This schema matching is described in Chapter 13.

Simply, the act of making predictions is the act of eliminating unlikely alternatives (Smith, 1975b). When considered this way, predicting is not wild guessing but a systematic evaluation of alternatives and the selection of those that match the reader's expectations of the author's meaning. It should be evident, then, that predictions are difficult and are likely to be incorrect when the reader has had limited experience with the topic and is unfamiliar with or cognitively not ready to process the language and stylistic features used by the author.

There are advantages to having the reader regularly make decisions to accept, modify, or reject assumptions about the author's meaning. This allows the reader to create meaning without having to worry about loading short-term memory with extraneous visual and auditory information. It is when teachers stress accurate processing of all visual clues that many readers attend only to the passage's surface features instead of to its meaning.

Students develop prediction strategies when encouraged to predict. Some students can intuitively predict, but others have learned not to do so. Their instruction has led them to believe that only word recognition accuracy is valued; they may withhold any attempt at prediction for fear of being wrong.

To make predictions, students must know what information to select and how to confirm their predictions. Some of the types of information students should use in making their predictions is discussed in this chapter. In this section, a discussion of a prediction strategy is included that can be used for discovering the general message of the author.

The information used for making predictions differs among students. We know that children in different stages of development differ in how they think and use language. For example, in one research study, third-grade students showed a different cognitive style from sixth graders by selecting more concrete answers to questions; the sixth graders selected more abstract choices (Lundsteen, 1974a). Therefore, to develop proficient predictors, teachers must be aware of each student's level of thinking.

Self-guided Reading–Thinking Lesson

One method to foster prediction strategies for the general meaning of a story is based on the guided reading–thinking lesson described in Chapter 4. The involvement level of the teacher makes the difference between a guided lesson and one in which the student develops a sense of predicting. When the teacher's actions totally structure the students' actions, the lesson is a guided one. When the teacher gives students greater responsibility for selecting information and creating purposeful questions, he or she is helping them move toward independence. For example, the introductory sequence of questions for a guided lesson of "The Eagle and the Boy" (see Figure 5–1) might be the following:

Title and Picture, First Page of Story

What do you think the story is about?
Where do you think the story took place?
Have you ever read any other story about a human and an animal?
Based on the title, what do you think the story will be about?

After students are guided through several stories using the principles of a guided reading–thinking lesson, they are ready to make predictions about a story. The teacher's repetitive use of the guiding questions establishes a pattern for students to follow. The following is a possible introductory sequence of questions for a lesson that fosters the student's independent prediction strategies.

Title and Picture, First Page of Story

Looking only at the picture and title of the story, what questions can you now ask about it?
After reading the first page of the story, what questions can you now ask about the story?
Do you want to change any of the questions you asked before you read the page?

This sequence of questions illustrates how the responsibility for setting reading purposes is shifted to students. The following responses show how students with different levels of thinking and language maturity might react:

The Eagle and the Boy

One day the Indian boy, Waukewa, was hunting along the mountainside. He saw a young eagle with a broken wing. It was lying at the base of a cliff.

The bird had fallen from its nest high above. It was too young to fly and had fluttered down the cliff. Now it was so badly hurt that it was likely to die.

FIGURE 5–1
Source: Fay, L., Ross, R.R., & LaPray, M. (1981). *The Rand McNally Reading Program, Level 9,* "Moonbeams and Microscopes." Chicago: Riverside. Reproduced by permission of Riverside Publishing Company.

I bet this story is just like the one I saw on television where the boy helps the eagle and then later, when the boy's in trouble, the eagle helps him.

We could probably ask, "What's going to happen between the Indian boy and the eagle?" Usually when a story has two people in the title, the story is about what happens to them. What's going to happen to the eagle? The eagle probably won't die because they wouldn't have put him in the title if he did. The story's probably about how the Indian and eagle become friends and help each other.

For those who know the story, these predictions, although produced by students of different maturity levels, are accurate. Both students have definite, self-created purposes for reading the story. How well the students are able to predict depends largely on the pattern of questions the teacher asked in earlier lessons.

Unless confirmation is expected, asking students to make predictions is not effective for developing an understanding of the relationship between reading and thinking. To do this, students should be asked whether their predictions were accurate and whether their responses can be justified. In this way, reading is not just reading and answering questions—it becomes active and purposeful. Students become conscious of reading as an attempt to match the purpose of the reader to that of the author so the latter's message can be understood.

Fostering Student Collaboration During Guided Reading

To reiterate the social nature of learning to read and write: Reading and writing tasks involve social contexts and interactions with others, they are extensions of our daily cultural and subcultural activities, and they are social–cognitive processes through which students learn to function in society. An educational implication of these ideas is the development of social interactions among students as a means for developing their comprehension monitoring abilities. One technique for promoting student collaborations is through peer-interaction groups (Hittleman, 1982a; 1982b; 1983; 1984a; 1984b).

Peer-interaction groups are small groups of students cooperatively planning and conducting reading lessons. Although students eventually conduct lessons without teacher help, teachers first need to guide and model the format and procedures of peer-interaction groups. (See Chapter 12 for discussions about the nature of groups and readiness for group activities.)

Peer-interaction groups provide students with opportunities to discuss a story with their peers and receive feedback on their oral and written questions and comments about the author's intent. Cooperatively, students examine the text; make predictions about its purpose, meaning and difficulty; and confirm or disconfirm their predictions. The story reading is done silently and usually, but not necessarily, independently. Students' activities are derived from two models: a directed reading–thinking activity (Stauffer, 1975) and peer conferencing of written products (C. Hittleman, 1983).

Students are not ready for peer-interaction groups until they can self-guide the reading–thinking lesson. Teachers can help make that happen by giving students greater responsibility for selecting information and creating purposeful questions. After students are guided through a number of lessons in which the teacher has used the directed reading–thinking approach principles, students begin to stimulate their own activating, agitating, and proving. As students learn to be responsible for guiding their own reading, they become active, purposeful readers and become conscious of reading as an attempt to find evidence to support and validate predictions about the author's intended meaning. This, then, is a first step towards comprehension monitoring.

The peer-conferencing model was developed as a way for students to get feedback on written drafts from their peers as they are trained in the techniques of responding to others' writing (C. Hittleman, 1983). The peer-conference training model is a 15-session structured procedure that begins with the teacher as owner, authority, and modeler of the the writing process and ends with the transfer of ownership, authority, and responsibility to students.

Through techniques based on this training model, students learn to be effective members of a peer-interaction reading group. Instead of responding to a known and visible author, however, students learn to respond to an unknown, absent author.

In sessions 1 to 5, students as a class become aware of the DRTA format as the teacher models aloud what a reader might think and how he or she might make decisions about setting a purpose for reading and questioning an author's possible purpose. The teacher also provides a model of how students can give each other feedback for making changes in their decisions. After the teacher models reading, the students and teacher make a list of appropriate thought-activating and agitating questions. The aim of these sessions is for students to learn how to focus their questions on what they perceive to be the writer's main intentions.

In sessions 6 to 10, students experience being peer-interaction group members. They treat the story as a product of one of their peers who happens to be absent. The teacher models the technique in a "fish bowl" situation by having students act as an audience while one group is guided through a peer interaction. After the peer-interaction group has completed their lesson, the other class members offer reactions and positive criticism. Each group gets a chance to be the model. Then all students use the technique in small groups as one group observes another and provides the observed group with feedback.

In sessions 11 to 15, students meet in peer-interaction groups, assume leadership for guiding the lesson, and make generalizations about effective and ineffective predictions and means for confirming or disconfirming their predictions.

During sessions 1 to 5, the teacher uses a prepared **story-specific study guide** which is constructed on the model of a DRTA (see Figure 5–2). The story theme, plot, and summary are provided for the teacher's reference and are not distributed to students. The teacher introduces the **general study guide** (Figure 5–3), which is appropriate for analyzing a great many stories, after students demonstrate that they can function in peer-interaction reading groups without teacher assistance and that they understand story structure and authors' literary techniques. This may occur during sessions 6–10 or 11–15, or it may not occur until much later. Therefore, some class groups may be using the story-specific study guide while others are using the general story guide.

In the story-specific study guide, the questions asked before reading the story direct students' attention to certain aspects of the story: the main characters, the setting, the plot structure, and the theme. In addition, the teacher's questions lead students to predict possible story development by directing their attention to the story title, various illustrations, the information on the first page of the story, and the author's choice of words. The students learn to participate as members of a peer-interaction reading group because the teacher encourages the students to confirm, question, or offer alternatives to their peers' answers.

During the reading of the story, students are encouraged to help each other in recognizing and analyzing unfamiliar words and in understanding confusing aspects of the story.

The questions asked after reading the story allow students to discuss their understanding of the story and to further confirm or disconfirm their earlier predictions. They are encouraged to raise questions about the author's use of literary techniques, choice of words, and development of plot and character. The premise throughout is that understanding is not solely dependent upon the reader's skills and strategies, but may be influenced by the author's style or the text's format.

The after-discussing-the-story activity allows students to integrate their ideas and assume ownership of them. The oral interaction is a preparation for writing, which in turn helps students build cognitive patterns for understanding the written material of others (Hennings, 1982).

The general story guide is used only after students are familiar with the DRTA format as a result of teacher-led and student-led peer-interaction group activities. This study guide is a general checklist of procedures that students should have already internalized. When they have acquired skill in questioning and analyzing the author's story structure and intent, students can begin to assume the roles of author or critic. In this situation, one student role-plays the part of an author and tries to answer questions from the others who assume roles of literary critics or book reviewers.

In summary, peer-interaction reading groups help students become independent, interactive readers and assume responsibility for guiding their own learning. Through them, the teacher transfers control and monitoring of their own understanding to students. What happens is that the metaphor of teacher as classroom manager becomes teacher as teacher (Pearson, 1985). An underlying premise of this approach is that answers to questions are not absolutes and that misunderstandings are part of the learning process. Reading is whole-language based; for that idea to be an underpinning of an instructional program, teachers must give students opportunities to develop their reading strategies in language contexts with their peers. The peer-interaction reading groups provide those contexts.

Deletion Procedures

Another way to develop a sense of prediction is through deletion procedures. In Chapter 10 the cloze procedure and the OP–IN procedure are presented as informal, silent-reading comprehension tests. Their use in developing students' prediction strategies is discussed here because researchers have found that students' reading-comprehension strategies can benefit from its use and that students can use the procedures as means for becoming comprehension monitors (Baker & Brown, 1984; Jenkins & Pany, 1981).

A cloze passage is made by systematically deleting one or more words from a paragraph and replacing each deleted word with a blank line of uniform

FIGURE 5–2
Study Guide I: Story-Specific

"Henry, Midge, and the Crystal Ball" by Keith Robertson in *Riding the Sunrise*, by T. Clymer and others. The Ginn Reading Program, Level 12, pp. 21–29.

Synopsis (provided as information for the teacher; not included in students' guide): Henry and Midge run the Henry Reed Baby Sitting Service. Belinda is constantly running away and hiding. The two devise a scheme that fools Belinda into thinking they have magical powers to see wherever she goes.

BEFORE READING THE STORY

Does the title give you any idea about what happens in the story? Do the words *crystal ball* in the title and the picture on page 20 make you think this is a real story or a make-believe story?

Read the first two paragraphs on page 21. Since Henry and Midge are in the title, they are most likely the main characters. Are there any other important characters in the story?

This story is being told by someone. Do you know who is telling the story?

Where does the this story take place? When does it happen? What clues do you get from the paragraphs on page 21 or from the picture?

What seems to be the story problem? What do you think the words *crystal ball* have to do with the story problem?

Are there any words you do not know? What are they? (Discuss all words not known by any of the group's members.) Read the rest of the story. If something is not clear to you, you can ask someone in the group to help you or to explain it to you.

AFTER THE STORY IS READ

Is this a real or make-believe story?

How did the words *crystal ball* fit the story?

Was the story problem solved? Do you think it was solved only for this story or has the baby-sitting problem with Belinda been solved for good?

Did Henry and Midge and Belinda act like real people?

Would you change the story in any way? If so, would you

FIGURE 5–2
Continued

- change the way Henry, Midge, and Belinda act?
- change what Belinda does?
- change the story ending?

Why did the author write this story?

- Did he want to change your mind about baby sitting small children?
- Did he want to tell you a humorous story about baby sitting?
- Did he want to give you information about running a baby-sitting service?

While you were reading, were there any words you did not know? What were they? Were they important to understanding the story? What did you do to understand them?

AFTER DISCUSSING THE STORY

Write a two- or three-sentence paragraph that tells about the story, "Henry, Midge, and the Crystal Ball."
The paragraph should tell

- who Henry, Midge, and Belinda are,
- what the story problem is,
- why the words *crystal ball* are in the story title, and
- why the author might have written the story.

Discuss your ideas with the others in the group and make changes in your paragraph if you want to.

---

length. A cloze passage constructed for teaching differs in two ways from one constructed for testing. First, the systematic deletion is not limited to every fifth word. The cloze procedure can be used to teach first- and second-grade students with as few deletions as every tenth word. In the other grades, passages with deletions over every seventh word can be used.

To introduce students to the use of cloze, use this criterion: The words used to fill in the blank must make sense and must be located somewhere in the passage. This first step creates text-explicit responses (see the section on "Strategies for Teacher and Student Questioning" in Chapter 4). For example:

FIGURE 5–3
Study Guide II: Story-General

BEFORE READING THE STORY

Read the title page and look at the picture.
   Is this a real story?
   Does the title give you any idea about what may happen? Does the picture?
   Read the first page (two pages).
   Does the story seem to be about something real or make-believe?
   What is the story problem?
   What is the story setting?
   Who are the main characters?
   Are there any other important characters?
   What do you think will happen to solve the story problem?
   Are there any words you do not know? What are they? What did you do when you read them?

AFTER THE STORY IS READ

Is this a real story? Could it happen just this way in real life?
   How does the title fit in with the story problem?
   Is the setting a good one for this type of story?
   Did the main characters act real? Are their actions appropriate to how the story problem was solved?
   Why did the author write this story?
   Can the story be changed in any way? What changes would you make? Why?
   What did you do when you came to a word or idea you did not understand? Was it important to understanding the story?

AFTER DISCUSSING THE STORY

Write a two- or three-sentence paragraph that tells what the story is about, who the main characters are, and why the story might have been written.
   Discuss your ideas with the others in the group and make changes in your paragraph if you want to.

Huge crowds gathered at the _____ to watch the boat race on the Charles River. The most daring of the spectators climbed high on the bridge cables to see better. To others, this was more interesting to _____ than the boat race.

The second difference is that synonyms are accepted, since the purpose is to foster anticipation of what the author intended. When introducing the procedure, use short passages with a total of about five deleted words. As students become adept at predicting, longer passages with more deletions may be used. After students can complete most items, have them discuss the reasons for their choices. This activity is most effective when students question one another and give reasons for their selections (see peer-interaction groups and reciprocal questioning).

When using synonyms, do not emphasize getting the "correct" answer; instead, guide students by asking questions such as, "Does the answer keep the meaning the author wanted?"

An analysis of research on the cloze procedure as an instructional technique found that it is most effective (1) when developing reading comprehension or at least some of the skills involved in the comprehension process; (2) when discussion is focused on clues that signal responses and on the appropriateness of the students' responses; (3) when materials are carefully sequenced according to difficulty, length, or purpose; and (4) when selective-deletion systems aimed at particular contextual relationships are used instead of semi-random deletions. The cloze procedure is least effective when developing or improving word knowledge or vocabulary (Jongsma, 1980).

Another procedure for developing students' sense of predicting is the OP–IN procedure, which is similar to the cloze procedure (Pehrsson, 1975; 1985). Unlike the cloze procedure, in which only single words are systematically deleted, this procedure deletes more than one word at a time. Instructional material is prepared by deleting the main verb phrase and all the information following that verb in every other sentence. (Complete directions and guidelines for creating OP–IN passages are found in Chapter 10.) For example, a prepared passage might be:

By now the entire city was awake. Buses _____
and trucks _____.
Paula had never seen such confusion as this, and she could not understand why everyone rushed so. She _____.
Seeing several people coming at her like a herd of stampeding cattle, she jumped into the doorway of the drugstore on the corner.

The materials may be selected from any reading matter appropriate for any independent or instructional level. The passage can be read orally or silently, and the student should either write all the responses or tell them to the teacher. The student's responses are then used as the basis for discussing the use of semantic clues in the story.

The instruction associated with this procedure of developing anticipatory thinking involves an examination of three types of information: (1) grammatical acceptability, (2) semantic acceptability, and (3) contextual acceptability. In response to the passage about Paula, one student replied:

> Buses jammed the traffic and trucks blew their horns very loud. She yelled at them to stop.

The responses are grammatically acceptable as independent sentences. The first is also semantically and contextually acceptable. It is *interpretive* because the author's intended ideas are kept. The second, although semantically acceptable as a sentence, does alter the context. It is *projective* because the student is expressing his or her feelings about the incident and is not sensing the general feeling of confusion.

The following responses by another student are not contextually appropriate, although they may be grammatically and semantically acceptable. They are *fragmented* responses.

> Buses picked up the people and trucks made deliveries. She got on the bus.

In this response, the student does not relate to the information in the surrounding sentences. The first answer does not indicate that the buses and trucks were the sources of some of the confusion as the city awoke. The second answer seems to indicate that the student is responding to some prior knowledge that one can board a bus. This response is not acceptable according to the information in this passage.

Practice and instruction in anticipatory thinking combined with discussions about their answers' appropriateness to the passage helps students focus attention on acceptable sentence patterns and appropriate meanings.

Inquiry Lesson

Another activity that shifts responsibility for asking questions to students and away from the teacher is the use of an inquiry lesson (Olmo, 1975). This activity is aimed at increasing student involvement in a lesson and decreasing the amount of teacher talk to increase the level of students' thinking from fact stating to problem solving.

An inquiry lesson is devised as follows:

- Students, who have been randomly divided into four to six groups, are given packets containing different materials about the same general theme. The material is in various forms: textual material (books, magazine articles, etc.), pictures, recordings, and graphics.

- As a group, students examine, read, and analyze the material in the packet and prepare answers to questions the other students will ask them.
- In turn, based on the type of information in their folders, the students develop questions they will ask other students. (The type of information in each folder is the same; only the particulars differ.)
- As a group, students attempt to find a solution to the common problem linking the information in all packets.

For example, in a third- or fourth-grade classroom, the teacher might ask the students, "What problems do people who live in desert areas have?" Four packets are prepared, each of which illustrates the life and problems of people in four desert regions—the Sahara, the Gobi, the Australian desert, and the American Southwest. The folders contain information about the problems desert dwellers have in getting water, food, shelter, and clothing. For resources the students can use library books, newspaper articles, magazines and children's school newspapers, films, records, maps, encyclopedia articles, and large pictures or study prints.

As the lesson unfolds, students should gather information for questions that might be asked of them and should prepare questions to ask other students.

Throughout the activity, which might last from one to five days, the teacher acts as a resource person, providing additional information or suggesting where the students might find it on their own, and as interpreter, clarifying anything that the students do not fully understand.

Reciprocal Questioning

A procedure for developing students' ability to generate questions is reciprocal teaching/questioning. The research literature shows that students can easily learn this procedure (Baker & Brown, 1984; Manzo, 1969; 1985; Palincsar & Brown, 1986; Wong, 1985). In reciprocal teaching/questioning, the teacher and students, individually or in a group, take turns teaching and asking questions about a passage. (See the section on "Strategies for Teacher and Student Questioning" in Chapter 4.) The procedure's aims are to improve students' comprehension by providing active learning and to teach students to generate different types of appropriate questions. The teacher is a model of questioning behavior. He or she helps the student expand or modify questions by providing direct feedback about the questions through specific answers or requests for more information if the question is confusing.

Reciprocal teaching/questioning is used during language experience, directed reading–thinking, and peer-interaction group activities. The teacher starts by explaining that others can lead discussions, then draws attention to the types of questions to be used. The teacher can encourage students to act as the teacher with the question, "Who would like to try being the discussion leader?" Prereading questions can be used to focus on purpose setting (acti-

vating thought by examining story information and hypothesizing about the story plot and theme). Postreading questions can be used to focus on verifying predictions, clarifying understandings, and integrating meanings (agitating thought by requiring evidence and extending ideas beyond the passage).

Strategies for Understanding Textual Material

As students develop predicting and confirming strategies, they learn to reconstruct the author's meaning by understanding the following text-reading strategies: (1) sentence-reading strategies, (2) paragraph-reading strategies, and (3) longer selection-reading strategies. A study of language cues shows how authors build their messages. By recognizing, responding to, and creating these cues, students become independent readers.

To reiterate, these strategies do not have the traditional names associated with comprehension skills. These strategies should, however, increase students' understanding (as revealed by their ability to get the main idea, follow directions, and so forth).

The idea of students taking meaning cues from language structure is not new. What is new is that the structures are not treated in isolation. By using them in context, students realize that comprehension is a set of processes operating on specific features of language (Bormuth, 1969a). These specific features are visual presentations of language signals to which the students respond normally in oral language. They learn to respond to oral language signals without a formal knowledge of grammar and rhetoric (Bormuth, 1969a). Therefore, the study of language signals lets students answer the following questions (Christapherson, 1974) without knowing the correct grammatical terminology:

- *Who* or *what* caused an event?
- *Who* or *what* was directly affected by the event?
- *What* was used to perform the event?
- *Where* did the event take place?
- *Who* or *what* benefited or suffered from the event?
- *What* was the outcome of the event?
- *What* descriptions and identifications were given about the event?

Some of the general signaling systems of which elementary and middle school students can develop an awareness are (Bormuth, 1969a)

- the meaning of words;
- the ways word affixes influence meaning and syntactic function;
- the ways deep structures are assigned to sentences.
- the ways surface and deep structures of sentences govern word and phrase meanings;
- the ways structures are assigned to paragraphs and larger units of discourse and how those structures are used to modify sentences, paragraphs, and section meanings; and
- the identification of antecedents of pronouns and other referring words.

Much of what is discussed in the next sections and chapters deals with cohesion and coherence. Authors achieve cohesion in their text through relationships. The interpretation of one idea in the text depends on the successful interpretation of another. Cohesion is created by a type of redundancy that links one phrase with another. Coherence is something the reader establishes as he or she reads connected discourse. It is the cognitive correlate of cohesion (Chapman, 1983; Irwin, 1986a; Moe & Irwin, 1986).

Cohesion is text-related and is created through cohesive ties. Identifying what certain words refer to or stand for is coherence. The following are common cohesive ties:

Pronouns

Some spiders are hairy all over. *They* are called wolf spiders.

Deleted nouns

Then the cloth is put into different liquids. *One* cleans the cloth. *Another* makes the cloth stronger.

Proverbials

He was not very smart, but he knew he could not stop. If he were to *do so,* the tiger would eat him up. So he continued.

Synonymous Terms

The horse arrived at the barn door just before feeding time. *The building,* however, was locked up.

The pin was set with precious jewels. Each *gem* glistened in the sunlight.

Arithmetic Pronouns

As the group approached, Bill could recognize *the three* who had visited him last night—Mr. Watkins, Mr. Stevens, and Mr. Olivera.

Prosentences

When you talk or sing or shout, the air passing between your vocal cords makes them vibrate. *This* is what makes the sound of your voice.

Strategies for understanding the general signaling systems of English text are discussed in the next sections and in Chapters 6 and 7. These strategies are not hierarchical. Although it seems logical to begin with word- or sentence-reading strategies before dealing with paragraph-reading strategies, there is no need to limit instruction to graphophonological information or to sentence reading and writing until these are mastered. The result is unnatural. It is rare to find words isolated from sentences, sentences isolated from paragraphs, and paragraphs isolated from longer discourse. The specific strategies used with students, then, depends on their capabilities for processing units of language. Strategies are both presented and learned cyclically and not linearly, and student lessons should contain word-, sentence- and paragraph-reading/writing strategies with increasingly mature discourse.

Sentence-reading Strategies

The specific strategies students need to understand sentences are

    1. Recognizing and using *who* or *what* in the sentence.

Felice got into the blue truck.

The animals in the zoo stared back at the children.

2. Recognizing and using the action being done by the who or what of the sentence.

Raymond *hugged his aunt and uncle.*

More and more people *are interested in how to protect wild birds and animals.*

3. Recognizing and using the information signals indicating where something is or is done. These signals are *under, over, in, on, at, to, between, among, behind, in front of,* and *through.*

The class had its morning recess *in the school gym.*

Jocie took careful aim and shot the ball right *through the hoop.*

4. Recognizing and using the information signals indicating when something is done or happens. These signals are *before, after, later, while, as, now,* and *then.*

Frank was able to get inside his house *before the thunder and lightning started.*

After breakfast, we all started to clean up the yard.

5. Recognizing and using the information signals indicating how something is done. These signals are words with the adverbial ending *-ly,* and the words *like* and *as.*

They walked *quietly* up the steps.

Like safari hunters, the children, stalking their older brothers, crept through the weeds.

6. Recognizing and using the information signals indicating how long or how much something is. The signals for this information are *for, about, almost, as long (much) as,* and *until* (and any measurement).

The cat sat *for hours* waiting for the canary to leave its cage.

The teacher gave Alice *until Monday* to finish her project.

7. Recognizing and using the information signals that indicate a *condition* exists. These signals are *is, seems,* and *appears.*

Harry *is* the name of my pet cat.

Nobody *seems* happy with my answer!

8. Recognizing and using information that indicates what kind of thing something is. The clues for this information are the possible transforms of the condition sentences.

The *tired* quarterback looked at the clock and wished the game was over. (The quarterback is tired.)

High in the tree sat a *reddish* bird I had not seen before. (The bird appears red.)

9. Understanding how some information in a sentence is movable without changing the meaning of the sentence.

The architect *skillfully* drew the lines of the house.

Skillfully, the architect drew the lines of the house.

Once in a while we like to bring home pizza for supper.

We like to bring home pizza for supper *once in a while.*

10. Understanding that different sentences can have similar meanings.

Sandra painted the furniture to match the drapes her mother made.

The furniture was painted by Sandra to match the drapes made by her mother.

11. Recognizing and using the information signals indicating that the sentence contains descriptive information. The clues to information about someone or something are *who, which,* and *that.*

Once there was a little gray mouse *who lived with his mother.*

Since everyone *who wanted to help* had arrived, it was now time to think of some way to get the skunk out.

All of a sudden, Jean remembered the cows *that were waiting to be milked.*

The test questions, *which seemed unanswerable by all the students,* covered everything that they had learned about the geography of Asia.

12. Recognizing and using the signals for replaced information. The clues to the replaced information are *I, you, he, she, it, they, we, us, them, their, his/her, your, our, him, this,* and *these.*

As the young mouse grew, *she* became more curious about the world.

Aunt Harriet landed the plane on *her* ranch.

Fran liked to tease *her* cat, but Sally thought *it* was a silly thing to do.

"Wait until you see *this*," shouted Randy, running to the other kids with *his* stamp collection.

> The teacher should note that pronouns such as *it*, *these*, and *those* many times do not replace just one word but groups of words or entire ideas.

13. Understanding that words are often left out of a sentence and that the reader has to mentally replace the omitted information. The clue that information has been omitted is when questions beginning with *what* or *did what* can be asked at the point the information was omitted.

While everybody was eating the hot pancakes, Leslie made some more. (More what?)

When the coach shouted, "Run!" all the players began. (Began doing what?)

14. Understanding how different sentences can be connected together and can be separated into other sentences. The signals to understanding sentence connections are a variety of conjunctions that seem to signal four types of relationships:
    a. *Joining.* The relationship brings together ideas that are similar. The common joining signals are *and*, *moreover*, *furthermore*, *in addition*, *too*, and *also*.
    b. *Excluding.* The relationship discriminates, negates, or rejects ideas. The common signals are *not*, *not this*, *neither/nor*, *but*, and *except*.
    c. *Selecting.* The relationship takes a subset of items from a larger category. The common signals to selected information are *one*, *the other*, *both*, *some*, *part*, *a few*, *either/or*, and the quantitative pronouns.
    d. *Implying.* The relationship is one of effect/cause, result, necessity, proof, or condition. The common signals are *if/then*, *if not this . . . then that*, *although*, *though*, *because*, *since*, *so*, *in order*, *as*, *unless*, *before*, *where*, *when*, *how*, *why*, *however*, *therefore*, *nevertheless*, and *hence* (Henry, 1974).

In addition to instruction about various sentence strategies, students need instruction in recognizing, using, and understanding these strategies as they apply to groups of two or more sentences. Often, authors place additional information (such as the when or where type) in later sentences. Students must recognize the signals that indicate the additional information and understand the relationships among the sentences. They also need opportunities to make these relationships in their own written sentences. In the following examples, additional information, or the referent of replaced information, is in a previous sentence. The signals are in italics.[1]

> They all tried to lift the first bar. *But* only Stan Moijeski, Pete Pussick, and a stranger from Johnstown could lift *it*. Then Pete and Stan and the stranger moved on to the next bar. Pete and Stan each got *her* off the ground, but the stranger from Johnstown had to give up. (Level 10, page 166)

> So Esther filled the big jug again and hurried home. *Her* mother was awake when *she* got there. (Level 10)

> *That's* what people all over the world do. *They* wear what the people around them wear. (Level 10)

> Another young woman from a different tribe in South Africa wears a blanket of wool. *She* folds *it* into a cape around her shoulders. (Level 10)

Paragraph Strategies

A paragraph is more than individual sentences that are grouped—it is a set of relationships among its sentences. The teaching of paragraph-reading and paragraph-writing strategies focuses on how paragraphs are structured and their function in longer discourse. First the focus is on following the flow of an author's ideas through a paragraph, and then it is on the various structures authors use when constructing paragraphs.

To understand and construct paragraphs, students must first recognize who or what a paragraph is about. The normal signals for determining who or what a paragraph is about are repeated and replaced words.

Repeated words are content words found in most sentences of the paragraph. By noting these words, a reader can follow or construct a flow of ideas and determine the agent of the paragraph. It is rare to find paragraphs with the same word or words repeated throughout. The following paragraph has been constructed for illustration and can be used to introduce students to the concept of repeated words.

> There are many kinds of storms. Some of the most common storms are rain storms, ice storms, wind storms, and snow storms. Hurricanes are a kind of storm that are known for their strong winds. Another type of wind storm is called a typhoon. Storms of different kinds occur all over the world.

---

1. These examples and those following in this chapter, except where otherwise noted, are from Fay, Ross, & LaPray (1981). The reading series levels are noted in parentheses.

More often, authors use substitute words that are repeated throughout a paragraph. Pronouns are common substitutes: *he, she, him, her, his, hers, it, its, their, them, they*. By mentally replacing the substitute word with its referent, readers can follow the author's flow of ideas, as in the next example.

> A dolphin cannot live out of the water. Its whole life is in the ocean. It is born in the ocean. The dolphin's mother teaches it how to stay alive in the ocean. It eats nothing but fish from the ocean. (Level 8)

A commonly held belief is that all paragraphs have a main idea. This does not always seem to be the case, however (Robinson, 1983; Santa & Hayes, 1981). Most paragraphs have a topic or a unifying idea, but not all paragraphs have a single, main point. For example, the following paragraph has a main point, or generalization, stated in its first sentence.

> A dolphin is among the fastest swimmers in the ocean. It can swim faster than the fastest person, and faster than many fish. Often it follows ships. It can keep right up with a ship, swimming and jumping and playing. (Level 8)

However, the following paragraph, although it has a topic, does not have a specific main idea. It is part of a larger main idea and only serves to add more information in a descriptive form.

> Now the monkey knew the name of the older sister too. He waited until they had left the tree, and then he climbed down and went home. (Fay & Anderson, Level 11)

The topic has to do with some action of the monkey, which is part of the larger idea of the monkey using various schemes to get information and pass it on to another animal.

Readers must realize that authors organize ideas about a topic in various ways. The notion of a main idea is only one major organizational writing pattern an author uses (Robinson, 1983). Readers need to learn what the various writing patterns are and the signals that will help them recognize these patterns. The various writing patterns are not unique to one level of reading material—they are found at all levels and in all subject areas. The differences between the same pattern at different levels are in the concepts, sentence patterns, and vocabulary of the authors. By creating these patterns in their own writing, students can understand and appreciate an author's task and purpose.

There are six main paragraph patterns (Robinson, 1983).

Enumeration. The enumeration pattern is relatively easy to recognize. It has a topic statement followed by subordinate statements that list the subtopics. The common signals of the enumeration pattern are numbers, and the words *another, more, also, one kind,* and *another kind.*

The following paragraphs illustrate an enumeration pattern.

> There are many different sounds. There is the sound of the wind rushing through the trees. There is the sound of raindrops hitting against your window. There is the sound of a train whistle, of a door closing, of footsteps, of a cat's meow. There are the sounds of birds singing, of a baseball when it is hit by a bat, of your mother calling you home from playing, of chalk on a chalkboard. (Level 10)

> Musical instruments are often played together in an orchestra. There are four main kinds of instruments used: strings, woodwinds, brass, and percussion. (Level 10)

Sometimes the enumeration pattern spans several paragraphs. Signals within the title, topic heading, or a paragraph indicate the use of this pattern. In the following example, the story title and the signals in the first two sentences indicate that the enumeration pattern will be used in succeeding paragraphs.

All kinds of Spiders, All Kinds of Places
There are many different kinds of spiders. Spiders live in almost every part of the world. They live in dry places. They live in the far north and in the highest places in the world. (Level 7)

Sometimes the enumeration pattern is introduced in a longer selection. The following paragraph introduces the enumeration pattern and later paragraphs complete the pattern by listing other kinds of horses.

> To us, probably the most familiar work animal is the horse. There are many different kinds of horses. One kind is the draft horse. It was bred in England and France hundreds of years ago. (Level 10)

Generalization. The generalization pattern is closest to what is traditionally called the main idea. In the generalization pattern, authors make a broad statement and then provide support for it through examples, explanations, or reasons. The generalization pattern is distinguishable from enumeration in that the generalization is a statement containing an idea or belief. The enumeration pattern indicates only that there are various types or kinds of a particular thing. The generalization can stand alone without the supporting ideas; the enumeration statement is incomplete without additional information.

In the following example, the generalization is found in the first sentence. In the generalization pattern, the words *for example* can be included after the first sentence to introduce the other sentences.

> With his hands the conductor tells the players just what kind of sound he wants. He may want the violins to be the loudest and the timpani to be very soft. Or maybe he wants the trombones to be the loudest with no violins playing at all. Maybe he wants everyone to play softly, or slowly, or as fast as possible. (Level 10)

In the following paragraph, the generalization is determined by combining the information found in the first two sentences. The other sentences provide information illustrating the generalization.

> Some very small spiders live on flowers and leaves. They change color to look just like the flowers they are sitting on. On red flowers, the spiders are red. On sunflowers, they are yellow. On leaves, they are green. (Level 7)

Comparison and contrast. In this pattern, two related ideas are compared or contrasted. Sometimes the two ideas are signaled by *but, however, although, yet,* and *even though,* as in the following paragraphs:

> Even though burros look sad and sleepy, they are very intelligent animals. People are always surprised at the clever tricks burros think up to get out of working. (Level 10)

> Ned thought that his father looked both funny and sad as a clown. The white and red and black pants made his father look funny. So did the bits of red hair stuck on all over his head. But the black rings around his eyes and the big white mouth he painted made the face seem sad. (Level 7)

Sequence. At first, the sequence pattern seems similar to enumeration. In the sequence pattern, however, the order of ideas is most important. There is no way to reorder a sequence without changing the author's meaning. In the enumeration pattern, the order of the ideas can be changed without altering the author's intended meaning. The common signals of a sequence pattern are *first, second, third, last; before, after, while;* and *then, later.*

The following set of paragraphs illustrates the sequence pattern:

> After the cotton is dried and cleaned at the gin, the workers put the cotton onto trucks, and the trucks take it to cotton mills.
>   At the cotton mills, the cotton goes through many machines. Some machines clean the cotton. Other machines make it into thread. Other machines make the thread into cloth. (Level 7)

(Notice the enumeration pattern is also a part of the paragraph development of the second paragraph. These paragraphs were taken from a selection in which the main pattern is sequencing. However, one step in the sequence is further explained by the enumeration of examples.)

Effect/cause. The effect/cause pattern is one of implication. One idea is subordinated to another in a relationship showing its dependency on that idea. Commonly the effect/cause relationship is signaled by *if . . . then.* Other signals also show this pattern: *because, so, in order that, unless, as a result of, since, so that, where,* and *when.*

The following paragraph illustrates an effect/cause pattern. Notice that the absence of signal words in this example forces the reader to supply the relational signals.

> Frogs and toads go deep under the water and into the mud. The mud keeps them warm, and they can sleep all winter. (Level 7)

In the following paragraphs, the effects and causes are in separate paragraphs:

> Trash and garbage cause other problems. Garbage dumps made fine homes for rats, flies, and other pests. These pests were often the cause of sickness.
>   So garbage men tried digging deep pits in the ground for the trash and garbage. But trash and garbage sometimes made drinking water bad. Drinking water comes from the ground. When underground water ran through the trash and garbage pits, the water became bad. (Level 8)

(Notice how the first paragraph in the previous example contains an effect/ cause relationship signaled by *cause.*)

Question and Answer. In the question and answer pattern, both parts are needed to complete the idea of the author. Too often, either the question or the answer is thought to be the main idea of the paragraph.

In the following example, the information needed to answer the question is signaled by the word *why*. The information, then, should be a reason. In other question/answer paragraphs, the information needed to complete the pattern is signaled by *how, when, where,* and *what*.

> But why doesn't the spider stick to its own web? For one thing, the spider knows which threads are sticky and which threads are not sticky. And the spider has a special oil on its feet. If the spider has to walk on a sticky thread, the oil keeps it from getting caught. (Level 7)

(Notice how the signals "for one thing," and "and" signal that two answers will be enumerated for the question.)

Longer Discourse

Rarely does a reader deal with individual paragraphs; paragraphs are generally part of longer discourse. Within these longer selections, paragraphs serve a function. Each is not autonomous, but serves to expand, clarify, or change in some way the main concept the author wishes to convey to the reader.

According to Robinson (1983), the author's flow of ideas in longer discourse is followed when the reader recognizes the paragraphs' functions: (1) introductory, (2) explanatory, (3) narrative, (4) descriptive, (5) definitional, (6) transitional, and (7) concluding.

Introductory paragraphs begin a whole selection or a new idea within a selection. The following paragraphs contain common signals that inform the reader that a story is beginning. Some of the signals are figures of speech. Students gain the ability to recognize these signals through being made aware of their use in their textbooks and in their own writing.

> A long time ago, at the edge of a dark and gloomy forest, there lived an old man and his wife. They were very poor, and their only pleasure lay in eight beautiful children. Even though they loved all eight of their children dearly, their favorite was the youngest, Erendel. (Level 9)

> Maybe I should tell you a little bit about Ceaser before I begin my story. Ceaser was a big, dapple-gray horse. He and I used to work for the fire department. You see, a long time ago the fire wagons were pulled by very big, fast horses. (Level 8)

> I had heard a lot about a young dolphin that spent a summer with the people of Opononi. I thought it would make a good story for my newspaper. So I went to Opononi to talk with the people there. (Level 8)

When a paragraph introduces a new idea within a longer selection, it often follows a transitional paragraph. Therefore, the recognition of introductory paragraphs within longer selections is dependent to some degree upon the reader recognizing that the author has changed the flow of ideas and has introduced another idea or set of ideas.

Explanatory paragraphs explain, inform, tell about, or provide some factual support to an author's idea. The internal organization of the paragraph may take the form of a paragraph pattern discussed earlier. The explanatory paragraph category encompasses most paragraphs in a long selection. Often, these paragraphs have signals that relate to the ideas in a previous paragraph.

In the example paragraph, the first sentence ties the paragraph to a preceding paragraph and continues the explanation of an idea:

> Not too many years ago, it was simple. Garbage men took trash and garbage far outside of town to dump it. The garbage dumps and trash heaps were ugly and smelly. But they were far from town so people did not see them or smell them. (Level 8)

The next paragraph is signaled to be an explanatory one by *the oxen* rather than by *oxen* alone.

> In America, the oxen helped settle the western part of the country. They pulled settlers' large, heavy wagons thousands of miles across the country. In India they pull big, clumsy carts filled with grain. In Portugal they plow the muddy fields in the spring, and they pull carts loaded with wine barrels and other goods. (Level 10)

The word *too* in the first sentence of the next paragraph signals that the paragraph continues explaining an idea introduced elsewhere.

> Some kinds of butterflies fly south, too. One kind is a big orange and black butterfly. Every year, on the same day, these butterflies begin their trip. It takes them a long time to get where they are going. (Level 7)

Narrative paragraphs are found in narrative selections and are used to advance the story line or explain the actions of a character. The following paragraphs illustrate how narrative paragraphs are used.

> Lee ran through the MAIL ROOM door. She saw another door marked OUT. She pushed the OUT door, but on the other side was a door marked IN. People came and went through both doors. (Level 8)

> Mr. Pepperkorn whistled the song all the way to the hospital. He wanted to whistle it there, too. But there were signs everywhere that said QUIET PLEASE. So Mr. Pepperkorn walked quietly up the steps and into Ruthie's room. Then he hugged Ruthie and she hugged him right back. Ruthie loved her grandfather very much. She thought she had the nicest grandfather in the world. (Level 7)

> He went on for miles and miles. Sand was getting in his shoes. The hat made his head hot. The trunk was beginning to hurt his back. Even the

boxes he had carried for his master had never hurt his back. And he still didn't know what was over yonder. It seemed as far away as ever. (Level 8)

Descriptive paragraphs describe an event, person, or thing. These paragraphs do not advance the story line; they provide descriptive information.

One music box had a golden bird. The bird sat on top of a tree. On another box girls and boys danced up and down. On another, Goldilocks ran around the three bears. (Level 7)

Draft horses have large bones and heavy, strong muscles, especially in the chest and legs. They are usually over five feet tall at the shoulder. They are gentle and patient, and they can work long, hard hours without getting tired. (Fay & Anderson, Level 11)

Definitional paragraphs provide the meaning of some term used by the author. In narratives, these paragraphs usually do not advance the story line or add information about the author's main concept. They often can be omitted from the selection without breaking the flow of the author's ideas.

The smallest particle of mercuric oxide that you can see is still much larger than the smallest particle of a compound, called a molecule. A molecule is the smallest particle into which a compound can be divided and still have the properties of the compound. (Brewer, Garland, & Notkin, 1972)

Transitional paragraphs indicate the author is changing the flow of ideas. Besides signaling a change, some transitional paragraphs introduce a new idea. The following paragraph makes a transition to a story that has its own introductory paragraph:

Can you guess what happens to a landfill? Here is a story about what one town did with a landfill. (Level 8)

The following paragraph makes a transition and introduces a new idea:

But there are some parts of the world where a horse cannot go. A horse cannot live where the weather is very cold and cannot run through deep snow. So people in very cold countries have found other animals to work for them. (Fay & Anderson, Level 11)

Concluding paragraphs close the story or the author's ideas. Readers can learn to recognize the various signals that authors use to indicate the conclusion of their selections. The following paragraph ending a fairy tale has the traditional signals:

The enchantment was broken. Erendel and the Prince returned to their palace where they lived happily ever after. And Erendel was always very kind to bears. (Level 9)

The following paragraphs contain signals indicating the author is concluding a discussion or explanation. One common signal that authors use is to relate information to an idea introduced at the beginning of the selection. Another signal is to give a brief summary or restatement of the important ideas presented in the selection.

And now we begin our long swim up to the top of the ocean. Back we climb toward the sun and sky and trees and people and animals that we know. But we shall never forget, you and I, the wonderful watery world that lies deep within the Atlantic Ocean. And we shall never forget our sea monster, the octopus. (Level 8)

All over the world animals are moving loads for people. In some places machines are doing the jobs animals used to do. But there are some places in the world where machines cannot go.
And some people may never want to use a machine instead of an animal. After all, you can't pet an airplane or milk a tractor or whisper into a truck's ear. (Level 10)

Although the seven paragraph functions may be illustrated with isolated paragraphs, the teaching and learning of paragraph functions cannot be done with single paragraphs. Students should be given examples of the various paragraph functions to examine during the reading and writing of longer selections. From these experiences, they can form generalizations about the paragraphs and their uses.

DEVELOPING COMPREHENSION-STRATEGY LESSONS

The lesson for developing sentence- and paragraph-reading strategies consists of five phases: (1) identification of a reading task or situation, (2) an example of the situation, (3) a strategy for recognizing the situation, (4) guided application of the strategy, and (5) independent practice using the strategy.

The teacher should direct the first four phases of the lesson. Students should do the final phase to work out some problems independently or in small groups and to gain facility in using the strategy. The Chapter 5 appendix has two sample comprehension-strategy lessons—a strategy for reading sentences and a strategy for reading paragraphs.

The **identification phase** establishes the point of the lesson. During this phase, the teacher may give students information about what signals, patterns, or organization the author uses. Students are not asked to identify the signal or pattern. (If they can identify it, there is no point in completing the lesson.) The identification phase ends with a paraphrase of the strategy that will be stated in the third phase.

The **example phase** is, again, a teacher-directed phase in which another instance of the situation is given to students. In the sample lessons the example phase occurs when additional signals are shown. The teacher should decide how many examples will be given during this phase.

In the third phase, the **strategy phase,** students are given the strategy statement and all signals to be learned with the strategy. The signals for the strategy can be placed on poster paper and hung in the room for students' reference during the guided application and practice portions of the lesson. Once students are familiar with the signals, the poster can be removed.

In the **guided-application phase,** the teacher needs to give extensive guidance during the first example. Less guidance may be given for the last. This procedure—almost a weaning from teacher direction—lets the teacher observe students in situations of increasing independence. The last part of this phase is identical to the practice phase; therefore, if the students have difficulty, the teacher can repeat the first four phases using other sentences. Some students may need more than one "phase through" before they are ready to do independent practice.

The sample sentence-reading lesson deals with the strategy for recognizing and using signals for effect/cause. The material was prepared for use with students in the fourth grade. The sample paragraph-reading lesson deals with using substitute words to follow an author's ideas. In each case, students are given a worksheet with the example sentences. Although these exercises could be written on a chalkboard, teachers' experiences show drawbacks to this practice. First, if the related activities are done on the chalkboard, not all students get a chance to do all the tasks. Second, if the students are required to copy example sentences, the task could be tedious for them, and their attention could be directed away from the main purpose of the lesson. Therefore, two worksheets are recommended for each strategy lesson: one with the examples of phases one to four, and one with the practice sentences of phase five.

STRATEGIES FOR USING READER GUIDES AND SEMANTIC ORGANIZERS

The development of students' pre- and post-reading and pre-writing comprehension can be aided through the use of reader guides and semantic organizers. These are graphic representations of text structure and information organization. Using reader guides and semantic organizers, students realize what they know about a topic before reading or writing and what they have learned after completing the task.

Reader Guides

To help students become aware of how authors organize ideas, the teacher can give them a guide to the author's flow of ideas. The guide should be sized to fit the text page. On the guide, the various paragraph functions found within the selection are identified. In addition, various paragraph structures are shown. From its use, students will gain insight into how an author constructed a particular piece of reading matter. More important, students will see that authors have definite plans for organizing their ideas when they write and do not randomly place ideas on paper.

Reader guides may be introduced when students are reading selections of any length and fit either a narrative selection or an informational, nonfiction selection. To illustrate that this technique can be used with young readers, the example reader guide is made for first-grade material. Too often, comprehension development is left until after students have learned basic word recognition strategies. However, as stated many times previously, understanding must precede the recognition of individual words. (Note: The chapter on vocabulary and word-recognition strategies follows this chapter.) No student is too young to understand the strategies authors use in writing selections. What must be varied because of students' differing cognitive and linguistic maturity is the language the teacher uses for explaining the ideas.

Reader guides are constructed by dividing a piece of paper or a duplicating master into columns corresponding to the pages of a selection. The reader guide is aligned with the page and each column is identified by its corresponding page in the selection. Some selections, such as the one in the example, may need more than one sheet or master. The less mature the reader, the more necessary it is to write complete sentences on the guide. As the reader gains maturity, sentence fragments, phrases, and single words can be used to identify the author's organization and development of ideas.

The reader guide in Figure 5–4 shows the patterns used by an author. The map does not explain the author's ideas; it merely points out how the author put the ideas together. Whether the students understand the author's ideas can be determined through the guided-thinking strategies and the questioning techniques discussed in the previous chapter and this chapter. Since the prime purpose of this chapter's strategies is to help students develop a sense of independence, instruction with a reader guide emphasizes the information students need to recognize organizational and writing patterns so they can reconstruct the author's message.

Although the story, "The Terrible Lizards," does not contain paragraphing in the usual sense, typographical features are used to differentiate between ideas. Notice the use of double spacing between certain groups of sentences. Examination of the entire piece reveals that these spacings correspond to paragraphing—all sentences between the spaces are intended, it appears, to be read as a unit.

Using a reader guide, then, allows teacher and student to identify the various writing patterns used by authors. By recognizing these patterns, students can locate what it is authors wish to say about a topic. However, locating an author's ideas depends on students knowing the concepts presented and understanding the relationships among them.

Story Structure Guides

Students' proficiency in reading narratives is aided when they develop a sense of story organization. Narratives are constructed generally with five main elements:

- *Characterization* Every story has a cast of characters. Some are important to the main story line and others play incidental or minor parts. In addition, each character can be identified by some distinguishable, identifying trait.
- *Plot* Every story is constructed around some general outline or problem. The plot is the basic framework within which the story unfolds and the characters operate. Often the plot takes the form of a problem that is the impetus for the characters to act. Many stories are recognized as having similar plot structures; they differ, however, in the characters and specific events.
- *Events* The events of a story are the specific, sequential happenings that provide the flow of the story. Events are recognized as those things the characters do, or as those things that happen to the characters.
- *Other information* Stories contain information that cannot be considered events. This information takes the form of explanations about what or why something is happening or has happened. It also takes the form of description. Although this other information is important to the understanding of the story, it does not convey the story action.
- *Theme* Most stories have a theme or message. The message relates to the moral issue(s) humans face during a lifetime. For expository or informative writing, the message is the author's main thesis. The theme in narratives should not be confused with a statement of the plot. A statement such as, "A young girl seeks the help of her brother in finding out what a 'shadow' is only to find out what a 'silhouette' is," states the story's plot. This story outline could be developed to exemplify various themes, such as, "Sometimes it is hard to get answers to your questions."

Students learn the five story elements when they are confronted with their first oral or written story. Once students understand these five aspects, they can identify them in the stories they read or hear. Also, they begin using the story elements as a basis for reconstructing an author's ideas and as a scheme for recalling the story. During lessons, a reader guide can be used to identify the different aspects of the story.

Direct instruction about story parts can be taught to students in two phases (Spiegel & Fitzgerald, 1986). The first consists of six lessons conducted over a two-week period. The procedure for this first phase is to review earlier lessons,

I. This tells when

FIGURE 5–4
Reader Guide
Source: Fay, L., Ross, R.R., and LaPray, M. (1981). *The Rand McNally Reading Program, Level 6,* "Red Rock Ranch." Chicago: Riverside. Reproduced by permission of Riverside Publishing Company.

introduce and describe one story part, get several examples of the story element from students, provide them with some nonexamples of the element, and then reinforce the learning. The second phase consists of ten lessons conducted over five weeks. The procedure of this phase is to review, complete an activity requiring the application of knowledge of two or more story elements, and summarize. The activities are story production, sequencing of story parts, and **macrocloze,** in which one story element is deleted from a short story and students have to determine the missing part.

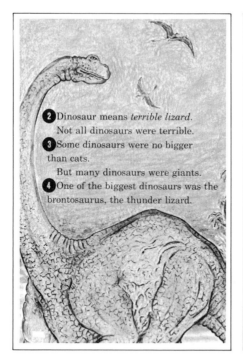

2. This gives a meaning.

3. This tells what they were like.

4. This tells what will come next.

5. This describes, or tells about, one kind of dinosaur.

FIGURE 5–4
Continued

Semantic Organizers

Another way to develop students' understanding of complete stories is with semantic organizers. Some educators refer to them as semantic maps, semantic webs, or graphic organizers. Semantic organizers are created to show relationships among groups of information (Heimlich & Pittelman, 1986; Pearson & Johnson, 1978; Pehrsson & Robinson, 1985). When students understand organ-

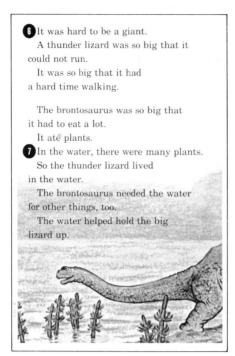

6. This tells more about it.

8. This gives a list. What is
   it a list of?

7. There is a cause and result
   here.

FIGURE 5–4
Continued

izers and make their own, they become actively involved in the reconstruction of an author's messages. Figure 5–5 contains examples of semantic organizers.

One type of semantic organizer teaches students basic semantic relationships using verbs and nouns (Pehrsson & Robinson, 1985). With this type of organizer, an action verb or a noun is placed in a center box surrounded by four other boxes. Three of the boxes contain related words or pictures. The fourth is a nonrelevant item. For example, in the center box is the word *ride*. In three of the boxes are pictures or words representing a bus, car, and bicycle. In the fourth box is a representation of a pencil. Students are to indicate the nonappropriate item.

In another type of semantic organizer, the story action is linked with the agent of that action, with the instrument of the action, and so on. These links

9 When the land changed, the plants changed.

But the brontosaurus did not change.

10 The brontosaurus couldn't eat the new plants.

It couldn't find food.

And where there was no food, the brontosaurus couldn't live.

After a long, long time, all the thunder lizards were gone.

11 Today we find these things that the brontosaurus and other dinosaurs left.

12 Lizards are still around today.
Dinosaurs are the great-great-great-granddaddies of these lizards.

But the great-great-great-granddaddies, the terrible lizards, are gone.

9. There are two different ideas here.

10. This information is given in an order.

11. The last sentence tells about the picture.

12. There are two different ideas here.

FIGURE 5–4
Continued

can be made through questions such as: What happens? Who causes it to happen? To whom or what does it happen? With what is it done? Where? When? How? These answers are then linked with additional actions that are linked with other agents until a map of the story is formed.

In a third kind, story information is organized inductively (drawing conclusions) or emotionally (Cleland, 1981). An inductive web organizes information by generalizations or conclusions about the characters and their interactions with other characters. An emotional web organizes the story information by the attitudes, feelings, or impressions of the characters.

As when introducing all comprehension strategies, the teacher should model how semantic organizers are created. For example, demonstrate to stu-

1. Concept webs

2. Story action web—"The Bell of Atri"

3. Emotional web—"The Bell of Atri"

FIGURE 5–5
Semantic Organizers

dents how organizers for the paragraphs about sounds and musical instruments (page 130) are made. To start, for the paragraph about sounds:

- Draw a box and place sounds in it.
- Draw lines like spokes encircling the box.
- Put one sound at the end of each spoke: wind in trees, raindrops hitting window, train whistle, etc.

For the paragraph about musical instruments:

- Place the words *musical instruments* in a box.
- Draw a line to another box and place *play in orchestra.*
- Draw four lines from that box and place *strings, woodwinds, brass,* and *percussion* at the end of each of those lines.

After several demonstrations, guide students in building their own organizers and allow them to collaborate with peers. Each type of organizer (noun/verb, story action, inductive, emotional) should be demonstrated before students attempt to develop their own. As a class or in small groups, prereading semantic organizers can be modified after reading, and postreading semantic organizers can be used as brainstorming for writing.

ACTIVITIES FOR RECONSTRUCTING MEANING

The following illustrate some of the many activities that may be used to improve student strategies for constructing and reconstructing an author's messages. With slight changes, each can become a writing activity.

- Provide students with pictures and sentences. Have them read the sentences and correctly match them with the appropriate picture. This task can be made more difficult by using pictures that have similar scenes or activities so that only by using the information in the sentences can students distinguish among the pictures. The length and complexity of the identifying sentences should be adjusted to meet students' reading and language maturity.

- The previous activity can also be used with paragraphs. Instead of limiting the paragraphs to descriptions of the pictures, however, paragraphs can be written or selected from other sources that relate to, but do not describe fully, the information in the picture. For example, a series of pictures might be used that show a scientist in a laboratory, someone preparing a meal, and a mechanic working on a car. The paragraphs could be a recipe, the steps in an experiment, and directions for repairing a flat tire. Or, using the generalization paragraph organization: a reason for safety in the laboratory, the need for cleanliness in the kitchen, and an appeal for wearing safety clothes when using tools.

- Provide students with opportunities to read directions in real situations. Many students do not have the opportunity to play certain games at home; they can learn these games by reading the directions in school. Other situations for learning to read and follow directions are constructing model planes or cars and learning card games. Many books exist that explain card games of varying complexities for various ages. Reading directions such as these should not be considered a frivolous activity. Board games and card games can be enjoyable, challenging recreational activities. Model building is not an activity for the young alone—many adults build model railroad cars and model aircraft as a hobby. Since the direction formats are generally the same within each of the three categories mentioned, students can begin to learn about them and develop the necessary vocabulary as part of their school learning.

- Provide students with sentences that contain the same words but are punctuated differently. Have students read the sentences orally using the correct intonation to convey the intended meaning. For example, one group of sentences might be:

  "Frank," said Marty, "Let Jimmy do it!"

  Frank said, "Marty, let Jimmy do it?"

  Or, let students read sentences such as the following to show, through different intonations, what the meaning of each sentence might be.

  I like boxing bears.

  He can't imagine flying fish.

- Provide students with an opportunity to expand basic sentence patterns through the addition of different information. For example, information such as *where, when, how,* and *why* can be added to the following:

  The puppy cried.

  The teacher gave everyone a book.

  Another activity might be to give students sentences with one type of information omitted. Have them complete the sentences using the appropriate type of information.

  The cat sat _____ watching the birds at the bird feeder.

(where)

  _____ gave me a new pen for my birthday.

(who)

  This activity can be extended for use with paragraphs by constructing a paragraph in which different types of information are omitted. The teacher or another student can ask for the information without revealing the story. After students' answers have been added to the paragraph, read the completed paragraph.

- Provide students with sentences in which some information appears in a different place in each sentence. Have students determine whether the meaning has been changed by the shift of information, and have them justify their decisions. For example:

  The cow ate the apples behind the barn.

The cow behind the barn ate the apples.

Behind the barn, the cow ate the apples.

Slowly, Jaye opened her eyes and got out of bed.

Jaye slowly opened her eyes and got out of bed.

Jaye opened her eyes slowly and got out of bed.

Jaye opened her eyes and slowly got out of bed.

Jaye opened her eyes and got out of bed slowly.

- Provide students with a sentence. Have them select from a group of other sentences the sentence that indicates accurate information about the group. For example:

Mother planted five new rosebushes in the garden.

Add *only*. Some possible constructions:

Only Mother planted five new rosebushes in the garden.

Mother only planted five new rosebushes in the garden.

Mother planted only five new rosebushes in the garden.

Mother planted five new rosebushes only in the garden.

Mother planted five new rosebushes in the garden only.

Or again:

My brother plays with the toy duck.

Add *in the bathtub*. Some possible constructions:

In the bathtub, my brother plays with the toy duck.

My brother in the bathtub plays with the toy duck.

My brother plays in the bathtub with the toy duck.

My brother plays with the toy duck in the bathtub.

- Provide students with cut-up sentences. First, type a sentence on construction paper or oaktag. Then cut up the sentences into word groups or individual words. Have students arrange the parts of the sentence to make a logical statement. For example, the sentence parts could be

the	we	check	
rent	the	for	gave
in the race	this Saturday	landlord	
will be running	Harold	the	

This activity can be extended by typing out the sentences in a paragraph and giving students clues as to how the paragraph should be organized.

- Provide students with a variety of puns, jokes, and riddles. Together, examine cartoons and comic strips to identify how meanings are conveyed through dialectal writing and typographical features. Have students explain what in the joke or cartoon creates the humorous situation. For example, what creates the humor in the following?

  Why is the letter F like Paris?

  (Because it is the <u>capital</u> of <u>France</u>.)

  Discuss what a reader must know before a joke, pun, or riddle seems humorous.

- Provide students with domino-type cards. On the cards write the words *who*, *what*, *where*, and *how* or words that provide similar information. A sample dominoes game might be the following:

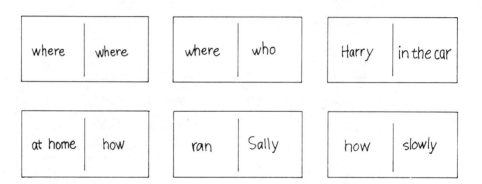

This game follows typical domino rules. For example, a domino with *where* and *where* is matched at either end to another domino with *where* or one with *at home*. A domino with *Harry* and *in the car* is matched at one end to a domino with *who* and at the other end to a domino with *where*.

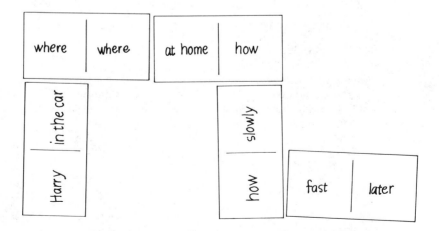

- Provide students with a story that has simultaneous or overlapping actions. Have them identify the signals for actions using *as soon as, meanwhile, at the same time, while* and the like. On a time line, have them map out the time relationship among the various events.

- Provide students with sentences or short paragraphs that describe a situation. Have them act out the situation as it appears on the paper and have other students determine what is being enacted.

- Provide students with a story that has accompanying illustrations. Have them decide which sentences in the story relate specifically to each picture and whether the pictures provide any information needed to understand the story that is not given in any of the sentences or paragraphs.

- Have students create probable stories using story frames of setting, character(s), problem, major events, and ending (Wood, 1984). Select significant concepts and terms from a story that is to be read. Give these to students and have them categorize the words according to the story frame. Then have students write a probable story based on the frame:

    The story takes place ——————. —————— is a character in the story who ——————. A problem occurs when ——————. After that, ——————. Next, ——————. The problem is solved when ——————. The story ends ——————.

Have students read the original story and compare it to their predicted one. Then have them modify their predicted story to be a summary paragraph.

- Use primary basal readers as a source for sentence-combining activities (Reutzel, 1986). Because many primary readers have simple sentences and sentences from which subordinating and coordinating elements are omitted, it is possible to have students rewrite the stories. Have students join two equally important sentences with *and, but, or, for, however,* or *moreover;* and subordinate one sentence to another using conjunctions such as *before, after, since,* or relational connectors such as *who, which, whose,* and various prepositions. When students mature in their ability to compose sentences, stimulus sentences can be selected for more advanced readers. For example,

    We clean. Grandpa may take us to a pond.

    After we clean, Grandpa may take us to a pond.

A variation is to have students analyze complex sentences in which common connectives are used. Have students dismantle each sentence to examine its root sentence. For example,

    Mama looked confused for only a moment, and then she brightened right up and moved busily about the room.

    Mama looked confused for only a moment.

    Mama brightened right up.

    Mama moved busily about the room.

- Have students use InQuest, an investigative questioning procedure (Shoop, 1986). In this procedure, students read a story and role play a news conference about the events in the story. After each role-playing incident, have students evaluate the interview. Stress that students incorporate the following ideas: getting longer responses to questions; following yes/no answers with "why?"; and using a variety of question patterns.

- Give students opportunities to develop mental imagery abilities (Fredericks, 1986). Mental imagery is developed in stages: Have students create images of concrete objects; have them visualize and recall familiar objects, scenes, or past experiences outside the classroom; have them listen to high imagery stories that use common experiences or knowledge; have them create their own mental images as they read stories.

In helping students develop mental imagery, use the following guidelines: understanding images is different for each person; there are no right or wrong images; mental imagery ability is developed over time and through varied experiences; mental imagery is stimulated through a series of open-ended questions; and, most important, time must be devoted to discussing each student's images.

RESOURCES FOR THE TEACHER

The following resources were selected because they contain exercises that relate specifically to the strategies discussed in this chapter. Many basal reading series contain lessons and exercises that correspond to the reading strategies for reconstructing meaning discussed previously; the following were selected, however, because they have easily identifiable components relating to one or more strategies. The exercises in these components often are at varying levels of difficulty or maturity.

Teachers should not expect these materials to teach, but they are excellent sources of examples to use in lessons. As with all instructional materials, teachers should select only those that are appropriate for the age, language development, and reading maturity of their students.

Thinking about reading, grades 2 to 6, Series 1 & 2.

The lessons are created on the directed reading–thinking activity model, with prereading predictions, during reading predictions, and postreading story mapping.

CROFT skillpacks: Reading comprehension. Old Greenwich, CT: Croft.

Separate primary and intermediate skillpacks offer classroom practice in selecting details, translating details, identifying signal words, selecting the main idea, determining implied details, identifying organizational patterns, and inferring the main idea.

Specific skill series. Baldwin, NY: Barnell Loft.
Supportive reading skills. Baldwin, NY: Dexter and Westbrook.

The two series have multileveled sets of booklets of exercises in several areas. Titles in the Specific Skill Series that complement the strategies in this chapter are "Detecting the Sequence," "Using the Context," "Drawing Conclusions," "Getting the Main Idea,"

"Following Directions," and "Cloze Connections." Appropriate titles in the Supportive Reading Skills series are "Understanding Word Groups" and "Understanding Questions."

> *New practice readers* (2nd ed.). New York: Webster Division/McGraw-Hill.
> *Reading for concepts* (2nd ed.). (1970). New York: Webster Division/McGraw-Hill.

These multileveled series contain stories about many topics. Each story is followed by a series of questions that require a different type of thinking strategy.

> *The thinking lab series: Junior thinking lab*, grades 2 to 4; *Think lab*, grades 3 to adult; *Think lab* 2, grades 5 to adult. Chicago: Science Research Associates [SRA].

This series contains activity cards, puzzles, and worksheets to develop students' creativity and reasoning abilities.

> *The thinking skills development program: Primary thinking box*, grades K to 3; *Thinking box I*, grades 3 to 5; *Thinking box II*, grades 6 to 9. Westchester, IL: Benefic Press.

This program has activity cards, filmstrips, and cassettes. The activities are structured around various thinking operations and draw their content from a variety of subject areas.

> *Reading, thinking, and reasoning skills program*, grades 1 to 8. Austin, TX: Steck Vaughn.

This is a series of fourteen books containing various categories of thinking strategies: categorizing, analogies, sequencing, implying, judging, synthesis, evaluating, comparing and contrasting, and restructuring.

> *Strategies for reading: Sentences; words in context; paragraphs; longer selections*, grades 6 to 8. Boston: Allyn & Bacon.

These are four books for developing comprehension strategies similar to those presented in this text. Each lesson is constructed according to this chapter's suggested format for developing strategies for learning lessons.

> *The skill-by-skill series*, grades 2 to 6. Cleveland: Modern Curriculum Press.

This series of books is organized in six areas: getting the main idea, literal and interpretive comprehension, facts and details, vocabulary, following directions, organizing information, and using reference materials.

> *Spectrum of skills: Reading comprehension booklets*, grades 4 to 8. New York: Macmillan.

This is a set of multileveled booklets intended for the intermediate and upper elementary grades.

> *Activity cards*, grades 2 to 6; and *Basic skills activities cards*, grades K to 3. Palos Verdes, CA: Frank Schaffer Publications.

These are sets of index-size cards that require students to read, solve problems and riddles, create things, work out relationships, and use their imaginations.

> *TODAY reading comprehension tactics, cloze power*, grades 3 to 8. Huntington Station, NY: Instructional/Communications Technology.

These three workbooks provide students with instruction in how to make predictions for the completion of cloze procedure maze technique in informational passages.

> *Thinking skills*. Pacific Grove, CA: Midwest Publishing.

These are several books dealing with critical thinking, analogies, puzzles, logic in easy steps, and inductive thinking.

> *SRA Schoolhouse: Comprehension patterns.* Chicago: Science Research Associates.

This kit contains multilevel exercises to help determine the meaning of words, sentences, and paragraphs. The exercises, on individual activity cards arranged in units, provide practice with a variety of sentence and paragraph patterns.

The following text has sample lessons that are models for many of the strategies highlighted throughout this chapter. It is a practical book in which the authors present sample lessons and also explain why and how they work.

> Goodman, Y. M., Burke C., and Sherman, B. (1985). *Reading strategies: Focus on comprehension.* New York: Owens.

Extended discussions about semantic organizers and specific lessons with various types of organizers are in the following.

> Buckley, M. H., & Boyle, O. (1981). *Mapping the writing journey.* Berkeley, CA: University of California, Bay Area Writing Project.
> Heimlich, J. E., & Pittelman, S. D. (1986). *Semantic mapping: Classroom applications.* Newark, DE: International Reading Association.
> Pehrsson, R. S., & Robinson, H. A. (1985). *The semantic organizer approach to writing and reading instruction.* Rockville, MD: Aspen Systems.
> Piccolo, J. A. (1987, May). Expository text structure: Teaching and learning strategies. *The Reading Teacher, 40*(9), 838–847.

The next item is a menu-driven computer program that guides students through the development of semantic organizers. The organizers can be printed and used for study or writing activities. There are additional packages that map stories from five basal reading series (for Apple and TRS–80 microcomputers).

> *The semantic mapper.* Gainesville, FL: Teacher Support Software.

DISCUSSION QUESTIONS AND ACTIVITIES

1. Rewrite the following statement by Johnson (1975) so that it would be understandable to a group of teachers who do not understand whole-language principles: "Whether a concept is meaningful thus depends upon the associational background of the learner and also the semantic structure of the concept within the linguistic community" (p. 427).

2. The following statement by Smith (1971) has implications for teachers whenever they give students reading or writing assignments. Does Smith mean that students should never be asked questions?

> The more a reader expects to be asked questions on what he reads the more he will rely on visual information, and the more difficult will reading become. (p. 3)

3. Devise a series of lessons to demonstrate to a group of students the following principle as stated by Miller (1974): "Certain words place restrictions on the meaningful occurrence of other words within a sentence" (p. 854).

4. Select a story appropriate for primary-grade students. Create a reader guide that
   a. identifies the main characters of the story;
   b. shows the flow of the main events of the story;
   c. identifies information that is important to the story but that does not carry the main action; and
   d. points out where the theme or moral of the story is stated (or implied).
      Use the guide as the basis for a lesson in which students are to recall the story's major information.

5. Select two stories, one appropriate for primary-grade students and the other appropriate for upper-grade students, and analyze the sentence and paragraph patterns used in each. How do they differ in construction? Use the patterns that occur most frequently as the basis for an informal test to determine whether the pupils can recognize and understand those structures.

6. Review current reading instructional materials to determine whether their authors would agree with the following statement by Harker (1973b): "Comprehension results from a dynamic cognitive process and not from the rigid application of a set of predetermined skills" (p. 381).

7. Select some current and popular reading instruction materials. From them select sentences that show description, attitude, or mood. Devise a lesson using those sentences to develop the concept that sentences do not necessarily show action.

8. Create different deletion-procedure exercises from the same passage for the following purposes:
   a. To improve predicting and confirming.
   b. To understand a particular syntactic structure of English.

9. Relate Guthrie's statement (1983) to the development by teachers of student-comprehension monitoring.

   The act of teaching is the art of communicating rules for social interaction and language use simultaneously with the structure of subject matter and the processes of literacy. Teachers orchestrate these themes to make music of the mind. (p. 95)

FURTHER READING

For those wanting additional information about the structure of English sentences, the following two small books present that clearly and concisely:

Waddell, M. L., Esch, R. M., & Walker, R. R. (1972). *The art of styling sentences: 20 patterns to success.* Woodbury, NY: Barron's Educational Series.

Haden, S. (1975). *A primer of transformational grammar for rank beginners.* Urbana, IL: National Council of Teachers of English.

To better understand the structure and function of paragraphs, teachers might find it helpful to consult references on rhetoric and style. The following texts contain background information and teaching suggestions about cohesion.

Chapman, L. J. (1983). *Reading development and cohesion.* London, England, and Exeter, NH: Heinemann.

Irwin, J. W. (Ed.). (1986). *Understanding and teaching cohesion comprehension.* Newark, DE: International Reading Association.

Teachers often want to improve their own reading procedures. One popular book that does not follow a traditional "how to" format is the following:

Adler, M. J., & Van Doren, C. (1972). *How to read a book: The classic guide to intelligent reading.* New York: Simon & Schuster.

The next two texts contain specific techniques for strategy lessons on the structure of English. Although Robinson's text is written with examples from high-school materials, elementary and middle-school teachers can use it to learn how authors construct textual materials and to get ideas for developing lessons for their students.

Irwin, J. W. (1986). *Teaching reading comprehension processes.* Englewood Cliffs, NJ: Prentice Hall.

Robinson, H. A. (1983). *Teaching reading, writing & study strategies: The content areas* (3rd ed.). Boston: Allyn & Bacon.

CHAPTER 5   APPENDIX*

HOW TO READ A SENTENCE

Joe took a trip.

The sentence above is a core sentence. The basic or main information is presented in a core sentence. Most of the time more information is added to a core sentence.

Read the following sentence.

Last summer Joe took a trip.

What does the information <u>last summer</u> tell you?

WHEN Joe took a trip

We now add another kind of information to this sentence:

Last summer Joe took a trip to California.

What does the information <u>to California</u> tell you?

WHERE Joe went on his trip

Here still another kind of information is added:

Last summer Joe took a trip to California by bus.

What does the information <u>by bus</u> tell you?

HOW Joe got to California

WHEN, WHERE, and HOW information is not the only information added to a sentence.

FOR EXAMPLE

Sometimes the **how** information tells **how long** or **how much**.

Joe took a trip for three weeks.
Joe's trip cost him three hundred dollars.

And here yet another kind of information is added:

Last summer Joe took a trip to California by bus for his vacation

What does the information <u>for his vacation</u> tell you?

WHY Joe took a trip

This sentence now gives you four different kinds of information about the core. The information added to the core is underlined and labeled.

when
<u>Last summer</u> Joe took a trip
where   how   why
<u>to California</u> <u>by bus</u> <u>for his vacation</u>.

Three of these questions begin with a *W*, and one begins with an *H*. (Remember: three *W*s and an *H*.) Of course, all questions are not always answered in all sentences.

STRATEGY

Different kinds of information may be added to core sentences. Ask yourself **When? Where? Why?** and **How?** to find the kinds of information added to the core. Remember that additional information can be one word or several words.

TRY IT

The following sentence has several different kinds of information. Mark this sentence as you work through the steps that follow.

During the last tennis

championship, in Baltimore,

Connie Reed hurt her knee

because of a fall.

When did it happen? Underline this information and write *when* above it.
Where did it happen? Underline this information and write *where* above it.
Why did it happen? Underline this information and write *why* above it.

The core sentence is _____

_____

CHECK YOUR SENTENCE. It should look like this:

when
<u>During the last tennis</u>

where
<u>championship, in Baltimore,</u>

Connie Reed hurt her knee

why
<u>because of a fall.</u>

The core sentence is: *Connie Reed hurt her knee.*

---

*Strategy lessons from Robinson, A., Andresen, O., Hittleman, D.R., Patterson, O., & Paulsen, L. (1976). *Strategies for reading.* Newton, MA: Allyn & Bacon.

Read the following sentence. Mark the sentence as you work through the steps that follow.

For the first three days in its new

home, the kitten was afraid of

everyone because of the strange

surroundings.

Underline the information that tells **how long**. Write *how long* above it.
Underline the information that tells **where**. Write *where* above it.
Underline the information that tells **why**. Write *why* above it.

The core sentence is _____

_____

CHECK YOUR ANSWER. Your sentence should look like this:

　　　　how long　　　*where*
For the first three days in its new

home, the kitten was afraid of

　　　　　why
everyone because of the strange

surroundings.

The core sentence is: *The kitten was afraid of everyone.*

Mark the following sentence in the same manner.

The singing group at the dance sang

the latest rock hits for three hours.

The core sentence is _____

_____

CHECK YOUR ANSWER
　　　　　　where
The singing group at the dance sang

　　　　　　　how long
the latest rock hits for three hours.

The core sentence is: *The singing group sang the latest rock hits.*

You may have been tricked by the previous sentence. Note that the *where* information separated two parts of the core.

Mark the following sentences in the same way that you marked those previously. Underline and label the kinds of information added to the core sentence.

Remember, to find the information in each sentence, ask yourself:

when?
where? } This information is added to the core.
why?
how?

1. The varsity cheerleaders practiced their cheers at Waller High School every Tuesday and Thursday.

2. Yesterday afternoon the wreckage of the lost plane was found in the heart of the jungle.

3. After the storm the nurses at the hospital had to work overtime because of the injured people.

4. Helen promised to meet Roger for a quick cola at the drug store right after work.

5. For most of that long, hot summer night, the gang on Tompkins Avenue played their bongo drums just for laughs.

Check your answers.

[Note to teachers: In this section of the lesson, give students a longer selection which requires them to apply the learned strategy in context. Provide directions similar to the following.]

In reading the following selection, you will need to use the strategy of this lesson. As you read the passage, look for [insert strategy and signals]. As soon as you finish reading, go on to the questions that follow.

USING EXAMPLES
TO UNDERSTAND
IMPORTANT IDEAS

Writers organize paragraphs in certain ways or patterns. Their goal is to be sure you understand an important idea they want to give you.

One pattern is to present one or more examples of an idea they think is important.

Read the following paragraph.

People of the cold northern forests live in log cabins. Rain forest people live in huts made of grass and straw. In the dry lands of the world, some people live in homes made of sun-dried brick or mud.

In this paragraph, the writer presents a group of examples to tell about an idea. By "adding" up the examples, you can discover the idea in the mind of the writer.

The examples used are:
    people live in log cabins
    people live in grass huts
    people live in sun-dried brick homes
What are these examples of? These are examples of different kinds of homes where people live.

The writer's idea is: *People live in different kinds of homes*.

In this paragraph, the writer did not state the important idea in a particular sentence. You had to add up the examples to arrive at the idea in the writer's mind.

In the next paragraph, the writer states an idea and a number of examples to support it. Read the paragraph.

Many large cities have great colleges and universities. For instance, New York City has fine colleges such as Columbia University, New York University, the City University, and Fordham University. The city of Philadelphia has Temple University, Drexel Institute of Technology, and the University of Pennsylvania. Boston has colleges such as Harvard University, the Massachusetts Institute of Technology, Boston College, and Boston University.

In this paragraph, the writer states the important idea in the first sentence: *Many large cities have great colleges and universities*.

The words *for instance* signal that the writer is about to use examples. In paragraphs like this, writers often use **signal words** to help you find examples.

Your job in reading the paragraph was to add up the examples to be sure they supported the writer's idea.

The examples are:
    New York City has Columbia University, New York University, the City University, and Fordham University.
    Philadelphia has Temple University, Drexel Institute of Technology, and the University of Pennsylvania.
    Boston has Harvard University, the Massachusetts Institute of Technology, Boston College, and Boston University.

Some words used to signal examples are:
an example	for instance
for example	one of the instances
some examples	an instance
one kind	some types

By discovering the examples you can understand the writer's idea. In some paragraphs, signal words will help you find the examples.

FOR EXAMPLE

In the following paragraph the writer states an idea and gives some examples to support it.

Pull out the coins in your pocket. Do you have a Lincoln cent, a Jefferson nickel, a Roosevelt dime, a Washington quarter, or a Kennedy half dollar? These coins all have pictures of presidents of the United States on them. The United States often honors its presidents by putting their pictures on money.

In the paragraph, the writer has given five examples of money with presidents' pictures on them. By adding up the examples, you can see that they support the idea in the last sentence of the paragraph.

STRATEGY

In some paragraphs, the writer states an idea and gives one or more examples to support the idea. In other paragraphs, only examples are given and you must figure out the idea the writer had in mind. Discover the examples and you will be able to understand the most important idea of the paragraph.

TRY IT

In the following paragraph, the sentence with the writer's important idea has been left out.

Read the paragraph to discover what the examples are. Then add up the examples to figure out the writer's idea. Answer the questions after the paragraph.

Ball point pens are often thrown away after they're empty. Paper diapers are often used once and then thrown away. Garbage is often put into throw-away bags instead of garbage cans. Also, drinks come in cans that are discarded.

What is the same about all these examples? Choose the best answer.
The examples are about:
a. people and things
b. things thrown away
c. things we use

The examples are about (b) *things thrown away*.
What might be a good sentence to put at the end of this paragraph? Draw a circle around the letter of the best answer.
a. We throw away a number of things we have used.
b. We use things that are made to last long.
c. We throw away paper diapers after they are used.

CHECK YOUR ANSWER

You should have circled (a) *We throw away a number of things we have used*. The paragraph gives examples of some things that are used and then thrown away.
The following paragraph has only one example. Read the paragraph and answer the questions after it.

Dolphins have been known to have saved people from drowning. For example, a few years ago, a woman was swimming in Florida. She was caught by a strong wave and could not fight her way out of it. She had given up hope. All of a sudden something gave her a shove onto the beach. She looked back and saw a dolphin playing in the water. A man on the beach told her that the dolphin had pushed her to the beach.

Draw a circle around the letter of the correct answer to each question:
What is the example about?
a. a woman swimming in Florida
b. a dolphin saving a woman
c. a dolphin playing by the beach
What is the important idea of the paragraph?
a. Dolphins may be found playing near beaches in Florida.
b. A woman was swimming in Florida.
c. Dolphins have been known to have saved people from drowning.

CHECK YOUR ANSWER

The example is: a dolphin saving the life of a drowning woman. You should have a circle around (b) *a dolphin saving a woman*.
The writer's idea is: (c) *Dolphins have been known to have saved people from drowning*.
Here is another paragraph with one example. The writer does not state the important idea in any of the sentences.
Read the paragraph and figure out what idea the writer wants you to know.

One of the oldest instances of a hidden message dates all the way back to about 600 B.C. A Greek named Aristagoras was told that a slave had come to see him. When he came into the house, the slave said, "Shave my head and look at it." Aristagoras shaved the slave's head. He was surprised to find a secret message from his father-in-law.

What is the most important idea in the paragraph?
a. Secret messages are not a new idea.
b. Slaves carried secret messages.
c. Secret writing was hidden under hair.

CHECK YOUR ANSWER

The correct answer is (a) *Secret messages are not a new idea*.

PRACTICE IT

Read the following paragraphs. Each paragraph has one or more examples. Use the examples to figure out the most important or major idea of the paragraph. Circle the answer to the question after each paragraph.

1. In many countries more than one language is spoken. Russian, for example, is the main language of the Soviet Union. But only half of the people living there speak Russian. The others speak one of 145 different languages. In China, a great many of the people speak Mandarin, the language of the northern part of China. The rest of the people speak other Chinese languages.

What is the most important idea in the paragraph?
a. Russian is the main language of the Soviet Union.
b. In China, a great many of the people speak Mandarin.
c. In many countries more than one language is spoken.

2. What if you had to think about blinking your eyes or ducking your head if a rock came at you? What if you had to think about pulling your hand away if you touched a very hot pot? In cases like these your body acts automatically, that is, so fast you really don't have time to think about it until later. If we had to think about everything we do before we did it, we would get hurt more easily.

What is the most important idea in the paragraph?
   a. Your body acts automatically, that is, so fast you really don't have time to think about it until later.
   b. What if you had to think about pulling your hand away if you touched a very hot pot?
   c. If we had to think about everything we do before we did it, we would get hurt more easily.

3. Without steel there could be no tall buildings, no modern railroad tracks or trains, no bicycles or automobiles, no machinery in our factories, no ships, tractors, airplanes, or modern tools. Our houses would be without refrigerators, canned foods, TV sets, and radios. There would not even be electricity, because the generators in the power plants that make electricity are made of steel.

What is the most important idea in the paragraph?
   a. Our modern world depends upon steel.
   b. Electricity could not be made without steel.
   c. Steel is too heavy to be used in everything.

4. A dormant volcano is one that has not been inactive long enough for scientists to know when it will break out again. Mount Larsen in California is an example of a dormant volcano. It erupted in 1915 and has been dormant since then. But some day it may erupt again.

What is the most important idea in the paragraph?
   a. Mount Larsen in California is an example of a dormant volcano.
   b. A dormant volcano is a volcano which has not erupted recently.
   c. Someday Mount Larsen may erupt again.

5. During the early years of our country, families had to be self-sufficient. They built their own houses, spun thread, wove cloth, and sewed their clothing. Families hunted for food in the forests and grew vegetables on small farms or in gardens. When people became sick or old, their families took care of them.

What is the most important idea in the paragraph?
   a. Building homes in the early years of America was hard.
   b. The early American family took care of its own needs.
   c. Children did many things to help their families in early America.

Check your answers.

USE IT

[Note to teachers: In this section of the lesson, give students a longer selection which requires them to apply the learned strategy in context. Provide directions similar to the following.]

In reading the following selection, you will need to use the strategy of this lesson. As you read the passage, look for [insert strategy and signals]. As soon as you finish reading, go on to the questions that follow.

Organizer

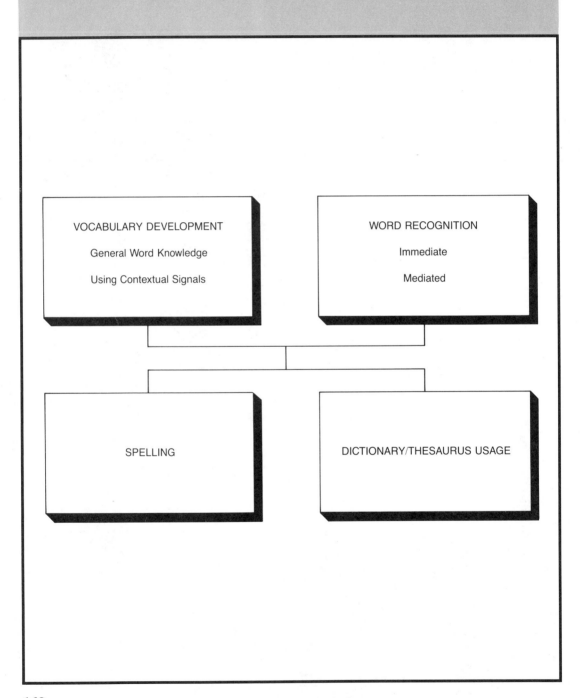

VOCABULARY DEVELOPMENT

General Word Knowledge

Using Contextual Signals

WORD RECOGNITION

Immediate

Mediated

SPELLING

DICTIONARY/THESAURUS USAGE

CHAPTER 6

Strategies for Vocabulary Development and Word Recognition

Focus Questions

- How can students' knowledge of concepts and words be developed and extended?
- How can students use context as an aid to word recognition?
- What strategies should students have for recognizing an unfamiliar word in print?
- How should students use the dictionary and thesaurus?

This discussion of vocabulary development and word recognition is placed after the discussion of constructing and reconstructing an author's meaning. This is because whole-language investigations suggest that individual word recognition occurs after the reader understands the author's message. Meaning is not derived from the synthesis of identified and understood words; whole-language researchers propose that the opposite is true: The sentence supplies the context for determining the meaning of the words.

The discussion in this chapter is based on the assumption that students come to school having a basic speaking and listening vocabulary. As previously demonstrated, a student's vocabulary, no matter how limited, forms the basis for literacy through a language experience approach. Strategies for understanding are developed for all levels of language maturity.

This chapter has ideas for (1) extending students' word knowledge, (2) developing students' strategies for determining the meanings of unknown words in context, (3) teaching students to use graphophonological information with sentences and other meaning signals for recognizing and writing words, and (4) developing students' strategies for using the dictionary and thesaurus.

One clarification needs to be made first. The term *word recognition* is used interchangeably in the professional literature with at least five other terms: *decoding, word perception, word identification, word analysis,* and *word attack.* In this text, **word recognition** indicates the processes by which a reader realizes what word an author has used and the meaning intended for it. A word may be recognized in various ways: The reader may already know the word; the reader may surmise what word is intended because he or she understands the general meaning of the passage; the reader may translate an unknown graphic form into a recognizable oral form; or, the reader may rely on some other source, such as a dictionary.

STRATEGIES FOR DEVELOPING AND EXTENDING WORD KNOWLEDGE

As stated previously, children come to school with existing listening and speaking vocabularies. As they progress in their education, two other vocabularies are acquired—reading and writing. For most people, the listening vocabulary is the largest because it has been developed the longest. The size of children's listening and speaking vocabularies when they enter school is largely determined by their prior language environment. The more restricted

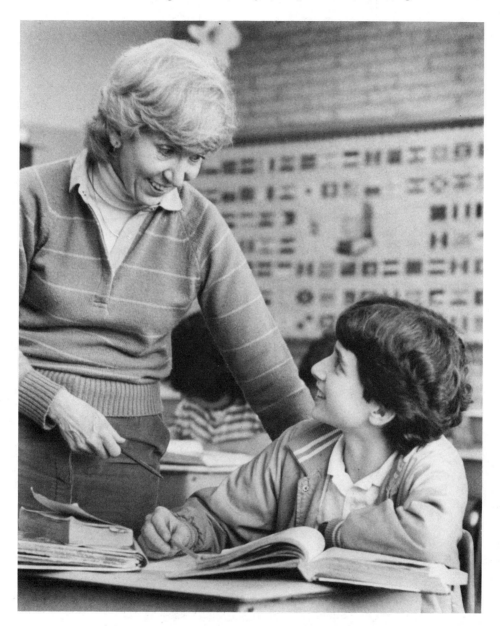

the language background, the less extensive the vocabulary and language patterns. All students, however, can increase their vocabularies by acquiring new concepts and their labels and by acquiring additional labels for already known concepts.

Reviews of research on teaching vocabulary revealed that many different activities successfully lead to increased vocabularies (Nelson-Herber, 1986;

Manzo & Sherk, 1971; Stahl & Fairbanks, 1986). A significant factor for helping students develop and extend their vocabularies seems to be the excitement teachers generate about words. When teachers demonstrate enthusiasm for words and transfer this excitement to students, all instructional activities seem equally effective. Another finding is that vocabulary knowledge is related to and facilitates growth in reading comprehension. A third is that although vocabulary is acquired through incidental learning, it is more effectively learned from direct instruction.

When teachers convey a positive attitude about vocabulary and its development, the following are additional features of a successful program:

1. Students are engaged with other students in the cooperative learning of new words.
2. Although it is possible to teach them, words that are not part of students' verbal community are not introduced.
3. Teachers provide continued and systematic attention to word meanings and their acquisition.
4. Instruction draws attention to word parts or word meanings.
5. A gamelike atmosphere, which fosters incidental learning, is a major source of vocabulary stimulation.
6. Teachers guide the development of contextual awareness, dictionary strategies, word derivations, and structural elements.
7. Words are encountered in many different contexts.
8. A few words are studied in depth, resulting in greater usage than exposure to many words.
9. The teacher's attitude toward vocabulary development is contagious and is rapidly acquired by students.

INCREASING GENERAL VOCABULARIES

Too often, vocabulary-development procedures encourage students to memorize lists of words and their dictionary definitions. Learning a word is no help, however, unless its usage is also learned. The techniques with the most effect on comprehension development seem to be those that include learning about the concepts of words and the contexts in which they are used (McKeown, Beck, Omanson, & Pople, 1985; Stahl & Fairbanks, 1986; Wixon, 1986).

Vocabulary development, then, should be concerned with teaching and learning a variety of conceptual relationships (Johnson & von Hoff Johnson, 1986; Williamson, 1974). Students must be able to recognize (1) members of the concept, (2) nonmembers of the concept, (3) unique characteristics that place members in a concept, (4) the range of sizes of members in a concept, (5) an act or activity peculiar to members of the concept, (6) the effect one concept has on another, (7) the cause-and-effect relationship between two or more concepts, and (8) what members of a concept depend on for continued existence.

For example, developing the concept *mammal* could include identifying animals such as humans, cows, platypuses, and porpoises as mammals; listing creatures such as spiders, snakes, and birds as nonmammals; understanding the terms *live-bearing*, *fur-covered*, and *mammary*; and comparing mice and elephants. Exploring these relationships will result in greater student understanding than will merely learning a label and memorizing a definition. Some concepts, of course, such as *possessing aspects of a color* (bluish, greenish) do not require an exploration of all the previously mentioned relationships.

Vocabularies can be developed and extended through the systematic study of semantic relationships (Anders & Bos, 1986; Burns & Broman, 1983; Johnson, 1984; Johnson & von Hoff Johnson, 1986). Throughout the school year, meanings should be identified as follows:

Symbols.   Nonverbal symbols are expressive gestures, traffic lights, road signs, flags, and emblems. The English language is a symbol, along with its derivatives (shorthand, Morse and other codes, Braille, and mathematical symbols).

Multiple meanings.   For communication to occur, there must be an agreed-upon meaning for a word—an accepted meaning by both the sender and receiver. Much confusion in communication can be traced to the use of words with multiple meanings. For example, *run* and *players* in the sentence *The run caused confusion among the players* might have different meanings for a baseball player, a stock broker, and a playwright. Understanding a term often requires fitting its meaning to the context—verbal, social, emotional, or historical.

In addition to these problems, there are other terms with abstract meanings, such as *kindness, democracy, truthfulness,* and *comprehension*. What such terms mean depends on who uses them, the person's values, his or her purpose for using the word, and his or her definition of the word. When a writer or speaker uses such terms, it is necessary to question, "What does this person mean? Is the intent to stir emotion or express opinion? Does this person mean the same thing that I perceive? Do I really understand what this person is saying?"

Denotations.   These are the specific meanings found in dictionaries. However, dictionaries are not published frequently enough to keep up with all the new words or new meanings of words (particularly technical ones), nor do they generally contain slang expressions.

Connotations.   These refer to the suggested or implied meanings of words apart from the things they explicitly name. This is a difficult aspect to understanding, for so many words have multiple or changing connotations. For example, a generation or so ago the word *square*, when describing a person, carried the connotation of true, honest, and forthright; today, the same word describes a person who is socially inept and out-of-touch.

Euphemisms.   These are substitutions of agreeable expressions for ones that may be offensive or be unpleasant. For example, *mortician* is a euphemism for *undertaker*. The word *plump* is less offensive than *fat*, and *slender* is more pleasing than *skinny*. Euphemisms require constant updating since they occur in usage long before they appear in dictionaries.

Functional shifts.   Functional shifts require an understanding not only of connotative shifts but also of shifts in parts of speech, such as a change from a verb to a noun. For example: *They* walk *to the bus stand each day; Joe went for a* walk.

Slang.   These are words and informal expressions used in varying degrees by all members of a community, and many are found in standard language. Discussions about who uses them, when they are appropriate, and special slang used by different groups—ethnic, geographical, age, occupational—can form the basis for understanding literature.

Technical language.   These are important specialized terms that come into popular use as people become aware of aspects of space, medicine, technology, or ecology.

Affective language.   Social adjustment and consumer wisdom concern everyone. It is important to realize that every form of communication has a bias—the sender expresses a message with meaning and intent and the receiver reconstructs it with another. When the two are not compatible, confusion or propagandizing can result. Children will learn that catchwords and slogans, such as *brotherhood of man*, or *good citizen*, often produce standard reactions.

Antonymy.   There are three kinds of antonyms. *Contradictions* are mutually exclusive (black and white); *contraries* allow for gradations (huge and small); and *reciprocals* deal with reverse or "undo" meanings (inherit and disinherit).

Metaphors.   These are direct or indirect comparisons between two apparently unlike things. Each metaphor consists of three elements: a topic, or the thing or idea to which attention is directed; a vehicle, or the thing or idea being used as the comparison item; and the ground, or the one or more traits that are implied links between the topic and vehicle. The seemingly anomalous comparison causes tension; when the tension is resolved, the metaphor is interpreted.

Developing General Vocabularies

For students to learn new words—new concepts and labels and new labels for already known concepts—they must be actively involved intellectually, emotionally, and physically (Donlan, 1975; Schwartz & Raphael, 1985). The purpose of vocabulary instruction is to develop students' independence in figuring out new words. This means that hearing a word, being given a word and its meaning, or finding the meaning of a word in a dictionary may not result in vocabulary growth. Students must be actively involved in learning new words so new words and concepts will be assimilated. Once learned, these words will remain part of the student throughout life.

In general, new vocabulary seems to be learned by factors of utility, application, elaboration, association with context, and memory load (Bruland, 1974; McKeown et al., 1985). Without some purpose for using new words, students will discard them as soon as they learn them. To remember, students need to use new vocabulary in their daily lives, both in and out of school. Once words are learned, there should be planned times for them to practice the words as part of their daily assignments. If too many words are studied at any one time, however, only a few of them will be learned.

Evidence exists indicating that students' reading comprehension is increased when they understand the meanings of words used in a text and when unfamiliar key terms are pretaught (Sorenson, 1985; Wixson, 1986). This is true even when reading from basals. When basal series are used in a reading program, certain misconceptions about basal vocabulary and the teaching of vocabulary can be avoided if teachers understand that

- all words are not equally learnable;
- words may have meanings other than the ones used in the passage;
- teaching a word does not ensure that it has been learned;
- pronunciation is not the object of vocabulary instruction; and
- older readers need as much direct vocabulary instruction as do younger readers.

To prepare effective vocabulary lessons, teachers should use several techniques. One technique for presenting words is semantic feature analysis (Anders & Bos, 1986; Thompson, 1986). **Semantic feature analysis** is done by determining a text's major ideas, listing phrases or single words that represent those ideas, determining which words represent higher-order and subordinate concepts; organizing the vocabulary into a relationship chart; distributing the chart before reading; and, after reading, discussing the concepts and relationships. Positive relationships are represented by a plus (+) in the chart; negative ones by a minus (−); no relationship is represented by a zero (0); and a question mark (?) indicates no consensus. A variation of the semantic feature analysis chart, called a **semantic comparison chart,** also makes visible students' prior experiences and stimulates discussion for discovering differences and similarities between the words and the text topic. But, it also shows differences and previously hidden similarities between concepts that are not members of the same category. Figure 6–1 contains a semantic feature analysis chart and a semantic comparison chart.

A. Semantic comparison
Idea: Ned thought his father looked both funny and sad as a clown.

Appearance of Ned's father	Clown features
+	white, red, black pants
+	red hair
−	black rings around eyes
−	big white mouth
+ = happy	
− = sad	

B. Semantic features — Important ideas

Vocabulary	Energy needed to cause physical and chemical change	Most energy today comes from fossil fuels	Fossil fuel supply is limited	Scientists finding ways to conserve fossil fuels
energy resource				
coal				
oil reservoirs				
refinery				
heat value				
acid rain				
conserve				
kerogen				
strip mining				
reclamation				
oil shale				
coal gasification				
petroleum				

FIGURE 6–1
Semantic Comparison Chart and Semantic Feature Analysis

ACTIVITIES FOR DEVELOPING GENERAL VOCABULARIES

To develop and extend students' vocabularies, teachers can do the following:

- Make a semantic word map, or a visual representation of a word's definition (Schwartz & Raphael, 1985; Stahl & Vancil, 1986). The map "zones" around the center zone that contains the word could be: "What is it?" (the general class of the word); "What is it like?" (the primary properties and those that distinguish it from others in the class); and "What are some examples?"

- Develop a vocabulary-rich program (McKeown et al., 1985). For sets of words, have students collaboratively determine the general meanings. Follow this with a class discussion of the discovered definitions and record them. Follow-up activities might be completing teacher-provided sentences to see the words used in context, student generation of sentences to create contexts, and comparing/contrasting words within sets to discover relationships. This activity can also be extended into natural contexts by encouraging students to be aware of these words when used outside the classroom and to independently bring examples to class of seeing, hearing, or using the target words.

- Help students develop an understanding of metaphors by having them classify items by physical features as well as affective, cross-sensory, and conceptual aspects. For example, discuss how houses can give a sense of newness or of age. Some houses, such as haunted houses, give rise to cross-sensory characteristics of noises; other houses elicit conceptual aspects of holidays.

- Develop lessons on the multiple meanings of words in which the meanings are situationally ambiguous. This is the kind of play on words that can drive adults to distraction once children discover how to manipulate language in this way! Because many children may not be cognitively ready, this activity might be most appropriate at the end of second or at the beginning of third grade. Books such as *Amelia Bedelia* and *Would You Put Your Money in a Sand Bank?* introduce this kind of language manipulation.

- Examine the metaphorical device of metonymy, which uses a part to represent the whole concept or uses one particular trait of something for something else. For example, if taken literally, the following sentences might cause confusion:

  Have you ever wondered how science got the computer to do so many things?

  Sally, be first base for today because we need Fran's arm on the mound.

- Create an essential word list about computer use (Dryer, Futtersak, & Boehm, 1985). A supplementary list for computer-assisted instruction can be made by examining representative software programs. Teach both the print and symbolic form of words such as <RETURN>, <ESC>, <esc>, ESC, Ctrl, and Alt. Also, provide learning time for terms such as *word processing program, microcomputer, random access memory, virtual drive, byte, megabyte,* and *display.*

- Develop action-packed vocabularies (Toothaker, 1974). Over an extended period of time, words that suggest actions, conduct, motions, responses, or behavior may be introduced. The advantage of this approach is that it promotes physical experiences. Two categories of words are used:

Muscular-action words are included in classifications such as traveling, driving reactions, motions with an object in front or behind, contracting, facial motions, eating, rubbing, upward or downward motions, leaping, moving to and fro, circular motions, irregular motions, fast and slow motions, and exertion.

Mental-action words are included in classifications such as memorization, language response, dramatic, musical, artistic, social, creative, mathematical, scientific and analytical, and discriminatory.

The difference between the two classifications is that the first pertains to actions that are more automatic or habitual than that of the second.

- Provide ample opportunities for new and interesting experiences. New concepts and words may be introduced during field trips, movies, classroom demonstrations, discussions with classroom visitors, and seasons and holidays.

- Provide opportunities for different social experiences. Use situations in which students have limited experience, such as using the telephone to find information or

order something, seeking advice or help from an adult who is not well known, reporting emergencies to the police or fire department, or visiting the home of a new friend who belongs to a different ethnic or cultural group.

This activity may be extended to cover other topics, such as developing a sense of social responsibility. Role playing provides controlled opportunities for students to practice various roles: giving orders or information, receiving orders or information, questioning, and mediating. There is a need in each situation for a careful examination of words that increase rather than hinder communication.

- Help students develop an interest in the natural environment. There is an almost universal concern for conserving resources and lessening pollution. The outdoors allows many opportunities for physical as well as emotional involvement as students learn to appreciate the beauty of nature. When it is not feasible to explore natural environments, articles or specimens can be brought to the classroom and set up as hands-on exhibits.

- Encourage students to study a hobby. Display the work of students or teachers who already have hobbies to stimulate other students to undertake their own. Even though some may never have their own hobbies, they will develop an appreciation of others' hobbies. These activities offer many opportunities for vocabulary development through labeling, organizing, and classifying.

- Compile new words around a theme. School events, special studies, literacy units, and holidays provide students with opportunities to learn words and concepts related to a theme. Sometimes the theme can be more general, such as friendship, humor, or moods.

- Help students develop an understanding of the figurative and idiomatic expressions in language (Foerster, 1974a). Idioms (expressions that convey meanings other than the literal ones) necessitate a degree of language sophistication to be understood and appreciated. Idioms can be analyzed by illustrating both their literal and figurative meanings through pantomime. Idioms may also be categorized according to their main source of metaphor, such as color, parts of the body, animals, food, clothing, solar system, plants, and marine life.

- Provide opportunities for students to explore the meanings of familiar words in new contexts (Deighton, 1959). In addition to the figures of speech mentioned previously, students can develop an extended understanding of (1) words used figuratively such as *ear, eye, face, foot, head, river, mountain,* and *road;* (2) relationship words with close meanings, such as *over/above, across/over, near/by/at/in, along/with/among/together, lower/under,* and *still/yet;* (3) judgment words that are used in a variety of situations but that may change in meaning because of their usage. These words include *cold, bad, beautiful, better, best, big, dark, deep, far, fast, fine, good, great, hard, heavy, high, hot, long, new, old, poor, rich, short, strong,* and *sweet;* (4) synonyms such as *stay/remain, sure/certain, small/little, glad/happy,* and *build/make;* (5) indefinite words that change in meaning according to the situation, such as *all, always, certain, every, sure, never, right, true,* and *whole;* and (6) idioms constructed from words such as *hold, bring, buy, clear, come, cut, put, make, get, go, in, down, up,* and *around.*

- Help students realize that vocabulary is constantly changing. Students should become aware of words that are used now but were not used a few years ago. Science and technology provide many examples of newly created words. Students with more mature language skills may also be able to study words that are no longer in current usage.

The changes in vocabulary are also noted in the changing meanings of words. As words are used more and more frequently, new meanings become attached to them. Although many professional writers and editors contend that some words are being misused, the final judge of the acceptability or correctness of a word in any given context is whether its meaning is understood by a significant portion of the population.

- Provide students with a vocabulary "capsule" (Crist, 1975). The capsule is comprised of a list of new words related to a specific topic that has been identified through a student survey. Introduce the new words and then allow students to talk among themselves using the words. Have students judge whether other students are using the words in the same manner as the teacher. At another time, students can use the new words in writing activities.

To recapitulate, students' general vocabularies (spoken, listening, writing, and reading) are built through planned activities that involve direct teaching as well as incidental learning. The enthusiasm of the teacher seems to be a key ingredient in a successful vocabulary-development program. Students are sure to respond to new words that are useful in their everyday lives and schoolwork if they are introduced in pleasant and pleasurable circumstances.

USING CONTEXT TO DETERMINE UNKNOWN WORDS

As students learn new vocabulary and extend their understanding of already familiar words, they should develop strategies for determining the possible meanings of unfamiliar words met in context. To use context clues effectively, students should know the various language patterns that signal an author's intended meaning.

In context, several textual constraint variables are in operation. These variables point out segments of the printed language that the reader is likely to use in determining word meanings at the sentence level (Aulls, 1970). These variables are (1) the position of the word in the sentence, (2) the grammatical class of the word, and (3) the types of grammatical structures in which the word is found.

Although context provides clues to the meanings of unfamiliar words, teachers should be cautious about encouraging the use of context clues alone (Deighton, 1959; Schatz & Baldwin, 1986; Stahl & Fairbanks, 1986). There is evidence that vocabulary instruction that includes both definitional and contextual information about to-be-learned words has the greatest effect on students' reading comprehension. Also, context clues work best when the target word is redundant in context and contributes little new information to the passage. In general, then, context clues do not reveal the meanings of low-frequency words in naturally occurring prose, and they may result in confusion as often as in correct word identification. Some limitations in using context clues in word study are

- context reveals meaning far less frequently than supposed. Although it is true that context determines meaning, it does not always show it.
- context reveals only one of a word's possible meanings. Since no word has a fixed, unalterable meaning, a single context will not suffice for all uses of the word.
- context seldom clarifies the whole meaning of a word. At best, context only provides clues from which the reader may infer the meaning of the unfamiliar word.
- vocabulary growth and expansion through context revelation is slow and gradual.

Therefore, as strategies for using context clues develop, teachers realize that

- what a context reveals about the meaning of an unfamiliar or unknown word depends on the reader's past experiences and knowledge (schemata);
- the portion of the context revealing, or providing clues to, the meaning of an unfamiliar word must be near the word; and
- there must be a clear connection between the unfamiliar word and the context that clarifies the meaning of the word.

Contextual Signals to Word Meanings

Contextual signals are aids to determining the possible meaning of an unfamiliar word. Contextual signals work partly because of (1) the reader's reasoning ability, (2) the reader's store of possible word meanings, and (3) the extent of the reader's knowledge of the topic (Burns & Schell, 1975). If the reader has the basic prerequisites for determining an unfamiliar word's possible meaning, the strategies he or she uses are hypothesis-generating and confirming.

According to Deighton (1959), context may indicate words' possible meanings through

1. *Definition.* Sentences containing forms of the verb *to be,* alone or in a verb phrase with the word *called,* often give the reader an explicit definition of an unfamiliar word.

A sculptor is a person who models, carves, or casts a work of art in solid material.

A person who believes in and campaigns for the careful use and protection of natural resources is called a conservationist.

2. *Example.* Sentences provide clues to possible meaning when they contain expressions such as *for example, such, such as, like, especially, other, this,* and *these.* If the reader knows the item used as an example, it may be possible for an unfamiliar word's meaning to be inferred.

Many new sporting arenas such as Cabo Hall in Detroit and Madison Square Garden in New York are being built as amphitheaters.

3. *Modifiers.* Sentences often contain unfamiliar words that can be understood because of a modifier used with that word. Modifiers can be single words, phrases, or entire clauses. Two important modifiers are relative clauses and predicate adjectives.

My grandfather's chronometer, which had a bright face, glistening black hands, and a loud tick, always made us eagerly gather around when he removed it from his vest pocket.

Delphinium are beautiful perennials that bed nicely with white lilies.

4. *Restatement.* Sentences containing appositives, that are punctuated with parentheses or dashes, and contain the words *in other words, that is,* and *or* provide many signals to unfamiliar words.

The parcels all were sent down a chute—a kind of slide—into the storeroom below.

The photograph was finished in sepia, or dark brown, tones.

5. *Inference through established connectives.* Sentences may show the possible meaning of an unfamiliar word through various grammatical patterns:
   a. **Parallel sentence structure.** A series—either in the same sentence or in succeeding sentences—often allows the reader to determine the meaning of unfamiliar words.

Each child brought a favorite musical instrument: Fred, his drums, Mary, her tambourine, and Warren, his horn.

   b. **Repetition of key words.** Often a writer will repeat an unfamiliar word throughout a paragraph. Each time the word is used, more information about its possible meaning is given. Or the writer might restate an idea, thereby giving additional clues to the meaning of an unfamiliar word.

   c. **Familiar connectives.** Sentences containing coordinating and subordinating connectives give the reader various clues to the possible meaning of an unfamiliar word.

Although Frances kept her room immaculate, her twin sister's room was always messy.

Other ways readers can discover an unfamiliar word's possible meanings are by using the sentence- and paragraph-reading strategies found in Chapter 5. Readers can begin to see the author's intended meaning as they question how the word is used:

Does it seem to be the *who* or *what* of a sentence?
Does it seem to indicate what is being done?
Does it seem to indicate what kind of thing something is?
Does it seem to tell how, how much, or how long something is happening?
Does it seem to mean something about where, when, or why something is happening?
Can the meaning be derived from other examples or reasons in the paragraph?

As students gain experience in using the sentence- and paragraph-reading strategies, they also learn strategies for determining the possible meaning of an unfamiliar word.

Contextual aids can also be found in illustrations, charts, tables, and maps that often accompany textual material. For example, students may not fully understand the meaning of *pedipalps* in Figure 6–2 until they refer to the drawing in the text. However, teachers should not assume that students can and will use illustrations. Relating visual information to its printed counterpart is a necessary strategy and skill that is gradually developed in all readers. (See Chapter 7 for a discussion of how to teach strategies for understanding illustrations.)

Using Context Signals

Students should not only learn context signals but also how they can be used to determine an author's intended meaning. The most practical place for getting teaching and practice material is in students' instructional materials. You can select the specific contextual strategies and the precise order in which to present them to students after examining the texts. When a basal series is used, it is best to follow the sequence of the series. Some basal series, however, do not provide continuous instruction in using contextual signals. When

Let's look at the spider's head. Most
spiders have a very strange-looking head.

This is because many spiders have four or
six or eight eyes. Even so, a spider cannot
see very much. A spider can tell only if it
is light or dark or if something is moving.

Most of the other parts of a spider's head
help it to catch food. The spider has two
small leg-like things, called *pedipalps*. It has
one pedipalp on each side of its head. The
pedipalps help the spider to hold an insect.

The spider has two jaws just in front of
its mouth. These jaws have fangs at the end.
When the spider catches something, it bites
the insect with these fangs. Poison in the
fangs puts the insect to sleep until the spider
is ready to eat it.

FIGURE 6–2
Illustration of Pedipalps

Source: Fay, L., Ross, R.R., and LaPray, M. (1981). *The Rand McNally Reading Program, Level 7.*
Chicago: Riverside. Reproduced with permission of Riverside Publishing Company.

they do offer exercises, they may merely ask students to ''use the context''
without specifying what they are to use and how they are to use it.

One lesson format for teaching contextual signals and the strategies for
using them is indicated in Figure 6–3. After students have learned various
signals, they should be given opportunities to apply their knowledge and gain
proficiency in using the contextual aids. The following suggested activities can
be used, with slight alterations, for practicing most of the contextual signal
strategies.

ACTIVITIES FOR USING CONTEXT SIGNALS

The following are some activities that promote the use of context signals as a means for developing reading comprehension.

- Provide a modified cloze passage. Instead of deleting every *nth* word, however, selectively delete one or two words from the paragraph. For each deletion give three or four possible choices that are grammatically correct. By examining the contextual signals, have students select a meaningful response. Afterward, let them discuss the reasons for their choices. For example:

    A cotton gin cleans the seeds from the cotton lint. Lint is the part of the cotton that is made into thread, then woven into cloth. Cleaning the cotton with a gin is called _____.
    linting   ginning   clothing

- Provide an opportunity for students to make their own sentences or paragraphs that show the meaning of an unknown word. Give each student a card on which an unfamiliar word is written. Have students use a particular contextual signal in writing their sentence or paragraph. Afterward, distribute their sentences and paragraphs among the other students and have them indicate the meaning of the unfamiliar word. For example, give students cards with words and signals similar to the following:

    escapade: a reckless or daring adventure
    signal: restatement using *or*

    character: someone in a story or play
    signal: example

- Play a variation of the game "Twenty Questions." Select a word unfamiliar to students. Have them ask a total of twenty questions about the word: The first ten on how the word can be used in a sentence and the other ten on possible meanings of the word. For example, students can establish the function of the word through questions such as: "Can it do something?" "Does it describe or tell what kind of thing something is?" "Can it be moved around in a sentence without changing the meaning of the sentence?" Once the word's function is known, students can focus on the word's possible meaning. The aim is not necessarily to guess the word but to determine its function and possible meaning.

STRATEGIES FOR EFFECTIVE WORD RECOGNITION

Word recognition by means of graphophonological signals is one aspect of reading instruction that causes many misconceptions. In most traditional approaches to word recognition there are three categories of subskills: phonics, structural analysis, and sight vocabulary. Phonics includes sound–letter relationships and the various rules for translating printed symbols into speech.

USING DEFINITION SIGNALS

The time of year when days and nights are the same length all over the earth (is called) the equinox.

You may not know the word *equinox*. The words *the time of year when days and nights are the same length all over the earth* are underlined to show you that they state the meaning of *equinox*.

The words *is called* signal the meaning of *equinox*. These words are circled to show you that they point to the meaning. Some other definition signals are:

or	who is, who are
that is	called, are called
is, are	means
which means	which is, which are

You can use definition signals to find the meanings of words you might not recognize.

FOR EXAMPLE

Find the meaning of *spontaneously* in the sentence below.

Spontaneously, (that is,) without planning, the team lifted the coach onto their shoulders.

A circle is drawn around the words *that is* because they are the **definition signal.**

The meaning of *spontaneously* is found after the definition signal. A line is drawn under the words *without planning* because they give the meaning of *spontaneously*.

You may have noticed that this sentence also has commas. Remember, commas may be used as apposition signals. Sometimes apposition signals and definition signals are in the same sentence. Both help you to find the meaning of unknown words.

STRATEGY

Definition signals tell you that the meaning of an unknown word or words is in the sentence. Use the definition signals and you will often find the meaning of the unknown words.

TRY IT

You may not know the meaning of *inflamed*. But you can find its meaning if you look for definition signals. Keep in mind the definition signals listed on this page.

The cut on Frank's arm became inflamed,

(or) red and sore.

What is the definition signal? Go back to the sentence and draw a circle around the definition signal.

You should have a circle around the word *or*.

What is the meaning of *inflamed*? Now draw a line under the words that give the meaning of *inflamed*.

You should have a line under the words *red and sore*.

FIGURE 6–3
Strategy Lesson for Context Clues

Structural analysis includes various rules for syllabication and the use of "root" words and affixes. Sight vocabulary includes any words that cannot be translated with phonics or structural analysis rules. Basic sight vocabulary usually refers to function words that do not have a direct referent, such as *of, from,* or *there*.

In a nonwhole-language interpretation of reading (commonly referred to as the traditional approach), it is assumed that reading progresses from decoding words to recognizing those words to creating sentences by reading all the

Check your sentence. It should look like this.

The cut on Frank's arm became inflamed, (or) red and sore.

Find the meaning of *amphibians* in the sentence below.

Amphibians (are) animals which can live

both on land and in water.

What is the definition signal? Draw a circle around it. What is the meaning of *amphibians*? Draw a line under it.

Check your sentence. It should look like this.

Amphibians(are)animals which can live both on land and in water.

Mark this sentence as you did those previously.

Doctors are finding out that overpopula-

tion, (which means) many people living in a

small place, can make people act strange.

Check your sentence. It should look like this.

Doctors are finding out that overpopulation, (which means) many people living in a small place, can make people act strange.

PRACTICE IT

The following sentences may contain words you do not know. Use the definition signals to find the meanings of the words in italics. Circle the definition signals and draw lines under the meanings of the words.

1. The *assassination*, (or) surprise murder, of Martin

   Luther King made everyone very sad.

2. Animals that eat other animals of their own kind

   (are called) *cannibals*.

3. Even today some people wear *ornaments*, (called)

   charms, to keep away bad spirits.

4. When I visited Canada last week, the weather

   was *frigid*, (that is,) very cold.

5. *Mercenaries*, (or) professional soldiers in a foreign

   army, were brought in to put down the rebellion.

Check your answers.

FIGURE 6–3
Continued

words together. As stated previously, the whole-language interpretation of the reading process is that sentences, rather than being the sum of the words they contain, are a major determiner of the words within their boundaries. A reader, therefore, only recognizes (that is, places into one's appropriate schema) the constituent words when the meaning of an entire statement is known.

This is not to say, however, that graphophonological information is not useful. It is, providing the reader has a clear understanding of its importance.

The main purpose for learning about graphophonological information is that it is helpful in turning ideas that are unrecognized in graphic form into sound to determine if the ideas are recognized aurally (Durkin, 1974). It is possible that certain words will only be familiar when they are heard—that is, they may only be in a person's listening vocabulary. When the visual form is translated into a sound form, a student might recognize the word. If the word is not in the reader's speaking or listening vocabularies, then no amount of decoding will benefit the reader. To reconstruct the author's intended message, the reader must rely on the contextual reading strategies discussed previously.

Clarification of Misunderstandings about Graphophonological Information

Of the three traditional word-recognition categories, phonics and structural analysis are of questionable value as they are usually taught. Any examination of current instructional materials shows that more pages are devoted to phonics than to reading comprehension. This seems a strange phenomenon since the meaning of a sentence often determines a word's sound representation!

Phonics instruction developed as an attempt to use the characteristics of the English alphabetic writing system. Alphabetic writing developed for the convenience of the writer rather than the reader; however, no written language has ever represented the phonemic structure of speech sounds exactly (Henderson, 1986; F. Smith, 1972). Normal reading does not involve decoding; readers do not understand words from their sounds. Instead, they attend as they read to the meaning of the spelling patterns of the words. If they did respond to the sounds of words, the following sentence (from F. Smith, 1972) would not provide confusion:

The none tolled hymn she had scene a pare of bear feat inn hour rheum.

In addition, the alphabetic system is only partially phonetic. Written English has two sets of relationships: (1) words that are related should look alike (*medicine, medication*), and (2) words that are not related should look different (*fare,*

fair). Obviously, these deviations from the original purpose of alphabetic writing (that is, to maintain a simple letter-to-sound relationship) have aided readers. The complex sound-spelling system of English, however, has become the basis for an idealized phonics instruction program. There is little relation between this phonic instruction and the realities of how beginning readers recognize words. Many practice exercises found in reading materials require students to identify phonic principles in already visually recognizable words. An example of this is found in exercises that ask students to mark the long and short vowel sounds in a list of words. Experienced teachers will verify that students experience the most difficulty in correctly labeling vowels in words unfamiliar to them.

In many current reading instruction texts, emphasis is placed on teaching the rules of syllabication. This instruction is based on the misconception that the written form is language itself, or the primary language form (Zuck, 1974). A careful examination of many of the syllabication rules reveals that they can be applied only after the pronunciation of the word is known. The reason is simple: Syllabication was devised for the convenience of the typist and typesetter (Waugh & Howell, 1975). The syllable divisions found in most dictionaries indicate the standard units of word divisions. They are not, however, intended as guides to pronunciation. For many English words, the pronunciation division differs from that of the written division. For example, the words *double, strengthen, pleasing,* and *molding* are words having different syllable divisions for writing and for pronunciation. Dictionaries divide words in pronunciation guides only as a visual aid to sounding out the words; these divisions have nothing to do with the rules offered as aids to decoding. Teachers, then, should understand the rationale for various dictionary subdivisions and use them for their intended purposes (Waugh & Howell, 1975).

In summary, in alphabetic writing it seems as though letters have a simple relationship to sounds, and that to know and apply these relationships is to read and write. This fallacy about literacy confuses decoding, or deciphering, with reading, or copying with writing. Teachers should not assume that knowing the likely sound relationship of each letter gives students access to words in print. It is possible for students to know their "sounds" and still be unable to reconstruct an author's message (Holdaway, 1986). Also, written words' syllable divisions often differ from the spoken syllable divisions. Because of erroneous instruction and because syllable boundaries differ in speech and writing, students may (1) apply syllable rules strictly and mispronounce many words; (2) pronounce words with additional syllables; (3) stress each syllable equally, thereby distorting the words; and (4) introduce additional sounds into the words (Zuck, 1974).

Teaching Word-Recognition Strategies

What you train students to do is what you get from them. This conclusion was drawn after a review of research about word identification (Johnson & Baumann, 1984). Students taught by an intensive phonics approach tend to do well at pronouncing words and at measures of phonics ability. Although students taught with a meaning-emphasis approach tend to produce more word errors, these errors are more semantically and syntactically appropriate than errors made by students taught by a code-emphasis approach, whose errors tend to be more phonetically appropriate. In addition, students can be taught to use and do use context to identify words: They make use of semantic cues at all levels. However, the application of syntactic cues seems to proceed developmentally. There is no evidence, however, that supports the effectiveness of syllabication or structural analysis instruction.

Word-recognition strategies are taught in the context of whole-language reading programs. To teach students how to use graphophonological information, teachers should understand (1) the sound structure of English, (2) the relationship between the sound structure and the written form of English, and (3) the spelling structures of written English.

Teachers should assume that students of all ages are familiar with sound structure when they come to school. (For a discussion of the structure of English, see Chapter 13; for information about students who speak divergent dialects, see Chapter 9.) In school, students become familiar with the written representations of the sounds they already know. Word-recognition instruction, then, should be directed toward teaching the written representation of the language and its relationship to the spoken language, and, most important, its relationship to the possible meaning of an author's message. The focus of word-recognition instruction in a whole-language approach to teaching reading is on the spelling structures of written English.

Together with learning the structures of English words, students learn that the purpose of a written code is to communicate the writer's feeling and ideas (Downing, 1975). The students' first and future experiences with the written language should stress its communicative function. Letter-to-sound relationships should always be taught in a context of constructing and reconstructing an author's thoughts and feelings.

There are two kinds of word recognition: immediate and mediated (F. Smith, 1972). **Immediate word recognition** occurs after a word's image and semantic features are generically stored in long-term memory and can be rapidly retrieved through either the context of the sentence or the internal features of the word. **Mediated word recognition** occurs when schemata for the word's image and semantic features and the procedures for its recall are not fully developed. In this case, a longer process of retrieval occurs through a combination of sentence context and internal features.

Immediate Word Recognition

Word recognition begins with the acquisition of a large repertoire of immediately recognized words. These may seem like the traditional "sight vocabulary"; however, instead of learning to recognize large numbers of words in isolation, students learn to recognize the printed form of objects and behaviors with which they are familiar. The relationship words (structure or function words) are learned as part of sentences or phrases that indicate the meaning they may represent. For example, the classroom can be filled with labels containing whole sentences. Complete sentences containing function words can also be used with pictures that illustrate their meaning. These aids, though common in primary classrooms, should not be considered immature for the upper elementary grades. Teachers of grades 5 and 6 might find labeled illustrations helpful in clarifying the meaning of *before* as students expand their understanding of its usage—*before* as an adverb, a preposition, and a conjunction. Other opportunities for developing immediate word recognition are classroom displays, bulletin boards, and readings containing repetitions of the words. Students' immediate word-recognition repertoire will constantly expand throughout the school years.

Mediated Word Recognition

Most exercises found in commercial instructional materials cover information and techniques for mediated word recognition. Much of this instruction (or practice, as is more often the case) attempts to develop in students an ability to decode, or translate into sound, unrecognized words. Teachers should remember that mediated word-recognition strategies allow students to recognize words that are in their aural vocabularies but not in their visual vocabularies. If the word is not in the students' hearing vocabularies, they will need to use the contextual strategies discussed previously. No amount of "sounding out" will help them recognize a word they do not already know by sound. Instead, they must try to approximate the word's meaning by using the surrounding context.

For students to use mediated word-recognition strategies, they should understand how the conventional spelling of words corresponds to their meanings and not to some surface feature—their pronunciations (Chomsky, 1973). Spellings are related to an underlying abstract level of meaning. Mature readers do not need to first pronounce a written word to recognize its meaning. Instead, they seek out and recognize the correspondence of the written symbol to some abstract lexical spelling of words. Lexical items are the meaning-bearing items of language. Therefore, instruction in mediated word-recognition strategies directs students' attention to features of the written word that, when combined with contextual signals, allow them to identify the word.

The acquisition of mediated word-recognition strategies depends on understanding two sets of information: (1) common letter clusters and (2) morphological units.

Letter Clusters
The results of investigations into how students translate printed symbols into sound representations indicate that readers seem to use a "structures approach" (Glass & Burton, 1973). Successful readers, when asked to read aloud,

did not use either rules of syllabication or rules of vowel control when they encountered an unfamiliar word. Instead, they seemed to group sounds according to various letter clusters appearing in the word. Examination of the materials commonly used in elementary grades revealed that 119 common letter clusters appeared in the materials (see Table 6–1).

It is possible and natural for students to learn three- and four-letter clusters as easily as they learn single-letter phonic units. These letter clusters are learned by examining words in students' listening vocabularies that are not immediately recognized. This system helps alleviate the problem of teaching vowel sounds. A vowel has a sound as part of a cluster and not because of a rule (Glass, 1965).

The teacher should present the clusters as part of whole words. Through direct teaching, students can learn to recognize the cluster and associate it with a common phonological unit. For example, the letter cluster found in *mate* is presented to students once they have in their speaking and listening vocabu-

TABLE 6–1
Common Letter Clusters

Common Letter Clusters Embedded in Whole Words

sat	bed	fall	*fowl*	her
sing	big	saw	bus	*hair*
set	lip	tel(l)	fil(l)	pal
sit	mud	*deck*	bite	*tied*
hot	lid	nice	mes(s)	few
him	den	tick	Tom	fire
top	hug	clif(f)	poke	*hear*
ran	hut	sink	tore	*real*
say	far	cob	*tow*	tea
sad	hem	sod	cast	bee
jam	cup	fog	cane	care
sun	mate	tub	meat	*deaf*
tin	tent	cuf(f)	glas(s)	*boat*
rap	test	rush	Bev	cue
sand	rake	table	kind	too
tack	hide	sight	toss	*out*
sum	lock	mis(s)	team	*pound*
tab	made	Ron	most	cure
bag	came	for	rol(l)	*nature*
told	cape	ful(l)	bone	fur
rash	face	*fact*	pale	fir
fish	sang	taf(f)y	save	raid
	sank	cook	rove	*auto*
	song	nation	folly	*boil*
			sage	

Source: Glass, G. (1973). *Teaching decoding as separate from reading*. Garden City, NY: Adelphi.

laries such words as *crate, date, fate, gate, plate, rate, state, skate,* and *slate.* As they learn other common clusters, they will be able to recognize such words as *inflate, debate,* and *rebate.* This approach can easily be combined with a program in which students learn to use mediated writing strategies.

Morphological Units

A practical approach to word recognition uses word parts that have invariant meanings and that, when combined with the reader's topical experience and knowledge of contextual signals, produce enough meaning so the reader can continue reading (Deighton, 1959). The difference between learning letter clusters and learning morphological units is the amount of word meaning information contained in the graphic unit. For example, the letter cluster contained in the word *fish,* though it may provide clues to the phonological representation of the word, does not indicate what the word means. On the other hand, the morphological unit *equi-,* found in the word *equinox,* gives the reader some idea of "equal." Table 6–2 contains some morphological units that have invariant meanings. Students in grades 4 through 8 should receive specific instruction in recognizing and understanding these units. Those in the primary grades may receive instruction in many of them as the need arises.

In devising lessons, teachers may need to identify the letter cluster or the morphological unit in words that are not part of a sentence's context. This may be done during the identification and example stage of the teaching lesson. The teacher, however, can develop within the guided application portion of the lesson an understanding of how the graphophonological information is combined with contextual information in recognizing unfamiliar words. Figure 6–4 contains a sample lesson for teaching mediated word recognition with morphological units.

A cautionary note is needed. Before young students are taught sound-letter relationship awareness, they must have developed a concept of "word" (Henderson, 1986). When they are ready to learn graphophonological patterns, they need time for this learning. Too often, teachers and publishers of commercial programs teach graphophonological relationships within one or two school years when the task should be accomplished throughout all the school years. Chapter 3 contains suggestions for introducing literacy to young students and strategies for determining their readiness to read and write.

SPELLING

The accepted definition of **spelling** is writing or naming in their correct sequence the letters that form a word. That of **learning to spell** is knowing or acquiring the basic correspondences between sounds and letters. To many people, nothing else is required. This belief has brought forth a plethora of programs and systems for teaching students graphophonological relationships. Another commonly held belief is that accurate spelling is a sign of an educated

TABLE 6–2
Morphological Units with Invariant Meanings

Units Found at the Beginning of Words

anthro- (man)	hydro- (water)	phil(o)- (love of)
auto- (self)	iso- (equal)	phono- (sound)
biblio- (book)	lith- (stone)	photo- (light)
bio- (life)	micro- (small)	pneumo- (breath)
centro- (middle)	mono- (one)	poly- (many)
cosmo- (universe)	neuro- (nerve)	proto- (first)
heter(o)- (different)	omni- (everywhere)	pseudo- (false)
homo- (same)	pan- (all)	tele- (far)
	penta- (five)	uni- (one)

Self-Explaining Compounds (Beginning and Ends of Words)

out	under	self	wise
over	up	way	

(Each of these has two clear meanings except *self*, which has only one.)

Common Prefixes With Invariant Meanings

apo- (different from)	extra- (additional)	mal- (bad)
syn- (same)	circum- (around)	intra- (within)
mis- (not)	com- (with)	equi- (equal)
intro- (within)	non- (not)	un- (not)
in- (in)	in- (not)	

Noun Suffixes Meaning Agent *or* One Who

-eer	-ess	-grapher	-ier
-ster	-ist	-stress	-trix

Common Mount Suffixes With Invariant Meanings

-ana (collection)	-fer (bearing)	-meter (mount)
-archy (rule)	-fication (process of making)	-metry (measuring)
-ard (one who)	-gram (written)	-phobia (fear)
-aster (mimic)	-graph (written)	-scope (something for viewing)
-bility (able)	-ics (facts)	-ee (one who receives)
-chrome (color)	-itis (illness)	
-cide (kill)	-latry (worship)	

Common Adjective Suffixes With Invariant Meanings

-est (superlative)	-wards (direction)	-most (superlative)
-ferous (bearing)	-wise (way)	-like (like)
-fic (process)	-less (without)	-ous (full of)
-fold (times)	-able (can)	-ose (sugar)
-form (shape of)		-ful (full of)

person and that the goal of spelling programs is to create flawless spellers. Whole-language advocates, however, hold these positions as untenable; they believe learning to spell means learning the underlying forms of the writing system for word creation and word recognition, and that learning to read and learning to spell are complementary processes (Chomsky, 1979; Henderson & Beers, 1980; Moffett & Wagner, 1976; Smith, 1982).

Misconceptions about spelling seem to be based on misunderstandings in general about language and in particular about English and its orthography. Some misunderstandings have been discussed along with ideas about phonics instruction and syllabication. What teachers need to realize, in addition, is that current research shows the developmental nature of spelling abilities (Anderson, 1985; Gentry, 1982; Henderson, 1986; Lehr, 1986; Lutz, 1986).

An analysis of students' writing from ages 4 to 10 found distinct stages in spelling strategies (Gentry, 1982). In the first, **precommunicative,** children use symbols from the alphabet to represent words, but they do not seem to know letter-to-sound correspondence. For example,

M F O
(Happy Birthday, Love, Wendy)

In the **semiphonetic** stage, children use letter combinations to represent words even though all the letters of a word may not be used. For example,

i diToda idi di siWk (Jenny)
(I did work today. I did do all my school work.)

In the **phonetic** stage, children begin to represent all surface sound features of words. For example,

VlitRin is the KiNG
fo ol the Rob theliensare
blak green ded yeenliodnd
blo.
Kef ries blak liein.
(Casey)
(Voltron is the King of all the Robots. The lions are black, green, red, yellow and blue. Keith rides the black lion.)

Then, children move into a **transitional** stage in which they begin to rely on visual and morphological strategies rather than sound.

Kermit
Kermit is smut.
he reds. he eat fliyes.
(Ryan)
(Kermit. Kermit is smart. He reads. He eats flies.)

USING MEANINGS
OF PREFIXES

Although is was January 2nd, Mr. Harris tried to cash a check dated January 15th. The bank teller said he could not cash a <u>predated</u> check.

The information in the paragraph can help you figure out the meaning of the word *predated*. You know Mr. Harris tried to cash the check before the date of the check.

You can also figure out the meaning of predated if you know the meaning of *pre*. The word part *pre* means *before*. Predated means: to date before. The word part *pre* is called **a prefix.** A prefix comes at the beginning of a word and changes the meaning of a word.

You can tell the meaning of the word *predated* from both sentence information and prefix information. A predated check is: a check dated before the time it is to be cashed.

The meanings of a few other common prefixes are:

Prefix	Meaning
pre	before
un	not
dis	not, away
inter	between, among
re	again, back

You can often use the information in a sentence plus the meaning of a prefix to figure out the meaning of a word.

FOR EXAMPLE

You know the meaning of *city*. A prefix is added to *city* in the sentence below. How does the meaning of *city* change?

At the <u>intercity</u> basketball game, James <u>rooted</u> for the Columbus City team, and Mary rooted for the Springfield City team.

The sentence tells you that Mary rooted for a team from one city and James rooted for a team from a different city.

The prefix *inter* means *between*. The basketball game took place between the teams from two cities. *Intercity* means *between cities*.

STRATEGY

Prefixes change the meaning of words. Use the meaning of a prefix and the information in sentences to help you figure out the meaning of a word.

TRY IT

You can get the meaning of the word in italics from the sentence information and the prefix information clues.

The lifeguard told the boys not to swim in the dirty water because it was <u>un-healthy.</u>

What sentence information helps you to figure out the meaning of *unhealthy*? You know the water was dirty. Swimming in dirty water is probably not good for you. What does the prefix *un* mean?

The prefix *un* means _____.

The prefix *un* means not. What is unhealthy water?

Unhealthy water is _____
_____
_____.

FIGURE 6–4
Strategy Lesson for Teaching Mediated Word Recognition

Check your answer. *Unhealthy water* is water that is not healthy, or water that is not good for you.

Read the following sentence and answer the questions.

> **The union leaders wanted the city workers to get a raise of ten dollars, but the mayor <u>disagreed</u> with them.**

What does the prefix *dis* mean?

Dis means _____.

What does *disagreed* mean?

Disagreed means _____.

Check your answer. In the word *disagreed, dis* means *not*. *Disagreed* means: did not agree.

Do the following sentence in the same way.

> **I thought I had looked over my composition carefully, but my teacher told me to <u>reexamine</u> it.**

Reexamine means _____

_____.

Check your answer. *Reexamine* means: to examine again or to look at again.

PRACTICE IT

The words in italics in the following sentences have prefixes. Read the sentences and answer the questions.

1. The cookbook said to *preheat* the oven to 400° and then to put in the food.

Preheat means _____.

2. The judge *disallowed* the lawyer's question because it was about the case.

Disallowed means _____.

3. Francine's father didn't want the *uninvited* guests to stay at the party with the people who should be there.

Uninvited means _____

_____.

4. The scouts were told to *repack* their bags after the inspection was over.

Repack means _____.

5. The Rio Grande River is an *international river* because it touches the United States and Mexico.

International river means _____

_____.

Check your answers.

USE IT

[Note to teachers: In this section of the lesson, give students a longer selection which requires them to apply the learned strategy in context. Provide directions similar to the following.]

In reading the following selection, you will need to use the strategy of this lesson. As you read the passage, look for [insert strategy and signals]. As soon as you finish reading, go on to the questions that follow.

FIGURE 6–4
Continued

The final stage, **correct,** is when children are aware of English spelling patterns and rules.

In a study of how young children develop the logic of orthography, beginning spellers went through certain patterns in the acquisition of English orthography (Henderson, 1986). It appears that the trial-and-error pattern of beginning spellers is similar to the trial-and-error pattern made by that of beginning speakers. The researcher suggests that instead of forcing children to develop the graphophonological relationships in a set manner, teachers should allow them to test what will work best for them. This point is reiterated throughout this book: Learning to read and write should be as easy for children as learning to listen and speak.

This leads to a second concept—invented spelling. **Invented spelling** refers to students' attempts to use their best judgments about spelling (Lutz, 1986). The study of written English's development (see Chapter 13) shows why there are many so-called discrepancies between English spelling and English pronunciation. Since English is alphabetic, the relationships that do exist between speech and print will be discovered by students as they develop literacy. One way to let students discover these relationships as shown by whole-language research is to allow students in the beginning (semiphonic) and later (phonetic and transitional) stages of written language development to spell words the way they think they should be spelled. These words are part of students' knowledge domains and as such provide an important motivation for acquiring their accurate representations to facilitate communication. The students' invented spellings show they already know the correspondence between sounds and letters. Students' patterns of invented spellings form the bases for instruction when they are encouraged to make educated guesses about spelling without fear of penalties for errors (Moffett & Wagner, 1976). Spelling improves with constant trying, since

> one of the best ways for the [reader] to gain experience with alphabetic representation and with the phonetic makeup of words is through word compositions, or writing words according to the way they sound. Children should be given much more practice in writing at the start. Writing in one's own invented spellings, according to the way words sound, is excellent experience when one is first starting to read, and many children can do this before they read. The practice that they get in attending to the sounds of words, in translating from pronunciation to print, and in the principles of alphabetic orthography are invaluable. (Chomsky, 1979, p. 121)

The complementary nature of spelling and reading result from the processes by which words are recognized. Reading and spelling both require visual memory, and the memory of words seen repeatedly in reading helps to standardize students' representations of those words. Visualizing words leads students to generalize about regular patterns of words and letters and helps them identify irregular words (Moffett & Wagner, 1976). As they read, students learn to recognize when a word "looks right," and, in turn, as they learn to spell already recognizable words, they analyze and remember the internal make-up of those words. As students gain experience with written language, they progress through stages in learning to spell and they develop more mature strategies involving deep levels of linguistic analysis and information. They become more aware of spelling principles and conventions (Anderson, 1985; Ehri, Barron, & Feldman, 1978).

Instructionally, students' spelling abilities are developed by embedding spelling instruction in whole-language experiences. Through an ongoing writing program to complement a reading program, students can gain a functional understanding of the complex nature of English's writing system, and they can use these connections with words they know to make the transition to a meaning-based interpretation of the writing system. The strategies and activities suggested for mediated word recognition are also appropriate for developing spelling instruction.

DICTIONARY AND THESAURUS USAGE STRATEGIES

Dictionaries tell what words often mean; they do not tell what words ought to mean (Downing & Sceats, 1974). Students turn to dictionaries because they see words (1) with meanings not revealed through the context, (2) that are not in

their oral vocabularies, (3) that need their precise meanings verified, or (4) with pronunciations that cannot be determined through mediated word recognition strategies.

Students may not use dictionaries because

1. The skills demanded for using them are too great. Some dictionaries are complicated in their format and presentation of information. Students are required to possess skills for selecting information, but they may not know what to select.
2. The information may be presented in a manner inappropriate for the cognitive level of the students. More recent dictionaries are overcoming this failing by adding additional concrete examples and eliminating definitions more complicated than the entry word (Downing & Sceats, 1974).
3. Students have no occasion to write their own sentences (Moffett & Wagner, 1976).

To use a dictionary successfully, students need to know some fundamental skills:

Locating a word.   To locate an entry word, students should know and use

- alphabetical order;
- guide words; and
- inflected or derived forms of words.

Deriving the pronunciation of a word.   To pronounce an entry word, students should know and use

- the pronunciation key to identify consonant and vowel sounds and associate them with the dictionary symbols;
- the pronunciation guide for blending the consonants and vowels into spoken syllables; and
- primary and secondary accent marks of the visual syllabic divisions.

Deriving the appropriate meaning of a word.   To determine the meaning of an unfamiliar word in relation to its context, students should know and use

- the basic dictionary definitions;
- illustrations, diagrams, and example sentences or phrases;
- the appropriate meaning for entry words with multiple entries or multiple meanings; and
- strategies for adapting the appropriate definition to the context of the word.

Some dictionaries made for elementary levels overcome the limitations stated previously by making dictionaries with differing formats for different maturity levels. The illustrations in Figure 6–5 show two levels of dictionary entries as published by one company. In addition, supplementary student guides or exercise booklets on the fundamental skills of dictionary use and practice are provided. Figure 6–6 shows one such practice lesson.

An important adjunct to the dictionary is a thesaurus. A **thesaurus** contains synonyms, antonyms, and related words. Students can learn to use a thesaurus when they learn to use a dictionary. A thesaurus helps to develop a sense of words. It helps students realize that synonyms do not always mean the same things and that different synonyms may be more appropriate in one situation than in another. Just as dictionaries should be written for students' cognitive and linguistic maturity, so should thesauri. The illustration in Figure 6–7 is from a beginning thesaurus.

To use a thesaurus successfully, students need to know some fundamental skills (in addition to basic dictionary skills):

---

game
A **game** is a way to play or have fun. Every **game** has rules. Some **games** are played with cards. All sports are **games.**

game |gām| —*noun, plural* **games 1.** A way of playing or having fun; an amusement: *As a game, we tried not to step on any of the cracks in the sidewalk. The baby tossed his food around as if eating was just a game.* **2.** A contest with rules and a purpose or goal that each side tries to achieve: *a football game; a game of cards.* **3.** Wild animals, birds, or fish that are hunted for food or sport.
—*adjective* **gamer, gamest 1.** Full of courage; brave; courageous: *He's a game boxer who'll never give up.* **2.** Ready; willing: *Are you game for a long walk?* **3.** Of or among animals hunted for sport or food: *The pheasant is a game bird.*

FIGURE 6–5
Two Levels of Dictionary Entries

Source: *My first dictionary.* (1980). Boston: Houghton Mifflin. *Beginning dictionary.* (1979). Boston: Houghton Mifflin.

Guide words

Look at that page.

It is the same as page 183 of **My Second Picture Dictionary.**

All the entry words on page 183 come between **oh** and **onion.**
They are the guide words.

Look again at that page.

Is the entry word **once** there?
If it is, draw a circle around it.

Below are some more entry words.

Look for each one on that page.

If you find it there, draw a circle around it.

What if you don't find it there!
It is on another page, between two other guide words.

---

oil	Oklahoma	one
olive	orange	old

FIGURE 6–6
Sample Dictionary Use Exercise

Source: Jenkins, W.A., & Schiller A. (1975). *My second picture dictionary exercise book.* Glenview, IL: Scott, Foresman.

Locating a word in an index.   Since a thesaurus is used for finding related words, students should first understand the principle of locating the word for which a synonym is desired and identifying the page on which that word and its synonyms are located.

Understanding the entries.   To select an appropriate synonym or antonym for a word, students should understand the form of a thesaurus entry.

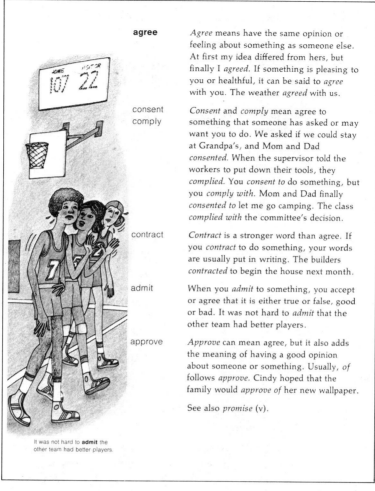

agree

Agree means have the same opinion or feeling about something as someone else. At first my idea differed from hers, but finally I *agreed*. If something is pleasing to you or healthful, it can be said to *agree* with you. The weather *agreed* with us.

consent
comply

Consent and *comply* mean agree to something that someone has asked or may want you to do. We asked if we could stay at Grandpa's, and Mom and Dad *consented*. When the supervisor told the workers to put down their tools, they *complied*. You *consent to* do something, but you *comply with*. Mom and Dad finally *consented to* let me go camping. The class *complied with* the committee's decision.

contract

Contract is a stronger word than agree. If you *contract* to do something, your words are usually put in writing. The builders *contracted* to begin the house next month.

admit

When you *admit* to something, you accept or agree that it is either true or false, good or bad. It was not hard to *admit* that the other team had better players.

approve

Approve can mean agree, but it also adds the meaning of having a good opinion about someone or something. Usually, *of* follows *approve*. Cindy hoped that the family would *approve of* her new wallpaper.

See also *promise* (v).

It was not hard to **admit** the other team had better players.

FIGURE 6–7
A Beginning Thesaurus Entry

Source: Schiller, A., & Jenkins, W.A. (1982). *In other words—A junior thesaurus.* Glenview, IL: Scott, Foresman.

Understanding cross references. To locate a desired word, students should know the means of cross referencing to other related terms.

These skills are the prerequisites for effective dictionary and thesaurus use. Students of all ages and grade levels may be proficient or deficient in these skills; once teachers have determined students' performance levels, instruction can be instituted to extend students' abilities.

ACTIVITIES FOR DEVELOPING DICTIONARY AND THESAURUS STRATEGIES

Once students know the names and the sequence of the 26 letters of the alphabet, activities such as the following can be implemented:

- Give students four to six noncontiguous letters and have them arrange the letters in alphabetical order. For example, students could arrange the letters *y, b, m, d, l, v* to *b, d, l, m, v, y*.

- Provide an interrupted sequence for students to complete. The sequence can be of contiguous letters: a, _____, c, d, _____, f, or the sequence can be noncontiguous and students must select the correct response from given items: d, _____, g, l, _____, o (z, a, f, h, n).

- Provide a list of words, each beginning with the same letter. Have students alphabetize them according to the second or third letters of the words.

- Provide sample guide words and a list of words that each begin with the same letter. Have students select those words that would be found on the page represented by the guide words. For example, the words *bear* and *began* are indicated as guide words. Have students decide which words would be on that page of a dictionary: *beat, beach, beg, below, bid, beaver,* and *beef.*

- Provide a list of words with inflected or derived forms. Have students indicate what the original form of the word is.
  The first stage of this activity could have students match the derived form to the original. As they become familiar with various spelling patterns and the changes that occur with the addition of inflected endings, they should be able to supply the original word without help.

- Provide a list of words spelled phonetically according to a dictionary pronunciation key. Have students match the phonetic spellings to the original spellings. As students' proficiency increases, give only the phonetic spellings and have students pronounce the words.

- Give students a list of dictionary definitions. Have them read the definition silently, then explain to another student what the entry word means.

- Give students separate lists of dictionary definitions and illustrations. Have them read the definitions and locate the illustration that matches each definition.

- Give students dictionary definitions and example sentences or phrases that help explain the word. Have them make their own example phrases and sentences in explaining the word to another student.

- Give students sentences that contain a word with multiple meanings. Have them refer to a dictionary and indicate which definition fits the meaning of the target word.

- Provide two sets of sentences, each containing the same multiple-meaning word. If a word has three meanings, each set should contain three sentences. Have students match the sentences in each set that have the same meaning for the word.

- Provide sentences in which a word's definition does not "fit" without some adaption. Have students rephrase the sentence so that the definition fits. For example:

  Michael grimaced with pain when the doctor gave him the injection.

  grimace: twisting of the face; ugly or funny smile

- Provide students with sets of riddles. Follow each riddle with a question containing two dictionary references. Students must solve the riddle after referring to each of the references. For example:

  I am a long-armed ape that lives in the trees of Asia. Am I a chimpanzee or a gibbon?

  I am sitting on a large porch alongside my house. Am I sitting on a piazza or a plaza?

RESOURCES FOR THE TEACHER

Many modern elementary-school dictionaries are written for different cognitive and linguistic maturity levels. The following publisher offers dictionaries and thesauri for elementary and junior-high grades. Each book begins with a series of lessons directed to the student for developing the fundamental skills for using the particular dictionary or thesaurus. Each also has an accompanying student exercise book.

Scott, Foresman, Glenview, IL.

My pictionary—for kindergarten and beginning grades
My first picture dictionary—for first grade
My second picture dictionary—for second grade
The Scott, Foresman beginning dictionary
The Scott, Foresman intermediate dictionary
The Scott, Foresman advanced dictionary
In other words: A beginning thesaurus, grades 3–4
In other words: A junior thesaurus, grades 5 and up

The following contain self-directed lessons for building and reinforcing dictionary skills and usage:

Moquin, L. D., & Nunes, A. (1973). *Dictionary skills*. North Billerica, MA: Curriculum Associates.
Lucken, J. A. (1981). *Activities for dictionary practice*. North Billerica, MA: Curriculum Associates.

The next series presents graphophonological information in the context of whole-language activities. The instruction integrates the study of spelling clusters with the study of sentences in language contexts. Each lesson starts with a chant (rhyme), then has "What Clues Do We Use?" "How Many Sentences Can We Make?" and "How Many Words Can We Make?"

Botel, M., & Seaver, J. T. (1986). *Language arts phonics: Strategies for decoding and spelling*. New York, NY: Scholastic.

The following is a set of multileveled booklets for the intermediate and upper elementary grades. Students answer questions, complete statements, supply details, and form generalizations.

> *Spectrum of skills: Vocabulary development.* New York: Macmillan.

The following series consists of multileveled sets of booklets containing exercises in several areas. Titles in each series that complement the strategies in this chapter are listed. These materials do not offer direct instruction but are useful for teaching and practice lessons.

> *Specific skill series.* Baldwin, NY: Barnell Loft.
> *Supportive reading skills.* Baldwin, NY: Dexter & Westbrook. Especially "Rhyme Time," "Reading Homonyms," "Learning to Alphabetize," "Using Guide Words," "Reading Homographs," "Mastering Multiple Meanings," "Recognizing Word Relationships," "Word-O-Rama."
> *Picto-cabulary series: What's in a name?* and *Word theater.* Baldwin, NY: Barnell Loft. (Booklets of various titles that present vocabulary for a particular theme.

The following publishers provide various booklets and duplicating masters for word puzzles and games. Teachers should review the materials first to determine their appropriateness for particular students.

> The Continental Press, Elizabethtown, PA 17022.
> Milliken Publishing Co., c/o AV Sales & Service, 166 Western Avenue, Albany, NY 12203.
> Scholastic Book Service, 904 Sylvan Avenue, Englewood Cliffs, NJ 07632.

The following is an excellent source of word games for extending students' vocabulary and understanding of word usage. Activities are graded by difficulty.

> Hurwitz, A. B., & Goddard, A. (1969). *Games to improve your child's English.* New York: Simon & Schuster.

Many trade books can be used for stimulating students' interest in words. The following is only a partial list of the many interesting and colorful books available.

> Longman, H. (1968). *Would you put your money in a sand bank? Fun with words.* Illustrated by Abner Graboff. Chicago: Rand McNally.
> Rothman, J. (1974). *The antcyclopedia.* Illustrated by Shelley Freshman. New York: Phinmarc.
> Hanson, J. (1973). *Antonyms: Hot and cold and other words that are different as night and day.* Minneapolis: Lerner Publications. (This book is part of a series of books on homonyms, homographs, synonyms, and antonyms.)
> Davidson, J. (1972). *Is that mother in the bottle: Where language came from and where it is going.* New York: Franklin Watts.
> Applegate, M. (1962). *First book of language and how to use it.* New York: Franklin Watts.
> Kraske, R. (1975). *Story of the dictionary.* New York: Harcourt Brace Jovanovich.
> Kohn, B. (1974). *What a funny thing to say!* New York: Dial.
> Adelson, L. (1972). *Dandelions don't bite: The story of words.* New York: Pantheon.

Paulson, R. S. (1959). *A is for apple and why: The story of our alphabet*. New York: Abingdon.

White, M. S. (1961). *Word twins*. New York: Abingdon.

Teachers may want to refer to the following articles, which are the sources for the idea in this chapter about developing an action-packed vocabulary.

Toothhaker, R. (1974). Developing an action-packed vocabulary. *Elementary English, 51,* 861–879.

Fraizer, A. (1970). Developing a vocabulary of the senses. *Elementary English, 47,* 176–184.

The following text presents word-recognition and vocabulary-learning strategies based on the same principles of thinking and learning the reading process as postulated in this text:

Johnson, D. D., & Pearson, P. D. (1984). *Teaching reading vocabulary* (2nd ed.). New York: Holt, Rinehart & Winston.

DISCUSSION QUESTIONS AND ACTIVITIES

1. To what kinds of word recognition instruction is Goodman (1972) referring?

   Schools may be teaching kids not to comprehend. They may be teaching them to match oral language with written language, which is very different from comprehending. (p. 1261)

   Examine some commercial reading instruction materials and determine to what extent Goodman's statement applies to each.

2. Observe a group of primary-grade students engaged in an activity. Through either note taking or recording, obtain samples of the variety of words they use. From the sample, select those that have multiple meanings. At another time, question students to determine whether they understand all the meanings of the words they used.

   Repeat this activity using students' instructional materials as the source of the words.

3. Examine the various reading materials for students in a particular grade to discover the authors' use of contextual signals for unfamiliar vocabulary and concepts. How often are difficult or abstract concepts introduced without giving contextual aids to their meaning? Collect samples of good use of context in revealing the meaning of words that might be unfamiliar to students in that grade.

4. Examine various dictionaries for elementary grades, paying close attention to the vocabulary used to explain the entry words. How many of the explanations seem confusing because they use abstract language? How many require students to find the meanings of other possibly unfamiliar words to understand the meaning of the entry word? How many of the teachers' guides suggest dictionary use to prescribe usage rather than as a tool for learning?

5. Prepare a short talk that might be given at a parent association meeting about the parents' role in developing their children's vocabulary. What suggestions would you make if the audience contained parents of varying educational backgrounds?

6. Plan a bulletin board display to interest students at a particular grade level in the etymology of words.

7. Make a series of informal tests to determine students' performance in the following areas:
   a. The understanding and use of contextual signals for meaning.
   b. The use of graphophonological information to pronounce unfamiliar written words.
   c. Locating a word in the dictionary.

FURTHER READING

The following article includes classic statements by advocates of each position on vocabulary development and word recognition and includes samples of research to provide a broad overview of the controversy.

Fox, D. (1986, April). The debate goes on: Systematic phonics vs. whole language. *Journal of Reading, 29*(7), 678–680.

The following texts, which have been cited in previous "Further Reading" sections, contain chapters about the lack of effectiveness of traditional phonics instruction.

Smith, F. (1978). *Psycholinguistics and reading.* New York: Holt, Rinehart & Winston.
Smith, F. (1982). *Understanding reading* (3rd ed.). New York: Holt, Rinehart & Winston.

The following is useful for additional techniques in developing and extending students' vocabulary.

Dale, E., & O'Rourke, J. (1971). *Techniques of teaching vocabulary.* Chicago: Field Educational Publications.

Organizer

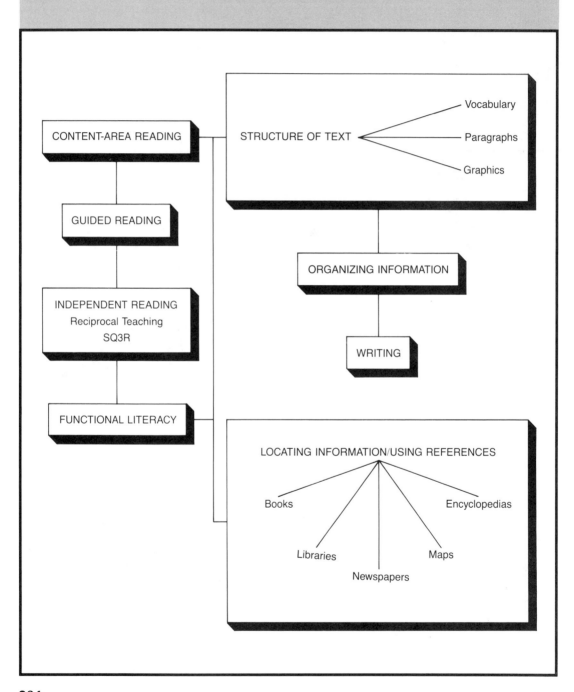

CONTENT-AREA READING

GUIDED READING

INDEPENDENT READING
Reciprocal Teaching
SQ3R

FUNCTIONAL LITERACY

STRUCTURE OF TEXT
- Vocabulary
- Paragraphs
- Graphics

ORGANIZING INFORMATION

WRITING

LOCATING INFORMATION/USING REFERENCES
Books
Libraries
Newspapers
Maps
Encyclopedias

CHAPTER 7

Developing Strategies for Content-Area Reading

Focus Questions

- What are the reading demands of content-area textbooks?
- What writing patterns, vocabulary, and graphic displays are commonly found in content-area texts?
- How can reading be guided in the content areas?
- What strategies are needed for locating and using information in reference materials?
- What strategies are needed for reading newspapers?
- What strategies are needed for organizing information?

To some degree, content-area specialists question the place of textbooks in content-area instruction and learning. Reading educators' concerns, however, are about the quality of texts. Because there are many content-area textbooks used in elementary schools, teachers should understand how to use them effectively. If school personnel choose a social studies, science, or mathematics textbook or series, then teachers should understand the typical reading demands imposed by those textbooks.

Textbooks are an important part of classroom instruction. Too often, textbooks are blamed for inadequacies resulting from teachers' and students' misuse. In classroom instruction, textbooks

introduce or overview a topic;
present new terms or concepts;
describe events or processes;
provide background or common experiences;
give specific facts;
provide substantiation for an idea or opinion;
are a source for instruction in study skills and for reading graphic materials; and
summarize a topic (Michaelis, 1972).

Many authorities in social studies, science, and mathematics instruction now emphasize a process approach to teaching and learning concepts, facts, and generalizations. This process approach is called the problem-solving approach in this book. The goal of this approach is to involve students in experiences that promote the development of language abilities so that they can communicate their ideas. The process in content-area instruction differs little from the creative problem-solving activities suggested in Chapter 3 and the comprehension strategies in Chapters 4 and 5.

To help students read content-area texts, teachers should know the specialized patterns used in writing and organizing such material (Alvermann et al., 1985; Armbruster, 1985; Davey, 1986; Holbrook, 1985; Robinson, 1983; Smith, 1964a; Strahan & Herlihy, 1985; Ratekin, Simpson, Alvermann, & Dishner, 1985). The following discussion synthesizes the findings of investigators who have analyzed the questions, directions, explanations, and various types of exercises used in content-area texts. It is through the structures and patterns of these components that the content-area specialist indicates how students are expected to think and work in a particular field.

THE STRUCTURE OF CONTENT-AREA MATERIALS

Content-area materials contain many of the same sentences and paragraph patterns discussed in Chapter 5. What makes content-area reading different from direct narrative is that certain patterns appear more often in content-area texts. The vocabulary load of content-area materials is also generally greater than that found in narration. The vocabulary load of content-area texts may cause students reading difficulties because of the large numbers of unfamiliar technical terms, unusual meanings given to familiar terms, and concepts in the same paragraph. Each content area, however, has its particular recurring patterns of vocabulary and paragraphs, and each pattern can be found in combination with other patterns.

The patterns described in this chapter are those most prevalent in texts intended for grades 3 to 8. Texts written for primary-grade levels usually have a style similar to that found in basal reading instructional materials for that level. Teachers should know, however, that specialized information in a narrative style can also present problems for readers. Teachers should examine the texts they use to determine which patterns appear and which ones may cause reading difficulties for students.

Written discourse having characteristics that interfere with students' attempts to reconstruct an author's messages is called "inconsiderate text" (Armbruster, 1984; 1985). Two text characteristics that allow readers to construct meaning are global and local coherence. **Global coherence** happens when the content (ideas) is integrated across entire chapters, sections, or books. **Local coherence** happens when ideas are linked within and between sentences and paragraphs. (See "Strategies for Understanding Textual Materials" in Chapter 10.) The characteristics of considerate text follow (Armbruster, 1985). The questions in Figure 10–13 are developed from these ideas and are used to identify considerate text.

Structure.   A logical, easily identifiable organization in which the headings and subheadings reflect a reasonable organization of the subject matter; introductions reveal content and structure; structure is clearly signaled throughout the text

Unity.   Addressing one purpose at a time; main ideas are obvious; information is clearly related to the main idea; transition statements help readers move from idea to idea

Coherence.   Clear relationships made between connecting ideas by explicit or obvious connectives; references are clear; the order of events in the text is easy to follow; graphics are clearly related to the text

Audience appropriateness.   Allowing the text to be understood by target students; the text contains information that is important for the target students to know

Truth.   Accurate information that is noncontradictory

THE STRUCTURE OF CONTENT-AREA TEXTS

The discourse of content-area textbooks is examined through (1) vocabulary, (2) paragraph structures, and (3) graphics. Vocabulary includes technical or specialized terms and the concepts they represent as well as familiar terms and concepts. The paragraph structures are those discussed in Chapter 5 with particular attention given to how patterns are used in content areas. Each content area has illustrative materials requiring certain reading strategies.

Vocabulary

Each content area has a highly specialized or technical vocabulary. For example, the following chart contains representative vocabulary from three content areas. The terms and the concepts they represent are generally unique to each area.

Specialized Vocabulary

Social Studies	Science	Mathematics
coastal	cochlea	parallelogram
mountain	bacteria	numerator
cases	spores	numeral
government	glucose	improper fraction
Tropic of Cancer	cytoplasm	congruent figures
adobe	molecules	divisor
latitude	particle	perpendicular

Students learn concepts and their labels during instruction. In mathematics and science, the specialized terms are often composed of morphological units that facilitate learning related terms (see Chapter 6). For example, psychrometer, thermometer, barometer, and chronometer are learned as instruments of measurement. Nevertheless, scientific and mathematical writing can be difficult to understand because of the special symbols and abbreviations involved.

Common Mathematical and Scientific Symbols and Abbreviations

$-$	(minus)	$\circ$	(degrees)	kph	(kilometers per hour)
$+$	(plus)	$<$	(less than)	C	(Celsius scale)
$=$	(equals)	$>$	(more than)	$\angle$	(angle)
$\times$	(times)	$\div$	(divided by)	$+$	(positive charge)
cm	(centimeter)	l	(liter)	$-$	(negative charge)
g	(gram)	mm	(millimeter)	$\rightarrow$	(direction of a force)

Mathematics reading may be difficult because the text has a mixture of words, numerals, letters, symbols, and geometric shapes. The reader must shift from one vocabulary form to another. The sample mathematics passages in Figure 7–1 illustrate the typical demands that are placed on the reader by the combined use of vocabularies—standard and mathematics.

When text contains unfamiliar terms and concepts, both students and teachers realize the problem; but the technical and scientific vocabulary is only one problem. Another is familiar terms with specialized meanings. Notice how the following sentences contain generally familiar terms used in special ways.

> Look at the vertical section of finely ground material in the *fault* between the layers of rock.

> What *forces* made the boat move?

Points, Line Segments, and Lines

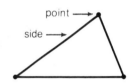

The **sides** of a polygon are line segments.
The corners of a polygon are **points.** Points represent exact locations in space. A dot is a model of a point.

A **line segment** is a straight path between two points. A line segment is part of a line.

This line segment is called *line segment PQ* or *line segment QP*. Points P and Q are **endpoints.**

A **line** is a never-ending straight path that extends in both directions.

This line is called *line RS* or *line SR*. The arrows show that the line goes on and on in both directions.

Centimeters

A **centimeter** (cm) is a metric unit of length.

A centimeter (cm) is about the width of a fingernail.

The height of the doghouse is 85 centimeters.

To the **nearest centimeter,** the crayon is 6 centimeters long.

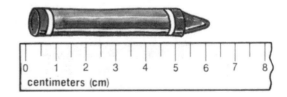

FIGURE 7–1
Sample Mathematics Text

Source: Merrill mathematics, level 4. (1987). Columbus, OH: Merrill, pp. 244, 321.

In addition, authors may use a term that has a different meaning in each content area, as the following sentences illustrate:

During the long months in prison, Austin's ideas began to *change.*

If I give the salesperson $10, how much *change* would I get back?

The force caused a *change* of state.

Other words that mean different things in different content areas are *operation, difference, division, property, product, revolution, planes,* and *positive.* When such words appear, students must try to understand the word's meaning in the context of the content area being read.

Another problem for students is the author's use of figurative language. Social studies materials, for instance, have many concepts that are stated figuratively. Some of these are important to the topic, and others are not. In the following example from a text intended for the fifth-grade level, figurative language is used freely. The terms illustrate some of the kinds of problems students might have reading this paragraph. (For additional ideas on problems with figurative language, see Chapters 6 and 8.)

Eager to get rid of Louisiana, Napoleon offered it at a low price which Jefferson delightedly accepted. In a single stroke, the United States expanded from the Mississippi to the Rocky Mountains. Though, at the time, many complained that most of the land seemed worthless and too dry to farm, later it would become the breadbasket of the nation. In making the Louisiana Purchase, Jefferson stretched the constitutional powers of the Presidency to the breaking point. The man who feared a strong central government helped to set a pattern for a long series of strong Presidents. (Davis et al., 1971, p. 94)

Paragraph Structures

The writing patterns used in the different content areas make certain common demands on the reader (Smith, 1964a). Generally, the reader is required to (1) select and evaluate information, (2) organize information, (3) recall information at the end of different time periods, (4) locate information, and (5) follow directions. Although these abilities are common to all reading, students' success is assessed only after the act of reading. For example, if students do not know what information to select or how to use the techniques and patterns of organizing the information, they are judged to be ineffective readers. By teaching students to recognize and use the structures and patterns in content materials, teachers prepare them to meet the demands of textbook reading.

In Chapter 5, six paragraph patterns are discussed: enumeration, generalization, comparison and contrast, sequence, cause and result, and question and answer. These patterns appear in general narrative, informational writing, and in textbook exposition. Additional information about these patterns and the structure of content-area texts is presented here.

The **sequence pattern** puts events in order. When used in social studies materials, events are put in chronological order. The reader must either understand the particulars of large periods in a specified order or fix an important date within a large unit. In addition to the time word signals, the reader must recognize the sequence of dates. In science writing, the sequence pattern provides an explanation of a technical process or provides detailed instructions for a demonstration or experiment. Intermixed with the sequence may be questions requiring students to make observations of the demonstration. While reading a sequence pattern in science, students are expected to follow explicit directions, observe events, explain results, and draw conclusions. The following is an illustration of this.

> Sounds are caused by vibrations. A vibration is made when an object moves back and forth. When you pluck a guitar string, it moves back and forth. The vibrations of the guitar make a sound. Sometimes you can see objects vibrate. The guitar string looks fuzzy as it vibrates. It looks fuzzy because it is moving. What other objects can you see vibrate? Look at the picture of the tuning fork. The tuning fork makes sound by vibrating. How do you know the tuning fork is vibrating? (Sund, Adams, Hackett, & Moyer, 1985, p. 187)

In the **comparison-and-contrast pattern,** an idea, event, person, or process is compared or contrasted with another. In some comparisons, one whole idea is explained using a closely related, more familiar idea. Or a comparison might be made by detailing the specifics of an idea and comparing them one by one. In another kind of comparison, two ideas are given but the comparison is implied. The reader must match the similar and dissimilar aspects of the two ideas; in other words, the reader provides cohesion.

> A reflex can be compared to the way a talking doll works. You pull a string and the doll says a word. The doll says the same word every time. The doll says the word only when the string is pulled. The doll's behavior does not change. (Sund et al., 1985, p. 173)

In social studies writing, the **effect-cause pattern** consists of a chain of causes and results, especially when the discussion is about large periods of history. The following example from a health text has effect-cause chains within the same paragraph.

> The cells that line your nose and sinuses make a liquid called mucus. Mucus traps dirt and dust. It also keeps your sinuses and the air you inhale moist. Sinuses are hollow spaces in the bones of your face. Sometimes too much mucus is made. This causes your nose to be clogged. You might have a runny nose also. This may happen when you have a cold. (Meeks & Heit, 1984, p. 72)

In addition to these patterns, content-area writing may contain others (Smith, 1964a, b; Robinson, 1983).

In the **topic development pattern,** a particular idea (topic) is developed in several paragraphs. This pattern can be recognized by a title or heading followed by an introductory sentence stating the topic. The complete development of the idea usually extends over two or more paragraphs, and the paragraphs within the topic development contain other patterns. The following passage from a text intended for use in the third grade shows how the development of a topic extends over several paragraphs. As is the case with many topic developments, the section contains a heading and a general statement about the topic that serves to introduce it.

Puerto Rico

Hola! Welcome to Puerto Rico—one of the most beautiful islands in the Caribbean Sea.

Puerto Rico is a very special place. It has long, white sandy beaches lined with tall, green palm trees.

The middle of the island has high mountains. They are partly covered with a blanket of thick green bushes, trees, and brightly colored flowers.

The weather in Puerto Rico is always warm. People can go swimming all year long. In the mountains, there are often heavy rainfalls, but it rains for just a short time. Soon it is sunny again.

Many different fruits grow well in such warm weather. Bananas, mangos, and pineapples are just some of the delicious fruits that are grown by farmers in the countryside, called *el campo.*

Puerto Rico has small villages and towns and some very large cities. The largest city is San Juan. It has many tall office buildings and hotels.

Many Puerto Ricans work in offices, stores, and other businesses. The people of Puerto Rico speak and write in Spanish.

Someday you may be able to visit Puerto Rico. Then you can discover for yourself that it is a very special place. (Durr et al., 1983, pp. 116–119)

Classification, a pattern similar to enumeration, is commonly found in science textbooks. Although the classification pattern may list various subclassifications, it emphasizes the conceptual subdivisions of information rather than the itemization of information. Like other patterns, the classification pattern may span several paragraphs.

Energy

Look at the systems on these two pages. In each system, the objects are interacting. It is energy that makes the objects interact. Each system can be called an energy system.

This hitting system is an energy system.

This crashing system is an energy system.

This sliding system is an energy system.

The hitting, crashing, and sliding systems are all energy systems. In each system, objects move. When the objects move, they have energy—motion energy. So all these energy systems can be called moving systems. (Berger et al., Level 3, 1979, pp. 148–149)

Another pattern found in elementary content-area texts is the **problem and solution pattern.** To understand the author's entire idea, students must understand both the problem and its solution. The following example illustrates this pattern.

Although there are many goods and services to choose from today, some families do not have enough money to buy some of the things they would like to have. Many families want color television sets, but it takes a long time for some people to save enough money to buy one. If they do not want to wait for the set until they save enough money, there is a way they can get it with only a small down payment. It is called installment buying, and it is a form of credit. The family can buy the set with a down payment if they promise to pay a certain amount each month. The set will cost more if it is bought this way, for the store will charge a fee for credit. But the family could be using the set while it is being paid for. (Davis et al., 1971b, pp. 186–187)

A pattern that is not a paragraph pattern but represents a style of writing found in social studies and its related materials is **propaganda.** Students at all school levels should know the general techniques of propaganda, such as "glad words" or glittering generalities, unpleasant words, testimonials, "plain-folks" implications, and stacking the cards. Although it is rare to find textbook authors using these techniques, sometimes they let their beliefs or feelings about a topic sway their presentation. For example, if a discussion of desert tribes included the phrase "have never even learned to store water," the connotation would be that the people of the tribe are incapable of learning. Also, the use of exclamation marks to indicate surprise or emphasis or to portray plain-folks implications and glittering generalities may have connotations of sarcasm or condescension. Last, some ideas are presented broadly and loosely, resulting in inaccurate statements. To offset its use, students need to recognize overt and covert propaganda in textbooks and related content-area materials.

Graphics

When graphic materials appear in content-area textbooks, teachers should not assume that students understand the related concept or process because it is accompanied by an illustration. Students must learn to interpret a particular graphic display and to alternately read verbal and graphic information. They must also learn to distinguish when an illustration is depicting the exception and not the rule.

Various graphic displays are used in content-area textbooks. Depending on the concept and the item to be illustrated, the types shown in Figure 7–2 and listed in the following paragraphs are found in textbooks.

Photographs.   Science, social studies, and mathematics texts often have black and white or color photographs to support and help explain the textual material.

Realistic illustrations.   Most content-area texts have drawings. These are realistic representations, in either black and white or color, of various objects. Some drawings directly support the textual materials. In such cases, parts of the drawings may be labeled. In addition, many content-area texts have illustrations for decoration. In these cases, the illustrations indirectly support the text by showing related objects or events.

Representational illustrations.   In some drawings, real objects are recognizable; in others, the objects have been stylized to highlight various components of the objects. Color is sometimes used to differentiate the components.

Diagrammatic illustrations.   When an object or process is shown symbolically, geometric shapes may be used to represent real objects or events. Diagrams for illustrating a process or a relationship do not show the entire structure of an object or its complete function. In such cases, the diagram directs the viewer's attention to one aspect of the process or relationship.

Charts, graphs, and figures.   Some information is best represented in a symbolic form so the reader can compare or contrast quantities. In such cases, graphs or figures let the reader see degrees or amounts of difference or similarity without having to process as much numerical information.

Maps.   Maps are representations of geographical areas. To understand maps, the relationship between the physical word and the symbolic representation must be understood. Maps can be (a) political—showing governmental boundaries of nations, states, cities, or towns; (b) physical—showing land forms and altitudes; (c) specialized—showing information such as weather patterns, population dispersion, industrial development, or natural resources; or (d) combinations of the three types.

The use of graphics in content-area textbooks does not always facilitate learning (Hittleman, 1985). When readers cannot cope with or do not possess adequate strategies for the demands of switching from reading verbal material to reading visuals, then they will be unable to process the author's message. Some authors have used the term *interrupted reading* for reading the visuals of textual material. Since visuals are often an integral part of the message, the constant shifting back and forth might better be described as *staccato reading* (Albert, 1971).

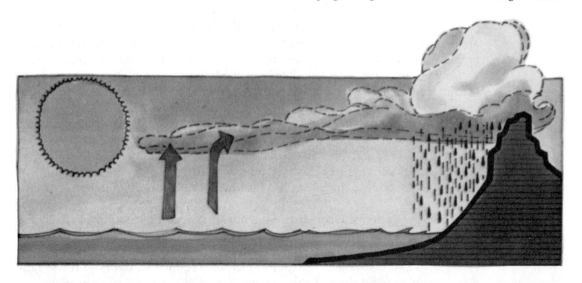

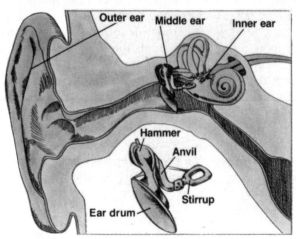

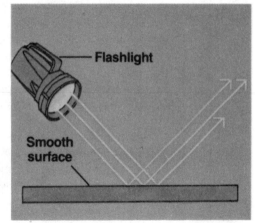

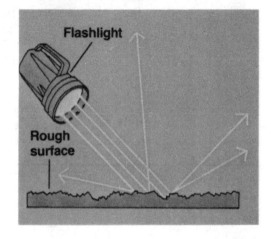

FIGURE 7–2
Typical Graphics in Content-Area Texts

Source: Sund, R. B., et al. (1985). *Accent on science, level 4.*
Columbus, OH: Merrill, pp. 243, 45; Meeks, L. B. & Hiet,
P. (1984). *Health 4: Focus on you.* Columbus, OH: Merrill,
p. 207.

The object of learning is to retain and later recall information; illustrations are intended to help in this process. However, students have problems remembering information from graphics unless the images are translated into semantic forms (Berry, 1980). In Chapter 13, a model of human memory shows both the imagery and semantic components of long-term memory. The images stored in imagery memory are not stored in a verbal code, but they are activated by associations from the semantic memory. For the verbal recall of information stored in imagery memory, a student must store both the image and the verbal code (oral or written language) for that image. A recounting of graphic information is not possible unless there has been a concomitant, immediate translation of the illustrated information into words, phrases, and sentences.

To help students reconstruct meaning from graphic materials, teachers need to know how confusion can be caused by visuals.

Photographs and illustrations.   Reading pictures requires students to relate new information to what they already know. When illustrations contain many details, students must have a schema for processing the information or they will be distracted by irrelevant details. Students need instruction in how to locate the focus point and how to examine other details in relation to that point.

Pictures are not real objects—only abstractions—so the viewer must realize that they show only a fraction of reality. Further, pictures cannot show a total picture; they depict only parts. Students must learn what part of reality is shown and use other illustrations to get the total context for the object or event.

Drawings and diagrams may oversimplify a continuous process by representing it in stages. Because the reader sees the process represented in stages, he or she may not realize the process is continuous. Teachers should provide instructions that relate these separate phases to something such as "stop action" in a video replay.

Estimating size.   Photographs, maps, diagrams, and illustrations do not always show the scale of objects. The scale from illustration to illustration in the same text is also not consistent. Small objects are shown in enlargements, and large objects are scaled down to fit the page. Close-ups show details that are not always essential to the understanding or recognition of the object. And, the perspective of objects may be distorted by the manner in which they are shown.

Good illustrations include a measure of scale such as a ruler or a common object of known size. Students need instruction in understanding these scales or in recalling concrete experiences with the reference object.

Color.   Color serves two purposes: functional or decorative. Functional color distinguishes the individual components of an object. Decorative color can give the viewer a false impression of the object and cause the viewer to focus on unimportant details. In addition, some colors detract from the illustrator's message.

Students should learn to question the use of color and how to disregard it when it is not relevant to the main idea of the illustration. This questioning can be learned by having students examine two pictures of an object—one black and white, one color—then deciding whether color adds to their understanding.

Movement.   All illustrations are static, yet they often represent movement. Lines and arrows are used to indicate enlargement, energy release, simultaneous action, movement, and reactions. Since these indicators do not exist in the natural world, students must superimpose them on reality whenever they transfer the information from the graphic display to reality (Albert, 1971).

Students can learn to make this transfer by using "clean" copies of the same illustrated objects or events. By covering the clean copies with clear plastic overlays on which the action lines are drawn, students develop an understanding about how the lines or arrows relate to the real objects or events.

Guiding Reading in the Content Areas

The same distinctions made in Chapter 4 between guided reading and independent reading of narration applies to the reading of exposition in content-area materials. For less-proficient readers, the teacher needs to structure the reading activity so students can determine the meanings intended by the author.

To reiterate, the guided reading–thinking lessons consist of five strategies:

1. Examining information to determine what is or is not already known.
2. Hypothesizing about probable meanings based on the information examined.
3. Finding proof of probable meanings based on the information examined.
4. Suspending judgment when information is not available to confirm or reject hypotheses.
5. Making decisions when information is available to confirm or reject hypotheses or deciding to seek additional information elsewhere.

The teacher can guide reading by asking questions that require students to make predictions. For example, using the information contained in a selection entitled "Before History Began," the teacher could ask for predictions about specific segments of the passage. The number of paragraphs that students read is determined by the amount of information they can process.

The following lesson illustrates how a guided reading–thinking lesson is structured for reading a sixth-grade social studies text.

Concepts

People have used technology since prehistoric times.

Ancient people independently in all parts of the world discovered farming. This might be the most important discovery ever made.

Growing crops and domesticating animals changed people's life-styles—hunters and gatherers began to live in permanent villages.

Concept: Ancillary

Archeologists are scientists who search for traces of ancient people.

Purpose

To provide pupils with new terms and concepts and specific facts about how the discovery of farming affected ancient people's life-styles. This is the second lesson in a unit entitled "People Are Toolmakers."

Guiding Questions

1. Subtitle, "Searching for Beginnings," special subsection on fourth and fifth pages of lesson (pp. 232–233); photograph and drawing of archeological dig.

   What do you already know about archeologists? What "beginnings" would they be searching for? You sometimes make guesses about things. What guesses do archeologists make?

2. Title page, "Before History Began," first subsection with pictures and time line.

   What does the picture show you about early humans' life-styles? When is the period "before history"? What does "history" mean? What information does the time line provide?

3. Second subsection, "The Age of Stone," second and third pages with illustrations.

   What is the age of stone? Where would it be on the time line on page 239? What questions does the author want you to answer as you read? Did you have an answer for them? What did you do when you couldn't answer the author's questions?

   Were there any words you couldn't figure out from the passage? Was the word important to understanding the author's ideas? What did you do when you couldn't figure out a word? What is important about the Stone Age? How do the pictures on the pages fit in with the information in the text?

4. Third subsection, "Farming in the Fertile Crescent." Before reading this section, read the subsection "Discovering Farming" on page 234. Why is this section set off from the text by a colored page? (Repeat

questions about the author's use of questions and unfamiliar vocabulary here and in the reading of each subsequent subsection.)

How is the information in this section told differently than the information in the other sections? Why is this information included in the unit? How does the story of the discovery of farming help you understand farming in the Fertile Crescent? What part of the world is shown in the map of the Fertile Crescent?

5. Subsection, "Farming in Other Parts of the World," one page with illustration.

How does the beginning of farming in other parts of the world compare to that in the Fertile Crescent?

6. Subsections, "Learning to Use Animals," "New Technology for Farming," and "A New Life Style," three pages with illustrations.

How were ancient people's lives changed because of using animals and the development of new technology? What did their new life-style become?

Guided Reading–Thinking Lesson based on Branson (1980) "Before History Began," pp. 229–239.

During a guided reading–thinking lesson, students' efforts are directed to applying their reading and thinking strategies. Throughout the lesson, teachers watch students apply their sentence-reading, paragraph-reading, and word-recognition strategies in reconstructing the author's ideas and constructing their own meanings. Since the aim of a guided content reading–thinking lesson is the acquisition of information, concepts, and facts related to a topic, the teacher's efforts should be directed toward that end. The guided reading–thinking lesson is useful when students cannot gain content-area information on their own. As they gain proficiency in acquiring reading strategies, teachers can use the lesson to direct students' attention to the application of those strategies.

For example, embedded within the text of the previous sample lesson are questions or directions for students to provide some information on their own. For this lesson, the questions require students to know something about the topic. Such questions as "Why do you suppose few bone and wood tools have been discovered?" and "How many of the foods discovered by ancient farmers do you eat fairly often?" interrupt reading and cause students to lose the direct flow of the author's main points. During the lesson, teachers need to guide students around the interrupting questions. After the material is read, teachers may return to those questions for discussion. It is possible that some students will still be unable to answer them. At these times, teachers can delay having them answered until students acquire additional information.

Students need the teacher's guidance for clarifying referential expressions in the passage (see Chapter 5, "Strategies for Understanding Textual Material"). The use of anaphora—using a grammatical substitute to refer to a preceding word or phrase—is typical of elementary and middle-school social studies textbooks. Depending on students' level of understanding referential constructions, teachers need to guide them in identifying the referents in statements such as the following:

This is just a moment of time compared to prehistory . . .

They ate fruit, nuts, roots, seeds . . .

That happening has been called perhaps the most important discovery ever made.

Those countries didn't exist when . . .

Those broken bones and tools must be made to tell a story.

As you know, that is when history began.

STRATEGIES FOR INDEPENDENT READING IN THE CONTENT AREAS

Students need ways for independently reading textbooks in the content areas. Techniques for teaching students self-directing strategies include *SQ3R* and reciprocal teaching.

Survey–Question–Read–Recite–Review

Survey–Question–Read–Recite–Review is known by the acronym SQ3R (Sargent, Huus, & Andresen, 1970). This technique benefits students because

students move toward an independent approach to reading and using textual materials in the content areas.

students develop procedures for adapting their reading strategies to reading an expository style of writing.

students develop strategies for integrating the reading of both textual and graphic information.

students extend their understanding of creative problem solving to acquisitions of specific knowledge and generalizations in the content areas.

The SQ3R technique should be taught to all students. The format of the comprehension strategy lesson given in Chapter 5 is modified for presenting the SQ3R steps to students. The technique can be introduced to students at any grade level. Although the procedures must be modified to meet individual student proficiencies, the SQ3R plan, once learned, will serve students throughout their school years. It provides them with a format into which they can fit their ever-increasing reading strategies and skills.

The phases of the SQ3R plan are:

Survey.   In the survey phase, students determine what kinds of knowledge or information the author expects them to understand. It is a "taking stock" of what they know about the topic and a determining of what they do not know. Through a survey of the reading materials, students predict the reading demands of the materials and what difficulties they may encounter in their reading.

Specifically, students examine the heading and subheadings, look for terms that are written in boldface or italics, examine graphic displays for the kinds of information they portray, and look for signals to the organization of the textual material.

Question.   In the question phase, students set tentative hypotheses about the author's ideas. These hypotheses or predictions become their purposes for reading the text. During the questioning phase, students ask themselves what they know about the topic and what it is the author wishes them to know after they have read the text.

Specifically, students create questions to be answered during and after reading the passage. One source of these questions might be those posed by the author at the beginning or end of each subsection. Another might be the collection of subheadings in each section. For example, in the passage "You Are Part of the World" (Beattie & Greco, 1980, pp. 184–189), a selection from a third-grade social studies text, the subheadings are

You Are Part of the World
Goods Around the World
Services Around the World
Cooperation Around the World
Tools Around the World
Language Around the World

These subheadings are from the thirteenth lesson in the unit "What Are Groups?" From a survey, students determine that people from all parts of the world share goods, services, tools, and some form of language. (The concepts of goods and services were presented in a previous lesson.) To form specific purposes for reading, students could ask questions such as

How are we part of the world?
What goods are used around the world?
What services are used around the world?
What cooperation takes place around the world?
What tools are used around the world?
What types of languages are used around the world?

In addition, students can predict from the text's illustrations that the passage contains information to answer questions such as

How are goods traded between the United States and other countries?
What other transportation services do we share with other countries?
How do we help hungry people around the world?
Can all people understand picture signs?

The question and survey stages can be combined so students can alter the questions or suggest others from the information surveyed in the photographs, drawings, and diagrams (a representation of different ethnic groups in the world, the flow of goods from the United States to other nations, a bus station, health and food in Asia and Africa, a telecommunications satellite, and international road signs).

Since textbooks have the same format and structure throughout, once students learn SQ3R and the strategy of forming predictions about a selection, they can locate cues to the author's message efficiently.

Read. In the read phase, students locate information suggested by the questions created during the previous two phases. Specifically, students read for two general purposes: (1) to find the answers to the questions they created, and (2) to find other important information that they did not predict through specific questions. This second aspect of reading is important, since questions might not cover all the author's main points. Students now must distinguish between passage information they predicted would be there and information they did not predict.

Some authors use aspects of the survey and question stages in structuring their textual materials. However, it does not always result in a considerate text. The following passage gives students a predetermined question to help focus their attention on important ideas. But, notice the information and question at the end of the last paragraph. This information is related indirectly to the passage's main point, and the final question directs students' attention away from that point. Only by viewing reading as creative problem solving will students realize this.

What is Culture?

Human beings are different from animals. Our hands are different. The way we think is different.

Another difference between humans and animals is that humans have culture (KUL-chur). Culture is the human way of living. Tools, language, institutions, and beliefs make up culture.

Human beings use tools for almost everything they do. We use tools to eat. We use tools to work.

Human beings use language (LANG-gwij) to tell others what they are thinking. How are the people in the pictures using language?

Another part of culture is institutions (in sti-TOO-shuns). Institutions are ways people do the same things over and over again.

Holidays are institutions because we celebrate them in the same way each time. Schools are institutions because we do the same things in all schools.

Beliefs are part of culture too. A belief is something that a person thinks is true. Some people believe that walking under a ladder is bad luck. Do you have this belief? (Beattie & Greco, 1980, pp. 91–93)

Recite. In the recite phase, students answer the questions posed during the survey and question phases. The recitation is the immediate recall of information from the portion of the passage read. Some students can read only one subsection at a time; others can read the entire section. In either case, students get immediate feedback from the teacher and the other students about their success in using reading strategies. During this phase, students make decisions about what information supports ideas or has an additional "human interest" effect.

Specifically, in the recite phase students take each question and form an answer to it. The answers can be oral or written, depending on the lesson purpose. After all questions for a section or subsection are answered, students identify other passage information. If the information is important to the topic, then they form and answer a question. A discussion follows about the information's importance to the author's idea and why its occurrence was not predicted. Students learn whether a clue was missed or whether no clue was given.

It is during the recite phase that students show their ability to reconstruct the intended message of the author through a self-guided reading–thinking activity.

Review.   In the review phase, which takes place at a later time such as in a study or review session, students again answer the questions formed during the survey and question stages. Since a purpose for studying a content area is to develop a store of information and concepts, remembering is a desirable characteristic of proficient students. However, understanding an author's message should not be considered synonymous with remembering; understanding of a topic does not ensure recall of its ideas (Pauk, 1973). Therefore, students take some additional steps to retain the learned information. The recite phase deals with the immediate remembering of information; the review phase deals with long-term retention. The most efficient time to use the review phase is within 24 hours of completing the recite stage, and then periodically thereafter.

Specifically, in the review phase students take the questions from the survey, question, and recite phases and answer them. At first, they do not refer to the text or to their written answers, but they do check their answers against previous answers or the text. This provides immediate feedback about the amount of information they remember and lets students realize what information needs additional study. Or, students and teachers together decide whether the information that was forgotten is important and should be relearned.

If relearning is needed, there is evidence showing that merely rereading the text will not result in remembering (Pauk, 1973). What may occur during rereading is "seeing" already-known information. What is needed after a first reading is a different approach to the same information.

Content-area texts are not meant to be the singular source of students' learning. There are limitations to the effectiveness of texts as informational resources. The technique suggested here, the SQ3R procedure, helps students become proficient independent readers. Yet, because of factors within students, the reading materials, or the situations in which the reading acts are undertaken, the technique may not be successful at a particular time. Other learning and teaching procedures should then be sought and used.

Reciprocal Teaching

Reciprocal teaching is a technique that incorporates self-questioning, summarizing, predicting, and teacher modeling. It is taught to students through an interactive dialogue (Palincsar, 1984). (Strategies for self-questioning and for teacher modeling are in the Chapter 4 sections, "Strategies for Teacher and Student Questioning" and "Fostering Student Collaboration During Guided

Reading." Those for predicting are in Chapter 5, "Prediction Strategies" and "Survey–Question–Read–Recite–Review." Strategies for summarizing are in Chapter 5, "Semantic Organizers," and this chapter, "Strategies for Organizing Information" and "Activities for Content-Area Reading.")

After students are familiar with the four activities of reciprocal teaching, the technique is taught (Palincsar, 1984):

1. Students are given an expository passage.
2. The teacher calls attention to the title and asks for predictions based on the title.
3. A segment of the passage is assigned for reading and the teacher tells students that he or she will lead the discussion. The teacher also explains that after a few lessons, one of the students will be assigned the role of teacher.
4. The students silently read the passage segment.
5. The teacher asks a question (see step 2), summarizes, and answers the question.
6. The teacher guides students to complete questioning, predicting, and summarizing through the remainder of the passage. Students are prompted with: "What question do you think a teacher might ask?"; instructed with: "Remember a summary is a shortened version; it doesn't include a lot of detail."; redirected with: "If you're having a hard time thinking of a question, why don't you summarize first?"; and encouraged with: "Who can help us out with this one?"
7. Using the fish-bowl procedure, other students in the class are asked to comment on the lesson.
8. After students become teachers, the adult teacher gives praise and feedback specific to the student teacher's participation, such as: "You asked that question well; it was clear what information you wanted,"; and models with: "A question I might have asked would be . . .," or "I would summarize by saying . . . ."

ACTIVITIES FOR CONTENT-AREA READING

The activities discussed in Chapter 4 for developing questioning strategies, in Chapter 5 for developing sentence- and paragraph-reading strategies, and in Chapter 6 for developing general vocabularies, contextual signals, and dictionary/thesaurus usage are continued and extended for content-area reading. Students need many opportunities to independently use their strategies in narrative and expository reading materials. In addition, the teacher can do the following:

- Extend the use of the SQ3R procedure to reading word problems in mathematics (Maffei, 1973). The extended SQ3R procedure would have the following implementation:

Survey.   Skim the word problem and locate and list any unknown words.

Question.   Write a direct question about the problem.

Read.   Read the problem and list all the word facts in a logical order.

Reflect.   Translate all the word facts into number facts.

Rewrite and solve.   Write the word problem as a mathematics problem and solve it.

Review.   Reread the word problem, putting the answer into the correct statement.

- Provide time for the translation of diagrammatic information into standard English sentences. At the beginning, students can match sentences to the appropriate diagrams. As they become proficient at interpreting visual displays, they can create their own sentences. For example, give students an illustration and three sentences from which they are to select the one describing the ideas that match the drawing.

    This activity can be extended for use with maps or incidental or decorative illustrations. Have students select information from the passage that comes closest to explaining the illustration. Or have them write a paragraph or explain to another student the information given in the map or illustration.

- Provide opportunities for using information learned in one content area in other situations. Have students create stories, plays, poems, radio broadcasts, or murals in which the content information is used. For example, after studying erosion in science, have students act out situations in which they assume the roles of town engineers planning the construction of a new road in a hilly section of town. Or, after studying Latin American customs and cultures, have students play travel agents preparing a tour group for a visit to Latin America.

    Students may observe models for this activity by reading stories and books in which content information is important to the plot. For example, Aileen Fisher's

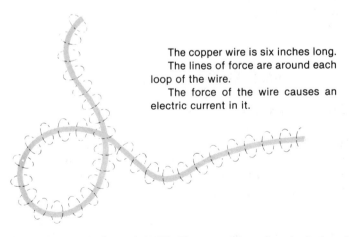

The copper wire is six inches long.
The lines of force are around each loop of the wire.
The force of the wire causes an electric current in it.

Source: Brewer, A. C., et al. (1972). *Elementary science: Learning by investigating.* Chicago: Rand McNally, p. 98.

Summer of Little Rain might be read after studying about weather, or Patricia Lee Gauch's *This Time, Tempe Wick?* could be read after studying the Revolutionary War.

- Provide chances for students to relate the lives of interesting or important individuals to the study of a topic. Have them read and discuss biographies of individuals who either contributed to a topic or were greatly influenced by it. For example, during a study of plants, the lives of Heinz, Booker T. Washington, Burbank and others could be studied and their contributions explored.

- Have students explore the everyday application of content-area concepts. For example, during a science unit on machines, they could read repair manuals and "how-to-fix-it" books, or during social studies units, travel books. Or, as one teacher did, take students into local shops in the community to learn the practical applications of science (*New York Times*, 1987). Have students ask managers of beauty salons, plumbing stores, ice cream parlors, and other businesses about the scientific techniques that apply in each business. Have students keep records of their observations, organize the information, and prepare a report on their findings.

- Use children's literature as an aid in content-area instruction. Trade books can be effectively used to make complex ideas clear, to illustrate many practical ideas of the content areas, to encourage and stimulate expression in speaking and writing, and to foster the growth of vocabulary. There are many informational books written about the physical world, people and places, history, and mathematics that can be used to extend students' knowledge and understanding. After acquiring the background through class exercises, students will have the necessary prerequisites for undertaking independent reading of many more books.

- Provide students with simulation strategies that approximate what a reader does when reading independently (Herber & Nelson, 1975). This gives them direct instruction in reading with good understanding. To begin, read a passage and ask questions about the author's major ideas. Then, use the answers to the questions to make up a set of exercises:

  - The first set consists of several statements to which students respond as well as the pages and paragraphs where information to support or refute those statements can be found. Students should indicate whether they agree or disagree with the exercise statements.
  - The next set is made up of a set of statements similar to those in the preceding set, but the teacher does not tell students where additional information may be found.
  - he third set provides questions to be answered as well as where pertinent information can be found.
  - In this set of exercises, the questions have no references to pages or paragraphs.
  - When students are able to do the preceding exercise, give them a reading assignment in which they are required to create their own questions and answers.
  - When they are able to read the content-area text at their level, have them read a passage and make their own statements of concepts and ideas.

- Provide exercises that lead to an understanding of the relationship between standard English sentences and mathematical sentences. Research findings on reading in mathematics underscore the importance of a particular language factor—verbal reading ability (Aiken, 1972). The exercises should promote student understanding of the mathematical sentence as an English sentence by providing examples of mathematical structures that parallel English structures (Lacey & Weil, 1975). First, establish that the mathematical sentence is read from left to right. Then teach basic symbol and word associations:

and   is synonymous with *plus*

is   is synonymous with *equals*

=   is the equivalent of *is*, and *these are the same number of things*

+   means *and, increased by, plus*

−   means *minus, subtract, decreased by, diminished by*

≠   means *is not equal to*

>   means *is greater than*

<   means *is less than*

×   means *times, product, multiplied by*

÷   means *quotient, divided by, ratio*

Using these symbol and word associations, have students

- read $7 + 4 = 11$ as "seven and four is eleven";
- read "seven plus four is eleven" and write $7 + 4 = 11$; and
- compose transformations of the algorithm: Seven added to four equals eleven, and adding seven and four is eleven.

Follow this with sentences about subtraction, multiplication, and division. Compound sentences can be written after some other symbols are learned:

∨   means the conjunction *and*

∧   means the disjunction *or*

≥   means *is greater than or equal to*

≤   means *is less than or equal to*

≮   means *is not less than*

≯   means *is not greater than*

Sample sentences might be:

Six plus ten is less than twenty, $6 + 10 < 20$
and   ∨
twelve plus ten is greater than four. $12 + 10 > 4$

Nine minus one is not equal to two, $9 - 1 \neq 2$
or $\wedge$
nine plus two is greater than ten. $9 + 2 > 10$

- Extend students' abilities to read graphics. Have them make accurate associations between diagrams and real events. Give them a diagram to read showing the energy/force interaction between two objects. Have them relate the event to a real-life situation—a bat hitting a ball, two cars colliding, or a dish breaking on a hard floor.

  Or, have students link an image with language to describe the image. Using a representation drawing of an eye indicating how an object is imaged on the retina, have students label the parts of the illustration.

  Also, give students opportunities to transpose information in illustrations into sentences—oral and written. For example, after examining a map showing the "New World" areas claimed by European countries around 1700, model for them by explaining, "The color *orange* shows the land claimed by the government of France. This area is in the middle of what is now the United States and goes from where the Mississippi River enters the Gulf of Mexico northward to Canada. It includes the areas around the Mississippi River, the Arkansas River, the Missouri River, the Ohio River, and the St. Lawrence River."

- Use an interactive-strategies approach to content reading (Haggard, 1985). The three aspects of this activity are the following.

Content-directed reading–thinking activity

- Students, working with partners, list everything they know about a general topic (7–8 minutes).
- The teacher announces the focus of the reading assignment.
- Students predict which ideas they have listed will appear in the reading. New ideas are added to the list (2–3 minutes).
- Students read the assignment, noting how well they predicted.

Group mapping activity

- Students individually map (semantically organize) their interpretation of the text without referring to the reading (10 minutes).
- Partners share maps and help each other with organization and content.
- The teacher leads group map sharing and follow-up discussion.

Vocabulary self-collection activity

- Students and teacher choose words from the assignment they believe the class should learn. Each team gives one word.
- The teacher leads the discussion as words are defined.
- The teacher and students choose the class vocabulary list from the pool of words.
- Students record the words and definitions. Words not chosen are added to personal lists or a general file.
- Students put the vocabulary words on maps.
- The teacher leads a final discussion and makes appropriate assignments for follow-up activities.

■ Have students graphically represent text patterns (Horowitz, 1985b). For example,

time order	$A \text{ (event)} + B + C = [\text{ idea }]$
effect–cause	$A \rightarrow B \rightarrow C \rightarrow \ldots$
problem–solution	$[\text{problem}] \begin{array}{l} \rightarrow S1 \\ \rightarrow S2 \ldots, \text{ or} \end{array}$
	$\begin{array}{l} [\text{ P1 }] \rightarrow \\ [\text{ P2 }] \rightarrow \end{array} [\text{ solution }]$

■ Use a listen–read–discuss model (Manzo, 1985). Have students listen to a lecture about a topic, then read the information in their text. Lead a discussion about the topic. During the discussion, ask the following questions:

  ■ What did you understand best from what you heard and read?
  ■ What did you understand least well from what you heard and read?
  ■ What questions or thoughts did this lesson raise in your mind about reading and learning or about other things?

STRATEGIES FOR LOCATING INFORMATION AND USING REFERENCE MATERIALS

Fully independent readers use many types of reading materials for obtaining information. The strategies discussed in this section are those needed to locate information (1) in books, (2) in libraries, (3) in encyclopedias, and (4) on maps, globes, and atlases. In some of the literature on reading in the content areas, these strategies are called *study skills*. In other places they are labeled *functional reading skills*. It does not matter what name they are given however; they are prerequisites for independent, lifelong self-instruction.

These strategies are discussed without reference to a specific grade level; however, they represent the locational and reference strategies that students need by the end of elementary and middle school. Instruction should be given after determining both the reading demands placed on students by the instructional materials being used and students' abilities to meet those demands.

Locating Information in Books

Beginning with their first contact with books, students learn the purpose of the various parts of a book as well as procedures for using those parts to locate information. Specifically, students learn to use

1. The title page to obtain information about the author, illustrator, and publisher of the book.
2. The table of contents to locate topics and general areas of information.

3. The index to locate specific facts or details.
4. The introduction, preface, and foreword to find out both the author's purpose for writing the text and the basic framework of the book.
5. The copyright page to obtain information about the relevance or recency of the information in the book.
6. The glossary for the definitions of words as used by the author.
7. The bibliography to locate other sources of information on the topic or to check the author's source of information.
8. The appendix to obtain supplementary information about the topic.

In addition, authors use signaling devices to identify important information. Such signaling devices are italicized words or boldface type, colored type, brackets, underlining, and colored or shaded boxes around sentences or whole paragraphs. A careful analysis of various book formats shows other techniques that authors and publishers use to help readers locate and identify information.

Locating Information in Libraries

Libraries are organized so that information may be easily found. Once knowing how to use a library is mastered, that knowledge is always useful. Some people erroneously think the purpose of a library is to store information. Museums are the storehouses of information; libraries are the circulators of information.

To effectively locate and use the information in a library, students need strategies for using the following:

The card catalog.   The card catalog lists all books in the library. From the catalog it is possible to locate a book if the author, the title, or the subject area is known. Some libraries use separate file drawers for each of the three references, but most school libraries mix the three types of cards. The strategies students need for using card catalogs are

- identifying the author's name;
- identifying the book's title;
- identifying the subject heading; and
- understanding the library classification code.

The library arrangement.   Most school libraries use the Dewey decimal classification scheme to arrange and locate their books. Table 7-1 shows the two most popular classification schemes—the Dewey decimal and the Library of Congress. Most school and public libraries, however, do not catalog popular fiction or biographies by the Dewey decimal system. General fiction is arranged according to the first letter of the author's last name, and biographies are arranged according to the first initial of the biography's subject, preceded by the letter *B.*

TABLE 7–1
Library System Classifications

The Dewey Decimal Classification			
000	General Works	500	Pure Science
100	Philosophy	600	Technology
200	Religion	700	The Arts
300	Social Sciences	800	Literature
400	Language	900	History

The Library of Congress Classification			
A	General Works—Polygraphy	M	Music
B	Philosophy—Religion	N	Fine Arts
C	History—Auxiliary Sciences	P	Language and Literature
D	History and Topography (except America)	Q	Science
		R	Medicine
E–F	America	S	Agriculture—Plant and Animal Industry
G	Geography—Anthropology		
H	Social Sciences	T	Technology
J	Political Science	U	Military Science
K	Law	V	Naval Science
L	Education	Z	Bibliography and Library Science

Special collections.   Libraries have pamphlets and pictures arranged alphabetically according to topic. In addition, libraries have record and filmstrip collections and magazines. Older students can learn to use the *Reader's Guide to Periodical Literature* to locate information in the magazine collection.

Strategies for Using the Encyclopedia

The encyclopedia is an excellent source of information about a wide range of topics. It is also sometimes thought that the encyclopedia is an irrefutable source. A commonly heard statement is, "It must be right . . . I read it in the encyclopedia." Although the encyclopedia might look more authoritative than other written works do, it can, of course, be in error. The "facts" about the same event may be recorded differently in different encyclopedias (Wehmeyer, 1975). Students need to note and examine contradictions when encountered, and they should not accept information as true just because it is in an encyclopedia.

Before using an encyclopedia, students must understand (1) the type of information contained in it, (2) the purposes for which the information has been collected, and (3) the relative value of the information.

To find and use the information in an encyclopedia, students need strategies for using

- the encyclopedia index;
- the information on the spine of each volume;
- the guide words;
- the cross-references;
- the boldface type and parentheses used in the main entries; and
- the bibliographies at the ends of articles.

Although encyclopedias are scholarly attempts at presenting information concisely, they do have the following limitations:

1. The size and scope of encyclopedias do not allow them to have current information on all topics. This is especially true in natural and political science, in which essential data change rapidly.
2. Some encyclopedias are cognitively and linguistically too demanding for children in the lower grades.

These limitations are overcome by some encyclopedia publishers. For example, specialized, limited-scope scientific encyclopedias are available. Many publishers also market limited-scope encyclopedia series that are written especially for young children. These child-oriented encyclopedias are written in a style and format approximating that found in many elementary content-area textbooks. The same guidelines for judging the considerateness of a textbook are used for judging the readability of an encyclopedia.

Strategies for Locating Information on Maps

Maps are representations of the earth's physical features. The type of representation that most closely approximates the earth is the globe. However, it would not be practical to use globes for all the different kinds of information that maps can provide. Therefore, a prerequisite for using maps is understanding the element of distortion that occurs when maps are drawn. The distortion is the greatest on maps that show the location of many features of the earth's surface. The greatest distortion occurs on world maps, the least on maps of extremely small areas of the earth.

To find and use the information found on maps and globes, students need strategies for using the following:

Map projections. The two most common map projections used in elementary content-area texts and school atlases are the Mercator projection and the polar projection. To develop true perspective of the relative size, shape, and placement of geographical positions, the amount and type of distortion created by each projection should be understood.

Different types of maps.   The purposes of physical or relief maps, political maps, and certain special maps need to be understood as well as the features that make each map different.

Map symbols.   Map makers use standard symbols for indicating geographic locations (lakes, cities, rivers, highways, political boundaries, and direction).

Map colorations.   Understanding the relationship between map color and actual land color is essential to map use. Although some colors on physical maps relate to actual land formations—blue for water, green and brown for landforms—the colors on political and special-purpose maps have no relationship to the concepts they represent.

Scales of distance.   Not only are maps not representative of the real distances found on earth, but distance scales and sizes differ from one map to another.

Map legends.   Most maps provide a legend explaining symbols, color, and scale.

STRATEGIES FOR READING THE NEWSPAPER

Newspapers fit into any school's content-area reading program. They are a current, constant source of information about events. In addition, they can fit a wide range of reading abilities—something in almost every newspaper can be read by elementary and middle-school students.

Almost any newspaper can be used for instruction, but it is probably best to use one familiar to students that they will also read independently. Once the basic strategies for reading newspapers are learned, the same information can be compared in two or more newspapers.

The following are strategies for finding and using information in newspapers.

Newspaper content.   Every newspaper has a variety of information, such as

- news stories, which are factual, interpretive, or speculative;
- human interest stories;
- opinion articles, which are either editorials or essays signed by columnists;
- sports stories;
- business and finance articles;
- entertainment articles, news, reviews, time tables;
- comics and puzzles;
- weather reports and forecasts;
- advertisements; and
- obituaries.

Content organization. Each newspaper organizes its contents in a particular manner that remains constant over a period of time. Familiarity with a newspaper's organization facilitates locating information on a particular topic.

News and feature article organization. News stories are written with the most current news at the beginning of the article. The introductory paragraph usually has answers to the five Ws: who, what, when, where, and why. By reading further into an article, information that appeared in earlier stories can be found. Feature stories and opinion articles are written in a more narrative style.

The newspaper is a source of information that can be used for developing skills and strategies in all content areas. Words related to social studies and science topics can be found daily in the newspaper. Most important, students meet these words in a context that clarifies their meanings. Photographs, maps, charts, and diagrams are used extensively in newspapers and supplement the graphic displays in content-area textbooks. Human interest stories, reviews, opinion articles, and political cartoons show how the "facts" found in textbooks and encyclopedias are used by different people to influence others in their thinking. And, certain newspaper sections, such as advertisements; radio, TV, and movie schedules; the business pages; and the sports sections provide examples of the utility of arithmetic skills in students' daily activities.

ACTIVITIES FOR DEVELOPING NEWSPAPER-READING STRATEGIES

The following strategies develop effective newspaper reading at different grade levels. If funds are available, each student should daily get a copy of a newspaper. (This is not unreasonable since every student could receive a newspaper for an entire month for the cost of a typical workbook.)

- Develop a sense of the newspaper's content. Have students work in small teams to list the different kinds of information found in a newspaper. This activity can be modified to meet the reading abilities of a wide range of students. Younger students can name the types of information while the teacher records them on the chalkboard or a permanent chart. Older students can make their own lists.

- Develop a sense of current events. Each day have students locate news articles of local, national, and international concern. This activity may be coordinated with map study by marking on a class map the locale of each story.

- Develop a sense of a news story's organization. Have students use their knowledge of sentence information to figure out how news writers use the same signals as do other writers for the location of information.

- Develop a sense of headline writing. Use headlines from several stories and have students find the information in each story that is the basis for the headline. Extend this activity to develop a sense of figurative language, puns, and connotations in headline writing. Have students write headlines for stories or rewrite the headlines of newspaper stories.

- Develop a sense of purposeful letter writing. Have students select an item from the newspaper—a job advertisement, an editorial, a mail order ad—and write a letter in response to that item. When appropriate, have them mail their letters.

- Develop a sense of the newspaper as a continuous resource and reference. Give students a topic study sheet. The topic should be current and reported on daily for an extended period. Such topics deal with political or social issues or a sports series. The format and content of the study sheet help students draw conclusions about the topic. The guide in Figure 7–3 is a model that can be modified to meet students' abilities.

- Develop an understanding of the use of propaganda techniques. Using advertisements first and moving to articles of familiar stories and events, have students analyze any propaganda techniques. Have them try to determine, by comparing the product to the advertisement (whenever possible) or by comparing several articles written about the same event or topic, whether propaganda techniques are used and the extent to which they influence thinking.

- Develop an interest in the biographies of interesting or important people. By reading newspaper feature stories and obituaries, students can learn to appreciate the contributions of various people to the topics they are studying in the content areas. If a biography or autobiography exists about a person, have students compare the person's life as portrayed in books, feature stories, and obituaries.

Topic: SOCIAL ISSUES | 21

COMIC STRIP: ROLE ANALYSIS

Select 4 or 5 comic strips from your local paper. Analyze them according to the criteria below for at least a 4-week period. Write a report which summarizes your findings, indicating what the comic strips are saying about the "American way" of life.

Occupations
1. What occupations do the male characters have?
2. What occupations do the female characters have?
3. Keep a list of the main characters for whom **no** occupation is mentioned.
4. If children or teenagers discuss future occupations, which jobs are boys interested in? girls?

Environment
1. What is the location of the action of each comic strip? (home, office, parks, city streets, etc.)
2. In which of the above settings do women most often appear? In which settings do men most often appear?
3. In "home" or "family" settings, what activities are men engaged in? women?

Dialogue
1. What topics are discussed in each comic strip (politics, education, the home and the family, etc.?)
2. What can you tell about the attitudes of the characters towards each other from the dialogue?
3. Who discusses what? (that is, can you make any generalizations about topics that women discuss? that men discuss? teenagers?)

FIGURE 7–3
Topic Study Sheet: Newspapers

Source: *The Associated Press Newspaper Reading Skills Development Program.* Project File #21. (1974). New York: AP Newsfeatures.

STRATEGIES FOR DEVELOPING FUNCTIONAL LITERACY

The purpose of schools is to prepare young people for survival in general society. To some people, this means learning, in addition to reading, writing, and arithmetic, the "basics" of knowledge presented in the content areas of science, social studies, and mathematics. Many of these people also believe that functional skills are to be learned by students who do not have the competencies for learning information presented in the content areas.

Functional literacy, however, is for all students—those performing in a superior manner in school and those having learning problems. It is not an either/or instructional decision. Functional literacy skills are needed for living and working in our highly industrialized society. Sophisticated technology and complex laws and regulations require us to be able to deal with a great variety of printed matter, not all of which reads like a book.

What is meant by **functional literacy?** A general definition is the ability to use certain skills and knowledge with the level of competence needed for meeting the requirements of adult living. *Functional* means the ability to read or write. This is determined in part by what is read or is written. Within this concept, there is no general level of literacy to be attained by all people. The level and degree of competence needed in a particular situation are different depending on the person and the purpose(s) for performing the reading or writing task.

Functional reading differs from general reading. General reading is described and discussed throughout the major portion of this text and its purpose is mainly for informing or entertaining. Although reading is an active search for meaning, the reader's usual overt response during and after general reading is passive. There is no immediate action to be taken because the reader acquires information and concepts for a delayed response. Functional reading, on the other hand, is done with an action in mind. There is usually an immediate need for action resulting from the active search for meaning, and the reader makes an active, overt response as a result of the reading situation.

General and functional reading tasks also differ in their organization and format. General reading material is usually organized in paragraph form. On the surface, each piece of general reading appears similar. But functional materials vary noticeably in their organization, style, and format. Even within a group or type of functional material there is great variety, as can be seen by comparing a classified want ad, a telephone directory ad (Yellow Pages), and a department store advertisement.

Results of research conducted as part of the Adult Performance Level Project show there are many kinds of literacy tasks (Northcut et al., 1975). Literacy, in its broadest sense, is possessing all the skills needed to perform in all aspects of society. Table 7–2 contains a matrix showing the interaction of society's skills and aspects.

The literacy skills areas are reading, writing, identification of facts and terms, computation, and problem solving. The first three areas deal with understanding and using written materials. "Writing" means the ability to handle everyday writing. "Identification of facts and terms" is recognizing words in the contexts of society (on doors, signs, maps, labels, etc.). "Computation" is more than performing the four functions—it is understanding daily-living arithmetic problems and manipulating numerical quantities. "Problem solving" is knowing appropriate and alternative solutions to problems of everyday living (schemas).

The aspects of society in which functional tasks are performed are community resources, occupational knowledge, consumer economics, health, and government and law. "Community resources" include recreational activities, transportation facilities, obtaining documents, and using informational sources. "Occupational knowledge" includes knowing job requirements, obtaining vocational counseling, selecting jobs and occupations, and applying for and holding jobs.

TABLE 7–2
Sample Functional Literacy Skills Appropriate for Elementary and Intermediate School Students

Aspects of Society →	Community Resources	Occupational Knowledge	Consumer Economics	Health	Government and Law
Skills ↓					
Reading	reading a bus or train schedule	reading a poster calling for newspaper deliverers	reading a sales slip	reading a label on a medicine package	reading a ballot in school elections
Writing	writing a letter for information about recreational facilities	completing an application for a summer camp job	writing for a magazine subscription	answering questions on a medical form	writing rules for a club
Identification of Facts/ Terms	knowing what *daylight savings time* is	knowing the difference between a job and an occupation	knowing what propaganda is	knowing what the different hospital services are	knowing the meaning of *mayor, governor*
Computation					
Problem Solving					

"Consumer economics" includes knowing and demonstrating an understanding of purchasing practices. "Health" includes understanding the principles and practices that lead to mental and physical health. "Government and law" includes understanding the structure of government and how the functions of the legal systems delineate the rights and obligations of all citizens.

Elementary and middle-school students encounter situations requiring functional literacy. The materials in these situations requiring the skills of functional reading, writing, and identification of terms are the following:

Advertisements.   The purposes of these are to identify something that is available: classified ads for a job, a product or item, or a service.

Blanks and forms.   The purpose of these is to file information for obtaining a product or service.

Lists.   These are sources of information that are needed to do another task.

Directions.   These provide instructions for specific products and services.

Legal documents.   The purpose of a legal document varies with the specific document. Some are for immediate response—tickets and tax statements—and others are for delayed response or storage of information—wills and birth certificates.

Visuals.   The purposes of visuals are to clearly identify how information from different areas is related and to draw attention to some needed information. These include transit maps, store and office signs, and street and highway designations.

Schedules.   These put information into time sequences and allow for planning immediate and future responses or actions.

There are some general guidelines for teaching the reading and writing of functional literacy materials in all classes and at all levels of literacy.

1. Use real materials. Students need instruction on dealing with materials that are met in real-life situations. The use of watered-down or altered materials gives students a false sense of the demands of life or the demands of survival reading and writing.
2. Teach the purpose for doing each functional task.
3. Point out the contrasting features of general and functional reading materials.
4. Teach the specialized vocabulary. Each type of functional material has concepts and terms that appear consistently. Identify them for learning.
5. Base instruction on performance. Involving students in concrete experiences with functional materials is the key to instruction and learning.
6. Use problem-solving situations. All communication skills are learned in situations where students have a reason for receiving and sending ideas. These are role-playing situations in which the students learn the schema of the situation and the verbal skills for acting them out.
7. Extend the activities into real life. Students recognize their abilities as they use their skills outside of school.

There are many ways to bring functional tasks into the classroom. In each case, the material, its content, specific tasks, and purposes must be appropriate to students' ages, background, and language and thinking abilities.

In language arts or English instruction, use advertising, legal writing, forms and applications, telephone techniques, resumé writing, catalog reading, and order writing.

In social studies instruction, use immigration documents, transportation, occupations in social fields, contracts, city resources, money and money substitutes, and financial services.

In mathematics instruction, use occupations in related fields, time zones, measurements, computation of salaries and benefits, budgeting, visuals showing proportions, and inflation.

In science instruction, use consumer products, packaging, applications for medical help, and safety measures.

Instruction in functional literacy tasks helps develop competence in using real-life materials and provides students with practice in actual functional situations. It gives them problems that they can relate and react to. The goal of functional literacy instruction is to develop realistic alternatives in real situations.

STRATEGIES FOR ORGANIZING INFORMATION

Once students locate information, it may be necessary to put that information in an organized form. When students work on projects or write reports, they often must take notes or create outlines. The strategies for organizing information develop as students learn about different writing patterns; however, unless their purpose for organizing information is real and relevant, activities in organizing may be meaningless tasks. The strategies for organizing information discussed in this section supplement the presentation of semantic organizers in Chapter 5.

A common form of organizing information is the outline. In elementary and middle school instruction, the outline can take different forms. Sometimes a simple list is sufficient. At other times a more detailed outline with multiple levels is needed. Whatever form is used, students must know the relationship between it and the writing pattern from which the information is obtained.

In many instructional materials, outlining is used exclusively with paragraphs written in the generalization pattern (see Chapter 5). However, other patterns can, and should, be used to illustrate the uses of outlining. These patterns include topic development, comparison and contrast, enumeration, and classification.

An outline is not the only way in which information can be organized. Depending on the purposes for organizing the information, the uses to which the information will be put, and the amounts of information to be recorded, other means for organizing information are semantic organizers, charts, graphs, time lines, and diagrams.

For example, if the learner's attention is on the general categories of behavior observed in zoo animals, then the outline form may be appropriate. But if students' attention is on the differences or similarities among the behaviors of various animals, then a chart might be more appropriate for recording and organizing information.

Some behaviors seen in zoo animals are:
1. *the ways they move*
2. *the sounds they make*
3. *the ways they eat*
4. *the ways they protect themselves when they rest and when they move about*

Strategies for Using Outlines

The concept of outlining can be introduced by a simple listing of information about a topic. For example:

Materials Needed to Test Minerals

set of minerals	piece of granite
hand lens	magnet
scissors	steel file
piece of glass	piece of tile
penny	

More complex outlines result from using paragraph patterns to identify important ideas of the author. For example, in the following paragraphs, a cause-and-effect relationship is established. A useful outline would emphasize that pattern.

Water Pollution

Many substances are dumped into rivers, lakes, and oceans. Factories are often built near water for just that reason. Most towns dump untreated or only partly treated sewage into the water. Drains and toilets at home and school carry away many different wastes.

Polluted water affects ecosystems in several ways. Some wastes are poisonous. They kill or injure plants and animals in the water. People and other animals who drink or swim in polluted water can also get sick.

Some wastes have a different effect. Wastes from food and paper mills, for example, are food for decomposers. The decomposers in the water digest the wastes. The problem is that digesting wastes uses up the oxygen in the water. A polluted river or lake can get very low in oxygen. Then fish and other animals in the water die, just as you would if you could not breathe.

Sewage is food for decomposers too. It also acts as a fertilizer. It makes plants in the water grow and multiply. A polluted lake can end up looking like a bowl of thick pea soup. As the plants die, they provide more food for the decomposers. The oxygen shortage gets even worse.

Water pollution problems can be lessened. Wastes can be treated before they enter our waters. Some wastes can be kept entirely out of the water. It costs a lot of money and energy to prevent water pollution. And

Water Pollution

Source of pollution	Effect of pollution
1. poisonous wastes	1. kill or injure plants and animals; people and animals get sick
2. digesting wastes	2. use up oxygen in the water; fish and other animals die.
3. sewage	3. acts as fertilizer; makes plants grow too thickly in water; uses up oxygen.

people have to want to keep the environment as clean and healthy as possible. (Berger et al., Level 6, 1979, pp. 272-275)

After students understand the relationships between major concepts and supporting concepts, the formal structure of an outline may be introduced. The most common outline form is as follows:

Title
I. Major concept
    A. Supporting concept
    B. Supporting concept
II. Major concept
    A. Supporting concept
    B. Supporting concept

Developing Outlining Strategies

The concept of outlining should be introduced in stages. The first stage helps students develop a sense of the relationship between a main concept and supporting concepts. The second stage extends this by requiring students to find appropriate supporting concepts. In the third stage, students use the outline form and fill in both the major concept and supporting concepts.

Stage 1: Relationship between Main and Supporting Concepts
Provide students with a paragraph and a list of the major and supporting concepts. After students read the paragraph and identify the paragraph pattern, have them complete the skeleton outline. For example,

> Human beings get energy from carbohydrates and fats. When you eat grains such as rice and wheat, you get carbohydrates. Starchy roots like potatoes or cassava also provide carbohydrates. Cassava is the main food in parts of Africa.
>
> Sugar is another source of carbohydrates. The white stuff you sprinkle on cereal comes from sugar cane or sugar beets. But you also get sugar from many other foods. For example, raisins, honey, and even onions give you sugar.
>
> Fats have the highest energy value. Americans get most of their fats from meat, cream, butter, margarine, and nuts. In the body, fats are changed to fatty tissue. About 15 per cent of a healthy body is fatty tissue. It helps keep you warm and protects delicate parts of the body. (Branson, 1980, p. 106)

I. _____

   A. _____

   B. _____

Human energy comes from foods with carbohydrates.
Sources of human energy are found in foods.
Human energy comes from foods with fats.

Stage 2: Finding Appropriate Supporting Concepts
Provide students with a paragraph and a partially completed outline. After they read the paragraph and identify its pattern, have them complete the outline. For example,

> Nomads depend on their animals for almost everything they need. How does this remind you of the Plains Indians and the buffalo? The animals give good milk, from which tasty cheese can then be made. The desert people shear the hair of their goats and camels. Then they weave clothes or blankets or tents. The nomads sleep on rugs made of sheep wool. When a group of nomads is ready to move, they pack up all their belongings and load them on their camels. Do you think nomads have a lot of things to pack? Could your family pack all their belongings and load them on an animal? Why or why not? (Davis et al., 1971, p. 170)

I. Nomads depend on their animals for their needs.

   A. _____

   B. _____

   C. _____

Stage 3: Locating Major and Supporting Concepts
Provide students with a paragraph and a skeleton outline of the major and supporting concepts. After reading the paragraph and identifying its pattern, have students complete the outline. For example,

> Crabgrass does not need seeds to produce new plants. If you try to pull up crabgrass, some roots break off and stay in the ground. Each piece of root can produce a new plant. When people try to get rid of crabgrass by pulling it up, they often cause more plants to grow. If a lawnmower cuts crabgrass, some of the cut up stems can root and produce more crabgrass plants. (Berger et al., Level 6, 1979, p. 45)

I. _____
  A. _____
  B. _____

Develop the strategies for organizing information over an extended period. Encourage students to experiment with different forms of organizing information. The logic of organizing results from emulating teacher models and attempting—sometimes unsuccessfully—to put information into a rational form. Through such opportunities to experiment, students will begin to understand, as they develop organizational strategies, what patterns are suited for particular kinds of information. Allow students to compare outline forms to semantic organizers as ways to organize information.

WRITING AS A STRATEGY FOR CONTENT-AREA UNDERSTANDING

Using information from the content areas in new and novel forms is a means for building on students' concepts and generalizations. All ideas from preceding chapters about using writing to develop understanding can be used in content areas, too. Students can use the information in relevant ways that enhance their understanding of the areas. **Relevancy** means using the ideas to solve problems that have an effect on their lives.

Using their postreading semantic organizers and outlines, have students write summary paragraphs. Because the organizers and outlines graphically present relationships among key ideas and details, students will gain additional understanding about text patterns. These paragraphs can become their study notes for examinations.

To create summary paragraphs, certain steps should be taken; the cognitive demands of summarization are dependent on the qualities of the text summarized, the educational setting, and the type of summary written (Hidi & Anderson, 1986). Two types of summaries are writer-based and reader-based. **Writer-based summaries** are those students create for themselves; these should be developed first. Begin with summarizing short segments of readable texts containing familiar ideas; keep the text present during summary writing to eliminate memory problems; have students use their writer-based summaries as notes and study tools. After students are comfortable with writer-based summaries, have them create **reader-based summaries,** summaries for which there is concern about audience—they are written for others to use.

Social studies and science textbooks that are high in concept density require active rather than passive reading. Teachers should teach students to focus on key ideas using a "dialectical journal." As students read, have them write out comments and questions about the author's ideas. These questions differ from those that are created for SQ3R or reciprocal questioning. In the dialectical journal, students write specific questions about the author's key ideas, examples and supporting ideas, and style of writing. The questions are not made before reading but are the products of students' thoughts as they are reading. For example, using the reading selection "What Is Culture?" (see p. 223), students' questions or comments during and after reading might be

During	After
How can you live a tool? (paragraph 2)	Culture is the way we live.
In two pictures the people aren't using language, they're pointing. (paragraph 4)	maby they're talking, not pointing.
Do all schools do the same thing? Even this one? (paragraph 6)	I don't think I know what institutions are.
It's bad luck to walk on cracks. (paragraph 7)	

Or, students use a reading log:

Before Reading:

What is the topic?_____

_____

What do I know about the topic?_____

_____

_____

What do I expect to find out about the topic?_____

_____

_____

During Reading:

What do I want to remember and talk about later? (List
words, phrases, pages or paragraph numbers, or questions)

_____

_____

After Reading:

How is the information organized?_____

_____

What signals are used to point out the organization?

_____

What new information do I know?_____

_____

_____

Other writing activities that help students build appropriate schemas about content-area topics are letter writing to real and imaginary people, fictitious journal keeping, and creating travel brochures. When studying explorers, students can act as sailors on the voyage and write home about their adventures. When studying the exploration of the Florida peninsula, they can report in a journal their periodic adventures, musings, and discoveries. The students can be lab technicians during important discoveries or pilots of the space shuttle. They can show their understanding of geography, climate, and resources in brochures for attracting tourists or industries to a specific city, state, or nation. Each of these activities requires students to reorganize information and transpose it into another form, adding to their growing schemas of the communicative process.

RESOURCES FOR THE TEACHER

Many instructional materials provide exercises in more than one content area. Whenever a resource has more emphasis in one area, it can still be a source of ideas for creating exercises in the other content areas.

Model Lessons. The following are sources of model lessons for developing reading and writing strategies in the content areas.

> Askov, E. N., & Kamm, K. (1982). *Study skills in the content areas.* Boston: Allyn & Bacon.
>
> Graham, K. G., & Robinson, H. A. (1984). *Study skills handbook: A guide for all teachers.* Newark, DE: International Reading Association.
>
> Readence, J. E., Bean, T. W., & Baldwin, R. S. (1984). *Content area reading: An integrated approach* (2nd ed.). Dubuque, IA: Kendall/Hunt Publishing.

The following are titles in the International Reading Association's Reading Aids Series (P.O. Box 8139, Newark, DE 19711):

> *Improving reading in science* (2nd ed.), by Judith Thelan, 1984.
>
> *Prereading activities for content area reading and learning,* by David W. Moore, John Readence, & Robert J. Rickelman, 1982.
>
> *Teaching information skills through project work,* by David Wray, 1985.
>
> *Teaching reading and mathematics,* by Richard A. Earle, 1976.
>
> *Using sports and physical education to strengthen reading skills,* by Lance M. Gentile, 1980.

Thematic Units. To develop content-area reading as a language experience, teachers can plan classroom lessons and activities using the available series of prepared thematic units. One source of such units are the curriculum bulletins prepared and distributed by city and state boards of education and departments of education.

Newspaper Reading. Instructional units for newspaper reading in the content areas may be obtained from the educational services departments of many local newspapers. The association of newspaper publishers, the International Reading Association, and local and state councils of IRA sponsor annual "Newspaper in Education" weeks. Local newspapers should be contacted. In addition, the following are resources for activities.

> Cheyney, A. B. (1984). *Teaching reading skills through the newspaper* (2nd ed.). Newark, DE: International Reading Association.
>
> McAuley, K. E. (1981). *The anatomy of a newspaper.* Washington, D. C.: American Newspaper Publishers Association Foundation.

The following contain specific instruction in reading and using newspapers. The kits can be used with the students' own newspapers.

> AP Newsfeatures. *The Associated Press newspaper reading skills development program,* Project File, 1974.

Newslab—Kit I: Grades 4–8; Kit II: Grades 5–9. Chicago: Science Research Associates.

Study Skills Kits. These materials deal with aspects of content-area reading. Each kit provides specific instruction and practice materials.

Study skills library (rev. ed.). Grades 3–9. "Science," "Social Studies," "Reference," and "Advanced Skills." Concord, CA: EDL Division/Arista Corporation. (These materials are also in workbook format.)

The next two kits offer instruction and practice in the strategies of organizing information.

Research lab, grades 4–8. Chicago: Science Research Associates.
Organizing and reporting skills kit, grades 4–6. Chicago: Science Research Associates.

The following has instruction in reading graphic displays.

Map and globe skills kit, grades 4–8. Chicago: Science Research Associates.

Study Skills Workbooks. The workbooks of basal reading series have activities for reading in the content areas. The following are workbooks prepared specifically for content-area reading strategies:

Be a better reader: Foundations A, B, C. Englewood Cliffs, NJ: Prentice-Hall.
Maps, charts, graphs for "Communities" (Level C); "Regions, Geography, Cultures" (Level D); "Our Country" (Level E); "The World" (Level F). Cleveland, OH: Modern Curriculum Press.
Success with maps, levels A–F. Jefferson City, MO: Scholastic.
Unlocking social studies skills: Map skills, graph skills, and research and thinking skills, for Middle and Junior High School. New York: Globe Book Company.

Functional Literacy. Not all books with functional reading and writing skills have actual representations of materials found in the real world. The following use fairly realistic materials:

Life skills reading books, grades 3–6. Palo Alto, CA: Creative Publications. (A series of books on making up favorite menus, using the telephone, using cereal boxes, reading menus, and using the Yellow Pages.)
Building life skills, levels D–F. Cleveland: Modern Curriculum Press. (A series of books dealing with functional reading in the home, neighborhood, community, and country.)

Content Reading Series. The following series aim at developing problem-solving and thinking strategies and at providing reinforcement of basic arithmetic computational facts. Each lesson is organized as a story problem.

Story problems, grades 3–6. *Techniques of Problem Solving* (TOPS), grades 3–12. *TOPS developmental workbooks* to accompany TOPS. Palo Alto, CA: Creative Publications.

One reading series, which focuses entirely on applying reading skills in content-area materials, has units at each grade level on general skills and reading social studies, mathematics, science, and literature.

Content readers, grades 1–6. New York: Harper & Row.

Nonfiction.   Some publishers produce series of nonfiction books and reference materials developed for the reading ability and cognitive maturity of elementary and middle-school students. Representing such series are

Let's-read-and-find-out science books. New York: Crowell Junior Books.

Milwaukee: Raintree Publishing Group.
The illustrated science encyclopedia, grades 3 and up.
Read about science, grades 2–3.
Reading about animals, grades 2–3.
A look inside, grades 4–12.
Machine world, grades 2–4.
Look at science, grades K–3.
Life cycles, grades 1–2.
Animals of the world, grades 4–9.
The money books, grades 2–6.

Washington, D. C.: National Geographic Educational Services.
Books for young explorers, grades K–3.
Books for world explorers, grades 3–8.

Schoolhouse world library, intermediate grades. Cleveland, OH: Schoolhouse Press.

DISCUSSION QUESTIONS AND ACTIVITIES

1. Explain what the following statement by Marksheffel (1969) means to you about reading in the content areas: "Reading has no subject matter of its own, whatever the reader reads is reading" (p. 129).

2. Explain what you think Shepard (1969) means by this statement: "The scientific method is as applicable to student development in the skill of reading science material as in learning scientific understandings" (p. 161).

3. Select a passage from a content-area textbook for middle grade–elementary students. Make reader guides that
   a. identify the major concept of the passage.
   b. show the location of the important generalizations.
   c. indicate the location of the important information supporting the major concept or generalizations.

4. Examine a chapter from three different texts of the same grade level on the same topic. Compare and contrast
   a. the organization and format of the chapter.
   b. the use of graphic displays and their relationship to the text.
   c. the style of language and vocabulary diversity.
   d. the amount of information following subheadings that does not relate directly to the subheadings.
   Rate three texts for their effectiveness in communicating with elementary or middle-school students and for their considerateness.

5. Select a content-area textbook and make a dialectical journal that students can use as a model for their own. Try out the procedures with students. What questions do

they ask? How do their questions show what they do or do not understand about the text?

6. Explain whether Gillham's comment (1986) applies to elementary or middle-school teachers.

> One explanation [for the difficulty teachers have in communicating the ideas of their subject in simple language] probably resides in the professional dichotomization of the teachers' role. On the one hand . . . teachers see themselves as subject specialists and on the other as professional communicators. For individual teachers the balance is different but the status of the subject specialists is almost always perceived as being higher than that of the communicator. (p. 5)

FURTHER READING

To develop reading strategies in elementary and middle-school content areas, teachers need a background in and understanding of the concepts and generalizations in each area. The following texts provide teachers with such information. The first is especially useful since it contains a series of "discovery lesson plans" that provide the basis for language experience units on a variety of topics across grade levels. Within each lesson, the thinking processes for both the lesson and the individual activities and questions are identified.

> Carin, A. A., & Sund, R. B. (1988). *Teaching science through discovery* (5th ed.). Columbus, OH: Merrill.
>
> Jarolimek, J. (1982). *Social studies in elementary education* (6th ed.). Riverside, NJ: Macmillan.
>
> Nichols, E. D., & Behr, M. J. (1982). *Elementary school mathematics and how to teach it*. New York: Holt, Rinehart and Winston.

Although the following were written for teaching secondary school students, many of their ideas can be adapted for elementary and intermediate students.

> Herber, H. L. (1978). *Teaching reading in content areas* (2nd ed.). Englewood Cliffs, NJ: Prentice-Hall.
>
> Laffey, J. (Ed.). (1972). *Reading in the content areas*. Newark, DE: International Reading Association.
>
> Thomas, E. L., & Robinson, H. A. (1982). *Improving reading in every class: A sourcebook for teachers* (3rd ed.). Boston: Allyn & Bacon.

The titles of the following explain their contents.

> Tchudi, S. N., & Tchudi, S. J. (1983). *Teaching writing in the content areas: Elementary school*, and *Teaching writing in the content areas: Middle school/junior high*. Washington, D. C.: National Education Association.

Journal articles in which instructional strategies are explained and illustrated are the following:

> Hollingsworth, C. R. (1985, March). Combining words and images: Photography in the classroom. *Journal of Reading, 28*(6), 556–559. (Describes how cameras, photos, writing, and reading are linked as tools to provide learners with methods to observe, explore, and respond to their environment.)

Horowitz, R. (1985, February). Text patterns, part I. *Journal of Reading, 28*(5), 448–454; and (1985, March). Text patterns, part II. *Journal of Reading, 28*(6), 534–542. (Explains and illustrates cues for recognizing and understanding text patterns.)

Kossack, S. (1986, December). Use the news: Comparison. *Journal of Reading, 30*(2), 266–269; and (1987, January). Use the news: Following directions. *Journal of Reading, 30*(3), 360–361. (Using the newspaper to teach text patterns.)

McGee, L. M., & Richgels, D. J. (1985, April). Teaching expository text structure to elementary students. *The Reading Teacher, 30*(8), 739–748.

Smith, R. J., & Dauer, V. L. (1984, November). A comprehension-monitoring strategy for reading content area materials. *Journal of Reading, 28*(2), 144–147. (A method for recording student cognitive and affective responses to text.)

Wong, J. A., & Au, K. H. (1985, March). The concept-text-application approach: Helping elementary students comprehend expository text. *The Reading Teacher, 38*(7), 612–618.

The next article contains a checklist for analyzing how content teachers are teaching reading strategies.

Shannon, A. J. (1984, November). Monitoring reading instruction in the content area. *Journal of Reading, 28*(2), 128–134.

Organizer

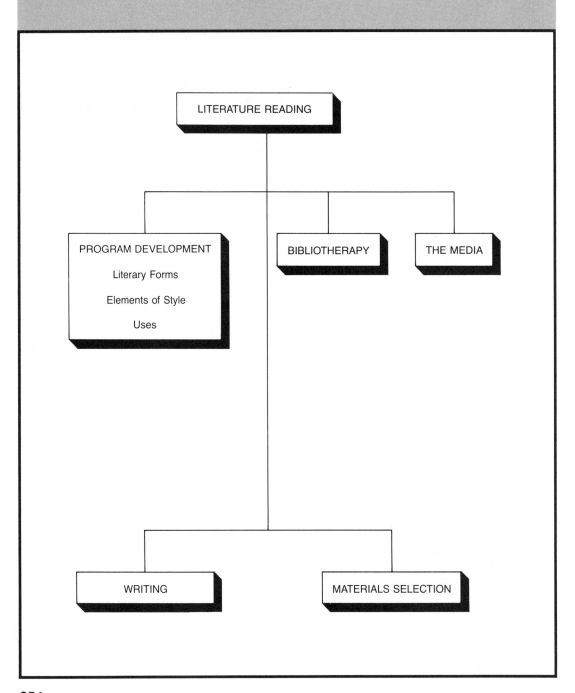

LITERATURE READING

PROGRAM DEVELOPMENT

Literary Forms

Elements of Style

Uses

BIBLIOTHERAPY

THE MEDIA

WRITING

MATERIALS SELECTION

Developing Strategies for Literature Reading

Focus Questions

- What is the purpose of a literature program in elementary school?
- What are the different types of literature available for students to read?
- How can literature of exceptional quality be identified?
- How can students and literature be brought together?
- What means are available to help teachers select literature for their students?

A successful literature-reading program creates an environment so filled with interesting activities involving books that students develop a lifelong desire to spend some of their time reading. Reading literature (as part of a whole-language reading program) leads students

to enjoy books and stories of all sorts;
to become acquainted with the literary heritage of their society;
to understand what constitutes "literature";
to apply knowledge gained from literature to their lives; and
to evaluate and appreciate literature and develop a personal taste from among the wide varieties and forms of literature (Huus, 1975).

What constitutes "literature" is difficult to state. To Huus (1975), it is classical or contemporary writing of such quality that children can understand what is read or heard. To Painter (1975), literature calls for power in using words and actions that lead to a well-knit plot, a strong theme that presents a basic truth, and realistic characters. It is seen as writing that reveals an author's knowledge of literary form and from which some wisdom may be apprehended. And to Lundsteen (1976), literature "portrays life and mind in language" and has three qualities: substance, sincerity, and memorable language (p. 181).

What literature is will probably never be defined to the satisfaction of everyone; yet, the three previous definitions have similarities. It may be best to consider literature not as something good or bad but as a continuum on which all authors' writings reside. At one end are the writings that are generally accepted as representing what is meant by literature. The aim of this chapter is to consider the elements that most will agree represent literary quality.

The United States and other English-speaking countries are melds of cultures. There is in these societies a growing appreciation of cultural pluralism. Literature programs in elementary and intermediate schools should aim at studying and developing a respect for the literary contributions of all cultural groups and for those of males and females in all aspects of society. The teaching of literature should seek to broaden and deepen students' experience. A reading program that does not explore literature reflecting the varying segments of society and that instead consistently promotes sexism and stereotyping through the literature it offers deprives all students of a full education.

Reading literature that treats society as pluralistic is congruent with the general purpose of any reading and writing program. A literature program is one way students can learn to empathize with the experiences of others and broaden their own experiences (Smith, 1960). Studying literature that reflects the diverse cultural groups in society can lead to an open-minded generation of students who accept the uniqueness and necessity of other life-styles (Jenkins, 1973). Reading the literature of other cultural groups leads to an understanding of the many similarities among those groups (Reed, 1976). By linking an understanding of linguistic sexism to reading the literature of diverse cultural groups, students can understand the nature of cultural values in general and the nature of their own values in particular.

For minority group students, the study of multiethnic literature is important for developing a healthy self-concept, which depends on a knowledge of and a sense of pride in one's family and cultural background along with a realization that one's own group is not the "center of the universe."

STRATEGIES FOR DEVELOPING A LITERATURE PROGRAM

To many, the teaching of literature may not be considered a critical part of the school reading program. A review of research on the teaching of literature reveals that it is used most often to supplement other subject areas or as material for teaching reading skills (Cullinan, 1974). However, without specific guidance, students will not develop a sense of reading literature for enjoyment or as a means of understanding the world. Teachers need to provide a planned, balanced program of instruction that offers the following components and that takes into account the difficulties of implementation (Huus, 1975).

Free choice of reading materials. Free choice is the opportunity to select, read, and even stop reading something selected without any intervention from an adult. A lack of materials or the structure of the schoolwide program may not always permit students to have a free choice of reading matter. Solving the problem of limited materials, however, may be easier than dealing with a situation in which students are restricted by a policy of required reading.

Daily reading aloud of a story or poem by the teacher. The teacher conveys to students a feeling that something is "good" not by extolling its merits, but by putting enthusiasm and feeling into reading it. The selection can be one that delights students because the author's words have magic, or it may be one that gives students new insights about some aspect of life. However, when reading aloud, teachers should be careful not to inject too much of their personalities into the story. Too often the focus of daily reading may be on the performance and not on the literature.

Guidance in finding a desired book. Through a teacher's or librarian's recommendation, students become aware of various books on a given topic or related to topics being studied in the content areas. The guidance a student gets from teachers and librarians depends on their experience and expertise.

Study of a common element through topical units.   The units can deal with a specific topic or subject area, a type or form of writing, or a style of writing. The development of topical units may be limited, however, by the availability of materials on that topic and by the availability of materials appropriate and appealing to students.

Opportunities for sharing books.   Students become interested in books they are reading or in the books others read as they share their ideas through discussion, reports, artwork, or dramatic presentations. Unfortunately, the sharing of books all too often replaces the literature itself. Although reports, art projects, and dramatizations are desirable, within the structure of a planned literature program they should not take precedence over the literature.

A planned literature program has provision for developing students'

1. strategies for distinguishing between real and make-believe;
2. strategies for recognizing the author's craft;
3. strategies for recognizing the mood, feeling, or tone of a story or poem;
4. strategies for recognizing and interpreting figurative language;

5. strategies for recognizing the major forms of fiction; and
6. strategies for extending their personal reading interests.

Recognizing the Categories of Literature

Material in a balanced literature program should be drawn from both classic and new literature. **Classic literature** comprises those stories, poems, and plays that provide continuity with society's literary heritage. It consists of long-enduring folk and fairy tales, myths and legends of other countries, and stories and books. **New literature** consists of modern fanciful stories, poems, and realistic works. Unlike the classics, which tie the reader to a cultural heritage, new literature more closely mirrors the child's world.

Teachers can present literature to students in various ways. One way is by reading different literary forms with different structural elements of style and use.

Recognizing Literary Forms

Categorizing forms of children's literature may be arbitrary, and many books represent more than one form. However, the following categories are useful in a guided literature program.

Fiction
The following are forms of fiction.

1. Realistic books and stories set in historical and contemporary periods. Many are everyday adventure stories that attract so many students. Also included are fictionalized biographies portraying real persons in realistic but fictionalized conversations and thoughts.
2. Fantasy stories, both traditional and modern, of magic and romance. The traditional fairy tales, myths, legends, and folktales have lasted in their appeal to students. Modern fantasy, science fiction, and American folklore have the same magic as traditional fairy tales (Higgins, 1970). (Some authorities classify animal stories as a separate category of literature; these will be discussed later.)
3. Pop literature, a form not considered literature by many, includes comics, jokes, chants in children's games, graffiti, and posters. However, there are many types of pop literature, and many of them meet the criteria of children's literature set out in this chapter.
4. Picture books are usually intended for young children. Their stories, although told in words, are carried through by the sequence of illustrations. Once the story has been heard, a child can look at the pictures and retell the story. Two subforms are picture books with-

out words, in which autonomous pictures are grouped by theme, and wordless picture books, in which the plot and characters are developed entirely by the illustrations.

5. Animal stories remain popular with children and adults. There are three types: animals that are talking beasts; animals that act like animals but talk; and animals that are seen objectively. The purpose of each is different. When animals are talking beasts, they are actually humans in disguise portraying human foibles. Stories in which animals talk but are still animals are stories of fancy. When animals do not talk or act like humans, the author is not free to interpret the animals' emotions, attitudes, or intentions. The animals, central to the plot, remain animals, and the readers are free to interpret the animals' behavior (Lundsteen, 1976).

Nonfiction

The forms of nonfiction are works that present information on topics in a literary style: biographies; personal narratives; technical or scientific explanations; essays; and books about other people, places, and cultures.

Poetry

Poetry often gets little attention in class, is seldom read to children, and is infrequently encouraged as a writing form (Terry, 1972). One reason may be that teachers themselves are unfamiliar or uncomfortable with poetry.

Poems have formal structure and use carefully chosen sequences of words. The structure and sequence of those words can vary; some of the forms popular with elementary and intermediate students are the following:

1. **Quatrains** are poems in four-line units with the second and fourth lines rhyming. Poems can contain several quatrains. This is the form most students use when they create poems.
2. **Couplets** are two-line rhyming units. Many poems have several couplets, sometimes of alternating rhythms, cadences, and rhymes.
3. **Haiku,** a form of poetry originating in Japan, has a seventeen syllable statement about nature in which the topic is usually not named. The form is arranged so the first line has five syllables, the second line has seven syllables, and the third line has five syllables.

   Rustling green branches
   Sweet music of singing birds
   Outside my window. (Fay et al., 1981)

4. **Cinquain** is a short poetic form of five lines:

   ▪ Stating in the first line a single thing—a noun
   ▪ Giving two words in the second line that tell what the thing might do—verbs

- Describing the thing in the third line—adjectives
- Stating in the fourth line a phrase that describes the thing
- Stating the word in the first line.

Snow
Floats, dances
Cold white sparkling
Sitting on my lashes
Snow. (Fay et al., 1981)

5. **Limericks** are nonsense rhymes usually making some humorous statement. Limericks have five lines: lines one and two rhyme; lines three and four rhyme; and the last line rhymes with the first two.

There was an old man with a beard,
Who said, "It is just as I feared!—
Two owls and a hen,
Four larks and a wren,
Have all built their nests in my beard." (Lear, 1966)

6. **Narrative poems** tell a long tale and may use a variety of forms and patterns.
7. **Free verse** does not follow any rhyme pattern, but its poetry is made from the sound, rhythm, and cadence of its words and phrases.

Plays

One form of literature particularly appealing to students is plays. Like poetry, plays are intended to be read aloud and heard. When plays are read, however, they are literature.

Reading, seeing, and hearing plays helps students appreciate the amount of information the reader must supply to recreate the author's message. Although there are various hints—stage directions and scene settings—the reader must provide much of the running commentary and interpretation that often appears in prose literature. Therefore, the study of plays for elementary and intermediate students should be a study of the relationship between a playwright's script and a prose writer's narrative. This experience prepares them to understand the dramas they will read in high school.

Recognizing Elements of Style

The study of *how* literature is constructed leads students to appreciate the author's craft. Enjoyment can more often be derived from watching an artisan when one understands the intricacies of the craft and the criteria for judging the artistic quality of the product. A book is more than just a story when one

© 1975 United Feature Syndicate, Inc.

follows the author in the development of a complex thought or the timbre of a phrase. What one writer of children's and adult literature asked about poetry is true for the study of all forms of literature: How does a poem [or story or play or novel] mean? By seeking an answer to that question, Ciardi (1959) feels that the way in which an author creates the work is important. What it means depends upon the reader's understanding of how it was written and his or her experiences.

Elements of style include the following.

Characterization

In developing characterizations, authors contend with three elements: credibility, portrayal, and uniqueness (Cullinan, 1971).

Characters are credible when they can be believed within the framework of a particular story. They must be integral parts of the author's story and make the action move in believable ways. Credibility ceases when a character performs some action or makes some statement that defies what the reader has been led to accept as the character's pattern.

Characters are portrayed according to the author's intent. Some characters may be described fully and the reader needs to add little from his or her schemata to "know" them. Others may be delineated vaguely because they are not central to the plot or because the author wishes the character to be indistinct. To appreciate an author's character portrayals, students should be familiar with various personality types.

Each character in a story should have some qualities that set that individual apart from the others; yet, each should have some qualities that are common to all humans.

Plot Development

In simplest terms, **plot** is the basic story outline; the **plot development** is how the story unfolds. If the author does not provide a purposeful sequence of events and a logical conclusion, readers might dismiss the story as unbelievable. In most narration, the plot order consists of a sequence of introduction, the development of a problem, the solution of the problem, and a conclusion.

Four basic plots appear in children's literature: romance, tragedy, irony–satire, and comedy (Sloan, 1985). Romance is literature in which wishes are fulfilled. The central character, or hero, is involved in a dangerous or marvelous journey, a struggle or ordeal, and a return. In children's literature, tragedy is an exploration of the central character's limited ability to have or make wishes come true. Central to tragedy is the death or catastrophic fall of the hero. Irony and satire express the contrast that exists between ideals and reality—irony illustrates the limitations of humans; satire attempts to change humans though ridicule. Comedy presents a positive view of the human experience—a picture of hope and renewal.

Figurative Language

The craft of an author is often appreciated through his or her language. The author's choice of words determines how the reader constructs the images of the story's characters and settings. An author might use straightforward language in reporting:

> As Jock nudged the cow into the barn and locked the door behind her, the clouds opened and the rain dropped in a sudden torrent. The lightning stabbed through the clouds, and in its momentary brightness Jock could see the trees tossing wildly in the wind that howled through the river walls and roared across the highlands. He cringed in spite of himself at the exploding thunder as he ran toward the house. It sounded as if the earth were splitting behind him. (Emery, 1965, p.6)

Or an author might use language full of images:

> The sea became a wildcat now, and the galleon her prey. She stalked the ship and drove her off her course. She slapped at her, rolling her victim from side to side. She knocked the spars out of her and used them to ram holes in her sides. She clawed the rudder from its sternpost and threw it into the sea. She cracked the ship's ribs as if they were brittle bones. Then she hissed and spat through the seams. (Henry, 1947, pp. 14–15)

The meaning of the story, both as intended and as perceived, is affected by the author's choice and use of words. Some of the ways to manipulate words are alliteration, personification, metaphor, and simile. In addition, an author can manipulate whole units of language to create moods.

Alliteration is the repetition of initial sounds to create an effect:

> "creepy-crawly caterpillar"

> And a noise that's a growl,
> and a roar,
> and a wheeze,
> and a whistle all stirred together. (Alexander, 1960, p. 7)

Personification is the portrayal of human traits by objects or animals:

> The galleon shuddered. From bow to stern came an endless rasping sound! (Henry, 1947, p. 15)

> Seashell, whisper in my ear
> All the secrets you hold dear. (Fay et al., 1981)

> The wildcat sea yawned. She swallowed the men. (Henry, 1947, p. 15)

Metaphor and simile are comparisons. Similes use the words *like* or *as*. (See Chapter 6 for ideas about developing students' recognition and understanding of metaphors.)

> The air was heavy, musky with an odor not unlike rotting fruit or aging garbage. (Monteleone, 1974, p. 93)

> It looked like a pile of broken twigs and oilcloth as it trembled and fluttered on the ground. (Monteleone, 1974, p. 104)

> The air about them quivered like a violin string. Then suddenly the string snapped, and the everyday world was all about once more. (Henry, 1947, p. 170)

Moods are suggested by images and words:

> For a while longer Tonka sat quietly on the mossy log in the sun, but the sun had little warmth even though it was late May. The last great Ice Age was over, but its cold lingered on. He drew his fox skin more tightly around his shoulders and looked away through the forest. Perhaps, he thought, he might see one of the beasts that the hunters of the tribe often killed and brought back to the cave where they all lived. But the forest was dark and forbidding, and he dared not venture beyond the stream to see what was there. (Hutchins, 1973, p. 10)

Theme Development

The theme of a piece of literature is the significance of the action or experience (Cullinan, 1971). It is the story's message—the author's purpose for writing the piece. Theme is a presence that transcends characters, plot, and setting. The most effective themes are often those that are implicit in the plot and characterizations. An explicit theme may tend to create an impression of moralizing or preaching.

The range of themes found in children's literature is immense. To appreciate an author's theme, however, students need to understand first that themes exist in literature. After that, students need experiences with themes to which they can relate. Unless they "know" a theme before it is encountered, there is no way it will be recognized within a story. Students, therefore, need guided reading of stories with relevant themes to build a storehouse of universal ideas (schemata) to which they can relate when reading independently.

Uses of Literature

Children's literature can be categorized by how it will be used (Cullinan, 1971). For example, literature may be classified educationally—by age groupings or reading levels; or it may be classified functionally—by the concepts that are to be developed, cultures, occupations, or animal survival. Also, a work may be classified according to the influence it has on the reader. This use is called bibliotherapy.

Classifying children's literature by its use is helpful only to the teacher. Students gain nothing from this classification scheme because it does not help them appreciate and understand an author's story and message. Therefore, although teachers may use this scheme for locating books, they should not use it for instructional purposes.

STRATEGIES FOR BRINGING CHILDREN AND LITERATURE TOGETHER

A successful literature program in the elementary and intermediate school is contingent on the teacher having a knowledge of children's literature and a positive attitude toward reading. Of the two, the second quality may be more important, because a teacher can always get help in selecting students' reading material. A positive attitude towards reading is something teachers must develop before they can instill it in their students. An appreciation for the author's craft is difficult to develop in others without being a habitual, appreciative, discriminating reader oneself. As indicated in Chapter 1, teachers need an awareness of the world beyond their technical training, and one way this is accomplished is through reading literature.

Using Library Resources

Wherever one teaches, the school library should be an integral part of the classroom reading program. The teacher should know what happens in the library, and the librarian should know the activities taking place in the classroom. When the library program is integrated with the classroom reading and literature programs, it becomes an adjunct to the classroom—the teacher is aware of the availability of library materials and the librarian of the individual abilities of the students. This joint venture leads to meaningful, effective, and valuable experiences for students, teachers, and librarians. (See Chapter 7 for library usage strategies.)

Classroom libraries can be built by borrowing books from the school library or local public library. Librarians can help select books and stories, or the teacher can refer to the resources indicated at the end of the chapter. Classroom libraries can be organized with books and other reading matter donated by students. With their parents' permission, students could lend the classroom library some books for the school year. Or encourage them to join book clubs and leave their books in the class library until the year ends.

Whatever means is used, students must have a source of reading material that varies in topics, difficulty, and interests; for example, books, short stories, magazines, plays, poems, and newspapers should be available.

SELECTING CHILDREN'S LITERATURE

The books, poems, plays, and stories chosen for a literature program should have literary merit. A review of often-used texts on using children's literature in the elementary school revealed that

- The factors that determine literary quality in children's literature are the same as those in adult literature: plot, content, theme, characterization, style, and form.
- The choice of subject matter and its treatment differentiate children's literature from adult literature, not the quality of writing or the depth of emotion expressed (Ladevich, 1974).

Besides selecting literature according to established criteria, teachers can judge literature's merit when students select material for their independent reading. Students need to satisfy a basic desire to stretch beyond their surroundings and themselves (Fenwick, 1968). When they consistently choose from among the same core of books and stories, there is evidence that those materials have some measure of literary quality. Therefore, teachers should be sure to consider students' tastes when books are being labeled as "fine literature" (Darkatsh, 1974).

Teachers need to differentiate among the many books published each year. The following questions (from Huck & Kuhn, 1968) can be used to judge children's fiction:

Plot

Does the book tell a good story? Will students enjoy it? Is the plot original and fresh? Is it plausible and credible? Do the events logically follow one another? Is there an identifiable climax? How do events build to a climax? Is the plot well constructed?

Setting

Where does the story take place? How does the author indicate the time? How does the setting affect the action, characters, or theme? Does the story transcend the setting and have universal implications?

Theme

Does the story have a theme? Is the theme worth imparting to students? Does the theme emerge naturally from the story or is it stated too obviously? Does the theme overpower the story? Does it avoid moralizing?

Characterization

How does the author reveal characters? Through narration? In conversation? By the thoughts of others? By the thoughts of a character? Through action? Are the characters convincing and credible? Do we see their strengths and their weaknesses? Does the author avoid stereotyping? Is the behavior of the characters consistent with their age and background? Is there any character development or growth? Has the author shown the causes of character behavior or development?

Style

Is the style of writing appropriate to the subject? Is the style straightforward or figurative? Is the dialogue natural and suited to the characters? Does the author balance narration and dialogue? What are the main characteristics of the sentence patterns? How did the author create a mood? Is the overall impression one of mystery, gloom, evil, joy, security? What symbols or signs has the author used to communicate meaning? Is the story's point of view appropriate to the purpose of the book?

Format

Do the illustrations enhance the story? Are the illustrations consistent with the story? How does the format of the book relate to the text? What is the quality of the paper? How sturdy is the binding?

Other Considerations

How does the book compare with other books on the same subject? How does the book compare with other books written by the same author? How have other reviewers evaluated the book?

The following questions (also from Huck & Kuhn, 1968) can be used to judge informational books for children:

Accuracy and Authenticity

What are the qualifications of the author? Are facts accurate? Is the book realistic? Are facts and theories clearly distinguished? Do text and illustrations avoid stereotypes? Is the book up-to-date? Are significant details omitted? Do generalizations go beyond present knowledge? Are differing viewpoints presented? In geographical books, is diversity revealed? In science books, is anthropomorphism omitted? Are phenomena given teleological explanations?

Content

Is this a general survey book or one of some specific interest? Is the coverage of the book adequate for its purpose? Is the book within the comprehension and interest range of the age for which it is intended? Do experiment books lead to an understanding of science? Are experiments and activities safe and feasible? Does the book present interrelationships of facts and principles? Do science books indicate related social problems? Is the book fresh and original? Does the book help the reader understand the methods of science and social science?

Style

Is information given directly or in story form? Is the text interesting and appropriate for the age level intended? Do vivid language and appropriate metaphors engender interest and understanding? Is the language pattern clear and simple or heavy and pedantic? Is there an appropriate amount of detail? Does the book encourage curiosity and further study?

Format and Illustrations

Do illustrations clarify and add to the text? Do different types of media maintain clarity of concepts? Are illustrations explained by captions or labels? Are size relationships made clear? Do size of type and use of space contribute to clarity? Are end papers used effectively?

Organization

Are subheadings used effectively? Do the table of contents and index help the reader locate information quickly? Does the bibliography indicate sources used by the author and sources for further reading by the students? Do appendixes extend information?

LITERATURE AND THE MEDIA

Television is often attacked as being the source of many of society's problems. A common complaint is about the effect television viewing has on students' reading performance. Parents and educators criticize the excessive time spent viewing television, the quality of the programming on television, and the effect television programs and product commercials have on students' academic success.

Much of this criticism may be rhetoric, since research shows that television's effect on students' reading achievement is limited. Studies done between 1961 and 1979 show the relationship between the amount of television viewing and reading achievement is not statistically significant (Neuman, 1980; Searls, Mead, & Ward, 1985). A survey of students' television viewing and their reading performance done between 1980 and 1984 shows that students watching television up to two hours a day read above average for their age groups. When students watch more than six hours per day, their television viewing is related to lower reading proficiency across age groups (NAEP, 1986). The hours spent in front of the set do seem to be negatively related to achievement in reading and success in school only when the number of viewing hours is excessive; however, most of the evidence is correlational, and a cause–effect relationship cannot be inferred from the results. Some researchers conclude that television and reading can be moved into a symbiotic relationship where interest in one can positively affect the other (Neuman, 1980; Searls, Mead, & Ward, 1985). Before definite conclusions can be made about the possible negative effects of television viewing on reading, there should be more controlled studies of the context in which television is watched, including the presence or lack of parental guidance, the types of programs viewed, and the quality of television programming.

There is no denying that media in any form influences children's perceptions and behavior. Media are vehicles for communication, and to deny their potential effect is to deny the communication process itself. The implication is not to whip television for other crimes present in society, but to exert the school's influence in developing the uses of television, film, radio, and records as forms of literature. There is good and poor content in each form of media; nevertheless, students can develop a "visual" literacy in which the cognitive and affective strategies acquired in a reading program are used for the selection and appreciation of information from these media. The "Resources for the Teacher" section of this chapter lists sources containing ideas about teaching through media.

Television programs and movies are art forms, and as such they are subject to the same critical analysis as stories, novels, plays, and poems. Students' critical thinking about story content in nonprint media programs can be fostered with the use of a media story-analysis chart (see Figure 8–1). After they view a program, have students complete the chart and then discuss their responses.

WRITING AND LITERATURE

Creative writing is the rearrangement of known linguistic and information elements into an original form or pattern. In this sense, all students' writing is creative when it contains students' own language. Two sets of schemata are needed to write creatively—language patterns and information. When students use what they know to produce something new, the act of creative writing has occurred. Readiness for creative writing is indicated by the acquisition of language patterns, structures of the different genre of literature, and a mental storehouse of information about a wide range of topics, events, and feelings.

Too often, creative writing is conceived of as unstructured, "free" writing; a time in which students write without direction about a topic of their own choosing. Although some of these aspects are present in creative writing, students cannot create unless they have the means to do so. When students parody a limerick, a television commercial, or a popular song, they are being creative. When they add to a list of events in an "add-on" story such as "This Is the House That Jack Built," they are being creative. When they write a mystery patterned after "The Return of Goldilocks" or another Encyclopedia Brown mystery, they are being creative. Creative writing is all these and more. It is the conscious arrangement of the known into a form that may not have occurred elsewhere.

STRATEGIES FOR USING BIBLIOTHERAPY

Bibliotherapy is based on the premise that books are dynamic and can change the attitudes, habits, and skills of the individuals who read them (Edwards & Simpson, 1986; Shepherd & Iles, 1976). When a reader engages in appropriate and meaningful reading, his or her personality is affected by that particular book, story, or poem. The result is that the reader may develop (1) an enlarged sphere of interest, (2) an increased social sensitivity, (3) the realization that

FIGURE 8–1
Media Story-Analysis Chart

Directions: Complete the chart after viewing a television program or a movie. Discuss your responses with your classmates and the teacher.

Title:

Characters
Who are the major characters? (List the characters from the program or movie, not the actors playing those roles.) _____

How do the characters act in the program or movie? What kind of people are they? _____

What are some things they do that make them different from other characters? _____

Do you think the actors did a good job playing the characters? _____

Setting
Where does the story take place? _____
When does the story take place? _____
How important to the main idea of the story is it that this setting is used? _____

Plot
What is the main idea of the story? _____

What are the problems of the major characters in the story? _____

Are there other, less important, problems? _____

How are the problems solved? _____

Logic
Is there anything in the story that did not make sense to you? _____

Do the characters act naturally? If they do not, is it important to the story that they act the way they do? _____

Source: Based on *Critical Television Viewing: A Language Skills Work-a-Text.* Developed by WNET/Thirteen. New York: Cambridge.

others have a life struggle, and (4) the realization that there is more than one solution to a problem (Corman, 1975).

As a process, bibliotherapy takes the reader through the following steps:

Identification.   The reader, vicariously participating with a character in a book or story, realizes there is some common trait or bond between them. The reader identifies with the story character and becomes ready to "live the other's life."

Catharsis.   After identification with a character is established, the reader experiences a release of emotions as the character works through a problem.

Insight.   When the experience results in a shaping and changing of the reader's manner of thinking, then bibliotherapy is effective. The reader realizes a transfer of the actions or attitudes of a story character can be made to a real-life situation (Corman, 1975).

The process is not a cure-all and should not be viewed as such. There is no guarantee that a particular book will influence any particular student or that the influence, if it does occur, will be in the desired direction (Corman, 1975). Bibliotherapy works best with individuals who are not severely maladjusted. Therefore, the following guidelines should be used whenever teachers attempt to change their students' interests, attitudes, or behavior by reading books.

1. Aim towards helping the student with a minor problem or question. Any seriously disturbed student should be referred to the school psychologist, guidance counselor, or nurse.
2. Avoid directly mentioning the problem. The intent is not for the teacher to become the therapeutic agent but to arrange a situation that may have beneficial effects.
3. Select books in which the content, characterizations, and situations are believable. Unless a book is real to the student, he or she will not be able to identify with a character.
4. Create situations in which students select books without coercion. The individual must "happen" upon the book or story. Since all people, children and adults, live with a romanticized image of them-

selves, any direct threat of that image is greatly resisted. The best results occur serendipitously (Shepherd & Iles, 1976).

5. Involve parents as a means for encouraging communication between them and their children. With training, parents can understand the rationale for using bibliotherapy, its goals, its appropriate use, and guidelines for selecting their children's books (Edwards & Simpson, 1986).

To use bibliotherapy in the classroom, teachers need books that naturally portray the problems and conflicts students meet in their lives. Sometimes a teacher wishes to affect the attitudes of an entire class; at other times, the situation may call for attending to the needs of one student. The following are resources for locating literature appropriate for use in working out problems of human relationships.

Tway, E. (Ed.). (1981). *Reading ladders for human relations* (6th ed.). Washington, DC: The American Council on Education. Available from National Council of Teachers of English, 1111 Kenyon Road, Urbana, IL 61801.

Council on Interracial Books for Children, Racism/Sexism Resource Center, 1841 Broadway, New York, NY 10023–7648.

ACTIVITIES FOR DEVELOPING LITERARY APPRECIATION

To encourage the development of students' literature-reading strategies, teachers should design activities to challenge students' thinking.

- Make a chart or "map" of a story's plot. Students should draw in the main plot and any subplots, indicating how important events are produced as the plots meet or diverge. The activity of the main and minor characters can also be traced by students in relation to the movement of the story's main event.

- Read or play a recording of a story up to a point near the climax. Have students discuss logical endings to the story according to the flow of events and what they know about the characters. Finish reading the story and compare students' endings with that of the author's.

- Select vocabulary from a classic piece of children's literature and discuss whether these words are still used in the same manner. Have students suggest what words might be used to "modernize" the story.

- Analyze the illustrations accompanying a work of literature. Have students decide whether the illustrations enhance the story or distract from it. Try to have students determine whether the illustration is appropriate to the particular story or poem in topic, style, and color.

- Analyze television programs and movies using the same criteria for judging the quality of children's fiction. Have students classify the program or movie according to its plot, theme, characterizations, and language style.

- Select a paragraph from a story and have students rewrite it by using different vocabulary that does not change the paragraph's meaning.

- Listen to different recordings of the same story or poem. Have students discuss the quality of the oral presentation in relation to their interpretation of the author's intended meaning.

- Compose stories and poems based on models students have studied. Have students make parodies of some classic fairy tales, stories, and poems by "extending" their use of repetitive elements. As they become familiar with plot structures, themes, and characterizations, have students compose their own stories and poems.

To extend students' understanding of characterizations and plot development, ask them to

- Prepare a story situation in which two or more characters from different books meet. The meeting should be a logical outcome of incidents in both books, and the conversation that ensues should be credible and consistent with the portrayal of the characters.

- Create a plot, events, and a theme for secondary characters in a story. Students are probably familiar with "spin-offs" that result when a minor character on a television series is highlighted in a new series. Have them create a spin-off based on a secondary character in a story.

- Select a plot from a familiar story and create a different theme. Have students decide how the characters might be portrayed differently for the theme to be significant.

To encourage students' interest in a variety of literary forms and styles, have them share their books through reports, art projects, and dramatizations. Ask them to

- Create collages, dioramas, "movie" boxes, posters, and book jackets that illustrate an important aspect of a story.

- Select an event and dramatize it in a puppet show. Students should make puppets that represent the characters in the story. The dialogue may be taken from the story, or it can be fictionalized.

- Encourage other students to read a book by using written advertisements or book auctions in which succeeding portions of the story are revealed for "a price."

- Study one author or illustrator in depth. Have students read as many works as possible by that individual as well as any available biographies. Then have them write or illustrate their own stories in that author's style.

RESOURCES FOR THE TEACHER

When teachers do not have the time, experience, or interest to assess all the books available to their students, they can get help in selecting reading material by referring to professional texts, book lists, professional journals, and publishers of exemplary literature for children and adolescents.

Professional texts, written to inform teachers of the entire field of children's literature, usually contain references to books, plays, and poems of exceptional quality. Comprehensive references are

Norton, D. E. (1987). *Through the eyes of a child: An introduction to children's literature* (2nd ed.). Columbus, OH: Merrill.
Huck, C. S., Hickman, J., & Hepler, S. (1987). *Children's literature in the elementary school* (4th ed.). New York: Holt, Rinehart & Winston.

Sutherland, Z., & Arbuthnot, M.H. (1986). *Children and books* (7th ed.). Glenview, IL: Scott, Foresman.

Cullinan, B. E. (1981). *Literature and the child*. New York: Harcourt Brace Jovanovich.

A good reference in paperback is

Larrick, N. (1975). *A parent's guide to children's reading* (4th ed.). New York: Doubleday. Available in paperback from Bantam Books.

Sources of ideas for incorporating literature into class reading and writing programs are

Burrows, A. T., Jackson, D. C., & Saunders, D. O. (1984). *They all want to write: Written English in the elementary school*. Hamden, CT: The Shoe String Press, Library Professional Publications.

Stewig, J. W. (1980). *Read to write: Using children's literature as a springboard for teaching writing* (2nd ed.). New York: Holt, Rinehart & Winston.

The following is a book for young people who enjoy writing. It is a practical guide for beginners who are serious about writing, but it is an idea and guide book, not a how-to-do-it book.

Tchudi, S., & Tchudi, S. (1984). *The young writer's handbook*. New York: Charles Scribner's.

When teachers feel unsure about making selections, there are ready-made sources on which they can rely. A classic anthology that should be on every teacher's desk is

Sutherland, Z., & Livingston, M. C. (1984). *The Scott, Foresman anthology of children's literature*. Glenview, IL: Scott, Foresman.

Ideas for scheduling authors for Author-in-Residence programs, Children's Literature Festivals, and Young Authors' Days are in

Melton, D. (1986). *How to capture live authors and bring them to your schools*. Kansas City, MO: Landmark.

Book lists are available for helping teachers select children's literature. These are "starter lists" to which other quality books can be added. Some lists are general and others are specific, depending on the agency compiling them. Two sources of general lists are

The Children's Services Division
American Library Association
50 East Huron Street
Chicago, IL 60611

The Children's Book Council
67 Irving Place
New York, NY 10003
(212-254-2666)

An annotated list of books arranged by reader age and compiled by teams of teachers representing the Children's Book Council and the International Reading Association results from field testing. The list contains those books children either selected to read or asked to be read to them. The two organizations compile and publish an annual list of "Children's Choices." Since 1974 these have been published annually in the October issue of *The Reading Teacher*.

Specialized lists are available that cover a wide range of topics. In developing literature programs for fostering an appreciation of the pluralistic nature of American society, the following lists may be useful. Others can be obtained from the ERIC Clearinghouse on Reading and Communication Skills, 111 Kenyon Road, Urbana, IL 61801.

Arth, A. A., & Whittemore, J. D. (1973). Selecting literature for children that relates to life, the way it is. *Elementary English, 50,* 726–728, 744.

Monson, D. L. (Ed.). (1985). *Adventuring with books: A booklist for pre-K–grade 6.* Urbana, IL: National Council of Teachers of English.

Sims, R. (1982). *Shadow and substance: Afro–American experience in contemporary children's fiction.* Urbana, IL: National Council of Teachers of English.

Stensland, A. L. (1979). *Literature by and about the American Indian: An annotated bibliography* (2nd ed.). Urbana, IL: National Council of Teachers of English.

The following specialized book list organizes books according to themes and provides a source of material for use with bibliotherapy.

Tway, E. (Ed.). (1981). *Reading ladders for human relations* (6th ed.). Urbana, IL: National Council of Teachers of English.

Various periodicals for children are listed in

Guide to children's magazines, newspapers, reference books. Washington, DC: Association for Childhood Education International.

Martin, L. K. *Magazines for school libraries.* New York: R.R. Bowker.

Seminoff, N. W. (1986, May). Children's periodicals throughout the world: an overlooked educational resource. *The Reading Teacher, 39*(9), 889–895.

Professional journals list and review current publications each month. The first two references are devoted entirely to children's literature. The others contain regular reviews of children's literature.

Bulletin of the Center for Children's Books. University of Chicago Press, 5801 Ellis Avenue, Chicago, IL 60637.

The Horn Book Magazine. Horn Book, Inc., 585 Boylston Street, Boston, MA 02116.

Language Arts. National Council of Teachers of English, 1111 Kenyon Road, Urbana, IL 61801.

The Reading Teacher. International Reading Association, 800 Barksdale Road, Newark, DE 19711.

The School Library Journal. R.R. Bowker Co., 1180 Avenue of the Americas, New York, NY 10036.

Several publishers are sources of materials for literature programs. Almost every major publisher has a division which makes children's books available in both hardcover and paperback. Some publishers reprint books in paperback and make them available to schools through book club plans. Others create filmstrips and recordings of popular books.

A. W. Peller & Associates, Inc.
   249 Goffle Road
   Hawthorne, NJ 07507

Creative Education
   Post Office Box 227
   Mankato, MN 56001

Dell Publishing Company
   245 E. 47th Street
   New York, NY 10017

January Productions
   249 Goffle Road
   Hawthorne, NJ 07507

Scholastic Book Services
   50 West 44th Street
   New York, NY 10017

Troll Associates
   Mahway, NJ

Weekly Reader Paperback Book Club
   Education Center
   Columbus, OH 43216

Xerox Education Publication Book Clubs
   245 Long Hill Road
   Middletown, CT 06457

Some publishers have literature anthology series. A good anthology series should contain selections with many topics, interests, styles, and forms. Exemplary series are

Bill Martin's big books; Bill Martin's instant readers; Bill Martin's sounds of language readers; and, *Bill Martin's sounds of our heritage readers.* New York: Holt, Rinehart & Winston.

The Random House achievement program in literature. (Consultants: Lee Bennett Hopkins & Tom Wolpert) New York: Random House School Division.

The following have teaching plans for selected children's books. Included are a wide range of activities and suggested further readings for each theme or book. Teachers can develop their own lessons for other books by following the format set out in the guides.

Literature enrichment activities for paperbacks. Littleton, MA: Sundance Publishers & Distributors. (Multiple copies of titles with student activity books)

Moss, J. F. (1984). *Focus units in literature: A handbook for elementary school teachers.* Urbana, IL: National Council of Teachers of English. (Contains lesson plans, activities, and bibliographies for thirteen sequences of stories and books)

Rhodes, L. (Ed.). *Link pak: Children's literature.* LINK—The Language Company, 1895 Dudley Street, Lakewood, CO 80215. (Literature extensions—instructional activities and ideas designed to extend children's experiences with books)

Roetinger, D. (Ed.). *Reading beyond the basal series.* Logan, IA: Perfection Form Company. (Activities for use with selected books)

Somers, A. B., & Evans, J. W. (1979). *Response guides for teaching children's books.* Urbana, IL: National Council of Teachers of English.

Weaver, C. (Ed.). (1981). *Using junior novels to develop language and thought: Five integrative teaching guides.* Urbana, IL: National Council of Teachers of English. (Guides for five prominent junior novels)

Other sources of activities related to children's literature are

Baskwill, J., & Whitman, P. (1986). *Whole language source book.* Richmond Hill, Ontario, Canada: Scholastic-TAB Publications.

Carlisle, J., Cook, C., & Moffett, G. (1983). *Classroom nursery rhymes activities kits.* West Nyack, NY: The Center for Applied Research in Education.

Graham, T. (1982). *Let loose on Mother Goose.* Nashville, TN: Incentive.

Schaff, J. (1976). *The language arts idea book: Classroom activities for children.* Glenview, IL: Scott, Foresman.

Ideas and resources for using television and other media in the classroom are in the following:

Becker, G. J. (1973). *Television and the classroom reading program.* Newark, DE: International Reading Association.

Dillingofski, M. S. (Compiler). (1979). *Nonprint media and reading.* Newark, DE: International Reading Association.

May, J. P. (1981). *Films and filmstrips for language arts: An annotated bibliography.* Urbana, IL: National Council of Teachers of English.

The American Broadcasting Company (ABC) and the Columbia Broadcasting System (CBS) produce special programming for school-age children and provide teachers with program scripts, links between the program and reading, and instructional guides for viewing selected regular programming. Information is available from

CBS Television Reading Program
    51 West 52nd Street
    New York, NY 10019

ABC Television Community Relations
    1330 Avenue of the Americas
    New York, NY 10019

DISCUSSION QUESTIONS AND ACTIVITIES

1. Find out what children are reading. Visit a school and public library and interview children about their book selections. Find out why they are choosing the books they do. Then interview teachers and librarians to find out what they think children are reading and should be reading. Compare the results of the two sets of interviews.

2. Study the criteria by which books receive awards. Information can be obtained from the Children's Book Council and the American Library Association. Select one

year's awards and compare the winner with the runners-up. Would your decision have been the same as the judges'?

3. Study the "visual literacy" movement in the media arts. In what ways do the criteria for quality and understanding differ between the judging of a visual story and a written story?

4. Explain what Huck (1968) meant in the following: "The ultimate experience of a story or a poem lies in the way it is told, not in just the facts or events it relates" (p. 45).

5. Is it true, as Barrett (1968) states, that

Only that book which helps the students to clarify and thus to define is going to be seen by him as relevant and will thus be for him an experience that has meaning; all other books will be irrelevant and meaningless. (p. 105)

6. Plan a topical unit for students in a particular grade level. Develop the theme of the unit with two or three literary forms and styles. Be sure to include selections appropriate to a wide range of reading abilities.

7. Plan a bulletin board display that will introduce students in the primary grades to the different types of literary forms.

8. Plan a book fair and contact local merchants or book suppliers about contributing books. Then plan a campaign to encourage elementary students and their parents to attend. If possible, work with a local parents' or teachers' organization to hold the book fair.

9. Explain what this statement by Koss (1972) means to you: "Relevance is a matter of applicability" (p. 992).

10. What is your definition of literature? Study how various authors define the term and then write your own definition.

FURTHER READING

In the first reference, the author discusses literature's place in elementary and middle-school education. She presents a theory with practical instructional suggestions for unifying the language arts so that literature becomes the center of language studies.

Sloan, G. D. (1975). *The child as critic: Teaching literature in elementary and middle schools* (2nd ed.). New York: Teachers College Press, Columbia University.

The following authors suggest ways to link literature to all areas of the curriculum.

Cowen, J. E. (Ed.). (1983). *Reading through the arts.* Newark, DE: International Reading Association.

Cullinan, B. E. (Ed.). (1987). *Children's literature in the reading program.* Newark, DE: International Reading Association.

Geller, L. G. (1985). *Wordplay and language learning for children.* Urbana, IL: National Council of Teachers of English.

Roser, N., & Frith, M. (Eds.). (1983). *Children's choices: Teaching with books children like*. Newark, DE: International Reading Association.

Tway, E. (1985). *Writing is reading: 26 ways to connect*. Urbana, IL: Clearinghouse on Reading and Communication Skills, National Institute of Education/National Council of Teachers of English.

The following text has children's literature organized in terms of social issues:

Rudman, M. K. (1976). *Children's literature: An issues approach*. Lexington, MA: D.C. Heath.

The following monograph, although it has examples mostly from the secondary level, contains ideas that can be used at all grade levels.

Weiss, M. J., Brunner, J., & Heis, W. (Eds.). (1973). *New perspectives on paperbacks* (Monograph No. 1). The College Reading Association. (May be obtained from Strine Printing Co., 391 Greendale Road, York, PA 17403).

The International Reading Association (Newark, DE) has published several collected articles on topics related to teaching children's literature.

Carlson, R. K. (Ed.). (1972). *Folklore and folktales around the world*.

Catterson, J. H. (Ed.). (1970). *Children and literature*. Huus, H. (Ed.). (1968). *Evaluating books for children and young people*.

Painter, H. W. (1970). *Poetry and Children*.

Painter, H. W. (Ed.). (1971). *Reaching children and young people through literature*.

Sebasta, S. L. (Ed.). (1968). *Ivory, apes, and peacocks*.

Strickland, D. S. (Ed.). (1981). *The role of literature in reading instruction: Cross cultural views*.

Tanyzer, H., & Karl, J. (Eds.). (1972). *Reading children's books, and our pluralistic society*.

The following, all published by the International Reading Association, are meant to help teachers with children who have problems with themselves as readers and learners.

Alexander, J. E., & Filler, R. C. (1976). *Attitudes and reading*.

Quandt, I. (N. D.) *Self concept and reading*.

Shapiro, J. E. (Ed.). (1979). *Using literature and poetry effectively*.

Spiegel, D. L. (1981). *Reading for pleasure: Guidelines*.

Periodically, issues of *Language Arts* focus on themes related to children's literature. For example, the March 1986 (Vol. 63) and the April 1985 (Vol. 62) issues deal with "Literary Discourse," and the March 1984 (Vol. 61) deals with "Children and Literature." Earlier volumes should be consulted for other related themes.

In addition to the articles on sex stereotyping in literature that occasionally appear in *The Reading Teacher* and *Language Arts*, the following are good sources of information about how to recognize it, how to teach students about it, and how to keep it out of your own and your students' writing.

Nilsen, A. P. et al. (1977). *Sexism and language*. Urbana, IL: National Council of Teachers of English.

Sheridan, E. M. (Ed.). (1982). *Sex stereotypes and reading: Research and strategies*. Newark, DE: International Reading Association.

Organizer

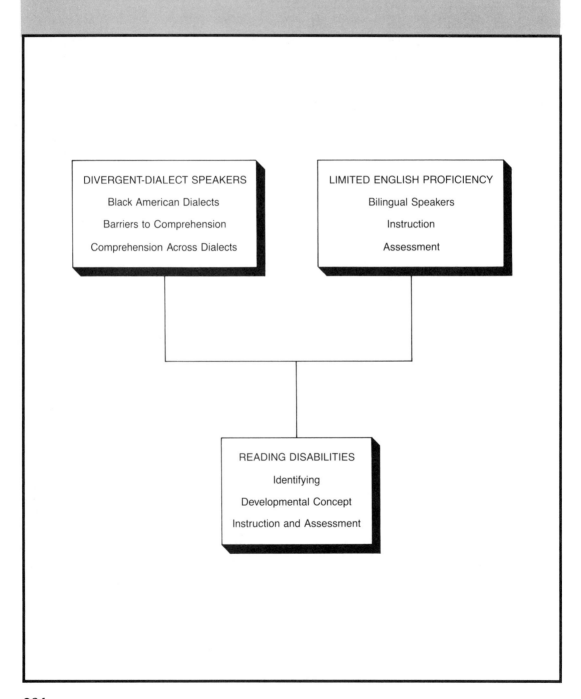

DIVERGENT-DIALECT SPEAKERS

Black American Dialects

Barriers to Comprehension

Comprehension Across Dialects

LIMITED ENGLISH PROFICIENCY

Bilingual Speakers

Instruction

Assessment

READING DISABILITIES

Identifying

Developmental Concept

Instruction and Assessment

Strategies for Students with Special Needs

Focus Questions

- What problems in learning to read and write are faced by speakers of divergent dialects?
- How can nonnative speakers of English become effective readers and writers of English?
- What are the characteristics of reading and learning disabilities?
- How can students with special needs be instructed in the regular classroom?

Students with special needs are those who may not succeed in regular education without some modification of instructional strategies. These are students who may be unable to function in school because of an inability to receive and transmit information effectively. Three types of students with special needs are discussed in the chapter: students with divergent dialects, students for whom English is a second language, and students having difficulties in learning to read. Since the vehicle for communication is language, an understanding of the nature of verbal and nonverbal communication is essential to understanding students' ineffectiveness in learning to read and write in school. Another type of students with special needs are those considered gifted and talented; they are discussed because they, too, have different instructional needs.[1]

THE NEEDS OF DIVERGENT-DIALECT SPEAKERS

In Chapter 8, cultural pluralism was discussed. The issues raised there are relevant to the discussion about students with special needs, especially those who speak a different dialect and have limited English proficiency. When classrooms have students with these characteristics, multicultural instruction should exist. **Multicultural instruction** is a multidisciplinary educational program with multiple learning environments that match the academic, social, and linguistic needs of students (Lynch, 1986; Syzuki, 1984). These needs may vary widely because of differences in race, sex, ethnicity, or sociolinguistic backgrounds. The result of these differing backgrounds is that students' development of academic skills and understanding about their and others' backgrounds is enhanced. Classes should and can be organized with consideration for the cognitive and linguistic competence that students have in their everyday lives (Au & Mason, 1981).

In all languages there are variations among speakers in the pronunciation of sounds, formation of sentences, use of emphasis, and meanings assigned to words. When an identifiable group of speakers consistently uses these variations, a dialect exists. American English speech is a family of dialects and each dialect is a legitimate form of communication for its speakers (Alexander, 1980; Goodman, 1969c). Within a language group, dialects have two dimensions (Foerster, 1974b). One is geographic and can be observed in regional dialect variations such as those heard in Maine, New York, and Texas. The other is closely allied with individuals' socioeconomic status. At one extreme of this

[1]The first edition of this chapter was written with Michele K. Heiman.

dimension is the speech of the poor and disenfranchised and at the other is the speech of the affluent and highly educated. Between them lie many other dialects. These two dimensions intersect so that each regional grouping has its own socioeconomic variations.

A dialect is not "slang," which is a deliberate word substitution within a dialect. All dialects can have slang expressions.

Standard American English is a dialect that has been arbitrarily set by society as the language of business, government, and mass communication. Standard American English is that language used most often by announcers and newscasters and heard on most national radio and television news and informational programs. It does not differ much from most other main dialects, and there is no one region that solely possesses this variety of the English language. The reason for this may be the extreme regional and social mobility within general society. The term *standard* for this language variety is probably unfortunate and misleading. Just as a standardized test score does not represent an ideal toward which all instruction should aim, the standard dialect is not a goal for American English speakers. Even its written form does not represent any extensively used spoken form and should not be used as the basis for oral-language instruction.

Black American Dialects

One of the largest groups of divergent dialects in American society is Black American English. An understanding of how Black dialects evolved helps clarify the differences between Black American English and standard American English. The history of Black American English is summarized as follows (Alexander, 1980; Stewart, 1966).

Africans were among the first immigrants to colonial America, being brought in as slaves. As did all immigrants, they faced the problem of learning the language of the new nation. As a result of slave trade, Pidgin English was formed. (**Pidgins** are hybrid languages used by native speakers of other languages.) Many Africans who were brought to America already spoke Pidgin English, as did many of the Americans engaged in the slave trade. The policy of slave owners and slave buyers to mix Africans of different language and cultural groups forced the Afro-Americans to rely on this means rather than their native tongue to maintain communication with others. The Pidgin English flourished and affected the English spoken by both slaves and slave owners.

Today, communities in many urban and rural areas display a range of dialects. Much dialect blending occurs as members of the different linguistic communities become mobile.

Unquestionably, the term *Black American English* is stereotypical, but many features of pronunciation, grammar, and lexicon are shared by many Black American speakers (Alexander, 1980; Labov, 1966). These features are acquired socially and are perpetuated socially. Two variations are recognized: standard Black English, the form used by educated Blacks for communication, and Black English vernacular, the form used by less-educated people (Wiig & Semmel,

1984). Research indicates how these two forms differ (Baratz, 1968). Examples of these differences are in Figure 9–1. Not all researchers agree on the form and frequency with which the features outlined in Figure 9–1 are found in Black American English, and some indicate that Black speakers predominantly use standard American English forms (Wiig & Semmel, 1984). It is best to view these features as those often used by most speakers in Black urban communities. No one uses them all, all the time.

Barriers to Comprehension

Barriers to effective communication are discussed in Chapter 13. Two of those barriers are relevant here: Communication is hindered because of different linguistic codes or because of "emotional static." The first barrier occurs when two or more individuals attempt to communicate in the belief their verbalizations are mutually intelligible. The other occurs when attitudes toward the backgrounds of divergent-dialect speakers interfere with the acceptance of their ideas and contributions in school.

For many years, speakers of divergent dialects (both of Black American English and other minority dialects) have been considered "disadvantaged" learners. Many people feel that such speakers' disadvantage results from their "substandard" speech and thinking patterns. Sometimes the term *culturally disadvantaged* is applied to students who are not prepared in their preschool environment to cope with school situations. These, however, are definitely misnomers; members of minority groups who are often given these pejorative labels have functioned in society as well as nonminority group members (Wheat, 1974). Individuals only become "disadvantaged" when they are taken from a familiar environment and are placed in an alien situation.

Students from minority cultures who are divergent-dialect speakers may come to school without the experiences that school personnel presume they have had. Success in school is hindered not because students are incapable of doing school tasks, but because they understand the tasks differently. They are unfamiliar with certain linguistic conventions used in school. The result is an apparent lack of understanding and an inability to do school tasks.

Literature about the effect on reading comprehension of speaking Black American English fails to cite specific causes. Although there is evidence of a high incidence of poor reading achievement among Black English speakers, there is no definitive evidence that it results from their language patterns (Rupley & Robeck, 1978; Dillingofski, 1979; Barnitz, 1980; Eberwein, 1982; Lucas & Borders, 1987; and Schwartz, 1982). However, there is some evidence of an attitudinal interference—many teachers hold negative attitudes toward "nonstandard language" (Lucas & Borders, 1987; Monteith, 1980).

The question of whether dialects interfere with understanding in school is further complicated by the introduction of a legal interpretation in addition to the educational interpretation. In 1979, a United States Federal district court judge in Michigan ruled that Black English is more than a dialect—it is a lan-

FIGURE 9–1
Features of Black American English

Phonological Features

Certain sounds may be omitted from medial and/or final positions:
/r/ from words such as *guard* (becoming /god/).
/l/ from words such as *tall* and *help* (becoming /taw/ and /hep/)
/t/, /d/, /s/, and /z/ in final clusters in words such as *past, bites, next* (becoming /pass/, /bite/, and /nes/)
Some final consonants may be lost in words such as *bat* and *hand* (becoming /bah/ and /han/)

Certain sounds may be similarly pronounced or interchanged:
/m/ and /n/ may be indistinguishable in words such as *ram* (becoming /ran/)
/th/ in initial position may become /d/ in words such as *them* (becoming /dem/)
/sk/ in medial or final position may become /ks/ in words such as *ask* (becoming /aks/)
/th/ in final position may become /v/ or /f/ in words such as *breathe* and *both* (becoming /breev/ and /bohf/)
/sk/ may be substituted for /st/ in initial position in such words as *street* (becoming /skreet/)
/e/ and /i/ may become indistinguishable in words such as *pen* and *pin* (becoming /pin/ and /pin/)

Syntactic Features

Certain transformations may occur in verb forms:
The present tense, third person: *He walks* becomes *He walk.*
The present progressive: *She is singing* becomes *She sing.*
The past tense irregular: *He took it* becomes *He taken it.*
Past perfect irregular: *He has taken it* becomes *He have took it.*
Future: *I am going to do it* may become *I'm a do it.*
Present habitual: *She is* (always) *doing it* may become *She be doing it.*
Past habitual: *He used to do it* may become *He been doing it.*

Certain transformations may occur in sentence structure:
Negation: *They don't have any* may become *They don't got none.*
Indirect questions: *I asked if he fixed it* may become *I asked did he fix it?*
Direct questions: *How did you do that* may become *How you do that?*
The subject: *My mother is there* may become *My mother, she there.*
Plural nouns: *Those pencils* may become *Them pencils.*
Possessive: *Phillip's book* may become *Phillip book.*

Source: Based on Alexander (1980); Baratz (1968); Wiig & Semmel (1984); and Zintz (1975).

guage different from standard American English. The judge ruled that because of this different linguistic background, Black English speakers in Ann Arbor, Michigan, were getting an inferior education. Although he did not rule that materials written in Black English were to be used for instruction, he did rule that teachers in the Ann Arbor school district should get sensitivity training about the needs of Black English speakers. The judge indicated that a problem arises when teachers refuse to recognize and accept in school the existence of a language accepted in the child's home and community (Monteith, 1980; Padak, 1981).

There are several important experiences that are prerequisites to successful school achievement (see Chapter 3). Students who get sensory and intellectual stimulation of the kind upon which school learning is based generally possess those prerequisites. Some students, however, do not have this background (they lack schemata) or receive instruction that interferes with their school achievement (Edwards, 1969). It is *not* that these students cannot speak and think; it is that what they do think and speak about is different from what they are asked to read and write about in school. Their cognitive, linguistic, and social backgrounds are different, not inferior.

Students come to school able to communicate with others in their immediate social environment. Evidence from research (Lucas & Borders, 1987) shows that dialect does seem to interfere with everyday classroom discourse. A breaking down of this barrier in communication seems to occur when there is an awareness by teachers and students of situationally appropriate dialect language use. It is only when students are confronted with the unfamiliarity of the school code and experiences (the language and concepts of school texts) that a barrier to communicating and comprehending develops.

Researchers have found that when two communicators who do not share many experiences or points of view try to communicate, they need to use an **elaborated code**—one that has extensive language signals. The factor controlling whether or not a message needs to be in an elaborated code is the extent to which the communicators share attitudes and experiences, or "context" (Erikson, 1968). High shared-context situations allow the use of a restricted code, since there is considerable overlap of speakers' experience and points of view. Low shared-context situations require elaborated codes. "As context increases the volume of necessary communication signals decreases" (Erikson, 1968, p. 496). The educational implication is that there is a need to develop common experiences and semantic labels among the divergent-dialect-speaking students.

Developing Comprehension Across Dialects

Allowing students to retain their dialectical patterns while giving them instruction in standard language patterns is what generally occurs in most schools. The written dialect (standard English) transcends all spoken dialects and permits effective communication between speakers of all dialects of English. The use of standard written forms with students' dialectical spoken forms becomes

ineffective only when teachers and students do not share a common context—
when a teacher does not recognize, accept, and understand students' language
patterns and students are made to feel their language patterns are inappropriate for academic work.

Instruction for speakers of divergent dialects is aimed at teaching them
about the structure of the material they read and write. They learn how to use

their own knowledge of language to predict what will be found in their books. They learn to approach the printed page with confidence and to use language cues to discover the author's meaning (Gillet & Gentry, 1980; Jalongo & Bromley, 1984; Lloyd, 1969). Learning to read for speakers of divergent dialects is no different than for speakers of standard dialect. When readers predict the meaning in printed matter, the result is "comprehension." Predictability is as crucial for divergent-dialect speakers as it is for standard-dialect speakers. If predictability is desirable, then it is logical to suggest that any student who speaks but does not read or write is guided *in the initial acquisition of literacy with predictable written language*—that is, by written language that closely matches their oral language patterns (Alexander, 1980; Gillet & Gentry, 1980. See Chapter 4, "The Language Experience Approach.")

The implications of this discussion about teaching students with divergent dialects are

1. Teachers must understand English and its many varieties. Whatever language students bring to school should be accepted as a legitimate means for communication.
2. If there is a difference between students' normal speech patterns and the speech pattern used in school, then school personnel must determine which items of language require attention because they inhibit communication. Analyze; do not criticize!
3. The development of literacy in all students is done with both teachers and students. Together they attempt to understand the alternatives available to them and to select those that seem comfortable and appropriate to the situation.

THE NEEDS OF STUDENTS WITH LIMITED ENGLISH PROFICIENCY

School programs for speakers of English as a second language exist in a variety of forms and for a variety of purposes. The issues surrounding these programs incite political, social, and educational concern because they are outgrowths of civil rights, equity, and anti-poverty movements (Nieto, 1986). The controversy will continue because demographers predict increasing numbers of immigrant children from Central and South America and Asia. Although educational and governmental officials agree on the goal—to make students competent in English—there is disagreement about program types, the extent of Federal government involvement, instructional methodology, and whether the programs are effective (Chambers, 1986; Chamot & Stewner-Manzanares, 1985a, b; Cummins, 1986; Fiske, 1985; Reed, 1985; Rohter, 1985; Rohter, 1986; Werner, 1987; Willig, 1985).

Most approaches intend to teach students to speak English. One approach, known as **English as a Second Language** (ESL) or **Teaching English as a Second Language** (TESOL), is organized like second-language programs found in many middle/junior and senior high schools and some elementary schools. The specific ESL teaching methodologies used have changed since the 1970s; current emphasis is on whole-language skills and learner-centered activities stressing the communication of meaning (Chamot & McKeon, 1984). Another approach, **bilingual education,** provides instruction in two languages. It has instructional periods in the students' native language and others in English (Chamot & Stewner-Manzanares, 1985a, b; McConnell, 1985; Schmitt, 1985). For instance, public-school bilingual programs sometimes conduct instruction in mathematics, social studies, and science in the native language and language arts instruction in English. Some parochial-school bilingual programs give religious studies in one language and secular studies in English. The most common type of program is called **transitional bilingual education,** which uses bilingual teachers who begin with students' native language and gradually introduce English. A third approach for nonnative English speakers is conducted in English but takes into account the linguistic and cultural features of the native language. These are called **education of the bilingual programs.**

Bilingual education and education of the bilingual are different. The discussion here focuses on the latter: the education of pupils for whom English is not a native language but who have achieved a degree of proficiency in spoken English so that they can receive reading and writing instruction in English. Here, these programs are called **programs for students with limited English proficiency** (SLEP).

Linguistic Characteristics of Bilingual Speakers

When an individual becomes bilingual, a language continuum is created (Ching, 1976). Proficiency in both languages lets the speaker "glide" at will from one end of the continuum to the other. What many teachers notice is a mixing of the two languages by students who are not totally bilingual. In some sections of the country, the pejorative terms *TexMex, Spanglish,* or *Newyorican* denote the language of individuals who mix Spanish and English. What teach-

Reprinted by permission: Tribune Media Services

ers must realize is that language differences or mixing language forms is not what interferes with reading. What does interfere with students' learning is the influence their language has on teachers and through teachers on the learning environment (Gumperz & Hernandez-Chavez, 1972).

There is evidence that code switching—alternating between two languages—persists wherever a minority language group has contact with a majority language group under conditions of rapid social change (Gumperz & Hernandez-Chavez, 1972). Alternating between languages serves definite and clearly understandable communicative ends (Silva, 1987). It does not represent "errors" or deficiencies by the speaker; it shows the creative use of alternative language forms to convey specific meanings. There is no way to predict when a switch in linguistic form will occur or to predict its particular meaning. The use of alternative language forms occurs when a speaker chooses certain words rather than their synonyms because of their connotations or their potential effect on the listener. It is a verbal strategy similar to making adjustments in speech to conform to the degree of formality in a situation. Teachers need to accept speech varieties as potentially meaningful and to interpret them in the context of the communication situation.

Not all educators accept the linguistic merging of other languages and English. For example, a group known as the North American Academy of the Spanish Language considers the use of anglicized Spanish words as unacceptable when an acceptable Spanish word exists (Chavez, 1987). Their efforts, however, may be a denial of the natural changes that occur when two languages, both of which are in evolution, exist together.

To interpret a message contained in a mixed code, speakers must share a cultural and linguistic context. They need common experiences, which are functions of home background, peer-group interactions, and education. When teachers are not familiar with the linguistic features of their students' native language, communicating with them may be difficult.

Strategies for Instruction

How then can teachers instruct bilingual students with limited English proficiency (LEP)? One thing they can do is to learn as much as possible about the students' language and culture, since evidence shows that LEP readers' background knowledge is a vital factor in comprehension (Anderson & Barnitz, 1984; Nelson, 1987). When teaching nonnative speakers of English, teachers should be sensitive to the students' cultural values: their aspiration levels, their value orientations, and their process of socialization. Whenever there are differences between the school's cultural value system and the local culture's value system, a breakdown in communication between teachers and students is likely. Effective communication is hindered when teachers fail to consider these differences, since "the basis for using language for information, action, or emotion in educational content is the assumption that the child has already mastered the essentials [of language]" (Mackey, 1973, p. 14).

Teachers can produce a learning situation in which nonnative speakers of English develop a sense of security, acceptance, and recognition. This should not be difficult, since such an environment should exist for all students to ensure successful school experiences.

Teachers need to know how English and other language(s) are similar or different in phoneme production, vocabulary, and syntax, and in how experiences and concepts are encoded. An analysis of other languages reveals potential sources of confusion and barriers to effective communication. For example, some students are reluctant to speak or write English because they are unsure of or confused by language forms that do not exist in their native language. Some are unfamiliar with English connotations of certain words or the appropriateness of certain words or phrases in a given context. The result is embarrassment or frustration whenever they must use English in situations for which they do not possess adequate English language skills. Teachers can avoid potential disturbing incidents and communication breakdowns by understanding the language system of LEP students.

There are various approaches to working with LEP students. The focus of this discussion is on strategies for reading and writing with the LEP bilingual student in typical classroom situations. The ideas are not exhaustive of the possible activities and exercises. As students learn about and use the structures and forms of English, they learn how these differ from or parallel those in their native languages.

The first step in improving students' reading and writing proficiency as well as in developing their self-concept is to link their oral language with reading and writing acts. This is accomplished by using the language experience approach (Amoriggi & Gefteas, 1981; Feeley, 1983; Gonzales, 1981; Moustafa & Penrose, 1985). The ideas in Chapter 3 for developing cognitive and linguistic readiness for reading and writing instruction and those in Chapter 4 for using the language experience approach to introduce students to literacy can be used with LEP students.

Oral and written language proficiency is further developed through activities that direct students' attention to significant features of English. LEP students gain fluency in English through tasks that have them do the following:

- Work with proficient English-speaking peers. Using peer-collaboration techniques, develop content-area activities as means for students to share their knowledge and solve problems in game activities.

- Learn key phrases and dialogues for school situations, such as greeting peers and adults; asking for assistance in obtaining information or school materials; and giving and receiving directions to the school office, library, and other classrooms (Feeley, 1983; Gonzales, 1981).

- Use predictable texts, songs, and chants to learn English language patterns and rhythm. Begin by having students listen to the material as they follow along in their own copies or enlarged texts. Allow ample listening and speaking before reading and writing; however, students may not need to be proficient speakers to read and write (Feeley, 1983).

The following activities might result in isolated drill unless they are integrated with learning across the curriculum. The content of the lessons should be selected from social studies, science, mathematics, and language arts topics. In addition to learning from the strategies and activities discussed in previous chapters, LEP students can gain proficiency by participating in the following.

- Have students practice a series of pattern drills (Saville-Troike, 1973) that include

  Mimicry. Students imitate a sentence attempting to use the teacher's intonational pattern. Use these sentences until students memorize them.

  Chain drill. This activity is similar to the game "Follow the Leader." One student makes a statement that is then repeated by other students.

  Substitution. Students substitute a word or phrase with another word, in most cases this is a pronoun.

Replacement.   Students replace a word or phrase with a synonym.

Conversion.   Students change the tense of the sentences in a predetermined manner.

Expansion.   Students add a word or group of words to a sentence.

Transformation.   Students change a sentences' word order so that a statement becomes a question, an affirmative becomes a negative, or an active becomes a passive.

- Help students develop a sense of adjective modification by expanding noun phrases. Students will learn the order of modifiers such as nationality, color, shape, size, quality, cardinal, ordinal, defining, and indefinite or inclusive.
- Help students develop a sense of adverb modification through tasks requiring the placement of adverbs in sentences. Make a distinction between adverbs that move without changing a sentence's meaning and those that cannot move because they qualify a particular unit within the sentence.
- Lead students to develop an understanding of common, multiple-use function words such as *have* and *do*. Have students learn constructions using *have:*

  > have + infinitive (to show necessity)
  > have + to have (to show necessity)
  > have + noun (to show causative action)
  > have + noun + verb (to show directives)

Resources for the Teacher

Cities and states develop guides for teaching LEP students. In addition, these series are designed to introduce and develop English for nonnative speakers. Most assume the intended audience have Spanish backgrounds. Teachers, however, should not assume all Latin American Spanish languages are the same and that the materials are appropriate in all situations. When they are used with students having other linguistic/cultural backgrounds the materials should be examined for relevancy.

The criteria given in Chapter 10 for selecting instructional materials can be used to assess material's appropriateness for your LEP program. Materials must be selected with care to ensure they reflect whole-language learning theory, integrate reading and writing activities with content areas, are appropriate for the students' age and ability levels, contain student-centered activities, and meet the students' academic language needs (Chamot & Stewner-Manzanares, 1985b).

> *English language support manuals*, levels A–O. Boston: Houghton Mifflin. (Has big books, word cards, instruction charts, transparencies, duplicating masters, and enrichment books)
> *I like English*, levels 1–7 (ages 5–12). Glenview, IL: Scott Foresman. (Has student books, teacher's manual, teaching cards, workbooks, and an audio book)
> *Reach out*, levels 1–5 (ages 4–11), and *New routes to English*, levels 1–6 (middle and junior high school). Riverside, NJ: Macmillan Publishing. (Have student books, teacher's manual, workbooks, cassettes, wallcharts, and informal placement tests)

Strategies for Assessment

Teachers can use formal and informal means to assess students' English language proficiency. Formal means are standardized instruments that measure students' skills in English or the native language. Informal means are teacher-made tests and inventories to measure students' understanding and use of English forms.

The information in Chapters 10 and 11 about informal and standardized assessment pertain to this discussion. Testing in language and literacy involves a linguistic interaction between tester and student. Since communication is context bound, the context of testing may limit students' performance. What may seem like a commonplace test can yield less-than-optimal results when the communicative expectations of students are not met (Guthrie, 1984).

Since standardized instruments may be of limited value to classroom teachers of LEP students, informal tests may be used to determine their readiness for and progress in reading instruction. The performance rating scale in Figure 9–2 is one means for localizing aspects of language which hinder students' progress in learning to read English.

To use the scale, observe students in a variety of social and educational situations. Or, set up a series of games in which students do learning tasks that show their language proficiency. For example, games can be played to auditorially distinguish between similar English phonemes—/shin/ and /chin/— or between contrasting elements in English and the native language—/hump/ and /jump/. Similarly, activities can show students' proficiency in using and understanding sentences and in selecting vocabulary when speaking, reading, and writing. The activities suggested in Chapters 3 through 7 and the exercises and activities in this chapter's section on instructional strategies can be used as analytical teaching situations. Always, the standard is the performance of the LEP students' native English peers.

The mistakes that students make during these activities mean more to someone who knows the learner's native language than to someone unfamiliar with it. Just as native speakers develop in identifiable stages, so do nonnative speakers. Consider students' "errors" as miscues that may result from an inability (1) to deal with contrasting forms of the two languages, (2) to understand a particular English language form, (3) to realize the ambiguity of a speech form, or (4) to use certain irregular English forms. By being aware of the linguistic and cultural features of students' native languages, teachers effectively assess the importance and meaning of the language divergencies.

THE NEEDS OF STUDENTS WHO HAVE DIFFICULTY LEARNING TO READ AND WRITE

The reading act is complex, and many characteristics of child growth and development bear on reading success. A single causal interpretation of reading difficulty does not, therefore, seem possible. Each student's difficulty in learning to read and write may be for different reasons. Assessment of each case

FIGURE 9–2
Performance Scale for Assessing Nonnative English Speakers

	LISTENING	SPEAKING	READING	WRITING
Pronunciation/ Spelling		———		———
Vocabulary: Word Meanings	———	———	———	———
Morphological Units	———	———	———	———
Sentence Patterns	———	———	———	———
Intonational Patterns:				
Oral Usage Related to Written Form		———		———

Ratings: The student compared with age-level peers understands and/or uses standard American English patterns:

1. Like a local native speaker.
2. With accent and some situationally inappropriate forms.
3. In most situations but must make conscious effort to avoid code switching with native language forms.
4. To small degree or haltingly.
5. Not at all.

means examining a student's performance in particular social and educational settings.

A growing trend among educators is to consider students having difficulty in school as having a "learning disability." When a difficulty in learning reading strategies exists, some educators use the term *dyslexia.* Other terms have been and are being used, but this term seems to persist. Among its users, the term is often used in ways that may seem confusing. Depending on the educator's conceptual background, the term can have several different meanings.

Historically, interest in dyslexia began in various branches of preventive and rehabilitative medicine, remedial reading, and special education. Now, those who study dyslexia include researchers of the sociological, psychological, political, and economic effects of reading failure. Basically, the result is two separate approaches, the medical and the educational, in the study and instruction of dyslexia (Lerner, 1985). Medically, dyslexia is viewed as an inability to read because of brain damage or central nervous system dysfunction. Educationally, dyslexia is viewed as an inability to read when no specific causes are evident. From a whole-language perspective, both definitions are limitative.

Reviews of the literature on researchers' use of the term *dyslexia* show that it is used in many ways. One review reveals that dyslexia defines a pupil's performance when there is (1) evidence of brain damage, (2) behavioral manifestations of central nervous system dysfunctions, (3) evidence of a genetic or inherited problem, (4) maturational lag, (5) reading retardation, and (6) an inability to learn through regular classroom methods (Lerner, 1985). Other reviews show lack of agreement among professionals about the criteria used for identifying individuals with learning and reading problems and lack of technical reliability and validity of tests used in selection procedures (Harber, 1981; Kavale & Nye, 1981; Olsen & Mealor, 1981; Shepard & Smith, 1983). Many educators use the terms interchangeably and consider them to have similar characteristics (Johnson, Schneider, & German, 1983; Harris, 1983; Lipa, 1984). The issue of defining dyslexia is important: Students labeled dyslexic are placed in special education classes or resource rooms and those called reading disabled are placed in remedial reading programs. Whatever the label and placement, students in both programs often get similar educational interventions (Johnson et al., 1983).

A current interest is in research indicating that dyslexia may be caused by abnormal prenatal development of the brain and by disproportionate development of the right hemisphere over the left hemisphere, which has the language control center. One newspaper headline heralded: "Dyslexia's cause reported found" (New York Times, 1987, p. C1). At the end of the article, however, the article stated that "whether brain research can lead to treatment for reading disorders is unclear . . . [because] reading is a culturally imposed function." Research about the specialized cognitive functions of brain hemispheres needs to be read and interpreted carefully. Much of the evidence cited comes from tests of doubtful validity, a lack of statistical evidence about whether the left and right hemispheres function differently, and an underestimation of the degree of interaction between the hemispheres (Shook, 1986).

In summary, many myths abound about dyslexia because there are no irrefutable criteria for determining who has a learning disability. The phenomenon now identified as dyslexia may actually be that which educators for many years labeled a reading disability. "There is little if any difference between learning by disabled children and many of the other children being seen by the reading specialist. A false dichotomy has been created because the two specialists imply different terms, different diagnostic approaches, and different remedial methods" (Hartman & Hartman, 1973; see also Taylor, Satz, & Friel, 1979; and Harris, 1980).

Difficulties in Identifying the Reading Disabled

There is considerable evidence to suggest that despite all the testing and data collecting done to identify students with learning disabilities in reading (dyslexics), the information has little influence on actual decisions of labeling students as learning disabled. It seems the decisions may be made independently of the data and whether or not the decisions are supported by the data (Sleeter, 1986; Ysseldke et al., 1982). What is needed is a move away from the search for causative factors within students to the specification of the social and task-based conditions under which different readers can and do learn (Lipson & Wixson, 1986; C. Smith, 1985). The determination of whether a student is experiencing difficulty in learning reading and writing strategies depends on the nature of the school tasks expected and the situation in which those tasks are done (Gillespie-Silver, 1979; C. Smith, 1985).

Why so many students seem to have a learning disability in school settings is not clear. One explanation might be that educators lack consistency in how they identify learning problems among different student populations, resulting in varying proportions and characteristics among labeled students (Sleeter, 1986). The variations result from differences in (1) the defining criteria, (2) the instrumentation used for measurement, (3) the methods used to analyze the data, (4) the characteristics of the sample drawn from school populations, and (5) the quality and extent of the subjects' instructional history. It seems that few estimates of the prevalence of students with school-learning problems are supported by findings from empirical studies.

The fact that different criteria yield different results makes it clear that final truths about readers with learning problems are difficult to discover. The particular pattern of deficits may be only an artifact of the investigator's decision to use one measure of potential instead of another.

A Developmental Concept of Disability

There seem to be two common frameworks in which reading or learning disabilities are placed. One is the deficiency concept. The **deficiency concept** states that students lacking certain vital skills cannot function. The adherents to this concept postulate that one or more traumas occurring in a student's life interfere with the ability to perform educational tasks. Taking their cue from the medical profession, they suggest that once causative factors are identified, correction procedures can be instituted. This thinking is, of course, much like that prevalent at the onset of the compensatory programs for the educationally disadvantaged. It is notable that these programs seemed to have failed whenever they were built on an erroneous concept of "disadvantagedness."

The **developmental concept** of learning disabilities posits that students' success or failure in school depends on whether (a) they are ready to perform certain tasks; (b) they are given appropriate reading and writing tasks; and (c) they are learning in supportive environments (Ames 1968; C. Smith, 1986). This concept demands that any single performance be evaluated in relation to preceding or subsequent development. Since human behavior is a function of structure, individuals seem to behave largely because of the way they have developed (Ames, 1968). Behavior, therefore, is patterned, predictable, and ordered, as is the physical organism.

Students who exhibit reading and writing learning disabilities often are considered different; yet, they may not be as different from other students as is usually thought. It may be more a matter of timing than of actual difference in potential. There is evidence that students having difficulty in school may have started too soon—they are educationally immature (Ames, 1968; 1983). To understand students (and to be able to work toward preventing disruptions in learning), each student's developmental history should be known. It is important to measure and identify students' stages of development. Those lacking the appropriate readiness will seem learning disabled; yet, what is missing might be the prerequisite conceptual background in thinking and motor abilities. For those who seem to be having a great deal of difficulty with learning, their problem may have roots in the child's individual nature or ability to learn (Ames, 1968).

The maturational process is linked to age. For some students, **maturational lag** (the slow or delayed development of brain areas that mediate the acquisition of age-linked development skills) may cause the apparent disability. Rather than representing a unique syndrome or disturbance, the pattern of deficits seen in dyslexic students often resembles the behavior patterns of chronologically younger students who have not yet developed certain skills. In such cases, the patterns of deficits vary as functions of the age at which certain skills first developed (Satz & Sparrow, 1970).

In addition to differing developmental growth patterns, students differ in their approaches to problem solving (Wagner & Wilde, 1973). Students' cognitive styles and/or conceptual tempos influence their problem-solving strategies. This may result from a blending of perceptual, cognitive, and personality factors. Individual problem-solving strategies range along a psychologically differentiated continuum. Students' places on the continuum may explain their strategies to organize their environment in meaningful ways. They might differ in their cognitive styles as placed on the following continuums:

Locus of Control (approach to the environment)

External _____ Internal

Field Articulation (organization of experiences)

Dependence _____ Independence

Mode of Conceptual Tempo (problem-solving reaction time)

Impulsivity _____ Reflective

Preferential Mode of Perceptual Organization and Conceptual Categorization (processing of stimuli)

Relational _____ Analytic

The locus of control is getting increased research attention. Evidence shows some students attribute their failure or inability to learn to factors beyond their control. They have learned to be helpless (Grimes, 1981; Stipek & Weisz, 1981; Thomas, 1979). These students seem to react to failure by lowering their expectations of success and by responding to problems according to sensory–perceptual information rather than an internal analysis of information.

If further research reveals differences in how students undertake problem solving, teachers can understand how students are "disabled" when they are expected to do tasks in a way not consistent with their approach to information processing. (See Chapter 13 for a discussion about the development of human thinking.)

Assessment and Instruction of Disability

When students exhibit learning problems, teachers should seek a cause. The cause can be sought through one of two types of assessment or diagnosis: status assessment or process analysis (Brown & Botel, 1972).

Status assessment is making an inventory: It lists the range and content of students' repertoires of responses. It is done with one or more standardized "diagnostic" tests designed to distinguish what tasks or items students do or do not know. To identify or diagnose students with reading/learning disabilities, the most common status assessment tests are predictive in nature. Norm-referenced tests predict those students who might not succeed. Diagnosticians assume a severe disability exists and intervention is necessary. (See Chapter 11 for a discussion about the limitation of norm-referenced tests.)

The second type of assessment, **process analysis,** looks at students' natural behaviors. In process analysis, the evaluator examines the sequence of steps or structures the learner uses to produce a response (Brown & Botel, 1972). Unlike status assessment, in which students might provide the "right" answer for the wrong reason, process analysis evaluates any performance in relation to preceding or subsequent functioning, the expected task, and the learning situation. The key to understanding process analysis is the ability to understand functional relationships.

Teachers use process analysis when they want to know how students perform the reading act and why they might not be proficient at it. The whole-language perspective in this text provides the framework for process assessment using the analytical assessment techniques explained in Chapter 10. In addition, teachers concerned about teaching students with learning disabilities are aware of the importance of whole-language approaches to learning and instruction (Kimmel & MacGinitie, 1985; Leigh, 1980; Reid & Hresko, 1981; Sinatra et al., 1984).

Learning disabilities should not be viewed as a strange phenomenon to be approached with reverence and awe. The teacher's task is not to require a student with a learning problem to meet any shortsighted, rigid requirements for which he or she may not be ready. Instead, the teacher's task is to adjust instructional expectations and provide alternative learning experiences appropriate to the student's development, cognitive style, information to be learned, materials to be used, and learning situation.

THE NEEDS OF THE GIFTED AND TALENTED

The idea that gifted and talented students are individuals with special needs has been exemplified in several ways. One is the passage of the Gifted and Talented Children's Education Act in 1978. In this federal law, gifted and talented are defined as

> . . . children and, whenever applicable, youth who are identified at the preschool, elementary, or secondary level as possessing demonstrated or potential abilities that give evidence of high performance responsibility in areas such as intellectual, creative, specific academic, or leadership ability, or in the performing and visual arts, and who by reason thereof, require services or activities not ordinarily provided by the school. (PL 95–561, Title IX, paragraph 1530)

The concern here is: Should gifted and talented students be given different educational programs for learning to read and write? Journal articles on this topic, organizations or special interest groups in major educational organizations, and conferences devoted to this topic all give an affirmative response. Many educators view the needs of the gifted and talented, especially in regard to reading and writing programs, as different. These needs include rapid pacing and timing; "going deeper" into a topic; less rigidly structured learning environments; provisions for critical thinking, reading and writing; and responses to ideas completely different from those of more ordinary students (Frezise, 1978).

However, if the factors that differentiate gifted and talented students' reading and writing instruction from others' are examined, the question should be answered negatively. First, there is some question whether gifted students read earlier than nongifted students. Evidence shows they may not, and they may have some difficulty acquiring literacy, despite the readiness they exhibit when entering school (Cassidy & Vukelich, 1980). Other recommended strategies are similar to those discussed throughout this text and are recommended for all students, regardless of their performance and ability. The instructional programs for the gifted and talented are to (1) provide less dependence on word-recognition programs and more on comprehension, (2) encourage the habit of reading widely through independent and recreational reading, (3) break away from the lock-set use of basal readers and their accompanying workbooks, (4) select well-written instructional materials that focus on ideas and events relevant to the students, (5) develop creative and critical reading skills, and (6) use peer groupings to discuss authors' ideas and styles (Labuda, 1974; Frezise, 1978; Witty, 1971).

An idea expanded on in Chapter 13's discussion of Piaget's stages of development is important here: In general, the results of Piaget's work indicates that children at each stage of development would benefit more from enriching activities than from attempts to speed up their education. If this premise is accepted, then reading and writing programs for gifted and talented students do not differ in kind from what is proposed for all students; they differ only in degree. Gifted and talented students benefit from an expansion of their abilities rather than an acceleration of them. They should not be pushed to higher levels of materials; they should be guided to gain greater maturity at their present levels of performance through a wider (not different) range of experiences and activities. Some gifted and talented students also need to develop a sense of the natural occurrence of "failure"—an incomplete assignment, the need for multiple revisions during the composition of a message, and the possibility that a prediction about an author's message or intent may result in an understanding different from that discovered by others.

What teachers can expect from gifted and talented students is a well-roundedness and a success orientation that may not be present in other students. This difference—level of performance—separates them from their peers and even threatens some teachers. Therefore, teachers and other students should be as sensitive to the gifted and talented as they are to other students with special needs. This can be done with the bibliotherapy techniques discussed in Chapter 8. The following have discussions about awareness of and sensitivity to the needs of gifted and talented students:

Fein, R. L., & Ginsburg, A. H. (1978, April). Realistic literature about the handicapped. *The Reading Teacher, 31,* 802–805.

Lass, B., & Bromfield, M. (1981, February). Books about children with special needs: An annotated bibliography. *The Reading Teacher, 34,* 530–538.

Tway, E. (1980, January). The gifted child in literature. *Language Arts, 57,* 14–20.

DISCUSSION QUESTIONS AND ACTIVITIES

1. Someone proposes to you that your students who speak Black American English be placed in a "special" class because they do not have the usual conceptual background, an adequate vocabulary, and the experience of handling written verbal symbols needed to remain in a heterogeneously grouped class. How would you answer?

2. Examine reading materials written in a Black American English dialect. In what ways do these materials meet or fail to answer the questions about reading materials given in Chapter 10?

3. The following statement about reading readiness is from Chapter 3. How can it be rewritten to replace "reading readiness" with "learning disability" so the basic intent and meaning of the statement is retained?

   In a Piagetian sense, readiness means possessing those skills and abilities of a preceding stage of development.

4. What factors need to be considered when administering, scoring, and interpreting the informal language-assessment procedures (including the miscue analysis) for bilingual and bidialectical speakers? How could features of their language patterns be misconstrued as errors?

5. Examine at least three definitions of dyslexia from current texts or journal articles. Do they contain common aspects? Prepare a statement for a parents' meeting that interprets these definitions in light of the information presented in this chapter and in Chapters 2 and 3.

6. Prepare a plan for students with reading or learning disabilities to overcome the difficulties with some remedial reading programs identified by Allington, Stretzel, Shake, & Lamarche (1986): There is little congruence between classrooms' or remedial settings' curriculum, goals, or instruction; and, remedial programs do not normally give students additional time for reading instruction.

FURTHER READING

Literature about teaching speakers of divergent dialects is also about teaching speakers of English as a second language. The following references give additional information about these topics.

Benderly, B. L. (1981, March). The multilingual mind. *Psychology Today*, 9–12.

Carter, C. (Ed.). (1982). *Non-native and nonstandard dialect students: Classroom practices in teaching English.* Urbana, IL: National Council of Teachers of English.

Cazden, C. B. (1972). Child language and education. In, *Dialect differences and bilingualism.* New York: Holt, Rinehart & Winston.

Ching, D. C. (1976). *Reading and the bilingual child.* Newark, DE: International Reading Association.

Feitelson, D. (Ed.). (1979). *Mother tongue or second language? On the teaching of reading in multilingual societies.* Newark, DE: International Reading Association.

Fox, R. R. (Ed.). (1973). *Essays on teaching English as a second language and as a second dialect.* Urbana, IL: National Council of Teachers of English.

Harber, J. R., & Beatty, J. N. (1978). *Reading and the Black English speaking child: An annotated bibliography.* Newark, DE: International Reading Association.

Laffey, J. L., & Shuy, R. W. (Eds.). (1973). *Language differences: Do they interfere?* Newark, DE: International Reading Association.

Office for Minority Education. (1980). *An approach for identifying and minimizing bias in standardized tests: A set of guidelines.* Princeton, NJ: Educational Testing Service.

Reed, C. E. (1977). *Dialects of American English* (rev. ed.). Urbana, IL: National Council of Teachers of English.

Rodrigues, R. J., & White, R. H. (1981). *Mainstreaming the non-English speaking student.* Urbana, IL: National Council of Teachers of English.

Seitz, V. (1977). *Social class and ethnic group differences in learning to read.* Newark, DE: International Reading Association.

Thonis, E. W. (1976). *Literacy for America's Spanish speaking children.* Newark, DE: International Reading Association.

Material is available about learning and reading disabilities; however, much of it contains the unfounded assumptions discussed in this chapter. The first text is a general reference that surveys the field and gives the reader background in various diagnostic procedures and teaching strategies. The second has ideas based upon whole-language principles.

Lerner, J. W. (1985). *Children with learning disabilities: Theories, diagnosis, and teaching strategies* (4th ed.). Boston: Houghton Mifflin.

Wiig, E. H., & Semmel, E. (1984). *Language assessment and intervention for the learning disabled* (2nd ed.). Columbus, OH: Merrill.

The following has a critical examination of some programs used with students with learning disabilities and has a template for evaluating other programs:

Kaufman, M. (1973). *Perceptual and language readiness programs: Critical reviews.* Newark, DE: International Reading Association.

For information about the relationship between learning problems and the functioning of the mind, many of the chapters in the following are excellent sources:

Chall, J. S., & Mirsky, A. F. (Eds.). (1978). Education and the brain. In, *The Seventy-Seventh Yearbook of the National Society for the Study of Education.* Chicago: University of Chicago Press.

A source of other books about learning disabilities is the following annotated bibliography:

Lee, G. E., & Berger, A. (Comps.). (1978). *Learning disabilities with emphasis on reading.* Newark, DE: International Reading Association.

The following contains articles with direct instructional applications for choosing books for readers with problems learning:

Ciani, A. J. (Ed.). (1981). *Motivating reluctant readers.* Newark, DE: International Reading Association.

Quandt, I., & Selznik, R. (1984). *Self-concept and reading* (2nd ed.). Newark, DE: International Reading Association.

Suggestions for instructional programs for the gifted and talented are discussed in the following:

Labuda, M. (Ed.). (1985). *Creative reading for gifted learners* (2nd ed.). Newark, DE: International Reading Association.

Witty, P. A. (Ed.). (1971). *Reading for the gifted and the creative student.* Newark, DE: International Reading Association.

Organizer

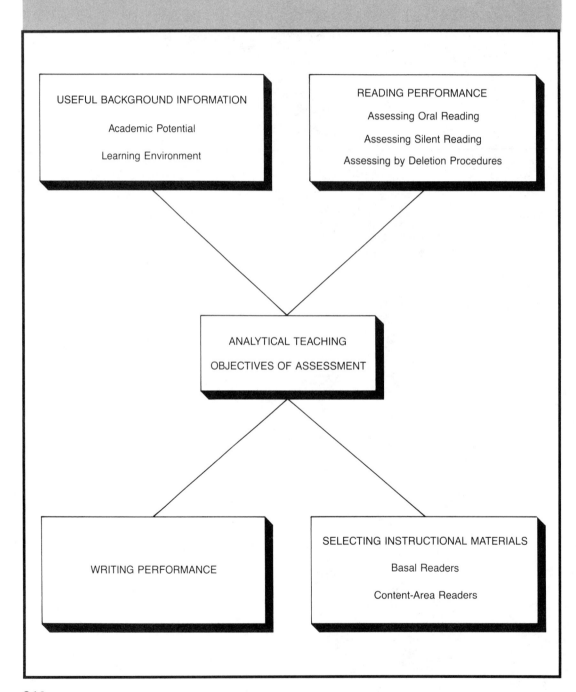

USEFUL BACKGROUND INFORMATION

Academic Potential

Learning Environment

READING PERFORMANCE

Assessing Oral Reading

Assessing Silent Reading

Assessing by Deletion Procedures

ANALYTICAL TEACHING

OBJECTIVES OF ASSESSMENT

WRITING PERFORMANCE

SELECTING INSTRUCTIONAL MATERIALS

Basal Readers

Content-Area Readers

Strategies for Analytical Teaching with Informal Instruments

Focus Questions

- What is analytical teaching?
- What information about a student's background and physical condition is relevant to reading and writing instruction?
- How can a teacher informally estimate a student's potential for doing academic work?
- How can a teacher analyze a student's oral and silent reading performances?
- What can be discovered about a student's reading performance by analyzing a writing task?
- What must be considered when selecting instructional materials for students?

Many teachers view testing and measuring as post-instructional activities. This testing and measuring, however, is only one type of assessment. Another kind—one that occurs continuously during instruction—is a check to ensure that teaching and learning are progressing in the desired direction. Both kinds of assessment are important to the overall instructional program, but the second kind is more important to the classroom teacher. The first type of assessment is called **summative assessment.** Examples are end-of-course final examinations and comparisons of two or more different types of instructional procedures after they have been in operation for a period of time.

Formative assessment, the other kind of assessment, evaluates an instructional procedure while it is in progress. Using it, teachers look at procedures to determine how many instructional goals have been accomplished and how well they have been accomplished according to an established standard. By undertaking formative assessment, teachers get feedback they can use to decide how to proceed. For this reason, formative assessment is often called **analytical teaching.**

ANALYTICAL TEACHING

The term *analytical teaching* has been selected over the more common one, *diagnostic teaching,* because *analytical* expresses more of the purposes of school assessment. The term *diagnostic* reflects a medical origin and implies a search for factors of failure. It implies, when applied to reading instruction, a search mainly for reasons why an individual is not reading well. It excludes assessing a reading performance that is successful.

Analytical teaching has five steps that the teacher undertakes as a continuous classroom activity. All five steps of analytical teaching may be undertaken one or more times a day or over a period of days.

Analytical teaching is

Describing.   Noting the performance of students without using any judgmental statements.

Classifying.   Placing students' reading performance in some schema of the reading process.

Inferring. Judging the quality of a student's reading performance by a set of standards. The standards can be applied to individuals or groups and should be consistent with the schema of the reading process.

Predicting. Deciding whether a student's observed reading performance needs to be modified and planning the teaching and learning that will follow.

Verifying. Deciding whether the plan instituted was effective. Verification occurs after planned instruction and learning by undertaking the steps of describing, classifying, and inferring. A decision is made to continue the plan or modify it.

Analytical teaching is not prolonged assessment. It is an ongoing activity in which the teacher constantly watches for patterns of effective and ineffective performance in students' reading or writing. Analytical teaching activities include the selection and recording of information during instances of students' oral and silent reading and writing.

Assessment is only as effective as the individual performing the evaluation. Teachers can become effective in devising and administering informal instruments and making instructional judgments that lead to appropriate programs for all students.

Although useful information about students' performances may be obtained through group comparisons, the analytical teacher identifies individual patterns of progress and needs. Elementary and intermediate students pass through the same developmental stages in their acquisition of reading and writing skills; however, no two students pass through the stages in the same manner, using the same pattern of strategies or language cues. Through analytical teaching, the teacher attempts to relate the developmental growth characteristics of all children to each individual student's needs.

Analytical assessment begins with an examination of the total reading and writing situations. The reading act model described in Chapter 2 may be used to help the teacher focus on individual and situationally specific tasks. Reading and writing must be examined during acts of reading and writing at different stages of development with different types of materials. Individual informal assessment procedures can be used to answer the following questions:

What is the student doing?
Is the student's performance appropriate for his or her age or grade?
Are there factors other than those directly related to the actual reading
    and writing processes that could cause the student's response or be-
    havior?

After a discussion about general objectives of assessment, this chapter presents procedures for obtaining information about students' academic potential and ways for obtaining information about oral and silent reading performance.

Then ways for assessing students' writing performances in relationship to their reading performances are considered. Last, some guidelines for selecting instructional texts are given.

OBJECTIVES OF ASSESSMENT

Reading and writing assessment programs, whether schoolwide or in a single classroom, are guided by certain objectives.

1. They are directed toward formulating methods of instruction.
2. They attempt to place reading performance and reading instruction in relation to the school's or class's educational program.
3. They are purposeful in that they have a place in the classroom's particular philosophy of education.
4. They are efficient so that the greatest amount of pertinent and useful information is collected and analyzed in the least amount of time.
5. They are continuous.

An assessment program begins with the selection of a test, or series of tests, that allows useful information to be collected. Tests, however, describe only the performance of an individual or group; they in and of themselves do not assess someone's performance. For example, if a test shows that a student has answered 16 of 25 questions correctly, all the teacher has is a description of that child's performance. What is needed is some measure of the child's reading performance. This is obtained by comparing the difference between the results of two or more tests or by measuring the results of a single test against some predetermined standard of performance. Still, this record of change or lack of change in reading performance is not yet assessment. **Assessment** is the qualitative or quantitative application of criteria for judging or evaluating the worth of performance. The process of assessing reading and writing performance, then, is the deliberate act of testing, measuring, and evaluating reading performance.

Analytical teaching, the conscious application of the principles of assessment, is really a matter of degree. The depth and thoroughness of analysis depends on the teacher's purpose. A full analysis of different students' reading and writing performances one or more times a year may be enough. On the other hand, a briefer, more frequent analysis of different aspects of the reading process may satisfy the teacher's plan. The amount and type of information collected should be consistent with the teacher's idea of the reading process and should fulfill an instructional purpose.

Information is collected about students' reading and writing performance for the purposes of instruction and administration. Information is gathered for instructional purposes when the effectiveness of the teacher's teaching or the students' learning or a combination of the two needs to be determined. Administrative decisions usually are not the responsibility of the classroom teacher. These decisions concern (1) the issue of accountability, (2) schoolwide effectiveness in comparison with other schools, and (3) predictions of long-range results of a project or experiment. For the classroom teacher, the selection and use of tests helps answer instructional questions such as

- What has the student done in the past?
- What can the student do right now?
- What can be expected of the student in the future?

USEFUL BACKGROUND INFORMATION

Often information about students' home situations, prior school and nonschool experiences, and attitudes toward reading and other activities gives the teacher insights into students' school behavior and, in particular, their reading and writing performances. Although this information in itself may not explain why students read and write the way they do, it may help explain why they do or do not respond to certain instructional activities and learning situations.

One source of information is students' school records. They often contain notations about previous achievements and home–school interactions, specialized reports or tests, and general impressions and evaluations. If school records are incomplete or unavailable, it might be beneficial to interview students and their parents, being sure to make clear that the information will be used only to help formulate programs geared to students' needs.

Sometimes students reveal their attitudes toward reading and their preferences for story content during discussions with the teacher or with other students. Teachers can use these attitudes and preferences as a guide when forming instructional programs with students who show reluctance to read independently or who resist conventional instructional materials.

Classroom teachers should observe students' behavior for signs of physical conditions that may impede school performance. In general, they should look for gross coordination problems, visual defects, or auditory deficiencies. Students who demonstrate speech problems also may need special attention. (Speech in this case refers to the physical production of oral communication.) At no time should teachers attempt to correct those deficiencies without proper guidance. It is a fallacy that children normally outgrow speech defects; generally, they must be corrected by knowledgeable personnel.

By noticing deviation from the behavior of other students in the class, teachers can identify those who need further examination by an appropriate specialist. It is good educational policy to bring to the attention of the school nurse, psychologist, speech teacher, guidance counselor, or principal any observations of deviancy. After consulting the appropriate school personnel, teachers may make a general recommendation to the parents about seeking further professional assistance.

Information about Academic Potential

When formal measures of academic potential are not available, a student's cognitive maturity and potential for academic performance can still be estimated. Listening comprehension seems to be directly related to reading. Listening comprehension is a reflection, among other things, of students' language development and knowledge of spoken words and sentences (Smith, 1975a). Since the cognitive processing of written language seems to be the same as the processing of spoken language, a listening comprehension test can be a good estimate of reading potential.

Informal tests are devised for particular classroom situations using a passage representative of the material students are expected to work with. After reading the passage aloud to students, ask them about its content to determine how well they understood the material. If students understood the material as it was read to them, then they have the potential for reading similar material.

To devise listening comprehension tests, the procedures discussed in the next section for developing informal tests of reading comprehension may be followed by substituting "listening" for "reading." Separate tests are developed for assessing students' listening comprehension of narrative and of informational passages.

Be aware, however, that attempts to measure comprehension may instead measure memory. The student who "understands" but does not retain that understanding over a period of time is different from one who does not understand at all. This issue is discussed further in a later section. In addition, be sure students' reading and listening performances are compared using materials of similar types and difficulties. Reading and listening comprehension often vary from one type of material to another.

Assessing the Learning Environment

In Chapter 2 the sociolinguistic nature of reading and writing was discussed, and the importance of considering the environment as part of any reading and writing act was noted. Literacy learning is a "process of gradual socialization to print, which is supported by formal and informal context for literacy in classrooms and other settings" (Bloome & Green, 1984).

Teachers need to examine their classroom's learning environment, which includes the physical, social, and procedural aspects of class lessons. The guidelines in Figure 10–1 may be used to focus on the context in which reading and writing are learned (C. Hittleman, 1984). Effective classrooms are identified by a large number of "yes" responses. (See Chapter 12 for a discussion about organizing for reading instruction.)

FIGURE 10–1
Assessing the Learning Environment

Classroom Environment

1. Are there reading materials available on a variety of topics and at various levels of difficulty?
2. Is there evidence that reading is a frequent and ongoing occurrence?
3. Are students' content-area texts often used to develop lessons?
4. Are materials used which allow students to transfer skills being taught to their own school and personal reading requirements?
5. Is there evidence of students' writings in all stages of development?
6. Are writing folders in active use?
7. Does ownership and authority over the writing process and product rest with the students?
8. Do students' purposes and needs determine writing tasks across all content areas?
9. Are thesauri, dictionaries, word lists, and writing aids easily accessible?

Prereading and Prewriting

1. Are students questioned about what they already know about the content of the reading selection (activating prior knowledge)?
2. Are students' responses mapped, categorized, listed, or arranged in some visual array to serve as a preorganizer for the reading?
3. Is needed vocabulary for the reading emphasized as it comes from the students' responses or included through the teacher's interaction in the prereading activity?
4. Are advance organizers provided for the reading selection—focus questions, structured overviews, SQ3R technique, or text-pattern analyses (cause/effect, sequential, comparison/contrast, superordinate/subordinate structures)?
5. Are students encouraged to hypothesize about what they might read in the selection?
6. Are provisions made for real or vicarious experiences on which to base writing?
7. Is time provided for journal writing, discussion, brainstorming, development of organizational strategies (concept maps, structured overviews)?
8. Is attention given to student-generated topics and provision made for writing the "universe of discourse?"
9. Is attention given to the audience and purpose for each piece of writing?

Developed by C. Hittleman (1984).

FIGURE 10–1
Continued

During Reading and Writing

1. Are students encouraged to jot down notes, questions, and ideas as they read?
2. Are students encouraged to take risks (predict a word or idea and look for confirmation based on further reading in the text)?
3. Are students encouraged to construct meaning from the whole text rather than try to memorize facts or details?
4. Is provision made for a rough draft—getting it down before it gets away?
5. Is time allowed for peer interaction to provide feedback and continued motivation?
6. Does the teacher act as coach: move among students, question and extend ideas, redirect focus as needed, and provide a model of self as writer?
7. Is provision made for feedback to students regarding content and meaning of their draft through peer conferences or teacher/student conferences?
8. Is provision made for multiple drafts to help students clarify their meaning and improve vocabulary and organization of their drafts?
9. Is attention directed to students' needs as shown in their writing by including one or two items for instruction and assisting with additional items for publication?
10. Are errors viewed as providing evidence about students' language development?

After Reading and Writing

1. Is there a return to the advance organizer, map, hypothesis, etc., to confirm, reject, or adjust original ideas predicted prior to reading?
2. Is some writing activity suggested to clarify the reading—short summary, questions still to be answered, arguments for or against ideas in the selection, and students' own preferences for writing purpose and audience?
3. Are students encouraged to discuss how the skills or content presented in the lesson can be applied to their other school or personal reading?
4. Is follow-up teaching carried out based on students' needs as shown during their reading?
5. Are written products displayed in the classroom, shared with others through oral reading, published in class books or newspapers, submitted to outside sources for publication, and kept in writing folders to record progress?

OBTAINING INFORMATION ABOUT READING PERFORMANCE

Assessments are made of students' oral and silent reading to determine the strategies they use when reading. As already noted, these are periodic analytic assessments. From them, teachers note changes students make in using their reading strategies and determine specific lesson content.

Assessing Oral Reading Performance

Researchers indicate that readers of all ages and levels of proficiency produce miscues (Goodman, 1969a; Hittleman & Robinson, 1975; Page, 1976). In assessing oral reading performance, the quality and not the quantity of the reader's miscues is important.

A **miscue** is an actual response in oral reading that does not match the expected response; the reader orally produces words that do not exactly reproduce the words or sentences on the page. Teachers can analyze students' oral reading miscues by answering a series of questions about the miscues. When the answers are tabulated and summarized, the pattern of the miscues can be evaluated (Burke, 1973, 1975; Goodman, 1969a).

Obtaining the Miscues

The analysis of miscues is made from an oral reading of an unfamiliar story. The story should be moderately challenging—one in which students make at least 25 miscues—but not so difficult that it frustrates students. The story should be selected from material intended for use at or one year above the grade level at which students are reading. In reading a challenging but manageable story, students reveal their reading strategies. The miscues students produce when frustrated usually do not indicate their normal approach to reading.

The exact number of miscues per hundred words that indicate whether a passage is "challenging" or "frustrating" cannot be determined through a formula. A teacher can only decide what material is too easy or too difficult for a student by doing miscue analyses. The factors making a story difficult for one student are not the same ones making it difficult for another student.

Each student's oral reading should be recorded on an audio tape or cassette recorder. This lets the teacher replay the student's responses at a later time. For the novice in miscue analysis, a recorder is essential. Often, miscues are missed or need to be reconfirmed. Intonational miscues are also difficult to judge without a second or third listening.

Place the recorder in a position that does not distract the student. Explain why the recording is being made but do not overemphasize its use. Ask the student to read the story aloud. Explain that no assistance will be offered during the reading, and at the end of the reading the student will be asked to retell the story. Directions can be given similar to the following:

> Please read this story to me. Read it out loud. While you are reading, I will not help you in any way. If you come to a word you do not know, try to do the best you can. You may skip the word if you cannot figure it out. However, I would like you to try to guess the word. When you are all finished reading, I will ask you to tell me about the story in your own words.

Tabulating the Miscues

All miscues should be written on worksheets that are copies of the story being read. The copies should faithfully maintain the line length of the story. On the worksheet, number each line for reference. Figure 10–2 shows a page from the story "The Bell of Atri." From that story, the sample worksheet in Figure 10–3 was made. Miscues are recorded on the worksheet.

Each miscue is indicated on the worksheet by some commonly accepted markings.

Substitution of a word. Write the substituted word above the word in the text. Spell nonsense words phonetically. A partial substitution, correct to the stopping point and then repeated, is not considered a miscue; however, it is marked on the worksheet.

He would like to put it in the art contest. *(look)*

I don't want it if it won't whistle. *(whee —)*

Insertion of a word. Indicate the placement of the inserted word with a caret.

"My prince," said the queen one *fine* day.

Omission of a word. Circle the omitted word or word part.

All day (long) the rain fell. It did(n't) whistle.

Reversal of two or more words. Draw a z-shaped figure between the words reversed. If more than two words are reversed, extend the horizontal lines to the end of the words.

Once upon a time there lived a prince.

(Read by the student as: One upon a time a prince lived there.)

Repetition of one or more words (to correct a miscue, to change a correct response, or to maintain continuity of thought). Underline the repeated word or words. Place a symbol in a circle to show the type of repetition.

The Bell of Atri

Atri is the name of a little town in Italy. It is a very old town and is built halfway up a steep hillside.

Years ago, the King of Atri bought a huge brass bell and had it hung in a tower in the marketplace. A length of rope reaching almost to the ground was fastened to the bell so that even a small child could ring it by pulling the rope.

FIGURE 10–2
"The Bell of Atri"

Source: Fay, L., Ross, R. R., and La Pray, M. (1981). *Young America Basic Reading Program,* Level 10. Chicago: Riverside. Reproduced by permission of Riverside Publishing Company.

A correction: Use a *c* in a circle.

All day long the prince rode his horse.

A repetition of a miscue, but the miscue is not corrected: Use a *u* in a circle.

He is painting a picture.

A repetition that changes or abandons a correct response: Use *AB* in a circle.

Jack ran to Pat's house.

The bell ⒸAntarg
of Atri

Arter Ⓝ
101   Atri is the name of a little town in Italy.

it   wee Ⓒ
102   It is a very old town and is built halfway

Ⓒ   the
103   up the side of a steep hill.

Artery
104   A long time ago, the King of Atri bought

Ⓐ   fine large bell
105   a fine large bell and had it hung up in a

Ⓒ   Ⓐ
106   tower in the marketplace. A long rope that

He
107   reached almost to the ground was tied;

T
108   to the bell. Even the smallest child could

his Ⓒ
109   ring the bell by pulling upon this rope.

Ⓐ just
201   "It is the bell of justice," said the King.

re Ⓐ
202   When at last everything was ready, the

Artery
203   people of Atri had a great holiday. All the

204   men and women and children came down

Ⓐ   L   It ⒸⒾ
205   to the marketplace to look at the bell of

t Ⓒ   Ⓒ
206   justice. It was a very pretty bell and was

207   polished until it looked almost as bright

as Ⓒ   A
208   and yellow as the sun

Ⓘ   look Ⓒ   the bell
209   "How we should like to hear it ring!"

210   they said.

Ⓒ
211   Then the King came down the street.

Ⓒ
212   "Perhaps he will ring the bell," said the

213   people. And everybody stood very still

214   and waited to see what he would do.

215   But he did not ring the bell. He did not

216   even take the rope in his hands. When he

Edward,
3rd grade

FIGURE 10–3
Miscue Worksheet

217   came to the foot of the ~water~ tower, he stopped

218   and ~rised~ raised his hand.

219   "My people," he said. "Do you see this

220   beautiful bell? It is your bell, But (it) must ~It's~ ~m-~ (C)

221   never be rung except in case of need. If ~rang skee~ (C) → *you never ring the bell*

222   any one of you is wronged at any time, he ~your 1.~ (AB) — *2. rung*

223   may come and ring the bell. And then the ~c-~ (C)

224   judges shall come together at once and ~j—~ (A)

225   hear his case and give him justice.

301   "Rich and poor, old and young, all alike ~Richard~ (C) ~alk~ (C)

302   may come. But no one must touch the rope.

303   Unless he knows for certain that he

304   has been wronged." (AB) *2. rung* ~1.~

305   Many years passed by after this. Many ~May~ → m

306   times did the bell in the marketplace ring; (A)

307   Out to call the judges together. Many (A) ~-ish~ ~m-~

308   wrongs were righted. Many evil people ~rungs~

309   were punished. (A) → ~was pun-~

310   At last. The rope was almost worn out. ~a~ ~T~ ~rung~

311   The lower part of it was untwisted. Some ~louder~ (N)

312   of the strands were broken. It became so ~strings~

313   short that only a tall man could reach it.

314   "This will never do," said the judges one ~w-~ (A)

315   day. "What if a child should be wronged? (N) → ~w~ (C) ~1. wrong did~ *2. rung*

316   He could not ring the bell to let us know it."

A repetition to maintain continuity: Use an *a* in a circle.

And you know that a prince must marry a princess.

Intonation miscue.   Indicate the student's intonation by punctuation or with arrows.

"Now why don't you get on your horse and go looking"

Tabulating the Retelling

At the completion of the oral reading, ask the student to retell the story. At first, do not give the student help. On an outline of the story (see Figure 10–4), record the information the student freely recalls. When additional information cannot be provided unaided, use general questions to guide the student.

Use the following considerations when creating questions and guiding a student's retelling.

> Questions should omit any information from the story not already given by the student.
> Questions should be general. The questions should be broad enough so the student cannot make conclusions about the story which would not have been formed from the reading of the story.
> Questions should retain all mispronunciations made by the pupil (Goodman & Burke, 1972).

Prepare general questions before the student retells the story (Goodman & Burke, 1972). These questions should be appropriate to a variety of situations and story plots, yet they can be just the encouragement a student needs for retelling the story.

Sample questions for guiding a student's retelling are:

> Tell me more about . . . (Use information already offered by the student.)
> Who was in the story?   or   Who else was in the story?
> What did (he, she, they) do?
> What kind of person was . . .? (Use characters student offers.)
> What else happened in the story?
> Where did the story take place?
> When did the story take place?
> What was the whole story about?   or   What kind of problem was the story about?
> Why do you think the story was written?   or   What did the author want you to know when he or she wrote the story?

The following conversation is an example of how a teacher can guide a student in the retelling of the story, "The Bell of Atri." From the retelling, the story outline in Figure 10–4 was marked and scored.

TEACHER: Can you tell me what you remember about the story?

STUDENT: I don't remember too much.

TEACHER: Well, tell me what you remember.

STUDENT: A king put up a bell. If someone was being bad they would ring it. And everyone would come and the bell . . . the rope got too short. And then the man, another man got another rope and put a vine on it. And then the king said leave it the way it is. And then the other guy wanted to be the minister. And he got gold and he was mean to his horse. He didn't feed him. The horse ate the leaves off the bell and he rang it and all the judges came. And they brought his master. And then they put him in a stall at the end. And one day there was a . . . The bell string got short and only a tall man could ring it. And then they made a new one. That's all I remember.

TEACHER: Can you tell me more about the horse?

STUDENT: He was starved. And he had nothing to eat and to drink so they put him in a stable and he began to eat. He had a lot of dinner.

TEACHER: Who put the horse in the stable?

STUDENT: The people after they found him.

TEACHER: Where did the people find him?

STUDENT: At the bell.

TEACHER: What was he doing there?

STUDENT: Eating the vine.

TEACHER: What happened when he ate the vine?

STUDENT: He rang the bell.

TEACHER: Why did the people think he rang the bell?

STUDENT: Because someone was being bad.

TEACHER: Who was that?

STUDENT: The master.

TEACHER: How was the master being bad?

STUDENT: By not feeding the horse. And not giving him shelter.

TEACHER: Can you tell me more about the judges?

STUDENT: I don't know. I forgot.

TEACHER: Why did the king put up the bell?

STUDENT: So if there were any person who was bad, another person would ring the bell and everyone would come.

TEACHER: And then what would happen?

STUDENT: They would punish him.

TEACHER: Who would they punish?

STUDENT: The person who did the bad thing.

TEACHER: Who would decide if the person was bad?

STUDENT: The king.

TEACHER: Can you tell me more about the minister and the master?

Characterizations (30 Points)

Identification (~~15~~) *9*

King of Atri

Men and women *people*

Judges

Man

Knight *minister / master*

Horse

Boys *5*

Theme of Story (~~20~~ Points)

Not to Be bad.

Justice applies to all creatures: animal and human.

Plot of the Story (~~20~~ Points) *10*

about a King and a horse   someone was mean to

How a faithful horse that is wronged brought retribution to his unkind master.

Main Event of the Story (~~30~~ Points) *14*

Took place in Italy

The King of Atri provided the town with a bell that had a long rope so even a child could

ring it.

The King declared it is the bell of justice and proclaimed that anyone who was wronged

should come and ring the bell. The bell would summon the judges to hear the case of the

king would punish

wronged.

The people of Atri had a holiday when the bell was finished.

Traits (~~15~~) *3*   *Edward, 3rd grade*

Hung the bell of justice

Curious about the bell

Heard cases of wronged; gave

order for new bell rope

Volunteered to fix rope

Once brave; now a miser

Mistreated; became lame and sick

Threw rocks at horse

FIGURE 10–4
Retelling Outline for ''The Bell of Atri''

STUDENT: The minister wanted to get the master's gold, but he wouldn't let
him. He wanted to keep it himself. That's why he wouldn't feed
the horse.

TEACHER: What happened when the bell string got short?

STUDENT: They fixed it.

TEACHER: How?

STUDENT: With the pine ivory. No, a grapevine.

Years passed and many cases were heard and settled. Finally the rope became worn *short* and

no longer reached the ground. Only a tall person could reach the bell rope to ring the bell.

Since there was no rope in the town long enough to hang to the ground, someone climbed

up and tied a long grapevine to the bell, instead. *King said to leave it.*

A knight who was once brave had grown old and become a miser thinking only of his gold.
the master was mean to
All day the miser sat and counted his gold. He neglected his horse who had been his best

friend and had carried him safely through many dangers. The knight could only think of how
someone wanted to be minister
much the horse would cost him so he left the horse to starve. *minister wanted to get the master's gold.*

The horse, grown lame and sick, was chased by the boys of the town and barked at by

the dogs.

One day, the horse wandered into the town when everybody was indoors. He came upon

the grapevine connected to the bell. The hungry horse begin to eat the leaves on the vine.

As the horse ate the leaves, the bell was rung calling the townspeople and judges.
at the bell
When they saw the horse, they knew he had been wronged. They realized that the horse

had called for justice against his master because of the way he had been treated. All the

townspeople explained how they had seen the horse mistreated.
master
The miser was called for. He was told that he must pay half of his gold to provide the once

faithful horse with food and shelter.

The miser grieved for his gold, and the townspeople were happy.
the people put
The horse was led to his new shelter and food.   *Total = 41*

TEACHER: Do you remember where the story took place?

STUDENT: No.

TEACHER: Can you remember what kind of place it was?

STUDENT: In Italy.

TEACHER: Can you tell me what the whole story was about?

STUDENT: About a king and a horse someone was mean to.

TEACHER: What do you call it when people who are bad get punished?

STUDENT: Judges.

TEACHER: Can you tell me why this story was written? What message did the
author want to give you? Can you think of it?

STUDENT: To not be bad.

TEACHER: Is there anything else you can tell me about the story?

STUDENT: No.

Tabulating an Informational Retelling

Although miscue analysis is used most often with stories (narratives), it can
also be used to assess students' understanding of informational material (Hittleman, 1980). The procedure for obtaining, recording, and analyzing the miscues remains the same as that for tabulating retellings from narrative passages;
what changes are the categories of the retelling outline. (See Figure 10–5 for a
sample informational retelling outline based on the passage, "Water Pollution,"
from Chapter 7.)

The categories of information listed on an informational retelling outline
are

- the major concepts or ideas,
- the important supporting concepts or ideas, and
- the specific details and examples used to explain or expand the major
  and supporting ideas.

The scoring can be apportioned: 25 points for major concepts, 25 points for
supporting concepts, and 50 points for details and examples.

Prepare general informational questions before the student retells the ideas
from an informational passage. Like the questions prepared for guiding a narrative retelling, they should be appropriate to a variety of informational passages.

Sample informational guiding questions are:

Tell me more about . . . (Use information the student has already offered.)

What did the author think was most important?

What are some more ideas about (examples of) . . .? (Use information
the student has already offered.)

What specific things are discussed in the passage?

What do you think is the most important idea?

Analyzing the Miscues

A student's miscues are analyzed to determine

1. how much the student's miscues change the author's intended
   meaning,
2. how effective the student's strategies for using his or her knowledge
   of language are, and
3. how effective the student's strategies are for recognizing words in
   context. (Burke, 1975)

FIGURE 10–5
Retelling Outline for "Water Pollution" (p. 242)

Major Concepts

1. Many substances are dumped into rivers, lakes, and oceans.
2. Polluted waters affect ecosystems.
3. Digesting wastes use up oxygen in the water.
4. Sewage acts as fertilizer making water plants grow and use up oxygen.
5. Water pollution problems can be lessened.

Supporting Ideas and Details

1. Factories, town dumps, and homes all put wastes into the water supply. Most towns dump untreated or partially treated wastes. Wastes come from toilets and drains.
2. Some wastes are poisonous and kill or injure plants, animals, and people. People and animals get sick from drinking or swimming in polluted water.
3. When oxygen is used up in the water supply, fish and other animals die.
4. When water plants grow, they fill up the water supply and die. This causes more pollution. Polluted lakes can look like thick pea soup.
5. Wastes can be treated before they enter the water supply, and some wastes can be kept out of the water. Preventing water pollution costs a lot of money. People have to want to keep the environment clean and healthy.

Analyze a student's miscues by examining whole sentences as finally produced by the student and answering a series of questions for each. Evaluate the final sentence with all the student's miscues, corrected miscues, and attempts at correction. If a miscue extends across a sentence boundary, judge the acceptability of the sentences together. For example, the following sentences on lines 305–307 in Figure 10–3:

> Many years passed by after this. Many times did the bell in the market place ring out to call the judges together.

were finally read as

> /May years passed by after this many time did the bell in the mark market place ring. Out to call the ish together./

Figure 10–6 contains a completed sample evaluation form.

Edward, 3rd grade

C–L	C–M	Q–1 Comprehension			Q–2 Knowledge of language	
Line no. of sentence	No. miscues per sentence	Meaning change			Acceptable sentence	
		No	Minimal	Yes	Yes	No
101	1	✓			✓	
102–104	4	✓				✓
104–106	2	✓			✓	
106–108	4			✓		✓
108–109	1	✓			✓	
201	1			✓		✓
202–203	1	✓			✓	
203–206	4		✓		✓	
206–208	3	✓				✓
209–210	2	✓			✓	
211	1	✓			✓	
212–213	1	✓			✓	
216–218	2		✓		✓	
220	1	✓			✓	
220–221	4		✓			✓
221–223	3			✓		
301–302	4	✓			✓	
302–304	3			✓		✓
305–307	4			✓		✓
307–308	2			✓	✓	
308–310	4		✓			✓
311	1			✓		✓
311–312	1	✓			✓	
314–315	1		✓		✓	
315	2		✓		✓	
Totals	57	12	6	7	15	10
		48 %	24 %	28 %	60 %	40 %

B–RS
Retelling Score
41 %

Note: The first part of the evaluation form is completed by examining the first 25 sentences containing miscues.

FIGURE 10–6
Miscue Evaluation Form, Part I—Sentence Meaning

Edward, 3rd grade

C–N	C–T	C–R	Q–3			Q–4		
			Grammatical function			Word recognition in context		
Line No. of miscue	Text	Reader's substitution				Similarity		
			Same	Different	Not Known	High	Some	None
101	atri	arteri	✓				✓	
102	is	it		✓			✓	
102	halfway	halfwee			✓	✓		
103	up	ups			✓	✓		
103	a	the	✓					✓
104	atri	artery	✓				✓	
109	this	his		✓			✓	
201	justice	juist			✓		✓	
205	of	it		✓				✓
208	and	as		✓			✓	
209	it	the fell	✓					✓
209	like	look	✓				✓	
212	perhaps	peerhaps	✓			✓		
218	raised	rised	✓			✓		
220	It is	It's	✓			✓		
221	rung	rang	✓			✓		
222	you	your		✓		✓		
222	wrouged	rung	✓				✓	
301	Richard	Rich and		✓		✓		
301	alike	alk			✓		✓	
305	many	may		✓		✓		
306	times	time	✓			✓		
307	judges	judish	✓			✓		
308	wrongs	rungs	✓				✓	
308	righted	right	✓			✓		
		Totals	14	7	4	12	10	3
			5 %	28 %	16 %	48 %	46 %	12 %

Note: The second part of the evaluation form is completed by examining the first 25 substitution miscues.

Miscue Evaluation Form, Part II—Word Recognition

The teacher asks a comprehension question (Q–1) for every sentence in which a miscue has occurred. The answer to this question indicates whether the student has changed the author's intended meaning. Note that the teacher judges the answer to the question in relation to the entire story plot and theme.

Q–1. Does the sentence as finally read by the student change the meaning of the story in relation to its plot and theme?

No: The sentence as finally read by the student does not change the intended meaning of the author.

Minimal: The sentence as finally read by the student moderately changes minor incidents, characters, or sequences in the story.

Yes: The sentence as finally read by the student greatly changes a major incident, character, sequence of events, or the theme in the story.

The teacher asks a knowledge-of-language question (Q–2) for every sentence in which a miscue has occurred. Each sentence with one or more miscues—not just substitution miscues but all types of miscues—is examined. The answer to the question gives an indication about the student's concern for producing acceptable language during oral reading. The teacher's criterion for judging acceptability is whether the student would produce such a sentence in spoken language.

Chapter 9 contains a discussion about judging the acceptability of the spoken language of students who speak divergent dialects of American English. The general rule is: If the sentence the student reads aloud contains elements of speech and language found in the normal, everyday speech of the student, the sentence and its miscues should be judged acceptable.

Q–2. Does the sentence as finally produced have an acceptable meaning and grammatical structure?

Yes: The sentence as finally read by the student is an acceptable sentence that could stand by itself as a meaningful and grammatically correct sentence.

No: The sentence as finally read by the student is not acceptable and could not stand by itself as a meaningful and grammatically correct sentence.

The teacher asks word-recognition-in-context questions (Q–3, Q–4) only when the student substitutes one word for another. Answers to these questions indicate the extent of the student's use of graphophonological cues and knowledge of grammatical functions.

The teacher uses the grammatical function question (Q–3) to determine whether the student's miscue is the same part of speech as the target word. In the case of nonsense words, the teacher should judge whether the student uses the word in the same grammatical function. For example, *Atri* read as /Artery/ is the same part of speech, but *Rich and poor* read as /Richard and poor/ is a different part of speech.

> Q–3. Does the miscue retain the same grammatical function as the word in the text?
>
> Same: The miscue is the same part of speech.
> Not known: It is difficult to tell whether there is a change in the part of speech.
> Different: There is a change in the part of speech.

In answering the sight–sound similarity question (Q–4), the teacher considers a word to have three parts. **High similarity** is when two word parts generally look and sound like the word, and **some similarity** is when one word part is similar to that of the word.

> Q–4. Does the miscue look like and sound like the word in the text?
> High: There is a high degree of similarity.
> Some: There is some degree of similarity.
> None: There is no similarity in any part of the word.

The first part of the evaluation form (see Figure 10–6) is completed by answering the comprehension and knowledge-of-language questions for the first 25 sentences containing miscues.

> In column C–L, write the number of the line on which the sentence begins.
> In column C–M, indicate the total number of miscues in the sentence. This number represents the sum of all miscues (not just the substitution miscues).
> In columns Q–1 and Q–2, complete the appropriate answers to the comprehension question (Q–1) and the knowledge-of-language question (Q–2).
> Calculate the totals for Q–1 and Q–2 by counting the number of checks and converting the totals to percentages.
> In box B–RS, enter the student's retelling score.

The second part of the evaluation form is completed by entering the first 25 substitution miscues.

> In column C–N, write the line number on which the miscue is located.
> In column C–T, write the word as it appears in the text.
> In column C–R, write the student's response (substitution miscue).
> In columns Q–3 and Q–4, place a check in the appropriate column for answering the grammatical function question (Q–3) and the sight–sound similarity question (Q–4).
> Calculate the column totals and percentages for Q–3 and Q–4.

The teacher then compares the score from the retelling and the percentages from the two parts of the evaluation form. The result is a profile of reading strategies indicating the student's strengths and weaknesses. From the individual profiles, the teacher can make a composite class profile to use in planning instructional procedures and class groupings. Figure 10–7 is an example of a class summary and profile sheet. Miscue analysis questions and a reproducible blank miscue evaluation appear at the end of the chapter for use in students' oral reading.

Interpreting Students' Miscues

The teacher analyzes students' miscues for their effect on the story's intended meaning as determined by the comprehension question (Q–1) and the retelling score (RS). In interpreting a student's miscues, the teacher compares the percentages for each column. Use the information in this section to determine Edward's reading strategies (Figures 10–4 and 10–6). An interpretation of his reading appears at the end of the chapter.

The first interpretation of the miscue profile is made by comparing the student's use of his or her knowledge of language (Q–2) to the comprehension question (Q–1) and the retelling score (B–RS). In reconstructing an author's message, a student may change the parts of speech of words. If miscues change a story's meaning, then there is evidence of a deficiency; however, some miscues that change a word's part of speech occur without major change in the story's meaning. This is possible because the student's miscues result in other miscues, and the sentence is adjusted grammatically. For example, the sentence beginning on line 203 of Figure 10–3 reads

> All the men and women and children came down to the marketplace to look at the bell of justice.

The sentence finally read by the student is a grammatically and semantically acceptable response:

> /All the men and women and children came down to the marketplace. Look at the bell of justice./

> What are Edward's strategies for recalling information from a story? What are Edward's strategies for using his knowledge of language to understand a story? Is there a difference between his understanding of the story and his recall of the story events?

The second interpretation is of the student's strategies for word recognition in context (Q–3). Clues to the student's strategies are obtained from answers to questions about how much the miscue (1) looks like the original word, (2) sounds like the original word, and (3) retains the same part of speech. Answers to these questions do not in themselves indicate the student's proficiencies as

Class Grade ___3___   Story ___"The Bell of Atri"___

Student's Name	C–1 Comprehension No Meaning %	C–2 Knowledge of Language %	C–3 Acceptable Sentence %	C–4 Word Recognition High Similar yes %	B–RS Retelling Score %	Effective Strategies
Alfred	45	65	85	90	40	word recognition some language sense
Betty	80	80	80	70	75	some word recognition language & meaning sense
Charles	15	40	60	55	30	some word recognition and language sense
Diane	85	90	95	98	90	all
Edward	48	60	84	84	41	*

* What effective strategies does Edward have?

FIGURE 10–7
Miscue Analysis—Class Summary Sheet

a reader; they only provide some insight into how the student's word-recognition strategies may affect his or her interpretation of the story. Miscues that have a low degree of sound or graphic similarity but do not change the story's meaning are not as important as miscues that do change the meaning of the story as intended by the author.

What are Edward's strategies for recognizing words in context?

Make the following comparisons to determine the student's effective reading strategies. You may have to refer to Edward's evaluation form and story worksheet for additional information when making these comparisons.

1. Compare the comprehension (Q–1) and retelling scores (B–RS).

Does Edward's retelling reflect the same level of understanding as do his miscues? Does his retelling score seem to be affected by memory factors?

2. Compare the knowledge-of-language (Q–2) and the comprehension (Q–1) scores.

> Is Edward producing final sentences that are meaningful by themselves but that change the intended meaning of the entire story?

3. Compare the grammatical function (Q–3) and knowledge-of-language (Q–2) scores.

> Is Edward making miscues that change words' parts of speech and then correcting them so that the final sentences are meaningful and grammatically acceptable?

4. Compare the word-recognition (Q–4) scores with the knowledge-of-language scores (Q–3).

> Does Edward use strategies mainly for recognizing individual words without using his knowledge of language for deriving meaning from the sentences? Which influences his use of strategies most—the words' sound and graphic structures or the words' functions in the sentences?

After the student's miscues are interpreted, the teacher completes a class summary sheet. Then the teacher can use the information in the class summary sheet (see Figure 10–7) for comparing students' reading strategies and for putting them in instructional groups.

The class profile sheet contains information about each student's reading of the same story. If using the same story is not possible, the teacher can use stories that do not differ in style, length, and difficulty of concepts.

On the class summary and profile sheet, the teacher should enter:

The percentage of sentences that resulted in no change in the story's meaning (Q–1).

The percentage of the sentences that were semantically and grammatically acceptable (Q–2).

The percentage of miscues that retained the same part of speech (Q–3).

The combined percentages of each student's *high* and *some* sound and graphic similarity totals (Q–4).

The score of each student's retelling (B–RS).

The strategies each student uses effectively.

The final step in miscue analysis is using the results of the class summary sheet for formulating classroom instruction. From the class analysis, it is possible to identify individuals or groups of students who need instruction in specific reading strategies.

Those having difficulty in retelling a story after oral reading might benefit from the guided reading and questioning strategies in Chapter 4 and the prediction strategies discussed in Chapter 5. Those students changing authors' meanings when reading orally might improve after receiving instruction on the prediction strategies and the paragraph and longer discourse reading strategies discussed in Chapter 5. For those whose oral reading responses are not meaningful and grammatically correct, the strategies on sentence reading in Chapter 5 might be helpful. If students need help in identifying words' parts of speech, they might benefit from lessons constructed from the information on sentence-reading strategies in Chapter 5 or that on contextual signals of word meanings in Chapter 6. Students needing to develop word-recognition strategies might benefit from the strategies for using graphophonological information discussed in Chapter 6.

What strategies would you recommend for Edward? Is there someone else in his class with whom you would group him for instruction?

Assessing Silent Reading Performance

Students' silent reading performances are assessed through (1) the oral retelling of a story or of an information passage read silently, and (2) deletion-procedure silent reading tests.

Oral Retelling
A student's silent reading comprehension is analyzed in a manner similar to that of assessing an oral reading retelling. After the silent reading, the student retells the story or recalls the information. The teacher offers no help and records the information on an outline as the student recalls it. The guidelines and questions for encouraging or guiding students are the same as those used during the oral reading retelling of stories and informational passages.

The student's responses on the oral reading retelling and the silent reading retelling are compared for patterns of similarity. The following questions may help in interpreting the difference between story or information recall after oral and silent reading.

For stories:

Is there a difference in the recall of main characters?
Is there a difference in the recall of details about the main characters' appearance, feelings, actions, and relationships?
Is there a difference in the recall of the major events?
Is there a difference in the recall of the plots?
Is there a difference in the recall of the themes?

For informational passages:

> Is there a difference in the recall of major concepts?
>
> Is there a difference in the recall of supporting concepts, details, or examples?

The comparison of the recall from oral and silent reading gives the teacher an indication about whether the interpretation of a student's reading performance obtained by the oral reading miscue analysis is the same when the student reads silently. Some of the common patterns emerging from the comparisons are the following.

Pattern 1: The silent reading recall score is greater than that of the oral reading recall score.

A possible reason for this is that the student, during oral reading, is attending to the pronunciation of words. Prior experiences may have taught the student that correct pronunciation, or at least attempts at such, is the important aspect of reading. Often a student's reading ability is judged not by a comprehension check, but by his or her ability to accurately pronounce the printed words. During silent reading, the student attends to the development of the story without undue concern for words' accurate pronunciations.

Pattern 2: The silent reading recall score is less than that of the oral reading recall score.

A student displaying this pattern may need the conscious effort applied in reading aloud to maintain involvement with the story. Such a student may be an active reader only when forced to put the written story into sound. The overt involvement may be keeping the student's attention directed at reconstructing the author's message. During silent reading, this student may have trouble selecting cues for reconstructing meaning.

Pattern 3: Both the oral reading and silent reading retelling scores are much below the comprehension score (Q–1) from the miscue analysis.

Here, the student may be giving the story information meaning at the instant of reading; however, the retention or recall of this information may be hindered. Such a student understands a story when miscues do not change the meaning of a story or when miscues that do change the meaning are corrected. The problem may arise from a lack of strategies for adequately storing the information. Or it may indicate a lack of adequate strategies for making an effective association among all the bits of information gathered so that recall is facilitated. As another possibility, a student displaying this pattern may find it easy to reconstruct surface features, but the student may not have strategies for reconstructing the author's deep structure.

When the student's oral and silent recall scores both fall below the meaning change score of the miscue analysis, the teacher may take a further step to determine the student's ability to understand the material by keeping the story passage open and allowing the student to refer to it during the retelling. This procedure is not effective with materials in which the entire story plot or the major concepts are carried in pictures. Nevertheless, most materials above the beginning reading levels have pictures that correspond to the story but do not show the entire plot and theme or major concepts.

If the student recalls more of the story content or information after referring to the text, then this may be further evidence that the student's ability to recall is interfering with the retelling. Such a student may need instruction in developing schemata and strategies for retaining and recalling information (such as those in Chapter 2 and expanded in Chapters 4 and 5). Recall is a desired trait to develop in students, but the ability to recognize information is also a important comprehension task. A student should not be deemed deficient in comprehension strategies because of limited recall strategies.

Assessing Reading Comprehension by Deletion Procedure Tests

Deletion procedures are the systematic deletion of words, phrases, or entire clauses from sentences. Students are required to reconstruct the author's ideas by writing in the missing word or words. Two deletion procedures are presented here—the cloze procedure and the OP–IN procedure. These comprehension tests are easy to make and score. Their value is in the insights they provide teachers about how students think through materials as they read. In Chapter 5, deletion procedures as an instructional technique are discussed.

The Cloze Procedure

The **cloze procedure** is a technique for systematically deleting words from a passage and having a reader replace the deleted word when reading silently. Figure 10–8 shows an abbreviated sample of a cloze procedure comprehension test.

Research substantiates the cloze procedure as a measure of students' silent reading comprehension. First, it seems the cloze procedure measures the reader's ability to understand linguistic structures; therefore, it is related to a reader's ability to understand the relationship between words and ideas (Horton, 1972). Second, since the cloze procedure requires the reader to exactly predict the deleted word and replace it, the cloze procedure measures the reader's ability to comprehend the author's ideas. Research based on psycholinguistic principles has consistently shown that a reader's comprehension is measured by how well the information surrounding the blank is used and how well the information taken from the text is used to get additional information. Also, studies show that a reader's performance on a traditional comprehension test (questions) cannot be distinguished from that person's performance on a cloze comprehension test (Bormuth, 1975). Hence, the cloze procedure measures, during reading, the mental processes commonly called *comprehension.*

My uncle is an anthropologist. That (1) _____ he studies all about
(2) _____ kinds of people and (3) _____ they act. He travels
(4) _____ over the world to (5) _____ people and to learn
(6) _____ about them.
    My uncle (7) _____ me that one of (8) _____ most important
things an (9) _____ does is talk with (10) _____ That isn't as
easy as it sounds, since that means he has to know how to speak many different
languages.

Answers:	1. means	2. different	3. how	4. all
	5. meet	6. all	7. tells	8. the
	9. anthropologist		10. people	

FIGURE 10–8
Sample Cloze Comprehension Test

Source: Fay, L., Ross, R. R., and La Pray, M. (1981). *Young America Basic Reading Program,* Level 10. Chicago: Riverside. Reproduced by permission of Riverside Publishing Company.

The steps for creating cloze procedure tests are standard (Bormuth, 1975). For the third grade and higher:

1. Select a 250-word passage.
2. Beginning with any of the first five words of the second sentence of the passage, delete every fifth word until 50 words are deleted. Always leave the first and last sentences intact. Do not delete punctuation and hyphens. Numerals, such as 1975, are deleted as whole words. Apostrophes are deleted with the word in which they appear.
3. Type the passage on a master, double spacing between lines. For each deleted word, type a line 15 spaces long. The spaces should be uniform in length, regardless of the length of the original word.
4. Provide students with instructions and a sample test before giving them the actual cloze tests. The instructions may be similar to the following:

    At the bottom of this page is a sample of a completion test. Your job will be to guess what word was left out of each space and to write that word in the space.
    Remember: Write only one word in each space. Try to fill every blank, and don't be afraid to guess.
    You may skip hard blanks and come back to them later. Wrong spellings will not count against you (Bormuth, 1975).

This untimed test is scored by counting exact replacements as correct responses. When the cloze procedure is used for measuring students' comprehension, the most efficient means is to use exact words as the standard for marking (Bormuth, 1975). In Chapter 5 the cloze procedure is presented as an instructional procedure. In such circumstances, deviations that retain the intended meaning of the passage are acceptable. To maintain consistency in interpreting the cloze procedure as a comprehension test, only exact replacements should be considered correct.

After the number of a student's correct responses has been determined, convert that number into a percentage. The following are guidelines for interpreting students' scores.

A score of 40 percent indicates the material is appropriate for instructional purposes.

A score of 60 percent or greater indicates material that can be read independently.

Scores below 40 percent indicate the material may be frustrating. (Jones & Pikulski, 1974; Bormuth, 1968)

Insights about a student's reading strategies can be obtained by examining the completed items within the context of the passage. Group the student's responses into four categories:

Fully acceptable. The response creates a meaningful sentence that retains the author's intended ideas.

Sentence acceptable. The response creates a meaningful sentence, but the sentence is not consistent with the author's intended meaning.

Partial sentence acceptable. The response is meaningful in part of the sentence and may retain some of the author's intended meaning. It is meaningful with either the immediately preceding or following words.

Unacceptable. The response does not create a meaningful sentence, and it is not related in any way to the author's intended meaning.

Additional insight about students' processes of understanding can be obtained by pointing to each completed cloze item and asking the student why the word was selected. When using this informal procedure, do not have the student read the entire passage aloud. Do not even ask the student to pronounce the answer. Just ask him or her to explain why the word was selected and note the types of clues the student used in determining the answer.

Although the cloze procedure test is a valid and reliable measure of comprehension, it has certain limitations (Hittleman, 1978). Some cloze tests may contain many deletions for which there are no contextual clues. Certain students, particularly those in the primary grades, should not be given cloze tests without some modifications. These were discussed in Chapter 5. Also, do not emphasize the writing of the responses; instead, give attention to the student's comprehension of the passage. In cases where the student is reluctant to write, accept an oral response. In such cases the teacher gets an indication of the student's ability to read and understand the passage. Last, a cloze test measures global aspects of comprehension and not specific substrategies. The test, then, should not be used to analyze students' specific strategies and skills.

The cloze procedure test is a quick and efficient way to estimate the appropriateness or "readability" of any book for use with particular students (Hittleman, 1978). With it, a teacher can estimate the level in which to place a student in a basal reading or content-area series. The cloze procedure test can also be used to determine whether students can read a text independently, whether they can read it only with the teacher's guidance, or whether they will be frustrated reading it.

When groups of students are tested for placement in any series of texts, they should be given higher-level materials whenever they score 60 percent or greater. Students scoring below 40 percent should be assigned to the last level at which they scored 40 percent or greater.

For example, a teacher could make a series of cloze tests to cover a wide range of texts in a basal series or in a content-area series. The test for the easiest level should be administered to the whole class. Those students who cannot achieve a satisfactory score may then be assigned to a text in that level. The remaining tests can then be given to the other students, and the teacher can continue placing students at their appropriate levels. Additional testing may be required for students showing that the first test is too difficult or the last test too easy. In a few days a teacher can match students with texts according to their ability to understand.

The OP–IN Procedure

The **OP–IN procedure** is similar to the cloze procedure in that words are deleted from sentences, but in this procedure entire portions of sentences are deleted. Figure 10–9 contains an abbreviated OP–IN procedure passage.

In the OP–IN procedure, endings are deleted from sentences within a passage (Pehrsson, 1975, 1985). The student is asked to write in the endings based on his or her perception of the author's ideas. From the student's responses a teacher gains insight about the student's comprehension strategies.

The steps for creating OP–IN tests for the third grade and higher are:

1. Select a passage with at least 29 sentences and remove its title.
2. Delete the last half of every other sentence. Sentences with an uneven number of words should retain the extra word in the first half.
3. If there are fewer than five words in a sentence, leave it intact and delete from the next sentence.
4. For every passage there should be at least ten OP–IN deletions.
5. In place of the deleted sentence endings, draw lines of equal length.
6. Provide students with instructions and a sample test before giving them the actual OP–IN tests. The instructions should be similar to the ones given for a cloze test. Be sure to remind students that they

FIGURE 10–9
Sample OP–IN Comprehension Test

"What did you buy?" Jenny asked.

"I was helping Mr. Sloan get ready for the auction, as I do every Friday. I saw a rolltop desk. I asked Mr. Sloan if I could buy it before the _____.

Then a man came in and insisted on buying it. I said 'no' but _____
_____.

Finally, I just left with the desk.

"That shouldn't make _____.

"But he followed me home."

Now Jenny began _____.

She parted the kitchen curtains and looked out the window.

Clouds floated over _____.

The sun shone brightly. Everything seemed peaceful. Then Jenny saw a man getting _____.

He was dressed in navy blue and had a bushy moustache. He was looking at their house.

Original OP–IN sentences

1. I asked Mr. Sloan if I could buy it before the *Saturday auction and he said 'yes' and so I did.*
2. I said 'no' but *he kept insisting.*
3. "That shouldn't make *you nervous, Mom."*
4. Now Jenny began *to feel nervous.*
5. Clouds floated over *the blue sky.*
6. Then Jenny saw a man getting *out of a small, green car.*

Source: "The Mystery of the Roll Top Desk," by Evelyn Witter, 1977, Chicago, IL: The Childrens Press.

can write as many words as they think are needed to complete each sentence. Encourage them to fill in every blank and to guess an answer when they're not sure. (Pehrsson, 1985)

This untimed test is scored by evaluating each sentence completion separately using a five-point scale.

Four points. The student's response is the same or similar to the author's intent.

Three points. The student's response is different, but it contributes to the author's topic.

Two points.   The student's response is different and fails to keep to the author's topic. It does, however, relate to a topic provided by the reader and makes sense out of the passage.

One point.   The student's response makes sense only in the context of that sentence and fails to contribute to the author's topic.

No points.   The student's response does not make sense.

Total the points for the entire OP–IN passage and divide by the total number of possible points in the passage. If the passage has 20 OP–IN deletions the possible points are 80. The resulting percentage is the "distance ratio" (DR), representing how much preparation the reader needs to understand the passage. Guidelines for interpreting the student's distance ratio are:

A DR score between 0–29 percent indicates the student can read this type of material rapidly and independently.

A DR score between 30–44 percent indicates the student needs minimal but some preparation before reading this type of material.

A DR score between 45–65 percent indicates the student needs normal preparation for being introduced to the topic and the related ideas.

A DR score between 66–100 percent indicates the student needs extensive preparation related to the topic prior to reading. (Pehrsson, 1985)

Insights about a student's reading strategies can be obtained by examining the completed OP–IN items within the context of the passage. Group the student's responses into one of the three following categories.

Interactive.   All OP–IN responses with point counts of four and three. The student understands the author's intended ideas about the topic.

Projective.   All OP–IN responses with a point count of two. The student does not understand the author's intended ideas but is relating the passage content to his or her own topic.

Fragmented.   All OP–IN responses with a point count of one or zero. The student does not understand the author's ideas and does not relate the passage content to any topic.

A category with 50 percent or more of a student's OP–IN responses is designated as the student's reading pattern. Students with interactive patterns might benefit from strategies for guiding them to independence in reading and writing such as those discussed in Chapter 5. Students with projective patterns might benefit from the teacher-guided strategies discussed in Chapter 4 and the content-area reading strategies in Chapter 7. Students with fragmented patterns should not read from texts with the maturity level of the OP–IN procedure test and should be tested with passages of lesser maturity. These students might also benefit from the vocabulary development strategies discussed in Chapter 6 and the guided strategies in Chapter 3.

OBTAINING INFORMATION ABOUT WRITING PERFORMANCE

Reading and writing use the same cognitive processes of knowing, reasoning, and inferring. Writing is the language production facility corresponding to the receptive processing of reading. Additional information about students' knowledge of and competence in using print is gained through an analysis of what and how they write.

Informal writing assessments are made of products composed by students after they have had at least one opportunity to review and revise their product. The composing process consists of (1) prewriting, (2) writing/drafting, (3) revising, and (4) editing. These phases are not discrete; they may occur simultaneously and recursively. Here, however, they are discussed as interrelated but distinguishable phases. (See Chapters 2, 3, 4, and 5 for other discussions of the composing process.)

In addition to its cognitive and psychological aspects, learning to write is a social process. Writing is learned most effectively in the community of a classroom where students and teacher interact and give feedback. Learning to write results from students' listening and responding to one another instead of working alone or with only the teacher. Teachers need to create an environment where students are encouraged to collaborate and learn from all members of the classroom writing community.

After a piece of written work is produced, either through a direct assignment or as a result of a spontaneous act, it should be analyzed to gain insights about students' understanding of the various schemata for communicating ideas.

Again, these schemata include the four factors of a communication situation: participants, the writing setting, topic, and task. A teacher judges students' competence in language by the appropriateness of what they write as compared to these factors. Students' competence also depends on where they are in the stages of development. This information is used with the rating scale in Figure 10–10 to judge the overall appropriateness of a student's writing sample and with the analysis checklist in Figure 10–11 to determine specific instructional needs.

When examining students' writing as communication, remember that there is no direct way to use writing for insight into reading comprehension. If students show they can compose a particular language pattern, you can assume that they have competence using that pattern in all language forms. Nevertheless, an inability to write or speak a language pattern does not indicate that a student does not have receptive competence.

For example, a student just beginning to produce one-sentence compositions would be given a rating of at least three for producing:

I wlkd to they zoo to see the amnis.

Here, the student has good communication for his or her developmental level. The participants, the story setting, and the topic are identified. The composition fulfills the task of recording an event—a class trip.

A task for a more mature student requiring a product with specific directions in sequence, however, would receive a rating no higher than two for producing:

FIGURE 10–10
Rating Students' Writing Performances

Use the information in Chapters 5, 7, and 13 on sentence patterns, paragraph structures, and the cohesiveness of longer passages to rate the characteristics of students' writing.

Establish the characteristics of the writing task to be rated before assigning the writing.

Rate a variety of writing samples in relation to students' language development.

1. Little or no presence of the characteristic(s).
2. Some presence of the characteristic(s), but communication of the idea(s) or story (stories) is impeded by incomplete schemata or is inappropriate to the participants, story setting, topic, or task.
3. Fairly successful communication of idea(s) or story (stories) through detailed and consistent presence of characteristic(s).
4. Highly inventive and mature presence of the characteristic(s) in communicating idea(s) or story (stories) and in relation to the development of the students' language and schemata.

How to Make a Swing
furst you need a tire
rope a latter nails and a
hammer. Now find a thick
branch and take the
latter and put it againt
the tree. Then get the rope and
tighe it tight around the
branch and hammer it to
the tree make sure its
sturdy.

Here, a student identified as being orally proficient in reporting ideas in sequence is not communicating well. Although the student does identify the participant and the topic, the student does not identify the task setting and the task. The tree and the branch are not set in any context. The sequence of directions is inconsistent, and there are few supporting details. In sum, the report does not give another student explicit directions for creating the swing.

Using the checklist in Figure 10–11, the swing composition can be analyzed additionally for specific aspects of writing. This student would be identified as needing instruction in identifying the rhetorical task, organizing ideas, choosing appropriate words, structuring sentences, and using mechanics ap-

FIGURE 10–11
Checklist for Analysis of Student Writing

Directions: Use more than one student writing sample in the analysis. Which of the following does the student need instruction in?

Rhetorical tasks

a. Understanding the purpose of the task?
b. Demonstrating a sense of audience appropriate to the task?
c. Using the required literary form correctly?
d. Maintaining a consistent point of view?
e. Providing the information content required by the task?

Organization

a. Developing a plan of organization?
b. Maintaining coherence within paragraphs and in the writing sample as a whole?
c. Using appropriate transitions?
d. Making generalizations?
e. Using pertinent reasons, details, and examples to support generalizations or conclusions?
f. Excluding irrelevant material?

Word Choice/Usage

a. Selecting and maintaining the level of usage appropriate to the task?
b. Using specific vivid words?
c. Forming words correctly?
d. Avoiding unnecessary repetition?
e. Using words accurately?

Sentence Structure

a. Avoiding sentence fragments?
b. Avoiding run-on sentences?
c. Using sentences of varied types and lengths?

Mechanics/Grammar

a. Developing spelling skills?
b. Using punctuation correctly?
c. Using capital letters correctly?
d. Improving handwriting?
e. Grammar—subject verb agreement, verb tenses, pronoun references?

Source: Bureau of English and Reading Education. (1982). *Writing test for New York state elementary schools, rater training packet.* Albany, NY: State Education Department, University of the State of New York. Used by permission.

propriately. For both writing samples, the students would be rated differently if they were identified as being of other developmental stages.

When assessing students' writing, the teacher must not use only a single sample to make judgments about their performance or about the relationship of their writing to reading comprehension. It is only by analyzing patterns of performance revealed in assignments requiring a variety of writing patterns that students' language competence is determined. Before making these assignments, teachers must have a clear concept themselves of the characteristics expected in written messages. These expectations are based on the knowledge of the nature of written messages, the purposes for which people write, and the appropriateness of the task to the student's developmental stage.

SELECTING APPROPRIATE INSTRUCTIONAL MATERIALS

A surfeit of materials can be found for use in instructional programs. The materials selected for use with a whole-language reading and writing program should be consistent with the information in Chapters 2 and 13 about language and its functions in communicating ideas.

Selecting Basal Reading Materials

In Figure 10–12 are critical questions for use as a guide in selecting materials for teaching reading. The accuracy of authors' claims to the relevance and importance of their information should be consonant with the insight gleaned from language study that can be applied to the teaching of reading and writing. (In Chapter 4, "Strategies for Guiding Students' Learning," are instructional strategies for use with basal reading series. Here, the concern is with evaluating the appropriateness of reading materials.)

Selecting Content-Area Reading Materials

Textbooks have a central place in content-area teaching. They are the main resource, whether desirable or not, that teachers use to select and organize information presented to students. Some teachers base their lessons solely on the books they use with their students (Hechinger, 1985).

Evidence shows that how textbooks are written has an influence on the amount and type of information students learn from those texts. Textbooks that are conducive to learning are called **considerate texts.** Teachers need to be aware of the problems inconsiderate texts present so they can help students read and understand those materials (Armbruster, 1984; 1985).

Figure 10–13 presents critical questions to use as a guide in selecting content-area textbooks (Armbruster, 1984; 1985). (Chapter 6 discussed instructional strategies for guiding student learning with content-area textbooks. Here, means for assessing the appropriateness of those reading materials are presented.)

FIGURE 10–12
Criteria for Evaluating Reading Series

Teaching Materials and Manuals

1. Do the manuals provide a means to mobilize students' prior knowledge and experiences (ways to activate students' schemata)?
2. Do the manuals provide suggestions for enrichment or remediation when and where needed?
3. Are teachers' lesson plans clear, purposeful, and connected to one another?
4. Are the supplemental materials pertinent and varied?
5. Are there suggestions to encourage independent language activities?

Appreciation

1. Does the series provide for assisting students in developing criteria to be critical, evaluative readers?
2. Does the series provide for assisting students to develop and extend their own tastes in reading?
3. Does the series help develop students' appreciation of the writer's craft?

Vocabulary and Language Development

1. Is attention given to linguistic readiness at the beginning stages of the series?
2. Are a number of different context-clue strategies taught and developed across the series?
3. Does the series provide for the recognition and teaching of substitution units (words used in place of other words, i.e., pronouns, synonyms)?
4. Does the series provide for the recognition and teaching of connectives (i.e., conjunctions, prepositions)?
5. Do the materials provide opportunities to relate reading to writing, listening, speaking, and viewing skills?
6. Does the language in the series move from students' natural language to more formal language?
7. Are vocabulary skills introduced at appropriate developmental levels?
8. Are multiple meanings of words taught?
9. Is new vocabulary presented in a setting of familiar words?
10. Is new vocabulary introduced in a variety of ways in meaningful, relevant context?

FIGURE 10–12
Continued

Text Content

1. Does the content reflect students' interests at progressive levels of development? For example,
   Primary Grades: contemporary life, fantasy, mythology, fairy tales
   Intermediate grades: curriculum content areas that look like content materials, humor, mystery, sports, science fiction (varied interest of students in specific areas)
2. Are sexist and ethnic stereotypes avoided in language and illustrations?
3. Is the vocabulary related to students' backgrounds?
4. Is the content related to students' backgrounds?
5. Does the series provide some classical literature as well as good contemporary material?
6. Are illustrations current, appealing, and relevant to the content?
7. Is the content factually accurate?

Text Structure

1. Do some selections build on previous selections so that there is continuity?
2. Do ideas presented gradually move from the concrete to the abstract?
3. When the primary mode of organization is expository:
   Are major ideas written simply, clearly, and highlighted?
   Is there a tight relationship between the main idea and vivid examples?
   Are less important ideas brief without vivid examples?
   Are important parts always written in the positive and never in the negative?
4. When the primary mode of organization is narration:
   Are the steps clear and identifiable?
   Are examples or explanations clearly subordinate to each item of the sequence?
5. Are narrative, expository, descriptive, argumentative/persuasive modes of discourse taught across the series?
6. Are organizational patterns taught as aids to comprehension (i.e., cause/effect, problem/solution, comparison/contrast, etc.)?

Continued on next page

FIGURE 10–12
Continued

Skill Development

1. Are basic comprehension/thinking strategies across the series introduced and taught at appropriate developmental levels (i.e., main idea, supporting details, inferences/drawing conclusions, understanding sequence, categorization) as opposed to just being tested?
2. Are skills usually taught and reinforced in relation to the content of the texts?
3. Are skills presented in a logical sequence?
4. Is enough practice provided to develop and retain skills presented in the series?
5. Are study strategies introduced and taught at appropriate levels of development?
6. Does the series provide for and develop instruction in the use of reference skills (i.e., table of contents, index, dictionary, thesaurus, card catalogs)?
7. Does the series provide for application of these skills through study strategies such as skimming, scanning, and surveying?
8. Are organizational strategies such as outlining and summarizing taught in the series?
9. Are test-taking techniques taught in the series?
10. Is attention paid to strategies for developing fluency in oral and silent reading?
11. Are opportunities provided to give practice in reading different materials at different rates for different purposes?

Assessment

1. Does the series provide criterion-referenced assessment related to the content at regular intervals?
2. Does the series provide for reliable assessment devices, independent of book content, at regular intervals?
3. Does the series provide for monitoring devices in a variety of formats (multiple choice, *Degrees of Reading Power*, grid responses, deletions)?

Parental Involvement

1. Is there a means, apart from test results, of informing parents about student performance?
2. Is there a means of informing parents of the roles they can play in extending students' language development?

Source: Developed by the Huntington Public Schools, Huntington, NY. © 1984. Used with permission.

FIGURE 10–13
Characteristics of a Considerate Textbook

Structure
Does the textbook have a logical, easily identifiable organization?

1. Do heading and subheadings reflect a reasonable organization of the subject matter?
2. Does the introduction reveal the content and structure of the material presented?
3. Is the text structure clearly signaled throughout the text?

Unity
Does the author address one purpose at a time?

1. Are main ideas obvious?
2. Is information clearly related to the main idea?
3. Do transition statements help the reader move from idea to idea?

Coherence
Are there clear relationships connecting ideas?

1. Are connectives explicit or obvious?
2. Are references clear?
3. Is the order of events in the text easy to follow?
4. Are graphics clearly related to the text?

Audience Appropriateness
Is the text written for a particular student population?

1. Can the text be understood by the target students?
2. Does the text contain information that is important for the target students to know?

Truth
Does the text contain the truth about the topic?

1. Is the information accurate?
2. Is there any contradictory information?

Source: Armbruster, 1984, 1985.

DISCUSSION QUESTIONS AND ACTIVITIES

1. Explain why a classroom teacher should examine students' reading and writing performances in classroom situations using typical classroom work rather than using standardized tests.

2. Using the informal procedures for assessing oral and silent reading explained in this chapter,
   a. compare the oral and silent reading performance of an elementary-school student.
   b. compare the oral and silent reading performances of two elementary-school students who are in the same grade level and are reading the same story.
   c. compare the oral and silent reading performances of two elementary-school students who are in different grade levels and are reading the same story.
   d. compare the oral and silent reading performance of an elementary-school student reading both a story and a passage from a content-area text.
   e. compare each of these previous reading performances with writing samples based on the written retelling of each reading selection.

3. Explain how to identify the significant characteristics to which Robinson (1975) refers in the following statement, and explain how a teacher might identify them.

   To study the reading process, two essential ingredients must be examined: the reader and the selection read. If the significant characteristics of each could be identified, then the interaction of the reader and the materials could be interpreted. (p. 11)

4. Construct cloze and OP–IN procedure comprehension tests using three different types of reading materials from the same grade level: a narrative story, a social studies passage, and a science passage. Administer the tests to
   a. a group of students at the same grade level; and/or
   b. students from each of three different grade levels. Identify students for whom the passages may be used for instructional purposes and students who may be able to read the passages independently.

5. The following statement by Bormuth (1975) has implications for classroom teachers when they construct tests to measure students' comprehension. Explain how the procedures for guiding retelling after oral and silent reading may help overcome some of the difficulties to which Bormuth refers.

   Test writers influence the difficulty of tests: two writers making a test over a single passage could produce tests of quite different difficulty, the one writer's test eliciting mostly low scores, and the other's mostly high scores. (p. 63)

6. Have one upper elementary-grade student orally read a basal-reader passage and a content-area passage. Score miscue analyses of the readings and compare the results. Do students' patterns of miscues differ on the two passages? If so, to what do you attribute the difference?

FURTHER READING

The following have articles about ways to informally assess students' learning of oral language, writing, and reading.

Jaggar, A., & Smith-Burke, M.T. (Eds.). (1985). *Observing the language learner.* Newark, DE: International Reading Association and the National Council of Teachers of English.

Pikulski, J.J., & Shanahan, T. (Eds.). (1982). *Approaches to the informal evaluation of reading.* Newark, DE: International Reading Association.

For those who wish to investigate in greater detail the administration and interpretation of miscues, the following texts will be helpful. The first is the manual for the full miscue inventory. It also contains three alternate procedures for using the inventory in classrooms. The other two contain articles explaining the application of miscue analysis in various educational settings.

Goodman, Y.M., Watson, D.J., & Burke, C.L. (1987). *Reading miscue inventory: Alternative procedures.* New York: Richard C. Owens Publishers.

Goodman, K.S. (Ed.). (1973). *Miscue analysis: Applications to reading instruction.* Urbana, IL: National Council of Teachers of English and ERIC Clearinghouse on Reading and Communication Skills.

Page, W.D. (Ed.). (1975). *Help for the reading teacher: New directions in research.* Urbana, IL: National Conference on Research in English and ERIC Clearinghouse on Reading and Communication Skills.

The following book has two purposes: to compile informal instruments that can be used to assess performance in all the language arts and to compile reviews of these instruments. The tests are listed by area, but there is a cross-reference index so that instruments appropriate to a particular age or grade level may be located. It is an excellent source of existing instruments and ideas for teachers to use in constructing their own informal assessment procedures.

Fagan, W.T., Cooper, C.R., & Jensen, J.M. (1975). *Measures for research and evaluation in the English language arts.* Urbana, IL: ERIC Clearinghouse on Reading and Communication Skills and National Council of Teachers of English.

In the following article, the authors explain a variation of the cloze procedure that can be used to identify children with comprehension problems and to monitor students' progress in comprehension development.

Guthrie, J.T., Seifert, M., Bumham, N.A., & Caplan, R.I. (1974). The maze technique to assess, monitor reading comprehension. *The Reading Teacher, 28,* 161–168.

The following two articles contain additional ideas for informally assessing students' language.

Clark, C.H. (1982). Assessing free recall. *The Reading Teacher, 35,* 434–439.

Pickert, S.M., & Chase, M.L. (1978). Story telling: An informal technique for evaluating children's language. *The Reading Teacher, 31,* 528–531.

An expanded discussion of the ideas about assessing students' writing is found in the following:

Greenhalgh, C., & Townsend, D. (1981). Evaluating students' writing holistically—An alternative approach. *Language Arts, 58,* 811–822.

The following nonprofit organization provides educators with evaluations of educational materials, equipment, and computer software in all subject areas. They publish their reports in monthly newsletters.

EPIE (Educational Products Information Exchange). P. O. Box 839, Water Mill, NY 11976

CHAPTER 10 APPENDIX

Edward's Reading Strategies

> What are Edward's strategies for recalling information from a story? What are Edward's strategies for using his knowledge of language to understand a story? Is there a difference between his understanding of the story and his recall of the story events?

Edward is able to recall major characters, but is unable to provide important traits about them. He does not understand the story theme and has only a general sense of the story plot. His recall of details deals mostly with events about the horse and the rope.

Edward's understanding of the story during oral reading may be greater than revealed by his recall. Seventy two percent of his miscues during oral reading have either no or minimal meaning change, indicating that he is making sense of the story as he reads. Also, his miscues result in generally acceptable sentences, revealing a knowledge of language. When his miscues result in unacceptable sentences, he often self-corrects those miscues.

> What are Edward's strategies for recognizing words in context?

During oral reading, Edward's miscues have a close similarity to the text, indicating that he is using graphic and sound cues. Many of his substitutions are self-corrected.

> Does Edward's retelling reflect the same level of understanding as do his miscues? Does his retelling score seem to be affected by memory factors?

Edward seems to understand more of the story information during oral reading than is revealed by his retelling. He does seem confused, however, by concepts important to the story theme and plot (for example, *justice*, *judge*, and *miser*).

> Is Edward producing final sentences that are meaningful by themselves but that change the intended meaning of the entire story?

Overall, as finally read, Edward's sentences are acceptable, indicating he has a knowledge of language. However, more than half of those sentences have at least a minimal change in meaning. Edward does not seem to have a full understanding of the story events.

> Is Edward making miscues that change words' parts of speech and then correcting them so that the final sentences are meaningful and grammatically acceptable?

Edward's substitution miscues are equally divided between retaining the same grammatical function and being different. Edward does self-correct many miscues so that his final sentences are generally meaningful and acceptable.

> Does Edward use strategies mainly for recognizing individual words without using his knowledge of language for deriving meaning from the sentences? Which influences his use of strategies most—the words' sound and graphic structures or the words' functions in the sentences?

Edward seems to be attempting to make sense of the story as he reads orally. He does seem to be using a knowledge of language together with the graphic features of the words when he encounters an unknown word. His uncorrected mispronunciations seem to be for difficult-concept words.

> What strategies would you recommend for Edward? Is there someone else in his class with whom you would group him for instruction?

Although Edward shows he is actively processing the story information and attempting to make sense of the story, he does not seem to be effective in his attempts. He would benefit from instruction in recalling story events with the aid of story organizers. Edward could be grouped with Alfred, who shows a similar pattern on the class summary sheet.

Miscue Evaluation Forms

C–L	C–M	Q–1			Q–2	
Line no. of sentence	No. miscues per sentence	Comprehension			Knowledge of language	
		Meaning change			Acceptable sentence	
		No	Minimal	Yes	Yes	No
Totals						
		%	%	%	%	%

B–RS
Retelling Score
%

Note: The first part of the evaluation form is completed by examining the first 25 sentences containing miscues.

C–N	C–T	C–R	Q–3			Q–4		
Line No. of miscue	Text	Reader's substitution	Grammatical function			Word recognition in context		
						Similarity		
			Same	Different	Not Known	High	Some	None
		Totals						
			%	%	%	%	%	%

Note: The second part of the evaluation form is completed by examining the first 25 substitution miscues.

Miscue Analysis Questions

Q–1. Does the sentence as finally read by the student change the meaning of the story in relation to its plot and theme?

No: The sentence as finally read by the student does not change the intended meaning of the author.

Minimal: The sentence as finally read by the student moderately changes minor incidents, characters, or sequences in the story.

Yes: The sentence as finally read by the student greatly changes a major incident, character, sequence of events, or the theme in the story.

Q–2. Does the sentence as finally produced have an acceptable meaning and grammatical structure?

Yes: The sentence as finally read by the student is an acceptable sentence that could stand by itself as a meaningful and grammatically correct sentence.

No: The sentence as finally read by the student is not acceptable and could not stand by itself as a meaningful and grammatically correct sentence.

Q–3. Does the miscue retain the same grammatical function as the word in the text?

Same: The miscue is the same part of speech.

Questionable: It is difficult to tell whether there is a change in the part of speech.

Different: There is a change in the part of speech.

Q–4. Does the miscue look like and sound like the word in the text?

High: There is a high degree of similarity.

Some: There is some degree of similarity.

None: There is no similarity in any part of the word.

Organizer

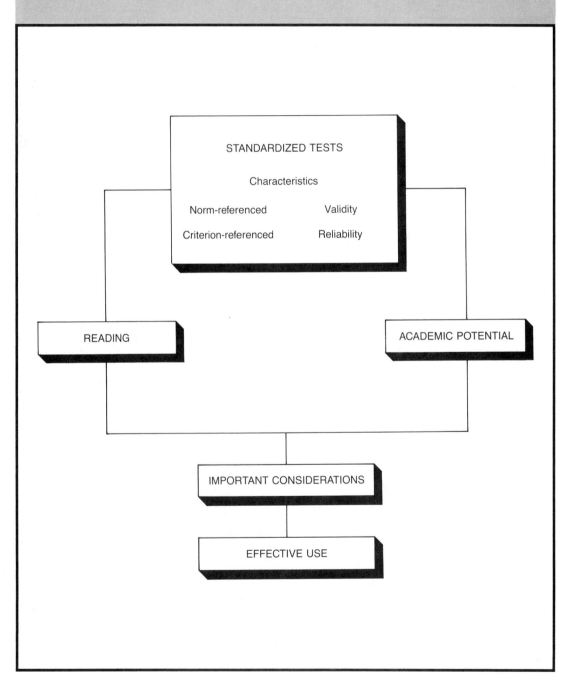

STANDARDIZED TESTS

Characteristics

Norm-referenced   Validity

Criterion-referenced   Reliability

READING

ACADEMIC POTENTIAL

IMPORTANT CONSIDERATIONS

EFFECTIVE USE

Principles of Analytical Teaching Through Standardized Tests

Focus Questions

- What are the characteristics of standardized tests?
- How can standardized tests be used effectively?
- What limitations do standardized tests have in analytical teaching?

This chapter presents ideas about using standardized tests for teaching analytically. To make insightful assessments that can be a basis for an instructional program, teachers should know (1) the purposes of schoolwide testing programs, and (2) the uses and limitations of standardized tests.

STANDARDIZED TESTS

A **standardized test** is one that has been experimentally constructed. The test author has followed accepted procedures and has researched (1) the content of the test, (2) the procedures for administering the test, (3) the system for recording and scoring answers, and (4) the method by which results can be turned into a usable form. Everything about the test has been standardized so that if all the directions are correctly followed, the results can be interpreted in the same manner, regardless of where in the country the test was given. Ideally, the results should mean the same thing to different people. A common misconception is that the word *standard* represents a goal to be attained. *Standardized*, however, means that the methods of administering, recording, scoring, and interpreting have been made uniform.

Characteristics of Standardized Tests

Standardized reading tests are of two main types: norm-referenced and criterion-referenced tests.

Norm-referenced Tests
Norm-referenced tests are used to compare the relative position of individuals in different groups. The test is given to a large number students. The average score (or median) is found by noting the raw score for which 50 percent of the scores were higher and 50 percent were lower. This score is then designated as the average for the group. For example, a hypothetical group of students take a newly constructed test in the second month of the fourth grade. The middle score of that group represents a grade equivalent of 4.2. If the test is given to other groups, such as third graders or fifth graders, the average scores can be obtained for those grade levels as well. The differences among the av-

erage scores for the different grade levels—the difference between 3.2 and 4.2, and 5.2 and 4.2—are determined through a mathematical procedure called *extrapolation*. It is also possible to obtain average scores for different periods of time during the school year. Many standardized-test publishers provide different sets of scores or norms for the beginning, middle, and end of each grade level.

A norm-referenced test measures the performance of a student compared to the norm, or standardizing, group. If a fourth-grade student achieves a grade equivalent of 4.5 in February, then that student has achieved a score equal to the average score of the fourth-grade norm group. The student's score is then interpreted as meaning he or she scored better than 50 percent of the norm population. A score of 5.5 would mean the student achieved a score equal to that of the average fifth grader in the norm group. It does not mean that the student is in the fifth grade or is doing fifth-grade work, however.

Norm-referenced tests are most useful for indicating how a student performs in comparison to other students when two other types of norms, the percentile and the stanine, are considered.

The **percentile** indicates how a student performs relative to all the students in the norm group. For example, students with a score in the 60th percentile scored better than 60 percent of the norm group, and 40 percent of the norm group scored better than that student did.

It is possible to create local percentile norms based on scores made by students in a particular class, school, or school district. In these cases, a percentile would show a student's performance in relation to his or her immediate peers. It is possible that local norms will not exactly match the national norms provided by the test publisher. A local norm may be higher or lower than the national norm. Consider, for example, the following hypothetical percentiles:

	National Norm Percentiles	Local Norm Percentiles
Vocabulary	45	55
Comprehension	45	40

These scores would mean that for the vocabulary test, a student who scores better than 45 percent of the national group in comparison scores better than 55 percent of the students at that grade level in the local school or school district.

The **stanine** scores are digits ranging from 1 to 9. Like percentiles, their interpretation is based on a relationship to a particular group. The fifth stanine is considered average, and the stanines on either side of the fifth are equally distant from the average. For instance, a student who scores in stanine 3 stands the same relative distance from the average as someone who scores in stanine 7. An advantage in using stanines instead of grade equivalents and percentile ranks is that stanines represent a range of scores, not just one particular score. Three students in the fourth grade with different raw scores could have different grade equivalents and percentile ranks; yet, their stanine scores might not differ. If their scores were within the same stanine unit, they would be considered to have performed equally well on the test. The following actual test scores of three students (Karlsen, Madden, & Gardner, 1976) illustrate this:

Reading Comprehension, Total

	Raw Score	Scaled Score	Grade Equivalent	Percentile	Stanine
Martha	48	446	3.8	41	5
Marc	51	460	4.1	49	5
Myra	52	472	4.5	56	5

In many schools, Martha and Myra would not be considered equal in performance. The use of the stanine scores, even with the seemingly wide grade-equivalent spread, makes it apparent that all three students performed, in comparison to the norm group, in the average range.

Stanines, like percentiles, are relative scores indicating performance relative to the group. Myra and Martha performed differently (from an absolute point of view), but compared to the peer group who took the test, they performed about the same. (A note of caution: Although stanines often classify two different scores as similar, they also may classify two similar scores as different if those scores fall close to the boundary between two stanines.)

Another example of using stanines to interpret scores is based on the following scores of two sixth-grade students on another actual test (Balow, Farr, Hogan, & Prescot, 1979). One student obtained a raw score of 49 on the reading subtest at the beginning of sixth grade (fall norms). The other achieved the same number of correct answers, but near the end of sixth grade (spring norms). As can be seen, they both have identical grade equivalents, although the scores mean different things.

Reading

	Raw Score	Scaled Score	Percentile	Grade Equivalent	Stanine
Harriett (Fall Norms)	49	753	65	7.8	6
Henry (Spring Norms)	49	753	58	7.8	5

Harriett, who received a grade score of 7.8 at the beginning of the year, would be considered high average in comparison to the norm group. But Henry, who received a grade score of 7.8 at the end of the year, would be considered average when compared to the norm group.

Many local school districts are reporting the results of standardized tests in a form called **normal curve equivalents** (NCEs). NCEs are similar to percentiles in that they range from 1 to 99; however, they differ in that NCEs are equally spaced units that can be used to compute averages and make comparisons. Percentiles cannot be added or subtracted from each other as NCEs can, and changes in percentile ranks at different points on the scale cannot be compared. For example, a student who performs at the 40th percentile at the beginning of the year and at the 50th percentile at the end has not made the same change as someone who performs at the 10th and then at the 20th percentile. Any student with a change of 10 NCE units, however, has made an equivalent change of performance, whether it has been from the 10th to the 20th or the 40th to the 50th NCE.

Criterion-referenced Tests

Criterion-referenced tests determine whether an individual or group has achieved a certain level of mastery. A criterion-referenced test is a set of standards or goals representing a group of tasks that students are supposed to master. Scores on this test, instead of showing placement compared to a group, show students' placement in relation to a set of goals.

To construct a criterion-referenced reading test, the test writer assumes a hierarchy of skills necessary to the reading process. The successful completion of certain tasks is presumed to be evidence of such skills. If a student can do a certain task, then that student is said to have mastered a particular aspect of reading. For example, a series of items may ask students to match words such as *under* and *over* to pictures showing those relationships. Or, students may be asked to read some paragraphs and mark their patterns of organization, such as time sequence or statement–detail. For each task there may be one or more items. When students can mark the appropriate answers for a series of items representing the task, then mastery of that task is assumed. Like norm-referenced tests, criterion-referenced tests can be made appropriate for different maturity levels of reading performance.

Validity and Reliability

Whether a standardized test is norm-referenced or criterion-referenced, it should have validity and reliability.

A test with **validity** measures what it says it measures. A reading test, for example, should indicate something about reading performance and the tasks should relate to aspects of reading. Of course, a test may be valid according to the test writer's definition of reading but not according to that assumed by the test user. For example, according to the definition of reading set forth in this book, a test composed entirely of word lists would not be considered valid.

Such a test is not concerned with testing the student's ability to reconstruct an author's message.

Reliability refers to the consistency with which a test produces its results. Think of an individual who is never able to keep appointments or is constantly disappointing others by failing to follow through with promises. That person lacks reliability. When a reading test cannot be trusted to give consistent, reliable results, then to classroom teachers the test is worthless. The reliability of a test can be found through statistical information provided by the test's publisher. If a publisher reports a coefficient of reliability between .90 and .99, then the test can be accepted as reliable. A test, however, can have a high degree of reliability but not have validity; whatever it may test—which may or may not be part of the reading process—it tests it consistently.

Standardized tests are usually accompanied by a directions manual that contains a variety of information about the test. This manual should be read carefully to find out

1. the intended purposes of the test,
2. the content of the test,
3. the manner in which the test is organized,
4. the recommended procedures for administering the test,
5. the publisher's estimate of its validity and reliability,
6. the various tables of norms (not included in criterion-referenced tests),
7. an explanation of how to interpret the scores, and
8. a discussion of how to use the test results.

The manuals accompanying norm-referenced tests also contain another bit of information that is often overlooked—the **standard error of measurement.** This number, which is usually, but not necessarily, expressed in grade-level equivalents, is an indication of how much the particular test's results could be wrong. No test produces precise estimates of a student's performance. The standard error of measurement is used to estimate how much a student's score actually differs from the one produced on the test. If a student scores a grade equivalent of 5.3 on a test with a four-month (.4 year) standard error of measurement, it can be assumed about 68 percent of the time that the student's real score is between the grade equivalents of 4.9 and 5.7 (obtained by adding and subtracting 1 standard error of measurement from the student's score). It is assumed about 95 percent of the time that the student's score is really between the grade equivalents of 4.5 and 6.4 (obtained by adding and subtracting the doubled standard error of measurement).

Standardized Reading Tests

A norm-referenced reading test usually has two sections: a vocabulary subtest and a paragraph-reading subtest. Separate scores are obtained for each subtest and some tests have a composite score. The vocabulary sections attempt to test a student's knowledge of specific words by having them match words to their

1. A large **boat**
   1) car
   2) house
   3) animal
   4) ship

4. He **speaks** fast
   1) drives
   2) talks
   3) runs
   4) eats

7. **Yell** for help
   1) ask
   2) beg
   3) look
   4) shout

> Do you know the shape of a sign tells what it means?
> A sign with three sides means to let the other car go first. A sign with four sides means to be careful. A sign with an X on it means that there are trains crossing ahead. A stop sign has eight sides.
> Know your signs and play it safe!

11. **Where would there be a sign with an X on it?**
    1) At a bus stop
    2) At a railroad crossing
    3) At a hosptial
    4) At a gas station

13. **What should drivers do when they see a sign with more than four sides?**
    1) Look back
    2) Turn to the right
    3) Slow down
    4) Stop

12. **What should drivers do when they see a sign with four sides?**
    1) Slow down
    2) Watch for trains
    3) Stop quickly
    4) Pull off the road

14. **What does a round sign mean?**
    1) Stop
    2) Slow down
    3) Keep going
    4) The story does not say.

FIGURE 11–1
Sample Questions from a Norm-referenced Test

pictorial representations or to appropriate synonyms. The student's comprehension is tested by a series of questions about different paragraphs or short selections. Figure 11–1 contains sample vocabulary and comprehension questions from a standardized norm-referenced reading test.

The following are widely used norm-referenced tests:

Comprehensive tests of basic skills: Reading, Form V, 1985. Monterey, CA: CTB/McGraw-Hill.

Intended grades: 1–12; Subtests: Oral vocabulary; oral sentence and story comprehension; visual and sound recognition (lowest level); word-attack skills; reading vocabulary; and reading comprehension of sentences, passages, and author techniques (primary and intermediate levels)

Gates-MacGinitie reading tests (2nd ed.). (1978). Chicago: Riverside.

Intended grades: 1–12; Subtests: vocabulary and comprehension

Iowa tests of basic skills: Reading. (1986). Chicago: Riverside.

Intended grades: Primary Battery (levels 5–8)—grades K–3.5; Multilevel Edition (levels 9–14)—grades 3–9; Subtests: vocabulary, reading, word analysis

Metropolitan achievement tests (6th ed.). (1985). New York: Psychological Corporation.

Survey Battery: Reading Comprehension.

Intended grades: 1–12; Subtests: vocabulary, reading comprehension, and word recognition

Diagnostic Tests: Reading.

Intended grades: 1–9; Subtests: reading comprehension, word part clues, word attack, and vocabulary in context

Sequential tests of educational progress: Reading. (1979). Menlo Park, CA: Addison-Wesley.

Intended grades: 1–12; Subtests: vocabulary and literal and inferential comprehension

Stanford achievement test: Reading. (7th ed.). (1984). New York: Psychological Corporation.

Intended grades: 1–9; Subtests: word study skills, reading comprehension, and vocabulary

Although a criterion-referenced test's surface appearance is similar to a norm-referenced test's, the differences are greater than their layout and format suggest. The criterion-referenced test measures students' mastery of certain specific objectives. Whereas a norm-referenced test cannot be used to pinpoint strengths and deficiencies, the criterion-referenced test can do just that without any reference to a norm group.

The following is a published criterion-referenced test:

PRI/Reading Systems. (1980). Monterey, CA: CTB/McGraw-Hill.

Intended grades: K–9+; Subtests: oral language, word attack and usage, comprehension, and applications

Some publishers try to combine the features of norm-referenced and criterion-referenced tests. A feature indicated for the *Metropolitan Achievement Tests* is that an "instructional reading level" can be obtained from either the reading survey or the reading instructional tests. The score represents the reading levels in current basal reading series and attempts to show an appropriate level of mastery at which instruction may be started. The *PRI/Reading Systems* has also correlated scores so that norm-referenced information may be estimated from criterion-referenced performance.

Another type of criterion-referenced test is the **functional literacy,** or life skills, test. (For a discussion of functional literacy, see Chapter 7.) A functional literacy test assesses students' performances in reading nonacademic materials in school, at home, and in the community. The items include reading and interpreting signs, street maps, advertisements, shipping catalogs, schedules, and directories. Figure 11–2 contains sample questions from a test of functional literacy.

FIGURE 11–2
Sample Questions from a Functional Literacy Test

OPERATING INSTRUCTIONS FOR PERFECTION OVEN

Checking Dial:
The reading on the oven thermostat dial shows that the BAKE area is from 150° to 500° and the BROIL area is from 375° to "Broil."

Baking:
Turn oven dial to ON and then set at desired temperature. If the dial is set above 300°, both BROIL and BAKE elements stay on until desired temperature is reached, then the BROIL element goes off. You will know when the desired temperature is reached, since the indicator light will go off.

11. What is the minimum temperature that may be used for broiling?

A. 375°
B. 350°
C. 300°
D. 150°

12. According to these instructions, what is the proper oven temperature for baking potatoes?

A. 500°
B. Not given
C. 300°
D. 375°

Oven Pot Roast

2–3 lb. Chuck Roast	3 large potatoes, peeled and quartered
1 tsp. salt	4 peeled carrots
1 cup water	1 medium onion, quartered
1 bay leaf	

Sprinkle salt over both sides of the roast. Place in roasting pan with 1 cup of water and 1 bay leaf. Cover pan and place in oven preheated to 325°. After 45 minutes add vegetables. Then allow to roast another 45 minutes or until vegetables are done. Serves 4.

78. From the recipe shown above, if you put the roast in the oven at 10:10 AM, at what time should you add the vegetables?

Source: Reproduced from *Life Skills Tests of Functional Competencies in Reading and Mathematics.*

The following are published tests of functional literacy:

Life skills: Tests of functional competencies in reading and math. (1980). Chicago: River-side.
    Intended grades: 5–12
Performance assessment in reading (PAIR). (1978). Monterey, CA: CTB/McGraw-Hill.
    Intended grades: 5–9; Subtests: two

One test different from all others is the *Degrees of Reading Power* (DRP) test. This test has a series of prose passages on a variety of nonfiction topics. Each test passage is formed by deleting seven words and providing five possible responses for each deleted item. (The DRP test is constructed on the principle of a modified cloze procedure; more information about the cloze procedure can be found in Chapter 10's section about deletion procedures.) Figure 11–3 contains sample questions from the DRP. The students' responses depend on their ability to comprehend the syntactic and semantic relationships in the passage. Their scores are reported in DRP units, which represent readability levels, or predictions of the readability of the prose they can read. The publisher also offers the readability in DRP units of commonly used instructional texts in various curricular areas so that the results of the test can be used for placement purposes. The Department of Education of New York State, which codeveloped the DRP test, uses various forms of it to measure students' progress in the third, sixth, and ninth grades and to determine whether the reading competence of high-school students qualifies them to receive diplomas. New York City uses the DRP as the principal means of student achievement in reading at all levels of the school system.

Degrees of Reading Power (DRP). (1980). New York: College Entrance Examination Board.
    Intended grades: 3–12.

Important Considerations about Standardized Tests

Both types of standardized tests—norm-referenced and criterion-referenced—have limitations and should be used judiciously. Some limitations are qualities inherent in the tests themselves and some result from misunderstandings about the capabilities of the tests and what they represent.

The following are limitations of norm-referenced reading tests:

1. Some tests overestimate an individual's reading performance.
2. The forms of a test that are supposed to be comparable may not be so.
3. Speed—how much time is allowed for different parts of the test—influences the results.
4. The validity of the different levels of a test may differ or be lost at different age levels.
5. The scores may be influenced by guessing.

It was sunny and hot for days.
Then the __S-1__ changed. It turned
cloudy and cool.

S-1 a) price   b) road
c) job   d) weather
e) size

It isn't safe to go out today. There
was too much __S-2__ yesterday. Many
streets are flooded with water.

S-2 a) rain   b) food
c) mail   d) noise
e) work

FIGURE 11–3
Sample Questions from the Degrees of Reading Power (DRP) Test
Reprinted with permission from Degrees of Reading Power Test Booklet, copyright © 1980 by
College Entrance Examination Board, New York.

6. The interpretation of scores may be misleading if the norm population differs from the users' student population.
7. The revisions made on tests sometimes result in different forms of
   the test not being comparable.
8. Test results do not always correlate with actual classroom performance.
9. The reading abilities sampled by some of the tests seemed to be
   limited (Strang, 1969).

The validity of a test is important. A reading achievement test may measure something entirely different from reading. For example, it may measure
general intelligence or problem-solving ability. It may also test specific aspects
of reading that are limited and provide only a partial picture of how a student
really functions.

Another important consideration about standardized tests is how the
scores may be interpreted and used for instructional purposes. The following
considerations guide the use of standardized tests in classrooms:

A score is not a judgment.   Judgments must be made by teachers and reflect the
value they place on any score.

A score is not high or low; it is only higher or lower than other scores.   This means
that any individual score is meaningless unless it is compared with another
score. Most commonly, the other scores are national norms. It is inappropriate,
then, to compare scores unless the group from which they were obtained have
the same characteristics as the norm group. Teachers should carefully examine
the manual to ensure that the national norm group contains students with
characteristics similar to those being tested.

*Grade-equivalent scores from one subtest are not comparable to those from another sub-
test.*   To determine whether two grade-equivalent scores differ, one of two
things must be done: (1) the stanine table must be checked to determine if the

scores fall within the same stanine. If they do, then no matter how large the difference seems between the two scores, they mean the same thing; (2) the standard error of measurement for each subtest must be added to or subtracted from the obtained score. If the range of the two sets of scores overlaps, they mean the same thing.

The grade-equivalent scores on tests given at different times of the year represent different performance levels.

If the results from an achievement test are used to compile a student's profile—a graphic representation of relative performance on a series of tests—then stanine scores may be the most useful. This is because they provide the same information—the student's performance on the various tests—about the performance of a peer group.

Criterion-referenced tests, too, have certain limitations. In regard to the validity of the test items, the comments made previously hold for criterion-referenced tests as well as norm-referenced tests. The classroom teacher needs to verify that the tasks represent aspects of reading. Other limitations of criterion-referenced tests are 1) a lack of empirical justification for the number of items used for measuring an ability to do a task, 2) the percentage of correct items needed for mastery to be demonstrated, or 3) the length of time allowed for administering the test.

When criterion-referenced tests are made, the question arises about the necessity to include items that test mastery of all reading skills. First, the concept of mastery is considered. As an educational goal, the idea of mastery has little support in the research literature (Johnston, 1984). Also, depending on how narrowly reading skills are differentiated, an unwieldy test might result. Researchers attempt to determine how many of the individual reading skills to test and the number of items for each skill to include; yet, some criterion-referenced test makers ignore any skills that are too difficult to explain or to measure with multiple-choice questions (Lyons, 1984). Also, some test makers are interested in determining student flow from performance level to performance level and not in comparing individuals with one another, so they are reluctant to use other test makers' normative procedures. Therefore, when teachers consider using criterion-referenced tests, the should take into account the following: *The criterion-referenced items should represent skills essential to learning to read, and the tasks must be evaluated in the context of a normal reading situation* (Pikulski, 1974b).

The second point is more important. The dynamic, interactive nature of reading is not easily specified in terms of discrete objectives and simple criteria (Johnston, 1984). Often students are asked to perform a task, perhaps to match words that contain a similar final-consonant cluster, that rarely occurs in actual reading situations. The matching task might be appropriate for a spelling situation, but it has limited utility in assessing an act of reading.

A cautionary note about the effect of examinations is necessary as a final word about all standardized tests (Bloom, 1969). Students, teachers, and administrators are affected by what each perceives to be the purpose of a test or testing situation. There may be, then, either positive or negative effects from the assessment depending on the attitudes of those involved. If the test is viewed as punitive—as they often are in some schools where the results of achievement tests are used for students' promotion or retention or for the evaluation of teachers—the entire learning process may be viewed as punitive as well.

Effective Use of Standardized Reading Test Results

Teachers can administer and interpret standardized tests in a classroom. To wisely use standardized tests, a teacher should know (1) the scope of the school testing program, (2) its relationship to the entire school educational program, and (3) the planned uses for the test results.

Teachers most often use test results for instructional planning. To analyze the results and to interpret them for students, parents, and other professionals, the classroom teacher must consider the following:

1. *The objectives of the school testing program.*   What are the administration's purposes for all testing that occurs in the school? How have these objectives been developed, and when was the last time they were reviewed?
2. *The content of the tests.*   What is the relationship between the content of the tests and the objectives of the instructional and testing programs? Who examined the tests to make this decision, and when was the test last reviewed?
3. *The pretesting arrangements.*   What information about the testing has been given to students, parents, and teachers? What attitudes toward testing are implicitly and explicitly expressed in this information?
4. *The testing schedule.*   What advance information has been given to teachers, students, and parents about who will administer the tests and when and where the testing will occur?
5. *The scoring of the tests.*   How will the tests be marked—by the teacher, auxiliary staff, secretaries, or machine? In what type of scores will the results be expressed—grade equivalents, percentiles, or stanines?
6. *The recording of the results.*   What test data are to be recorded? What forms will be used for recording the results? Which of the derived test scores will be recorded?
7. *The meaning of the scores.*   What interpretation of the scores will be given to teachers, students, and parents? What is the relationship between the test scores obtained and other data available about the students?
8. *The reporting of scores.*   How will the test results be reported to students and parents? When will the reporting take place and in what form?
9. *The use of the tests in the school.*   How will the test results be used by administration, teachers, school psychologists, and guidance counselors? In what way do these uses conform to the objectives of the testing program?

OBTAINING INFORMATION ABOUT ACADEMIC POTENTIAL

The process of reading is closely related to the entire process of thinking. Analytic teachers attempt to determine whether students' reading performances are commensurate with their maturity of thinking. To many, this may immediately bring to mind "intelligence"; however, the use of the term *intelligence* has led to many misconceptions about students' performances in school. There are different types of intelligence; in school there is concern with only one of them. The term that describes this one area is *academic potential,* which draws attention to specific abilities that directly influence students' school performance. For a discussion of how there are different types of intelligence for different types of tasks, see the discussion of Guilford's structure-of-intellect model in Chapter 13.

An estimate of a student's academic potential may be made from the results of a standardized individual or group test. Individual tests, which should be administered by a psychologist, psychometrician, guidance counselor, or another qualified person, require much time. Therefore, many schools regularly administer some type of standardized group intelligence, mental maturity, or academic potential test.

The following are widely used standardized group measures of academic potential:

> *Cognitive ability test.* (1985). Lombard, IL: Riverside.
>> Intended grades: Primary Battery (levels 1–2)—grades K–3; Multilevel Edition (levels A–H)—grades 3–12; Subtests: verbal, quantitative, and nonverbal
>
> *Otis-Lennon school ability test.* (1982). New York: Psychological Corporation.
>> Intended grades: 1–12
>
> *Test of cognitive skills.* (1981). Monterey, CA: CTB/McGraw-Hill.
>> Intended grades: 1–12; Subtests: sequences, analogies, memory, and verbal reasoning

The academic potential or mental maturity tests usually contain a nonverbal, or nonlanguage, subtest and a language, or verbal, subtest. Careful examination of the tests themselves will indicate that these terms do not accurately describe the tasks included on the tests. The subsections are tests of nonwritten and written language. Since reading is required on all the language, or verbal, sections of these tests, one can ask whether the test measures academic potential or reading achievement.

Because the results of group intelligence tests' verbal forms have such a high correlation with performance on reading achievement tests, the differences seem to arise mainly because of the two tests' errors of measurement (Strang, 1969). It may be wise, then, to estimate a student's potential for doing academic work by selecting a test that requires little or no reading or by using the results from subtests that require no reading.

Classroom teachers can be alert to discrepancies between test results and students' observed performances in class settings. When there is a question, students can be referred for further appraisal by the appropriate school personnel.

Some cautionary words must be given about using group tests of academic potential to predict students' reading potential:

1. Intelligence tests are not a sure measure of the innate ability to learn. They represent developed ability.
2. Intelligence tests show how individuals are functioning at the time the test is taken.

3. Intelligence scores for each student fluctuate from test to test.
4. Intelligence tests may lack validity.
5. Intelligence test scores should be interpreted according to the students' cultural backgrounds and home environments.
6. Intelligence test scores should be interpreted in accordance with students' language proficiency.
7. Intelligence test scores may be raised by practice and coaching (Strang, 1969).

Group tests of academic potential should be used with caution as part of analytical teaching. If the tests are administered, the results should be used as only one means for comparing a student's cognitive maturity with that of students of the same age. A student who matures at a slower rate or who has not had an equal opportunity to learn cannot be expected to perform in the same manner as other students do. Using group tests of academic potential allows for the identification of those students whose performance is markedly different from the others, but these tests do not disclose the cause for the difference. For this, further analysis is necessary.

DISCUSSION QUESTIONS AND ACTIVITIES

1. In order for a test to be valid it must first be reliable. Why isn't the converse of this statement true?

2. Examine a standardized reading test and its accompanying manuals. From your examination of the test items, does the test seem to measure what the author states it is supposed to measure? How many of the questions in the comprehension subsection can be answered from information contained in other questions and answers? Are there features in the layout of the test and its answer sheet that might confuse students and cause them to answer the test items incorrectly?

3. Prepare a statement for a parents' group, explaining in nontechnical language (1) the characteristics of a good standardized test and (2) some of the advantages of using standardized reading tests.

4. If there is no single standardized reading test that is best for all student populations, all instructional programs, and all school settings, how then should school personnel select a standardized test that is "best" for their situation?

5. Explain what the following statement means to you:

   A school instructional program is no better than the means by which it is assessed.

6. The meaning of grade equivalent is often misunderstood by many parents and teachers. Explain how the terms *grade equivalent*, as used on standardized tests, and *grade level*, as used on instructional materials, may be confused. How might school personnel clarify the meaning of these terms for both parents and teachers?

FURTHER READING

The following draws together information which is relevant to the problem of assessing students' reading comprehension.

Johnston, P.H. (1983). *Reading comprehension assessment: A cognitive basis.* Newark, DE: International Reading Association.

These short books address teachers' concerns about problems of assessment in reading instruction.

Blanton, W.E., Farr, R., & Tuinman, J.J. (Eds.). (1974). *Measuring reading performance.* Newark, DE: International Reading Association.

MacGinitie, W. (Ed.). (1973). *Assessment problems in reading.* Newark, DE: International Reading Association.

Scheiner, R. (1979). *Reading tests and teachers: A practical guide.* Newark, DE: International Reading Association.

The following is the latest in a series of yearbooks with which teachers should be familiar. It contains critical reviews and descriptions of standardized tests in all subject areas. These reviews can help teachers wishing to select tests for particular purposes.

Mitchell, J.V., Jr. (Ed.). (1985). *The ninth mental measurements yearbook.* Published by the Buros Institute of Mental Measurement. Lincoln, NE: University of Nebraska Press.

Periodically, standardized tests are reviewed in *The Reading Teacher* and *The Journal of Reading*, both published by the International Reading Association.

The issue of preparing students for taking standardized tests is a controversial one. The following, all available through the ERIC system, were written on the premise that students' full performance is measured only when they know what is expected of them and have a set of procedures for effectively dealing with the directions and formats of tests.

Jongsma, E.A., & Warshauer, E. (1975). *The effects of instruction in test-taking skills upon student performance on standardized achievement tests, final report.* New Orleans: University of New Orleans, Department of Elementary Education, ED 114 408.

Maryland State Department of Education. (1975). *Improving student attitudes and skills for taking tests.* Baltimore: Maryland State Department of Education, ED 128 352.

Sabers, D. (1975). *Test-taking skills.* Tucson, AZ: Center for Educational Research and Development, ED 133 341.

Organizer

```
                    ┌──────────────────────────┴──────────────────────────┐

        ORGANIZATIONAL PATTERNS              DEVELOPING GROUP ACTIVITIES

        Considerations for Selecting                 Group Functions

        School and Classroom Patterns                 Forming Groups
```

CHAPTER 12

Organizing for Reading Instruction

Focus Questions

- What kind of school instructional program is appropriate to the teaching and learning of reading and writing?
- What principles underlie the selection of a school or classroom organizational plan?
- How are strategies developed for student participation in group activities?

Reading curricula consonant with a whole-language approach are based on the premise that reading is using language and that the function of language is the communication of thoughts: "Reading is not reading without some level of comprehension, and reading materials, however simple, must have something to say; there must be some thought to be comprehended" (Goodman, 1969c, p. 2).

A whole-language instructional program in reading has educationally sound general curricular principles, has a theoretical foundation, and relates the means of instruction to what has been confirmed about human potential and human development. Bruner (1966) described some general characteristics of instruction which are summarized in the following paragraph.

Learning and problem solving depend on the exploration of alternatives, and instruction aids and guides these explorations. The teacher's role is to begin the exploration of alternatives, maintain the learner's interest, and constantly direct the learner's search for solutions to problems. Any idea, problem, or fact must be presented to students in a form simple enough so that any of them can understand it. The efficacy with which the information is understood and recognized depends on the interaction of certain variables. Instructional techniques should be selected with consideration for (1) the learners' ages, (2) the learners' styles of learning, (3) the subject matter, (4) the mode of presentation, (5) the concepts to be learned, and (6) the learners' conceptual capacities. The teacher can lead learners through sequences of statements and restatements that increase their ability to grasp, transform, and transfer what is learned. Essential to learning is a knowledge of results at a time when the knowledge can be used for corrections. Learners can be aided in developing self-sufficiency in problem solving by always translating the information to be learned into the learners' ways of solving problems.

Organized procedures for teaching reading strategies provides for multiple and varied learning situations. These procedures give specific guidance in the development of students' thinking strategies. The instructional activities and experiences allow the teacher and students to mutually assess the students' needs and are designed to allow development of those strategies relevant to students' learning needs and capabilities.

CONSIDERATIONS IN SELECTING AN ORGANIZATIONAL PATTERN

A reading program's structure is the school or classroom organizational pattern. Many beginning teachers wonder whether reading instruction should take place in a group or through individualized instruction. The decision, however, is not "either/or." The type of organizational pattern used in a school or classroom should be selected because it fits the learning environment. A school or class organizational pattern should be selected after considering (1) the concepts about learning and reading held by the school administration and the classroom teacher, (2) the recognized role(s) of the teacher, (3) the facilities available for instruction and the daily classroom interpersonal interactions desired, (4) the perceived needs of the learners, and (5) the subject matter and format in which the subject matter is presented.

Philosophical Assumptions

Different philosophical assumptions about learning underlie three current learning theories: the Behavior-Control Model, the Rational Model, and the Discovery–Learning Model (Nuthall & Snook, 1973). With the Behavior-Control Model, teaching is considered as a method of controlling both the students and the conditions of learning. In the Rational Model, the aim of teaching is to transmit knowledge. The Discovery–Learning Model has various descriptions consolidated in teaching models based on information processing. These models call for (1) the active participation of the student in the learning process; (2) the creation of attractive alternatives; (3) the encouragement and development of divergent, convergent, and creative thinking; (4) the rearrangement and transformation of evidence; and (5) the learning of the process of discovery through various kinds of learning. The psychological theory supporting the information-processing models is not as precise as that supporting the Behavior-Control Model. The Discovery–Learning Model, however, is strongly supported by the research of cognitive psychology, child development, and the study of creativity (this is discussed in Chapters 2 and 13).

A reading program consistent with the ideas in this book can be developed along the guidelines of the information-processing and Discovery–Learning teaching models. In such models, the instructional program aims at (1) establishing learning environments in which students accept some responsibility for educational decisions rather than merely following directives; (2) tying learning not only to performing some task but also to making decisions about what is appropriate at any given time; and (3) encouraging the generation of many answers, not simply accepting a right answer.

Teacher Roles and Activities

The roles teachers play in instructional settings depend on their perceptions of the expectations of others in the immediate social and educational system, the teachers' self-concepts, and their value systems. Teachers adjust their activities in response to factors within and outside the classroom context, sometimes to the benefit of students, sometimes not. Among the roles teachers play are reporter, model, problem-poser, counselor, diagnostician, systems manager, disciplinarian, experimenter, and consumer. No one role is more important than another; each is played because it is appropriate to the immediate classroom social context. Together, teachers and students determine the roles they will play, the behaviors that are and are not appropriate during different activities, and how each person's communicative behavior is to be interpreted (Bloome, 1983, 1985; Duffy, 1983; Morine & Morine, 1973; Rosenshine & Stevens, 1984).

An instructional program should be flexible enough to accommodate and develop the special talents of all concerned—teachers and learners—in a manner that is self-rewarding, educationally sound, and socially effective. Teachers should not be asking, "Which role should I perform?", but "Which role is appropriate for a particular instructional purpose, with a particular student or group of students, and with a particular subject matter?"

Effective teaching occurs when there is some explicit rationale for the relationship between what the teacher does and what students do. Good teachers provide directed instruction which consists of a predictable sequence of demonstration, guided student practice, feedback and corrections, and independent practice (Rosenshine & Stevens, 1984). These teachers ask "Do instructional activities take place as planned, and are they producing the outcomes intended?" Also, the relationship between the teacher's activities and the students' learning depends on the social system in the classroom. In school, the teacher has the right and the obligation to control and evaluate students. Learning depends on how this authority is used (Cohen, 1972; Weinstein, 1979).

Facilities

The physical environment most assuredly places limitations on the type of instructional organization to be implemented. Often, however, the size and arrangement of rooms and the age and construction of the school building can be used as excuses for adhering to one particular organizational pattern. The facilities of a school will not hinder a creative teacher who wishes to use a particular organizational structure or a variety of arrangements. The decision about what pattern or patterns to use need be influenced only indirectly by the school's physical conditions.

Reading is a social process; it is not so much the physical classroom that is important for creating effective reading instruction as it is the classroom climate. Teachers need to examine the social relationships between themselves and students to ensure that reading events are socially appropriate for learning information, values, and ways of thinking and problem solving (Bloome, 1985).

The Learner's Needs

Havighurst's (1964) evidence that students have a drive to learn remains relevant. It is not fully known whether this drive is innate or acquired. Some evidence points to the possibility of crucial periods in which certain learning is easier. The crucial period for learning language and communicative tasks seems to be the first 12 years of life. What is most evident, though, is that students need a curriculum in which teachers

1. provide experiences in exploring and explaining the unfamiliar in both the social and physical worlds,
2. offer experiences in a variety of sensory modalities and experiences while talking about these sensory impressions,
3. develop experiences with increasingly complex social relationships,
4. provide practice in the fundamentals of reading that are tied to relevant discussions and explanations of these fundamentals, and
5. allow for experiences in expanding control of language and meanings as expressed in speech.

Learning does not occur rapidly—at least not that learning needed for long-term decision making. Facts are learned quickly, but the processes of thought and communication are acquired slowly and cumulatively. These processes require practice and are undertaken with an anticipation of reward. Factors that influence the extent to which learning is acquired include intelligence, the mode or modes of learning, motivation, and the expectations developed through family relationships (Havighurst, 1964). (See Chapters 3 and 13.)

The school organizational pattern should reflect a responsiveness to students' needs in any learning situation. If the pattern does not meet the needs and purposes of all the learners, there is no need for the teacher to follow that one specific organizational pattern.

Subject Matter

Every subject area has some unique features of organization. Some subjects are more efficiently presented in certain formats and require certain strategies for their effective processing by the reader. Previous chapters further discuss strategies for reading and writing in specific subject areas.

SCHOOL ORGANIZATIONAL PATTERNS

The modern concept of school organization is that it should offer flexibility, which means it should provide options and alternative patterns for learning and teaching opportunities that would not otherwise be available. Classroom groups in a flexible organization are periodically created, do not contain permanent members, are modified, and disbanded. They vary in size according to the instructional task and students' capabilities, needs, and interests (Congreve & Rinehart, 1972; Unsworth, 1984).

There are various schoolwide and intraclass organizational patterns for reading instruction that can be used in elementary and middle schools. **Schoolwide plans** include:

Grade level classes. Classes are arranged by grade level, and all students of a particular age are grouped together.

Nongraded units. Random groups of students, selected and representing different age levels, are put together. This is sometimes called a *multiage grouping*.

Cross-class or cross-grade groupings. Students from different classrooms are regrouped for instruction in particular areas. For example, students with the same learning needs or who are performing in reading and writing at the same level are put in one class. The purpose of this regrouping is to reduce the range of students' abilities or performances; it is sometimes called the "Joplin" plan.

Team teaching. Instruction is planned by two or more teachers who are responsible for teaching a particular subject area or a particular group of children.

Learning laboratory. Special rooms, usually with a supervising teacher, are available for students to go to (either as a whole class or as part of class) for instruction in particular areas; this is sometimes called a *reading laboratory, skills center,* or *learning center.*

Differentiated staffing. This is a situation in which team teaching is based on teachers' skill differentiation. Also included are different levels of staff: master teacher, teacher, assistant teacher, paraprofessional, teacher interns (student teachers), and volunteers. The features of cooperative planning found in team teaching are part of this plan.

Departmentalization or scheduling. The school day is divided into periods and students move to different classrooms for instruction. Variations of this plan include "semidepartmentalization," in which students remain in a home room for language arts/reading instruction or language arts/reading/social studies instruction and then move to other classrooms for instruction in science, mathematics, arts, and music.
Intraclass plans include:

Homogeneous grouping. Students are placed in classes based on some characteristic—reading, intelligence, other test scores—to reduce the range of achievement in the group.

Heterogeneous (or random) grouping. Students are placed randomly without any attention to reducing the range of achievement or ability.

Individualized reading. Students select their own reading material, read at will, meet with teachers in conferences, have temporary groups for specific skills instruction, and share their reading experiences with other students.

Needs or activities grouping. A short-term grouping during which students share an instructional need or group project. The group may be formed because students have some common instructional need or because they are interested in jointly developing an activity or a project. No achievement or ability level limitation is imposed when forming these groups.

Independent or contract learning. Specific assignments are based on student–teacher contracts. The students' contracts, or learning assignments, are planned cooperatively by each student with the teacher, allowing the student options depending on his or her level of independence. The contract usually covers such things as the subject(s) to be covered, the material(s) to be used, the location for completing various parts of the assignment (classroom, library, skills center), the time limits, the manner of learning (self-instruction, teacher, peer teams), and the manner in which the assignment will be evaluated (student or teacher checking). Sometimes this is called *differentiated learning.*

Peer teams or peer collaboration. This plan is discussed in Chapter 5 ("Fostering Student Collaboration during Guided Reading").

Diagnostic/prescriptive instruction. Students are given individual assignments based on pretested needs and a follow-up evaluation to determine progress. This plan is used when the curriculum is based on a specific hierarchy of learning.

Open classroom. This is more of a concept than a specific organizational pattern. Teachers who use this classroom organization often have goals and attitudes about student learning and grouping based on a philosophy similar to that of the Discover–Learning Model. An open classroom is difficult to define and is usually described in terms of observable characteristics. Whatever its outward form, the essential philosophy of open classrooms is that "children are unique individuals whose learning needs can be met only in a free, active atmosphere where each child can pursue his [or her] particular interests and learning needs as they arise" (Blitz, 1973).

The previously discussed patterns of schoolwide and intraclass organizations are not mutually exclusive; many rely on other plans for their implementation. The question about whether to group or individualize the teaching of reading and writing has no simple answer. Research into the effective use of classroom organization for meeting students' individual differences substantiates the belief that all forms of school and classroom organization have at least some potential for promoting learning. A comparison of research between intraclass and interclass organization, heterogeneous and homogeneous groupings, and divided-day and whole-day instruction reveals implications for teaching (Oliver, 1970). The research indicates that the best organizational plan for a reading lesson permits appropriate teaching and learning for the teacher and the students. Research also indicates that homogeneous groups of students selected according to one criterion will still be composed of students with different instructional needs, and that teachers tend not to move students from group to group to the extent that individual differences would suggest is necessary.

This research does not make it possible to conclude that the advantages of the ungraded school outweigh its disadvantages. It seems that the claims of the proponents are excessive; many of the advantages claimed by those who favor the ungraded structure can be achieved by excellent teachers working in a traditional school organization. The literature shows there are many different types of ungraded organizations in schools, so it is hard to determine whether a cause-and-effect relationship exists between many of the advantages and disadvantages of these patterns (Kingston, 1969). The research on open classrooms shows there is not enough consistency to warrant an unqualified endorsement of the open classroom as a superior means of organization (Horowitz, 1979). In general, the term *open classroom* is used ambiguously, and so it has become difficult to determine the actual degree to which teachers have implemented openness (Marshall, 1981). The main advantage of ungraded and open structures is that they show the inflexibility and impracticality of the self-contained classroom as a form of organization.

A summary of the issues and principal findings of research on homogeneous and heterogeneous grouping by ability shows, in part, the following:

1. In a homogeneous grouping, there is consistent, positive value for students in general; a particular group of students can achieve more academically; and more efficient learning conditions are provided.
2. There is evidence of an unfavorable effect on the affective development of students because of homogeneous grouping.
3. No improvement of achievement under either homogeneous or heterogeneous grouping patterns seems to be a factor unique to the organization and could be considered a factor separate from curriculum modifications.
4. Teaching methods, materials, and other variables—not the type of grouping pattern—have a cause-and-effect relationship with achievement (Esposito, 1973).

Research on the sociological conditions for effective student/teacher interactions and the effect of classroom environment variables on learning verifies the conclusions found in the previously mentioned research. The physical characteristics of a conventional classroom seem to have little effect on the students' achievement, although the classroom environment may affect their nonachievement behaviors and attitudes. Instead, student growth and learning seem to be directly related to the type of classroom teaching to which they are exposed. Certain personal characteristics of a teacher may be as important in determining teaching success as any particular knowledge or set of skills is. (See "Teacher Roles and Activities" on p. 383.)

Another conclusion about learning in the classroom is that it depends on several interacting variables. In any determination of the success of a learning situation, the teacher should consider the developmental history of each member of the group, including background conditions, personality variables, cognitive variables, socioeconomic status, and sex. These variables seem to interact with the behavior of the participants in a certain environment (Randhawa & Fu, 1973).

In conclusion, no ideal organizational pattern exists for all instructional situations. A teacher's concern should not be one of selecting an open or individualized approach in contrast to a self-contained or grouped approach; instead, it should be determining how best to integrate the various kinds of instructional organization patterns and procedures into an efficient and effective learning climate. Organizational patterns can be viewed as administrative devices that never eliminate individual differences. Openness and individualization are as much attitudes as they are organizational procedures. Since there can never be a true homogeneous or heterogeneous group, organizing the classroom is not an end in itself; it is a means for realizing the goals and objectives of a relevant reading program. Throughout this text, ways have been presented in which the various organizational patterns are important to learning and teaching reading and writing.

The degree to which students undertake directed and independent study varies in different circumstances. In individualized instruction, each student does not need to work independently (which can sometimes be a lonely undertaking), nor does each one need to do something different from what all others do, nor do they need to work simultaneously. Individualized instruction means providing for the growing needs of every student by giving each the type of organizational structure he or she needs for learning.

DEVELOPING READINESS FOR PARTICIPATING IN GROUP ACTIVITIES

Bringing several students together for a lesson does not mean a "group" is formed. In the previous section, flexible classroom grouping procedures were suggested. The intent in this section is to focus on the purposes for forming groups. Teachers have many reasons for organizing groups, and the requirements for a student to join a group or to be included in one after it has been formed are flexible.

Whenever a teacher brings together several students for a particular purpose, a group still is not necessarily formed. Often, so called "groups" are nothing more than aggregations. A real group has an internal, interpersonal structure. When a few students meet with the teacher, and each communicates only with the teacher, then they are not functioning as a group. When each of the students communicates with the others as well as with the teacher, a true group is functioning.

A common misconception is that grouping means organizing students of somewhat equal ability. Usually what is meant is the students are reading "at the same level," or that they need "the same skill development." The result is usually an aggregation in which the teacher is presenting one lesson to a number of individuals. Although ability may be a desired criterion for inclusion in a group, it is not the hub about which a group is formed. The primary purpose for organizing any group is to simplify learning through joint problem-solving ventures.

When a true group exists, there are at least three functioning levels.

Groups function at the task level. This represents the original purpose for organizing or designing the group. Most groups to which individuals belong have an overt task need. Often, that is the level at which the members seem to operate.

Groups function at a maintenance level. Groups function with a changing system of relationships among its members. This is the group personality. The members of a real group are aware that they exist as a group, and they are confronted with the need to maintain the interpersonal relationships so that a working system exists.

Groups function at an individual level.   Each group includes individuals with their own needs. These range from the need to share experiences with others to the need for dominating others. Too often, because individual needs are masked, the functioning of the group breaks down. When members, consciously or unconsciously, place their needs and goals ahead of the main purpose of the group, the cohesiveness of a group lessens.

The group is efficient only as long as the members interact and maintain some balance among the three functioning levels. Learning to be a good group member is important. The group process can facilitate much of the learning that occurs in schools. Therefore, teachers must know when their students are ready to participate as members of real groups.

Group Functions

Although students may not be able to overtly identify the three functions of a group, they should have some awareness of a goal and the personal responsibilities of helping the group reach that goal. Following are some of the more common task and maintenance functions that can be carried out by group members (Gorman, 1974). Through guidance and modeling, the teacher can encourage students to take on different roles as the group operates.

Task Functions

Initiating.   Group members propose goals, define a group problem, and suggest ways for solving that problem.

Seeking ideas.   Group members request information and seek suggestions and ideas.

Giving information.   Group members offer information and ideas and state a belief or opinion.

Clarifying ideas.   Group members interpret or reflect on information or ideas already given, give additional information or examples, and suggest alternative solutions.

Summarizing.   Group members bring together others' ideas and offer conclusions for the group's acceptance.

Testing.   Group members test to see how much agreement exists among the group's members.

Maintenance Functions

Encouraging. Group members become responsive to others' ideas, suggestions, and opinions; accept their contributions; and recognize them for their contributions.

Expressing feelings. Group members sense the group's mood and feelings and express this to the other members.

Reducing tension. Group members help individuals in the group explore their differences.

Offering compromises. Group members attempt to resolve conflicts through compromise.

Facilitating communication. Group members make suggestions for sharing and discussing ideas and reconciling differences.

Setting limits. Group members state standards for evaluating the group's functioning and achievements.

In summary, it is impossible to talk about grouping without specifying (1) the group's purpose, (2) the situation in which it will operate, and (3) the expected learning resulting from the group's efforts. In a productive group, its members share concerns and aims, and they understand how group members constructively work together toward the completion of their goal. With the teacher's guidance and leadership, groups can be formed that allow individual members to function without losing self-respect or experiencing rejection from other group members.

Forming Groups in a Classroom

The nature and size of groups vary. The duration of a group depends on the task and the abilities of the group members. However, before classroom groups can function without chaos, students need to be familiar with certain routines.

It takes students varying periods of time to learn to become effective group workers. Some students may learn how in a matter of weeks; others may take years. Nevertheless, all can participate in the identification of the task- and maintenance-level functions. At the kindergarten and first-grade level this can be accomplished by organizing interest groups. For example, some students could develop a puppet show from a favorite story, some could design and build a class store, or some could collaborate in composing a book for the class library.

Next, students must know some of the techniques that will be the basis for their activity. Students must know how to

- handle specific materials such as phonographs, woodworking tools, tape recorders, and filmstrip projectors.
- follow the class routines for using supplies such as paper, crayons, paint, and paste.
- seek help from the teacher and from other class members.
- maintain class decorum so that no one is imposing on the abilities of others to do whatever activity they wish.
- do whatever is necessary when an activity is complete or cannot be completed at that time.
- work in special learning centers without adult guidance.

Finally, students must know how to work independently. There will be times when not all students are working at group activities or under the teacher's direct guidance. At these times, students should be able to work on individual projects or assignments. In these cases, students should understand how to

- allow others to work without interference.
- stay with a task until it is completed, or at least to understand how, why, and when a task may be terminated before its completion.
- move from one activity to another without requiring the help of others.

When a teacher complains that a class is uncontrollable or that students do not have the maturity to work independently or as effective group members, it may mean that the teacher has not established routines for efficient classroom practices. It is widely accepted that children are self-motivating. Without guidance and limitations, they seek their own ways to relieve boredom and frustration—two of the prime causes of uncontrolled classrooms.

DISCUSSION QUESTIONS AND ACTIVITIES

1. Explain how proponents of two different school or classroom organizational patterns might react to the following statement by Armentrout (1970):

   School has the obligation to provide flexibility and diversity for the vast differences and rates of growth children come to school with.

2. Explain what the following statement by Goodlad (1969) means: "Take the educational environment beyond school and classroom and learning can be humanized" (p. 59).

3. What has appeared in the professional literature about classroom organizational procedures—grouping, individualizing instruction, open classrooms—in the last year?

For students who are currently teaching:

4. Keep a one-week record of the different grouping procedures you followed in your classroom. What kind of activities did you use in each grouping? Would any particular instructional lesson have been more effective if done with a different grouping procedure? What kind of activities and groupings seemed to go together best?

5. Keep a one-week record of the different roles you used as a classroom teacher. Did you use the same type of role in all instructional situations? Did you use a different role for teaching arithmetic or social studies? Did you ever start out functioning in one role and find that you had to change roles? If so, what made you change?

6. Using the questions in Figure 10–1 as a guide, assess the context in which you are teaching reading and writing. For questions to which you answer "no," what can you do to effect a change in the classroom learning environment?

FURTHER READING

The following book deals with aspects of classroom organization that foster the integration of reading and writing instruction.

McVitty, W. (Ed.). (1986). *Getting it together: Organizing the reading–writing classroom.* Portsmouth, NH: Heinemann.

The following contains specific ideas about how to organize instruction in classrooms.

Lapp, D. (Ed.). (1980). *Making reading possible through effective classroom management.* Newark, DE: International Reading Association.

The following two books deal with behavior in the classroom and the relationship of teachers and students as encoders and decoders of language.

Clark, M.L., Erway, E.A., & Beltzer, L. (1971). *The learning encounter: The classroom as a communication workshop.* New York: Random House.

Gorman, A.H. (1974). *Teachers and learners: The interactive process of education* (2nd ed.). Boston: Allyn & Bacon.

Organizer

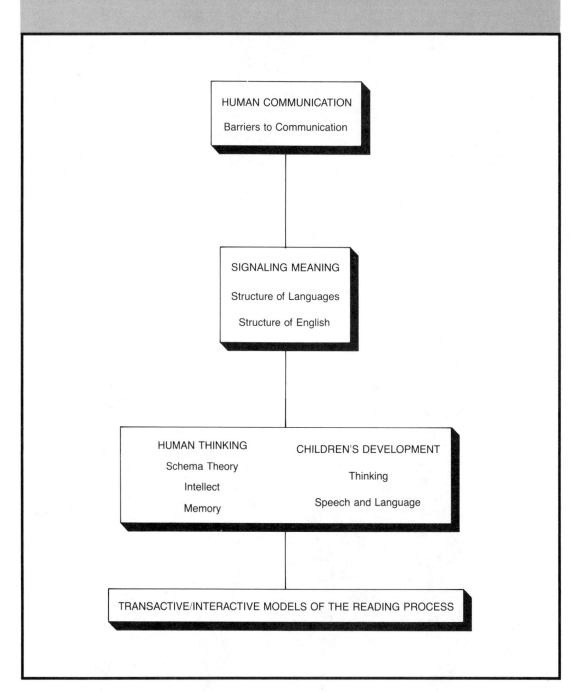

HUMAN COMMUNICATION

Barriers to Communication

SIGNALING MEANING

Structure of Languages

Structure of English

HUMAN THINKING

Schema Theory

Intellect

Memory

CHILDREN'S DEVELOPMENT

Thinking

Speech and Language

TRANSACTIVE/INTERACTIVE MODELS OF THE READING PROCESS

Human Communication and the Development of Thinking and Language

Focus Questions

- What do verbal and nonverbal communication systems have in common? How do they differ?
- What can cause a breakdown in the communication process?
- What are the basic structures of human language?
- How is meaning signaled in present-day American English?
- What are the developmental stages of growth in human thinking?
- What are the traits of human intelligence?
- What is the difference between the way information is retained in long-term memory and short-term memory?
- What are the developmental stages of language acquisition?
- What characterizes a transactive/interactive model of the reading process?

In a broad sense, communication is the way one mind affects another. Human communication is the process by which people share ideas. Language, the vehicle of human communication, consists of arbitrarily agreed-upon patterns of sounds and movements. In this chapter, the patterns of language and how they represent meaning are discussed. First, human communication is defined and factors that may cause breakdowns in the process are discussed. Then ideas about how all language and thinking are structured are presented, focusing specifically on how spoken and written English are structured. Next there is a discussion of how children develop the ability to think and use spoken language. Last, three transactive/interactive models of the reading process are discussed.

Knowledge of the nature of verbal communication allows teachers to better understand the reading and writing processes and to develop effective reading and writing instruction practices. The ideas presented in this chapter underlie the model of the reading act in Chapter 2 and the instructional strategies presented throughout the text.

HUMAN COMMUNICATION

Communication is the transmission of information from one person to another or from one group to another. It generally has three phases: transmission, perception, and evaluation (see Figure 13–1).

A message may be transmitted by actions that are verbal (in spoken or written language) or nonverbal (in previously agreed-upon or accepted patterns of meaningful signals or body movements). Another person perceives the message and may retain it for future reference. Or, after evaluating it, the receiver may respond. In that case, the receiver may become a transmitter, and the process of communication continues.

Human communication must be examined within the context in which it is used—its cultural situation. "Every cultural pattern and every single act of social behavior involve communication in either an explicit or an implicit sense" (Sapir, 1967, p. 75). Competence in using cultural patterns or codes is reflected in a person's ability to participate in social activities. This means that no type of communication, either verbal or nonverbal, is learned outside a social setting. Human communication is learned only in contact with other humans. How well people learn to communicate with others determines how well they function within that social setting. Therefore, it may not be possible to take on

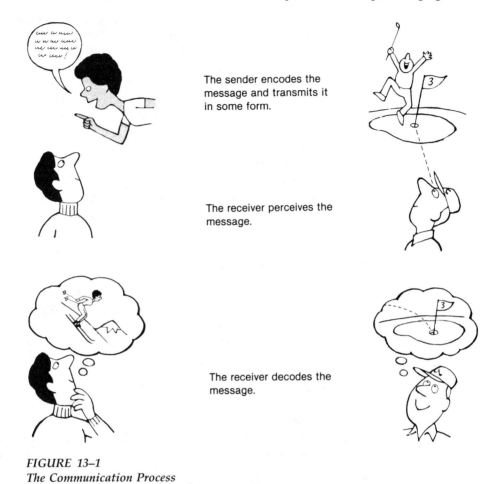

The sender encodes the message and transmits it in some form.

The receiver perceives the message.

The receiver decodes the message.

FIGURE 13–1
The Communication Process

the cultural practices of another group except through participation in that other group (Byers & Byers, 1972).

Nonverbal communication is sometimes called **paralinguistic communication.** It is the way individuals convey information, feelings, and attitudes without words. Paralinguistic communication is a form of language because, like verbal communication, it has patterns of cues and signals meaningful to members of a cultural group or social organization. The cues and signals are learned intuitively by the group's members. The paralinguistic system includes sign languages, body movements and gestures, pantomime and dance, and the intentional display of material things (kinds of clothing, cars, and houses, for example, express feelings, beliefs, and attitudes).

There is a strong relationship between a culture's verbal and nonverbal communication systems. So much so, in fact, that many verbal messages are conveyed on two levels: (1) the statement itself, and (2) the factors surrounding its interpretation. The receiver of a message unconsciously uses the nonverbal signals accompanying the message. The transmitter of the message may, either unconsciously or consciously, use paralinguistic signals. These signals may be used to help the receiver understand the message or to obscure the true meaning of the message. The role of gestures in daily communication is so important that "one may intuitively interpret the relatively unconscious symbolisms of gesture as psychologically more significant in a given context than the words actually used" (Sapir, 1967). In some cases this may create misunderstandings, as discussed in the next section.

Another set of signals to which all people respond are the intonational patterns of speech. The volume of a verbal message often conveys meanings that reinforce or contradict the message delivered verbally. In addition, voice pitch indicates attitudes and feelings. Often a listener responds to the openness of a speaker's voice—the hollow or resounding effect of the voice—instead of to the message itself. Listeners are also affected by the softness or sharpness of speech (drawls or tight-lipped staccato speech), as well as tempo, all of which influence the way a message is received.

In summary, human communication occurs through an arbitrary, systematic set of symbols associated with ideas, feelings, and attitudes. The nonverbal signals—signs, actions, gestures, vocal features—transmit meaning usually on a subconscious level. Both verbal and nonverbal signaling systems are learned intuitively in a cultural setting during interaction with others.

Barriers To Communication

Breakdowns in the communication process occur if an individual is unaware of the features of a communication code. The most obvious example is of two individuals speaking different languages. Yet there are subtler barriers to effective communication. These, because they may not be realized consciously, are confusing to both the message's sender and receiver. The subtler aspects of communication are important. Someone who is not familiar with these subtleties is likely to be baffled by the significance of certain kinds of behavior, even though he or she is thoroughly aware of the external forms and verbal symbols that accompany them (Sapir, 1967).

Although all communication depends on accord between the sender and recipient of the message, it is impossible to know ahead of time what the degree of agreement will be. Only after the message is sent and attempts are made to receive and evaluate it does a breakdown become evident.

Failures in communication may occur when

1. the receiver has a limited capacity. The person may have a physical or cognitive inability to receive and evaluate a message effectively.
2. unwanted emotional noise is interjected. Emotional noise may take the form of unstated assumptions, in the form of projected connotations for certain words, by the receiver about the intended mes-

sage. When the receiver's connotations differ from those intended by the speaker, the intended communication is not conveyed.

3. the message is transmitted in a confounding manner. The speaker might make ambiguous statements or deliver the message using nonverbal signals that contradict the verbal ones.

Effective communication results from active participation in a social group's life activities. All people learn language and culture in a collaborative activity with other members of that group. People become, so to speak, members of the "club" (Smith, 1983). They are deemed competent in a group if they can use the group's communication system. Skill in using verbal language is usually judged by looking at the message to see if it matches what was expected by the group. When there is a high correlation, the speaker is considered competent in using language skills. An individual's nonverbal communication competence is judged by examining what is occurring among communicators. When there is reciprocal understanding, efficient communication has occurred.

These insights have consequences for the classroom. "When we teach children how to participate in communication with others, we are teaching them how to learn" (Byers & Byers, 1972, p. 6). Often, an individual fails to learn because of a barrier to effective communication. Simple translation of a verbal message will not overcome the lack of communication between a teacher who speaks English and a student for whom English is a second language. Also, dialogues between speakers of different dialects are not always successful because of felt, but not conscious, linguistic or emotional static. Exclusion from the "club of learners" can be dramatic and lead to a person learning not to learn (Smith, 1983).

Effective classroom communication between the teacher and students and among students results from a classroom environment in which all share knowledge. Teachers should detect differing social or cultural viewpoints that impede communication. Once these are identified, a common system of communication can be developed, resulting in a reduction of classroom misunderstandings and conflicts.

SIGNALING MEANING

The following generalizations about language are accepted by linguists:

1. Language, any language, is a system of arbitrary symbols used for human communication. The key to understanding languages in general is that they are systematic. The structure of any language can be described and predicted.
2. All languages allow their speakers to deal with the world. No known natural language is any more advanced than any other is. Each language can express any experience understood by its users.

"There," said Amelia Bedelia.
She looked at her list again.

Dust the furniture.

"Did you ever hear tell of such a silly thing.
At my house we undust the furniture.
But to each his own way."
Amelia Bedelia took one last look at the bathroom.
She saw a big box with the words *Dusting Powder* on it.
"Well, look at that.
A special powder to dust with!"
exclaimed Amelia Bedelia.

So Amelia Bedelia dusted the furniture.
"That should be dusty enough.
My, how nice it smells."

FIGURE 13–2
Excerpt from* Amelia Bedelia *by Peggy Parish

Source: From *Amelia Bedelia* by Peggy Parish, illustrated by Fritz Siebel. Text copyright © 1963 by Margaret Parish. Pictures © 1963 by Fritz Siebel. Reprinted by permission of Harper & Row, Publishers, Inc.

3. Vocal symbols are associated by convention with objects, ideas, and actions. The language's users agree (usually implicitly) to a relationship between the sounds uttered and the concepts to which the sounds refer. The relationship of word to meaning, in short, is arbitrary.

4. Every language is unique and can be described only in terms of its own structure. Languages may be compared, but only their similarities and differences can be noted. The structure of another language or the rules of how one language signals meaning cannot be used to explain these procedures in another language. For example, a knowledge of Latin's rules for conveying meaning will not necessarily help in understanding English.

5. All used languages are constantly changing. Examples of changes in present-day American English are most evident in the new words entering the language and the new meanings being assigned to already existing words. More subtle changes are evident, for example,

in dropping the adverbial *ly* in a statement such as *Go slow!*[1] Other changes include the use of alternative pronunciations of words (/add VER tiz ment/ and /add ver TIZE ment/), variant spellings of the same word (*programmed* and *programed*), and the different ways for constructing what become accepted, grammatical statements (/I think I should go/ and /I think that I should go/).

6. The details of a language system must be learned in social settings.
7. A spoken language generally varies from place to place, with social or occupational status, and in differing social situations. No one form is more correct. Certain variations, however, may have greater social status.
8. Every language has built into its structure a factor of redundancy—the signaling of meaning in more than one way. For example, in the sentence /The boys are here/, the information regarding plurality is signaled by the /s/ and the form of the verb, /are/ (Wardhaugh, 1977; Marquardt, 1965).

A distinction is usually made between the *structure* of language and the *function* of language. Structure refers to the form of a language. Function refers to the purpose of language. **Pragmatics** is the study of a language's function. Aside from its role as a means of expressing and recording thoughts, language functions as the medium in which we think. In a subtle way, language may help shape our thought processes.

Because of increasing evidence that thought and language are mutually inclusive, some researchers have concluded that "thinking is always thinking in some language" (Schaff, 1973). Language is viewed as a template or screen through which the world is codified. The language of a society or group contains the categories into which the events of the world are placed. These are the schemata which were explained in a previous section. When a language does not have a specific category for an event, a distinction, or some aspect of reality, then one of two things may happen: (1) the event or distinction is ignored totally, or (2) it is placed into another category, and the two events, although observed by members of another group as different, are conceived to be the same thing. This is another way of saying that unless two people share similar social and linguistic contexts, then communication is impossible.

For example, American English divides the color spectrum into six main categories (red, orange, yellow, green, blue, purple) and then subdivides these categories into tints, shades, and hues—gradations of the colors. The result is that we "see" a vast array of colors on a paint-shop color chart. However, some native American languages categorize the color spectrum into four units and do not have or recognize as many color gradations as American English does.

---

1. A letter or word in slash marks, such as /t/ or /PRES ent/, represents its spoken form. When there is a possibility of confusion, examples are used. An italicized letter or word (*t, cat*) represents its written form.

The Structure of All Languages

In the 1940s, psycholinguistics originated when researchers combined the knowledge and insights from both behaviorist psychology (followers of Skinner and others) and descriptive linguistics (followers of those who examined and described the structure of language). In the 1950s, another version of psycholinguistics emerged. In this version, cognitive psychologists joined transformational linguists in studying the mind by studying language. This later version of psycholinguistics emphasized the powerful regularities of the underlying language system rather than the way sentences sound or look when people hear, speak, read, and write them (Malmstrom, 1977).

Many of the psycholinguistic insights discussed here start with the theory of language developed by Noam Chomsky called **generative** or **transformational grammar.** His theory is called generative because it tries to explain how speakers are able to produce, or generate, all the sentences of their language. A generative grammar is a system of rules from which speakers generate, or create, an indefinite number of sentence structures (Chomsky, 1965). Figure 13–3 represents the components of a natural language grammar.

Chomsky's theory postulates that languages have three components: (1) The **syntactic component** explains the formation of sentences, and the study of syntax examines how sentences are formed in a language; (2) The **semantic component** assigns meanings to strings of words, and semantics investigates how meaning is assigned and interpreted; and (3) The **phonological component** determines how strings of words are put into sounds and transmitted. Because attention is given in this text to written language, this component can also be called, without damage to Chomsky's model, graphophonological, and can be used to determine how words are written.

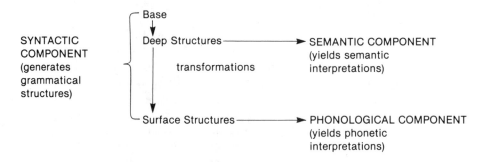

FIGURE 13–3
Chomsky's Transformational Theory of Grammar (1965)*

*Chomsky has recently modified his theory so that the semantic component interprets surface structures rather than deep structures. For this text's purposes, it will be worthwhile to ignore this refinement.

Chomsky's theory states that every sentence has a deep structure that determines its semantic interpretation. This **deep structure** specifies the basic syntactic relations among the elements of the sentence and is roughly the basic underlying meaning of the sentence. The **surface structure** is the sentence's form, either spoken or written. These are the only language forms we can observe and describe. The surface structure is produced from the deep structure through certain formal operations called **grammatical transformations.**

The syntactic component contains two subcomponents—the base and the transformation rules. The **base** is the collection of rules that define and determine the ordering of the sentence's parts. It also contains a dictionary of terms (a denotative lexicon). The relationship of symbols to referents in this dictionary is consistent, and there are no emotional or attitudinal overtones. The **transformation subcomponent** determines which of some alternative rules will be used to arrive at the surface structure. Here is an example of two sentences with the same deep structure (meaning) that have undergone different transformations and are represented by two different surface structures:

The hungry cat ate the bird.
The bird was eaten by the cat that was hungry.

The rules governing sentence production and transformations in all languages determine such things as word order, inflectional endings, and structure words.

Languages differ in the order of the subject and its modifiers and in the ways they may reorder words to change simple statements into questions.

Inflectional endings are used to indicate tense, parts of speech, plurals, mood, the status of the speaker or hearer, agreement among different parts of speech, and voice.

Structure words do not usually have any direct meaning in themselves but indicate relationships among other words. They also aid other words in expressing meanings.

Languages may use rules in one or more of these categories. The rules may be parallel or be completely different from those of another language.

The semantic component pairs the sentence's deep structure with its meaning. The semantic component interprets terms, "colors" the multiple meanings of words, deals with certain aspects of specialized vocabulary, places limitations on the common speech that may be used in various situations, and changes meanings within the context of a social situation.

The graphophonological component determines what sounds or graphic representations the message will have. This component also selects such things as intonational patterns, stress, accent, and pitch, and the junctures, or pauses, used by speakers.

It should not be inferred that any part of this process really goes on inside the speaker's head. The base, transformations, deep structures, and surface structures are convenient linguistic notions that help explain many phenomena. These notions may have biological correlates of some sort, though none have yet been identified.

Although Chomsky's work was an important breakthrough for understanding language structures, psycholinguists realized that his theory provided insights only about the construction of sentences, not longer discourse, and that it emphasized grammar, not meaning. In the 1970s, psycholinguistics became more interdisciplinary as anthropologists, sociologists, and neuropsychologists joined cognitive psychologists, linguists, and educators in studying language and language development in children. What emerged from this study was an area that has become known as **generative semantics.** Researchers in this area study language systems' meaning-producing structures. Their work shows that a study of the grammar of language does not indicate meaning; it is meaning that determines sentences' forms (Smith, 1978). The result has been a shift from studying specific, isolated samples of language (usually single sentences) to studying language in longer spoken or written passages and the purpose(s) for which they are intended and used.

Much of the work in generative semantics has been summarized by Graesser (1981), who identified six knowledge domains of natural language (see Figure 13–4): linguistic; rhetorical; causal conceptualization; intentional conceptualization; spatial; and roles, personalities, and objects. The nature of these language domains is consistent with the nature of schemata. (See the

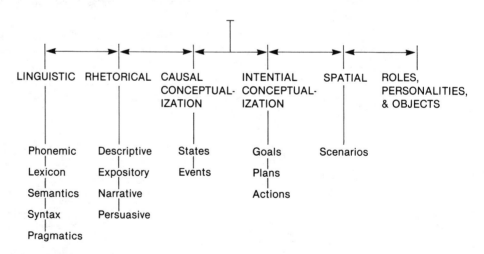

FIGURE 13–4
*Generative Semantics Knowledge Domains**

*Each domain contains information about the world and the way a language organizes and expresses that information. The domains are not discrete but interactive.

discussions in this chapter of the reading process as theorized by Rumelhart and Kintsch and of schema theory.)

Linguistic domain.   The linguistic domain contains rules that govern the use and sequence of sounds (phonemics), the assignment of dictionary meanings (lexicon), the grouping and ordering of words in sentences (syntax), the construction of meanings in sentences (semantics), and the use of language in dialogue and social situations (pragmatics). The linguistic domain contains many of the insights of transformational grammar theory. The least understood domain is pragmatics—the rules that govern the interactions of speaker and listener, author and reader.

Some pragmatics researchers have constructed a theory of shared, or common, knowledge. Their work shows that when the sender and receiver of messages share background knowledge or when the communication occurs in a specific social context, the form of the message becomes more limited and more abstract than when the communicators have less in common. For example, a master craftsperson is more likely to comment to an apprentice, "It won't fit unless it's rotated half a notch," than to say, "The cam, in order to be aligned with the indicator, needs to be placed in a position so that it is first turned to the left the distance of half of the space of one notch."

From the study of the linguistic domain, a new view of the link between syntax and semantics has developed. Called **case grammar** (Fillmore, 1968), this is much more than the transformational grammar proposed by Chomsky. In case grammar, the verb is considered the key element of a sentence, and sentences are examined for their underlying syntactic–semantic relationship(s). Therefore, verbs are studied and analyzed according to the function of nouns to verbs. There are six relationships between nouns and verbs:

> Agent (person or thing doing the action denoted by the verb)
> Object (receiver of the action)
> Instrument (object used in performing the action on the object)
> Manner (modification or explanation of the action)
> Time
> Location

These cases are thought of as explaining the *who, what* or *whom, with what, how, when,* and *where* in sentences and groups of sentences.

Rhetorical domain.   The rhetorical domain contains rules about how statements should be introduced, ordered, and interrelated in different kinds of language, novels, speeches, newspaper articles, and so on so that the message has the best chance of making an effect on the listener or reader. Rhetoric is usually descriptive, expository, narrative, or persuasive.

Causal conceptualization domain.   The causal conceptualization domain contains rules for how events and states are sequenced and how they are influenced in a nonintentional manner. **States** are the more-or-less stable characteristics of the communicator's physical environment and social conditions. **Events** are changes within these environments and conditions. Languages have various links to the way two or more events are related in a causal way; to the way a state is the causation of an event; and to the way an event results in a state. These links can be explicit or implicit in the language. For example, knowing that a person consistently reacts in the same way to specific actions or statements may influence the way another makes a request or offers a suggestion. Knowing this, a speaker might say "I have found that planting tomatoes at least one week after Mother's Day results in less loss to frost" instead of "Your plants died in last night's frost. You should always wait until later in May to plant tomatoes in this region."

Intentional conceptualization domain.   The intentional conceptualization domain contains the rules for organizing language according to the user's goals, plans, and actions. What the initiator of a message expects to achieve—a behavior, another statement, an act—and whether this goal is oriented toward the future or the past influences how something is said or written.

Spatial domain.   The spatial domain contains the knowledge and rules of the "scenarios" that create contexts for the communicator's actions, events, and states. In other words, the specific place and situation in which the communication occurs affects the structure of the message.

Roles, personalities, and objects domain.   The roles, personalities, and objects domain contains the rules governing the form of language used when referring to messages about social roles and personality traits, characteristics, and aspects. These rules also govern language form about stereotypes, impressions attributed to people, and the physical properties of inanimate objects or the personification of such properties. These rules usually call for the use of nouns and adjectives which, in conjunction with rules from the intentional conceptualization and rhetorical domains, might, for example, create the statement, "John is a radical anarchist." It is known that such labels will produce a specific action from others, which is the speaker's intent.

These six knowledge domains are not discrete. They interact throughout the communication process, and they control the formation of a message's surface structure. They control the sender's message and the receiver's perception and evaluation of the message. Whether the message is received as intended or whether the communication is hindered by some barriers depends to a large extent on the shared knowledge of the rules by both parties in the communication act.

Current psycholinguistic research shows that people usually focus on a message's meaning; they seem to remember the message's semantic and pragmatic aspects instead of the exact words in its surface structure. Therefore, any instruction in reading and writing must include attention to the total communication process and all features of language—not just to surface features alone.

The Structure of English

The structure of modern American English can be understood by examining its origin and changes. Following this discussion of English language history is a discussion of the semantic, syntactic, phonological, and pragmatic features of present-day American English, as well as a description of the features of written English and some of the differences between its written and spoken form.

History of the English Language

The known history of the English language dates from the sixth or seventh centuries when the Germanic Angle, Saxon, and Jute tribes invaded Celtic Britain. The Germanic languages belonged to the large family of Indo-European languages, from which almost all the languages of Europe and India are said to have descended. (Currently, however, no known language ancestor exists for all the known spoken languages.)

Texts written by English writers first appeared in the Middle Ages. The English used in the Middle Ages is currently called Old English or Anglo-Saxon. The English spoken from about 1100 to the Renaissance (about 1450 to 1550) is generally called Middle English. The language of Shakespeare, called Early Modern English, was spoken until about the beginning of the eighteenth century. The English spoken from that time to the present is called Modern English. These are general classifications and tend to distinguish social history, not language characteristics. Nevertheless, language historians use these distinctions to account for the major differences in language between these periods.

In its early periods, the grammar and vocabulary of English was influenced greatly by other languages. Old English was influenced by the languages of the Scandinavian and Norman invaders and conquerors. During the late Middle Ages, the strong influence of French caused changes. Early Modern English, spoken during the age of world exploration, was affected by the English people's contact with different cultures. American English from the 1700s on developed separately from British English through constant contact with various languages such as Dutch, Spanish, French, native American languages, German, Scandinavian languages, Yiddish, and Afro-American language.

The sounds of English underwent changes, too. Many of these changes are easier to follow through the Old English and Middle English periods because spellings then were inconsistent and were related more directly to words' pronunciations. After the Middle English period, spellings tended to be consistent and no longer were pronunciations always reflected in spellings. To identify the different present-day American regional pronunciations and to classify changes in these sounds, special records are now kept. Although consistent spelling patterns aid people today in written communication across regional speech patterns, they do not show the past and ongoing changes in pronunciations.

From this brief description of the development of present-day American English, it is possible to draw certain conclusions. Changes in English have occurred and continue to occur because of normal variations in society. As new ideas and technologies are produced, new language forms need to be invented to represent them. Also, as people move around the world, they create new language forms as they are first isolated and then begin to interact with other languages and cultures. These language changes can occur in pronunciations, word forms, sentence structures, and vocabulary (Malmstrom, 1977).

Semantic Features

The word *semantics* usually has a connotation of word meanings. **Semantics** as a language study, however, is concerned with the ability of speakers to interpret sentences. Semanticists study both the meanings or concepts attached to words, singly and in strings, and the relationship of meanings to syntactic and phonological structures.

In English, words have various functions as parts of a sentence. When words are discussed as such, they are called **parts of speech.** The term refers to the positions of certain words in sentences and the meanings those positions signal.

The first part of this discussion of semantics is not of semantics in its strict sense. It is, instead, a discussion of syntactic features that allow the reader to determine certain meaningful relationships between and among words and sentences. The syntactic functions of words (their parts of speech) provide the reader with signals to their meanings and to those of other words, phrases, and sentences. (The reader's use of these signals for understanding an author's message was discussed in Chapter 5, and strategies for developing and expanding students' understanding of words were discussed in Chapter 6.)

Content words can often be recognized by certain structural features and by the changes that occur in these words according to the part of speech they take in a sentence. For example, *know* becomes *knowledge* or *knowledgeable* and /NAY shun/ becomes /NAH shun ul/ or /NAH shun ul ize/ according to how they function as different parts of speech. In these cases, a signal to the meaning of the word can be found in the word itself.

The smallest sound unit in language is the phoneme. A sound by itself, however, usually does not convey any meaning; only combinations of these sounds convey meaning. These combinations, **morphemes,** are minimal meaningful forms.

The English language has two forms of morphemes: free and bound. A **free morpheme** is a group of sounds that by themselves signal meaning. For example, /walk/, /tooth/, and /pretty/ are free morphemes because they can be combined with other free morphemes to create sentences. A **bound morpheme** is a sound or group of sounds that signals meaning only when it is combined with other free or bound morphemes. For example, /s/ is a bound morpheme that signals meaning when it is combined with /coat/ to form /coats/.

Sometimes a morpheme can be both a free and a bound morpheme. For instance, /ball/ and /meter/ are considered free morphemes; yet they are bound morphemes in /football/ and /thermometer/. When written, the bound forms of the morphemes are spelled identically, but they do not always retain their original meanings or pronunciations.

Structure words are classified by the role they play in sentences. The various categories of structure words are

Noun markers.   Words such as /a/, /an/, /the/, /their/, /this/, /my/ and /some/ signal the appearance of a noun or noun phrase.

Verb markers.   Words such as (1) forms of /to be/, /to have/, and /to do/ used as auxiliary verbs and (2) other auxiliaries such as /well/, /shall/, /ought/, /may/, and /can/ signal an oncoming verb or verb phrase.

Qualifiers.   Words such as /very/, /too/, and /much/ signal the relative strength of an oncoming adjective or adverb.

Prepositions.   Words such as /up/, /down/, /in/, /out/, /out of/, /above/, and /below/ combine with noun forms to create phrases that modify other parts of speech.

Clause markers.   Words such as (1) the relative pronouns /who/, /whom/, /which/, /what/, and /that/ and (2) the subordinating conjunctions /if/, /because/, /although/, /even/, /while/, and /until/ all signal the onset of a dependent clause.

Question markers.   Words such as /who/, /how/, /where/, /when/, /what/, /did/, /are/, /is/, /have/, /do/, and /has/ often begin sentences and signal question transformations.

Negatives.   Words such as /no/, /not/, /never/, /nor/, and /none/.

The semantic features of English also refer to (1) definitions of words—both denotative and connotative, (2) the concept of unity and coherence, and (3) the context of the communication situation. The third point, the context of the communication situation, is discussed in the next section, "Pragmatics."

Dictionaries record the most common meanings of words, or their denotated meanings; connotative meanings are given to words because of how or when or by whom they are used. Connotative meanings transcend a word's specific dictionary definition. For example, one meaning of *club* is an organization of individuals with a common goal, purpose, or interest. But to some people, *club* implies an elitism, snobbery, and exclusion. Word meanings, therefore, develop within the context of sentences and longer discourse and are related to specific communication situations.

In addition, certain features of English indicate the coherence of a message or prose passage (Chapman, 1983; Irwin, 1986a,b; Schafer, 1981). When a message is coherent, it is tied together; there are no abrupt jumps or missing links between ideas.

The devices of cohesion are

Reference.   The use of pronouns to refer to another word.

Substitution.   The use of a synonym for the original word.

Ellipsis.   The deletion of an intended idea from subsequent sentences, as in "I went to the movies last night and enjoyed the show. So did Mary." (So did Mary go to the movies last night and enjoy the show.)

Connection.   The use of various terms (/therefore/, /although/) that connect or subordinate ideas.

Pragmatics

Closely related to the semantic features of language are the functions for which language is used. **Pragmatics** is the study of how and when language is used. The syntactic and phonological features of language are essential in signaling meaning; yet much of the meaning of a message results from the manner in which a speaker or writer uses language. This functional aspect of communication combines the other basic elements of communication—the content and the form of the message. The five dominant pragmatic functions of spoken English are

The controlling function.   Statements to direct or affect the behavior of another person as well as responses to control a situation. Examples are requests, suggestions, warnings, acknowledgments, refusals, and assents.

The sharing function.   Statements and expressions of feelings to others. Examples are praise, commiseration, ridicule, approval, apology, and rejection.

The informing function.   Statements to provide ideas and information to others. Examples are naming and giving examples, responses to information given by others, answers, questions, and denials.

The ritualizing function.   Statements that help sustain social relationships with others. Examples are greetings, thank yous, introductions, and teasing.

The imagining function.   Statements dealing creatively with reality through language. Examples are speculation, fantasizing, story telling, and dramatization. (Wood, 1981)

The social functions of a message can be obvious, as in /I want you to wear your mittens today/, or it can be implicit, as in /It's rather cold today; I think you left your mittens on the closet floor/. In the latter case, the pragmatic features of the message are hidden unless the complete communication situation is apparent, including the relationship between the message's sender and receiver. The speaker of the second message is performing a speech act and indirection (Ortony, 1984). **Indirection** is using one kind of speech act (here, informing) to achieve the goal of another (commanding). There is evidence that children first learn to attend to what is meant by a message and then learn to pay attention to what is said (Olson, 1981). This literal understanding of a message may be acquired as a result of learning to read and write.

In spoken language, the pragmatic features may be provided by nonverbal linguistic features such as sign language, symbols, and gestures; most communication involves the interplay of more than one function. For example, two functions come into play when someone controls a situation by using a ritualized means of introduction.

Syntactic Features

The typical English sentence contains a subject and a predicate. In English, the order of words in a sentence is important—the order of certain classes of words often signals meaning.

The main word classes, or parts of speech, are nouns, verbs, adjectives, adverbs, and structure words. A word's classification is determined more by how it is used in the sentence than by dictionary designation. The first four classes of words (nouns, verbs, adjectives, and adverbs) are considered **content words.** These words usually have basic referents and carry the content or subject of a message. The fifth class of words, **structure words,** have no meaning in themselves, but instead act as markers of content words and establish relationships among the classes of words or between groups of these word classes.

As stated previously, according to transformational grammar and semantics, a language has deep structures. Transformations may be performed on the deep structure of a message resulting in its surface structure. Linguists generally agree on the five common patterns of deep structure sentences. In the basic sentence patterns, the structure words are not considered important, since the meaning of the sentence is predominantly carried by the word order of the four content word classes and by the relationship of the nouns and verbs in the sentence. Sentence patterns that have undergone a minimum of transformations and whose surface features are similar to their deep structures are called **kernel sentences.** Strategies for reading and writing transformations of kernel sentences were discussed in Chapters 3 and 5.

The deep structure sentence patterns are

- Noun–verb or subject–verb structures

Birds fly.
He works happily hour after hour.

- Noun–verb–noun or subject–verb–direct object structures

Freddy threw the stick.
The gerbil ate the sunflower seed quickly.

- Noun–verb–noun–noun or subject–verb–indirect object–object structures

John gave Harry a watch.
Father gave me a new bat.

The following patterns are often considered noun–verb–noun patterns. Although the purpose here is to explain the general patterns of classifying English sentences (not to describe definitively all sentence patterns), these patterns are included for clarification.

- Subject–verb–direct object–object of preposition structures

Billy took a letter to school.

- Subject–verb–direct object–object complement structures

The class voted Jim door monitor.

- Noun–linking verb–noun or subject–linking verb–predicate noun

Walter is a monitor.

- Noun–linking verb–adjective or subject–linking verb–predicate adjective structures

Sheila is pretty.

Five common kinds of transformations that deep structure sentences can undergo are

Passive Voice

Kernel:	John gave Harry a watch.
Transformation:	A watch was given to Harry by John.

Questions

Kernel:	Freddy threw the stick.
Transformation:	Did Freddy throw the stick?

Negative

Kernel:	Walter is a monitor.
Transformation:	Walter is not a monitor.

Imperative

Kernel:	George gives Alice a new book.
Transformation:	George, give Alice a new book!

Beginning with It *and* There

Kernel:	Answering a teacher is wise.
Transformation:	It is wise to answer a teacher.
Kernel:	Birds are flying.
Transformation:	There are birds flying.

Not all English sentence patterns can be accounted for by the preceding categories, but most can. From these basic patterns, an unlimited number of sentences can be formed by applying rules governing the expansion and combination (also known as *embedding*) of whole sentences or parts of sentences.

Five common patterns of expansion and combination are

Compounding.   Words, phrases and independent clauses are combined to form compound subjects, compound predicates, compound objects, and compound sentences.

Kernel:	Carol sat.
	Carol waited.
	Betty sat.
	Betty waited.
Transformation:	Carol and Betty sat and waited.

Modification.   Adjectives, adverbs, qualifiers, adjective and adverbial phrases, and adjective and adverbial clauses are added.

Kernel:	The man gave away chickens.
Transformation:	The little man who wore a red hat gave away three chickens.

Apposition.   Words, phrases, or clauses are used to restate a preceding noun.

Kernel:	Gerald is secretary of the club. Gerald read the minutes of the previous meeting.
Transformation:	Gerald, secretary of the club, read the minutes of the previous meeting.

Subordination. Words, phrases, and clauses that are closely associated with and dependent on the main idea are added.

| Kernel: | John bought an ice-cream cone.
John was not really hungry. |
| Transformation: | Although John was not really hungry, he bought an ice-cream cone. |

Parallel structure. A series of ideas in the form of equally important phrases or clauses are added.

| Kernel: | The children had to read a story.
The children had to draw a picture.
The children had to write three sentences. |
| Transformation: | The children had to read a story, draw a picture, and write three sentences. |

Reading comprehension is partly the reconstruction of an author's intended meaning. It occurs when readers understand how a text's syntactic surface features result from the author's decisions about the six knowledge domains of natural language. Since more than one syntactic form of a message is possible in English, authors choose forms to reflect their knowledge of the receivers of the message, the intent of the message, and the situation in which the message is received. Previous chapters explained the various strategies for guiding students to maturity in reconstructing an author's possible meanings. The procedures are consistent with the notion of a reader reading like a writer (see Chapter 2).

Phonological Features

The human voice can make hundreds of different sounds, or phonemes. Each language, however, uses no more than a few dozen. Even though there is considerable overlap among languages in the phonemes used, no two languages share exactly the same ones. As explained previously, individual phonemes do not carry any meaning; meaning is assigned only to sequences of phonemes. Within a speech community, there is an implicit agreement to group sounds into a few dozen classes. When speakers of a language recognize two sounds as being significantly different, then two distinct phonemes exist. For example, the English sounds /t/ and /d/ are recognized as being distinct sounds.

All English speech sounds are made by the muscular movement of the speech organs as breath is expelled. Traditionally, phonemes are divided into two groups: consonants and vowels. A consonant is a speech sound in which the breath is stopped, hindered, or diverted as it is emitted. A vowel is a speech sound in which the vocal tract is open and the tone is selectively changed as it passes through the resonating chambers of the throat and head. Differences in the vowel sounds depend on the position of the tongue and changes in the mouth opening and cavity.

Some disagreement exists about the exact number of phonemes in English. There is greater agreement on the number of consonant phonemes than there is on the number of vowel phonemes. Generally, it is felt that 24 consonant sounds are used. Depending on the source and method of categorizing, however, this number may differ (Kean & Personke, 1976). In Chapter 6, some misunderstandings in teaching phonemes as part of reading instruction were discussed.

The categories of consonants are (1) stops, (2) fricatives, (3) affricates, (4) nasals, (5) liquids, and (6) glides (see Table 13–1). **Stops** are produced by impeding the flow of breath by either the lips or some part of the tongue. **Fricatives** are produced by forcing air through an opening restricted by the lower lip or the tongue. **Affricates** are produced in a manner similar to the fricatives except that the tongue touches the roof of the mouth just behind the front upper teeth. The stops and the fricatives can be either voiced (that is, the vocal cords vibrate) or unvoiced. The only difference between /f/ and /v/, for example, is that the latter is voiced. **Nasals,** all of which are voiced sounds, are produced by emitting the sound through the nasal passage rather than through the mouth. **Liquids** are produced by emitting air over or around the tongue. **Glides** are like vowels in that the stream of air is relatively unimpeded in the oral cavity, but they nevertheless act like consonants in the flow of speech. In most cases, the consonants occur in contrasting pairs—one voiced and the other unvoiced.

There is, as mentioned, much less agreement among speech and language researchers on the exact number of vowel phonemes in present-day American English. Since the production of a vowel depends on the position of the tongue, a very large number of different sounds can be produced. All could conceivably be considered vowel sounds. It is only through ear training during the speech acquisition process that individuals learn to distinguish a few of these sounds as the usable vowels for any language.

There is general agreement on the nine relative positions of the tongue during the production of English vowel sounds. In Table 13–1, "front," "center," and "back" refer to the placement of the tongue in relation to the teeth (front) or the throat opening (back). The labels "high," "mid," and "low" refer to the height of the tongue in relation to the roof of the mouth. The low vowels are generally produced with a wider mouth opening than are the mid or high vowels.

Vowel combinations are called **diphthongs** and are produced by combining vowels or by combining a vowel and a semivowel (or glide). In this way, there are over 35 possible diphthongs; however, in actual practice, English uses fewer (Kean & Personke, 1976).

It is no wonder that reading teachers are confused about the teaching of "vowel sounds." All speakers of American English know the vowel sounds; yet confusion arises when educators try to teach these sounds to students who

TABLE 13–1
The Phonemes of Present-Day American English

Consonants

		Stops			*Nasals*
*	/p/	pig, nipple, speak, rap	/n/		name, manner, fin
	/b/	big, tumble, stab	/m/		miss, hammer, ram
*	/t/	take, stop, little, fat	/ng/		ring
	/d/	dog, middle, mad			
*	/k/	kite, skate, tickle, back			*Liquids*
	/g/	got, bigger, rag	/l/		long, follow, fill
			/r/		rabbit, barrel, tear

		Fricatives			
*	/f/	fat, rifle, fluff			
	/v/	vote, savor, save			*Glides*
*	/th/	them, either, clothe	/w/		win, away
	/th/	think, ether, cloth	/y/		yes
*	/s/	sink, hassle, pass	* /h/		have
	/z/	zone, fuzz, quiz			
*	/sh/	shell, fashion, fish			
	/zh/	vision, mirage			

		Affricates
*	/ch/	chin, kitchen, such
	/dj/	fudge

*unvoiced

Vowels

	Front		*Center*		*Back*	
High	/ee/	feet			/oo/	pool
	/i/	it			/oo/	look
Mid	/ay/	table	/u/	up	/oh/	nose
	/e/	bed				
Low	/a/	act	/o/	ox	/aw/	saw
			/ah/	Amen		

	Diphthongs	
/ie/	pie, final
/ow/	cow, found
/oy/	boy, soil
/ai/	pail, stay, rake

already know them. When helping students associate the sounds of the language with the printed symbols representing these sounds, a great deal of frustration can be avoided if variant forms of the phonemes are recognized by teachers. No value judgment should be made regarding the various pronunciations themselves. Many people probably do not pronounce the words /idea/, /father/, /dog/, and /merry/ in the same way; the main difference lies in the way the vowel sounds are pronounced. Most people have learned to consider the variations in regional and individual speech patterns as normal and to treat variations in vowel sounds as usually insignificant to meaning. These two ideas about teaching vowel sounds have been discussed in Chapters 3 and 6.

Other features of spoken English are the phonemic elements of stress, pitch, and juncture. These elements make up the intonational pattern of language. **Stress** refers to the relative loudness of a syllable or word; there are usually four levels of stress: primary, secondary, tertiary, and weak. They are signals to differences of meaning. For example, one way people know the difference between the noun /record/ and the verb /record/ is by the shift in stress. Also, /GROWING corn/ is not the same as /growing CORN/.

Pitch is the relative level of a speaker's voice. English is considered to have four pitch levels. The following example shows that change in pitch level can signal a change in meaning:

```
                       ing
               go
/we are all                   home/

                              home/
               going
/we are all
```

The first sentence follows the normal intonational pattern for a declarative statement and the second follows the normal intonational pattern for a question.

Juncture is a phonemic element closely related to pitch; it refers to the pauses made between syllables, words, phrases, and sentences. Most of these pauses are so slight that they are almost imperceptible. Together with stress and pitch they combine to convey various meanings. Juncture allows the listener, together with other syntactic and semantic features, to distinguish between /Seymour/ and /see more/, /night rates/ and /nitrates/, /scenic/ and /see Nick/, and /syntax/ and /sin tax/.

Graphic Features

It is commonly heard that writing is talk written down. In a way it is. There are, however, several stylistic features found in one form that are not found in the other. Written language is not merely speech in graphic form, just as reading, though similar to listening, is more than "listening with the eyes" (Olson, 1981). These differences include features of syntax, semantics, pragmatics, and graphophonemics. The differences between the forms becomes most apparent when individuals attempt to transpose one form into the other (write down speech, read expository prose aloud).

Spoken prose and conversation differ in the use of tempo, juncture, and redundancy. Juncture in spoken prose is related to the written message and follows the pattern of punctuation. In conversation, juncture can be unpredictable. In spoken prose, tempo will be uneven. In conversation, there is much redundancy for emphasis and for maintaining the continuity of ideas. Also, the pronunciation of words—especially articulation deviations—often goes unnoticed in conversation.

Present-day written English is not directly phonetic. There is no longer a single, simple, one-letter-to-one-sound relationship. Sometimes, one letter represents a sequence of sounds, as in /x/ and *x*. In other cases, a sequence of letters represents a single sound, as in /th/ and *th*. There has been a tendency to retain a word's spelling from when it first entered the language or its spelling from its original language. For example, the /sh/ pronounced in *ocean* reflects the spelling of its Greek origin; the same sound in *nation* reflects the original Latin spelling.

There is difficulty, though, in drawing hard and fast conclusions about the differences between spoken and written English. First, there is a methodological problem in research. Researchers have used different types of oral language passages as a means for comparison, since it is impossible to obtain material on the same topic, intended for the same audience, and presented by the same communicator through both modes. Second, authors and speakers confront the problem of audience from different perspectives. An author must address unknown readers, in unknown context, and with unknown states of knowledge. Therefore, authors must use more explicit references and link propositions and ideas in a more logical manner than speakers do, who directly confront their audiences.

Keep in mind that a writing system is one symbolic form of a language—it is not the language itself. Both spoken and written languages have many levels. They both have a standard and nonstandard form and a formal and informal tone, and they both can be scholarly and edited, or slangy and unrevised. These variations should not be considered corruptions of the language. Language changes continually, and should it cease to change, it would no longer be adequate for human communication. Language change does not mean language decay.

The following concludes this section on understanding verbal communication:

The effectiveness of a communication is not related to the use of an extensive vocabulary, careful articulation of speech sounds, or perfect grammatical phrasing. Instead, it is based on the appropriateness of what we say. The message must be appropriate to the person, the setting (time and place), the topic being discussed and the task at hand. The competent communicator carefully weighs the factors of the communication situation:

1. participants: the person(s) involved in communication
2. setting: the time and place of the communication event
3. topic: the subject matter of communication
4. task: the goal or purpose of communication (Wood, 1981, p. 230)

HUMAN THINKING

Living entails thinking, and thinking entails resolving uncertainty (or at least attempting to). The term *problem solving* is applied to thinking that is aimed toward adjusting to a new situation or resolving some conflict. Psycholinguists are increasing their research attention to certain issues related to problem solving: how people develop this capacity, how it relates to the nature of language, and how it affects and is affected by the development of language. Their findings regarding human thinking and language are changing the general knowledge of thought and language. The following discussions represent a synthesis of current research on these topics. Although this information may be modified in the future, there is strong evidence that it will not change radically.

The basis for current ideas about the structure of human thinking is called schema theory. At one time the basis of thinking was believed to be the acquisition and use of concepts—categories of mental experiences learned by individuals during their lifetime. Although the idea of concepts is important to schema theory, the model of thinking involves much more than what is considered to be a concept.

Schema Theory

Schema theory postulates that a spoken or written text does not in itself carry meaning. Instead, meaning is created by using previously acquired knowledge (schemata). The theory specifies how knowledge transacts/interacts with and shapes incoming information and how this knowledge must be organized to support this transaction/interaction (Anderson & Pearson, 1984; Graesser, 1981; Hacker, 1980; Rumelhart, 1981).

Features of Schemata
Schemata are the building blocks of thinking. They are generic, not specific knowledge structures. These broad concepts are stored in memory.

Concepts, like schemata, are categories created for sorting out and responding to the world. These categories reflect the culture of people and help them organize their lives. Concepts serve to reduce environmental complexity, to identify surrounding objects, to reduce the necessity of constant learning to provide direction for basic life activities, and to order and relate different kinds of events (Bruner, Goodnow, & Austin, 1956). For a concept to be developed, there must be a series of earlier experiences that are similar in one or more respects. The common features of those experiences are generalized, and it is this general description of an idea or event that is considered a concept (Carroll, 1966). Schemata, though, are and do much more than concepts.

Schemata are structures for reproducing concepts. They guide interpretations, inferences, expectations, and attention. They are not merely memories of events but are an organized, structured set of summaries of the parts, attributes, and relationships that occur in specific events. Schemata are created after years of experience (Graesser, 1981).

One main feature of schemata is the collection of variables forming their structures (Graesser, 1981; Hacker, 1980; Rumelhart, 1981). These variables can be categorized in the six knowledge domains of language discussed previously: linguistic; rhetorical; causal conceptualization; intentional conceptualization; spatial; and roles, personalities, and objects (see Figure 13–4). The variables of schemata are like scripts or little plays stored in the memory. They allow people to know and understand activities that contain many ideas and ways of acting. For example, the scripts for such activities as "going shopping" or "going to school" may include:

	Going shopping	*Going to school*
Characters:	customers, clerks	students, teachers, principals
Objects:	goods, counters	desks, pencils, paper
Goals:	the customer purchases goods and pays the bill	students learn; teachers teach
Logical orders:	obtain item from shelf, go to check it out, total bill, pay	arrive at school, morning routines, day divided into periods or subjects, related activities, lunch, recess, dismissal

A second feature of schemata is that they can be embedded, or nested, one within the other. Some schemata contain subschemata. For example, in the shopping schema, there is the subschema of "bill paying." In the school schema, each learning activity or subject area may have its own information, rules, and actions.

A third feature of schemata is that they can represent levels of abstractness. Some schemata may be concrete, such as the schema for mixing colors from the three primary colors, and some may be abstract, such as that for relating stylized map features to real geographic properties.

A fourth feature is that schemata represent broad aspects of knowledge, not just definitions (Graesser, 1981). From such a view of schemata, it is possible to understand that people possess incomplete schemata for some aspects of the world. For example, to understand the schema of shopping, a person needs not only a definition of *shopping,* but also an understanding of the general components of grocery stores or supermarkets, the general attributes of stores, the actions of shopping, and the relationship between shoppers and sellers. This understanding may not necessarily be a complete knowledge of all aspects of all stores and all shopping instances. What is developed is a universal or generic understanding so a person can shop in a variety of food-selling establishments.

Last, schemata are a part of active processes. They are constantly used to examine incoming information in an effort to determine how it fits with existing schemata or whether it needs to be developed on its own as a new schema. This feature will become clearer as the processes of schemata are studied further in this chapter.

Processes of Schemata

Schemata are used for identification and schema application. At first, this may seem circular, but it becomes more understandable when schemata are thought of as (1) templates in the memory against which incoming information is matched, (2) organizers in the memory that specify how all previously learned information (schemata and concepts) will transact/interact with and shape new information, and (3) processors that specify how the incoming information must be arranged to support the transaction/interaction. It is almost as if what is already known determines what and how someone will understand and learn. Schema identification and schema application may work independently of each other or, as is more often the case, in an interactive, supportive manner.

Schema identification is a pattern-recognition process. A schema is activated by available information and is used to examine and evaluate the information's appropriateness—to determine how it fits into the broader, generic categories. For example, the incoming information may be a new experience with food shopping—perhaps shopping in an exclusive gourmet shop. The new data are then placed in perspective to already existing schemata about food shopping (broad and subschemata) so that appropriate behavior(s) for the information may be selected.

Schema application is a process of seeking out information to satisfy or embellish already existing variables of schemata. It is also a process that provides knowledge and a context for interpreting incoming information, generating inferences, and guiding a person's attention to specific aspects or parts of the incoming information. Schemata are then used to determine whether the information contains aspects that are consistent with or deviant from existing schemata. Schemata are corrected and adjusted according to new input; schemata, then, can be considered knowledge specialists that govern what messages are received and how they are received.

In summary, schemata are generalized descriptions both of the categories into which some of life's experiences are placed and of the hierarchial arrangement into which others are placed. They are private theories about the nature of the world, its objects, and events, and they guide predictions about how well new information conforms to the old. They allow people to make predictions about unobserved or new events and guide them in acting in conventional and novel situations. In this way *thinking* is the transaction/interaction among schemata, and *understanding* is realizing how any information conforms to or disagrees with what is already known.

The Structure of Human Intellect

Guilford (1967; Guilford & Hoepfner, 1971) classifies the kinds of thinking that can occur in adults. He does not attempt to explain the developmental nature of his structures. The basic implication of his theory is that there are different kinds of thinking for different situations. In the classroom, a student might be able to do certain mental activities and yet not be able to do others.

Guilford's structure-of-intellect model is not hierarchial in nature (see Figure 13–5). Guilford cross-classifies the various intellectual abilities that adults seem to possess. His model classifies the intellectual abilities in three different ways so that the subunits, or categories, of each ability intersect with those of the other abilities.

The three major classifications are *mental operations, contents,* and *products* (Guilford, 1967; Guilford & Hoepfner, 1971). **Mental operations** are major kinds of intellectual activities; they are what a person does in processing information. The five intellectual activities are (1) recognizing information, (2) remembering information, (3) creating more than one logical conclusion from known information, (4) creating a logical conclusion consistent with information known by others, and (5) comparing information and making judgments.

Contents, Guilford's second classification, are the ways information can be organized. The four kinds of contents are (1) the actual object or a realistic representation of it, (2) a symbol representing the object or other information, (3) a semantic representation of information (concepts or mental images), and (4) nonpictorial and nonverbal information.

Products, Guilford's third class, are the forms in which information is presented. The six categories of products are (1) individual items or bits of information, (2) classes of information (groups of items having a common property), (3) connections among items based on a definable relationship, such as time, space, or rank order, (4) complex structures of items organized according to a plan, (5) changes in information such as redefinitions or modifications, and (6) circumstantial connections among different information, usually through implications that cannot be verbalized.

When the three classifications are combined in the cross-classification model, the result is a block of 120 cells, or subunits. Each cell represents a combination of one type of operation with one type of content and one type of product.

In his explanation of the model, Guilford (1967) advises the reader not to suppose that the 120 abilities represent all the intellectual traits of human intelligence. There are reasons to suppose that the number might be much

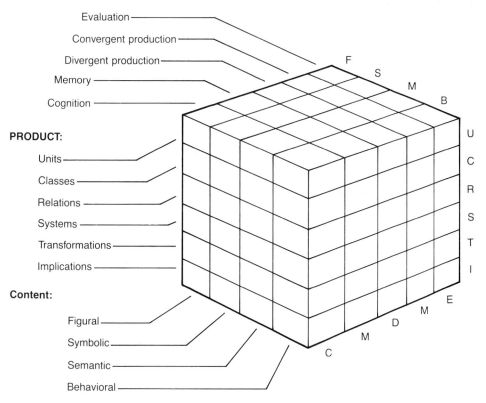

OPERATION:

- Evaluation
- Convergent production
- Divergent production
- Memory
- Cognition

PRODUCT:

- Units
- Classes
- Relations
- Systems
- Transformations
- Implications

Content:

- Figural
- Symbolic
- Semantic
- Behavioral

FIGURE 13–5
The Structure-of-Intellect Model

Source: J. P. Guilford. (1967). *The nature of human intelligence.* New York: McGraw-Hill. Used with permission of McGraw-Hill Book Company.

greater, since many of the cells seem to represent two or three kinds of related abilities. For example, figural memory of units may consist of an auditory and a visual memory. Cognition may consist of auditory abilities, visual abilities, and kinesthetic abilities. It appears that in the cognition and memory-operation categories, there may be some general differentiation of abilities along sensory–modality lines.

One classroom implication of Guilford's theory is that the concept of *product of information* is represented in different ways in the English language (Guilford, 1967). The information presented as units and classes are things or groups of things to which nouns are normally applied. Relations, the connections or bridges between two or more bits of information, are commonly expressed by prepositions. Systems are generally verbally stated arithmetic problems, outlines, mathematical equations, or plans. Transformations are generally expressed through participles (a verb in noun form such as *thinking* or *running*). The ability to use these various parts of speech and to understand their use may depend on certain and separate mental abilities.

The Structure of Human Memory

A growing body of research indicates that human memory has the structure of a multiple storage system (Kumar, 1971; Lindsay & Norman, 1977; Andre, 1979). The components of the system are a sensory register, a short-term memory, and a long-term memory.

From the available evidence there is some

> reasonably good agreement that permanent storage of information takes place either through chemical or structural changes in the brain. There is little or no disagreement that the immediate, ongoing activities of thorough, conscious process, and the immediate memories—sensory information store and short term memory—are mediated through electrical activity. (Lindsay & Norman, 1977, p. 421)

One possibility about the location of the various functions in the brain is that memories do not seem to be stored in specific locations. They tend to be found as patterns in different locations. Any specific memory, then, involves large sections of the brain. No one portion is absolutely necessary for memory processes; yet, the more sections that function together, the clearer the recollection is (Lindsay & Norman, 1977).

The human brain is amazingly complex; its parts seem to be interchangeable, or at least interdependent. This has not allowed researchers to identify the specific sections functioning as the memory system. If the brain should encounter injury in one section, its complexity allows it to use another section to do certain life-sustaining activities. What do seem to be localized are the specific regions where certain sensory stimuli enter the brain and the regions responsible for certain human activities. For example, motor areas, speech areas, and seeing areas have been identified. Still a mystery, however, is precisely how information is transferred from one region to another and what the exact process is of solving problems and storing, retrieving, and analyzing information. Although the exact physical nature of the brain's activities is not yet known, enough evidence is available to sustain a theory of a multiple storage system model of memory (see Figure 13–6).

The **sensory register** is where all sensory images are deposited by the sensory modalities. In half a second, a bit of registered information disappears. Information may also be forgotten or eliminated from the sensory register by the introduction of new information.

How is information, which will quickly disappear, transferred to the other memory storage systems? Transfer is best thought of as "copying" information. What information is copied into one system from another depends on the schemata. Each person uses procedures of selective attention. Information is se-

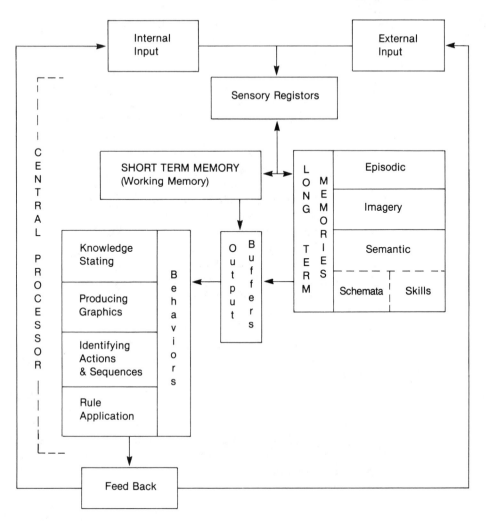

FIGURE 13–6
An Information Processing Model of Memory
After Andre (1979) and Gagne & White (1978).

lected from the sensory register according to the importance of the information to the individual. The information is then retained in the short-term memory storage. Everyone is aware of the phenomenon of "attenuating" when they direct their thinking to the heat in the room and do not listen to the lecturer, or when they divert their attention from a theatrical performance to the uncomfortable seats.

The phenomenon of selective attention has good and bad aspects. It is desirable because without it the collection of sensory inputs would be utterly chaotic. The world would be a jumble of sights, sounds, and smells. The procedure allows for the orderly selection of incoming sensory data based on what seems important at the moment. A negative feature is that more than one thing cannot be given attention in any one instant. Because of this it is difficult to keep track of two conversations simultaneously or to read a book and follow the progress of a sporting event on television without rereading many pages of the book or relying on instant replays of the sporting event.

The **short-term memory** is a working memory. It retains information for a longer period than does the sensory register. Information is generally retained for no more than 15 seconds. The capacity of short-term memory is much more limited than that of the sensory register; however, this limited information is much more select. The short-term memory may hold only about six units of information. However, meaningful information or closely related units of information are likely to be retained as one unit of information. For example, the letters x, y, l, and n would probably be retained as four discrete information units, whereas a rearrangement of those letters into a meaningful unit—*lynx*—would cause them to be retained as one unit.

Information is eliminated from the short-term memory by decay or replacement. Information is lost or forgotten after about six seconds or when new information enters the short-term memory to replace it. However, information may be retained for longer periods of time by a process of mental repetition (Lindsay & Norman, 1977).

The information transferred from short-term memory to long-term memory is under an individual's control, although it may be unconsciously so. The importance placed on information determines whether it is processed further (Kumar, 1971). An attentional aspect similar to that involved in the transfer of information from sensory register to short-term memory may be involved in the transfer of information from short-term memory to long-term memory (Kumar, 1971). The transfer strategies are an individual's conscious efforts involving the replacement of the information by other information, the storage of additional information, and the combining of information with past experience (schema formation).

Long-term memory may consist of three subunits: episodic memory, imagery memory, and semantic memory (Andre, 1979; Gagne & White, 1978). Episodic memory has dated events and temporal-spatial relationships regarding those events retained in a cognitive code (schemata). These memories are tied to places and time sequences. Episodic memory can be considered a diary of life's experiences.

Imagery memory contains both concrete and referential representations. These images are not stored in any verbal code; they are true images but can be activated by encoding, a process of getting associations from other long-term memory units. For example, a mental picture can be created by hearing or seeing the words *Mount Rushmore.*

The semantic memory contains all a person's abstracted or generalized knowledge about concepts, principles, rules, and so forth. These abstractions are broader than episodes; they are the schemata that enable comprehension of incoming information. Semantic memory also contains a network of interrelated schemata—ideas and the connections between them. Semantic memory may have two subsections. One is the clusters of information and relationships previously mentioned, and the other is a set of "action plans" or "routines." These are concepts and rules that guide the application of rules. It is the "knowing how" portion of memory that complements the "knowing what" portion.

This "knowing how" aspect of memory is called metacognition. **Metacognition** is the knowledge and control people have over thinking and learning activities (Baker & Brown, 1984). It is clusters of activities that allow people to know their thinking ability and the compatibility between themselves as learners and the learning situation. These activities can be considered self-regulatory mechanisms that active learners use during their attempts to solve problems. For example, the activities may include checking outcomes, planning next moves, checking on the effectiveness of strategies, revising strategies for other learning, and using compensatory strategies. Throughout this text, instructional strategies are stressed that allow readers to know how successful they are in applying them.

Long-term memory, the most important of the memory systems, is more permanent and resistant to forgetting. In comparison to the sensory register and short-term memory, the capacity of long-term memory is almost limitless. Everything to be retained for more than a few minutes must be placed in long-term memory. Here are stored all one's knowledge of the world, language and cultural rules, and strategies for creating meaning out of the world.

Any discussion of long-term memory is not complete without considering retrieval. If information is adequately stored (appropriate schemata exist and appropriate rules are applied to link new information to them), the recall of that information depends on several factors. These include the means of searching the memory, the means of beginning the recall process, and the length of time between input and recall (Berry, 1980; Gagne & White, 1978; Graesser, 1981).

Immediately after information is stored in long-term memory, a person can recall verbatim the message of the input. But over time the memory becomes more generalized. Information consistent with a person's general schemata is preserved. What an individual remembers is not so much the specific information that was received and stored but a generalization consistent with his or her schemata. Retrieval may also be affected by the recall process. For example, returning to the analogy of the shopping schema and, in particular, the sub-schemata of buying an item in a gourmet shop, recall might be started by thoughts about a particular dinner party (concept to detail). Alternatively, retrieval might be started by observing a particular food item and recalling the party at which it is to be served (detail to generalization).

These ideas have important implications for instruction. In previous chapters, instructional strategies for assessing and developing comprehension were discussed. Those strategies are built on the ideas presented here about schema theory, human intellect, and the structure of human memory.

THE DEVELOPMENT OF THINKING AND LANGUAGE IN CHILDREN

In this section, the development of verbal (syntactic and semantic) structures in the language of children is discussed. Phonological development—the development of the ability to produce the sounds of language—although interesting, has no direct bearing on the larger topic. The concern here is with the development of the thinking process in children as reflected in their development of language. Little will be said about the development of vocabulary, because evidence indicates that vocabulary development reflects the social situations in which the young child grows. This point was discussed in Chapter 6.

That language is learned as a process of communication is the most important result of the study of how speech develops in children. Young children seem to possess an innate ability to reduce and restructure adult language in a highly systematic way to fit their intellects. As children mature, there is a progressive differentiation in word usage and the use of syntactic structures (Brown & Bellugi, 1966). Children's language is not, however, a miniature copy of adult speech; until the child is almost mature, patterns are used that do not normally appear in adult speech. These patterns are remarkably similar from language to language (Slobin, 1979). Furthermore, language cannot develop primarily from the memorization of words and lists of sentences. The known limitations of young children's memories preclude memorization as the mechanism of language acquisition. Also, all speakers of a language are able to produce sentences that they have never heard previously.

Behavioral philosophy presents another view of how language is learned. However, psycholinguistic research demonstrates that the behaviorist view cannot adequately account for language acquisition (Lindfors, 1980). Specifically, the behaviorist approach to language acquisition cannot explain the uniformity with which language is learned by all humans, regardless of their ethnic, cultural, or geographic backgrounds; it cannot account for why or how children infer the deep structure from an exposure to only surface elements; and it cannot explain the short time period needed and the early onset of acquiring such a complex system of linguistic rules and applications.

Generally, children begin to speak around the age of one and a half years, a period that coincides with the Piagetian "preoperational thought" stage. Keep in mind that the preoperational thought stage is characterized by the internalization of the external world and that items and events are classified by attributes that the child can perceive. Vygotsky characterizes language acquisition beginning at this age as an internalized reflection of reality.

The following explanation of children's development of thinking and language is a synthesis of ideas and contributions of researchers and scholars in the field (Anastasiow, 1979; Halliday, 1975; Lindfors, 1980; Wiemann & Backlund, 1980; Wood, 1981). It begins with an explanation of children's thinking as conceived by Piaget and Vygotsky.

Development of Human Thinking

Piaget

According to Piaget, intelligence develops gradually over a long period. An individual shows this growth as differences in the way problems are solved at different developmental stages (Furth, 1970). Acquiring knowledge is not just adding new information to old information, but is an active process of incorporating new information (which Piaget, too, called schemata). A thing in the world is not an object of knowledge until it is related to something already learned. Then the new information is reorganized into a new, larger meaning or understanding. However, the manner in which people relate new information to prior knowledge depends on their psychological frame of reference, or cognitive structure. Piaget's four developmental stages (see Table 13–2) are an attempt to explain how a child thinks when progressing through the stages of cognitive maturity.

Piaget considered humans to be biological organisms. This means that they respond to their environment and their reactions are not merely responses to outside stimulation. Reactions are attempts to incorporate environmental information into the intellect (schemata). People then make some changes in their cognitive structure to meet the newly incorporated information. These are what Piaget called *assimilation* and *accommodation.* As a biological organization, people have an innate tendency to preserve the status quo. But, cognitive functioning is not static; it is a dynamic process in which people try to maintain a balance between assimilation and accommodation. The process of keeping this balance is called **equilibration.** It results in developmentally successive changes that lead from the most elementary and basic knowledge (shown by

TABLE 13–2
Piaget's Stages of Intellectual Development

Approximate Age (years)	Characteristics
0–2	**Sensorimotor Development** Acquires skills and adaptations which are reflexive in nature. Coordinates and integrates information from senses; operates with a sense of object permanency; exhibits goal-directed behavior.
2–7	**Preoperational Thought** Develops internal cognitive picture of external world. Begins language development; classifies on perceived attributes.
7–11	**Concrete Operations** Organizes through the logical structure of groups. Manipulates concrete ideas; develops concepts of reversibility and conservation.
11–15	**Formal Operations** Develops fundamentals of logical thought. Understands principles of causality and hypothesis testing.

adaptive reflex action) to abstract knowledge (shown by adult intelligent actions). The change represents a qualitatively different way of organizing and dealing with the world at each successive stage. These changes are cumulative, each building on the other, and they occur in four ways:

1. Addition—adding new information to an existing schema;
2. Substitution—replacing some or all information in a schema;
3. Inclusion—adapting old information to a new schema;
4. Mediation—using old information to bridge the gap to fit new information (Gray, 1978).

Intelligence, then, is a force that regulates a living organism so it maintains a stable relationship (equilibration) between the organization and its environment (Furth, 1969).

Piaget emphasized the effect of the environment. Although he stressed that children would progress naturally (mature) through the stages of development, he indicated other sources of change as well: biological, experiential, societal transmissions, and equilibration. Experience, he felt, could be passive—merely experiencing the physical world—or it could be "logicomathematical," actions stimulating change. Societal transmission, according to Piaget, are learning and education (Gray, 1978). Sketches of Piaget's four stages of development follow.

The **sensorimotor stage,** the first stage, occurs during the first two years of a child's life. During this time, the child develops the practical knowledge of the world that will structure all future knowledge of the world. The skills and adaptations developed during this stage are reflexive. The child organizes sensory information from the various sensory modalities and begins integrating this information in goal-directed, deliberate actions. Discoveries are still primarily through manipulation. The child begins to understand the permanency of space; however, there is no internalized representation of the world yet. During this period, language begins.

The second stage, the **preoperational stage,** is filled with experiments with objects in play. The child begins to establish relationships between experiences and actions. The child imitates adults and begins to internalize observations of adult activities. The result is that these internalizations become the basis for imagery and language development. Although the child is developing consistent representational skills (schemata), these are not always acceptable representations to adults. At first, the child identifies words and symbols with an object and its characteristics. A cow is a cow because it has "cowness." By the end of the growth period the child begins to understand the arbitrariness of symbol-to-object associations. Different things and people may be called by different names. Thinking during this period is "transductive," which means that information can be related from particular to particular but not from particular to general. The child's activity is limited to concrete actions. Relationships are made because objects have some features in common. For instance, associations may be based on environmental conditions rather than on some

inherent quality of the object. Things are grouped together because ''Mommy uses them in the kitchen,'' not because they are all round or made of metal. Last, the child cannot distinguish between the motives of the external world and those of the internal world. Egocentricity will not allow the child to take another's point of view. Thinking during this period is irreversible, which is shown by the widely known experiments on conservation of mass.

The **concrete operations stage,** the third stage, occurs about the ages of 7 to 11 and covers the largest portion of the elementary-school years. During this stage the child develops schemata of time, space, number, and logic. These control the child's understanding of events and objects, the logical structure of groups, and a sense of multiple classifications. The child realizes that objects have multiple characteristics and that the significance of each characteristic can change with a change of purpose. Objects can be grouped because they are red or round and then again because they are used for cooking or building. Although thought still remains tied to actual objects and events, the child has internalized the world. A need to manipulate objects physically no longer exists. By the end of this stage, the child can do mental arrangements of objects.

The fourth stage, **formal operations,** occurs during the ages of 11 to 15. In this period, the child develops an understanding of basic principles of causal thinking. The child can do experiments, deduce implications, and grasp abstract, logical thought, and hypothetical reasoning. The child, by the end of the period, can think through a full set of alternatives for a problem.

There is an important distinction between the thinking of elementary-school-age children and that of adults. Often adults make assumptions about the way children think that are erroneous according to Piagetian principles (Elkind, 1974). One misconception is that children and adults are alike in the way they think and different in the way they feel about things. The opposite may be true. Nevertheless, many adults treat children as if they do not have personal preferences or likes and dislikes and as if children's emotions are different from adults'. Another misunderstanding is that children learn by sitting and listening. From the description of Piaget's developmental stages, it seems children learn best by activity and movement. Children learn about the world through active manipulation of objects and ideas and by imitating the people they meet in their lives. A third misunderstanding is that children learn best by learning rules. Again, children learn by living and acting in the world, not by associating some abstract rule to a situation. A fourth misunderstanding concerns attempts to accelerate development. In general, the results of Piaget's work indicate that children at each stage of development benefit more from enriching activities than from attempts to speed up their education.

Vygotsky

According to Vygotsky (1962, 1978), a child's intellectual growth is contingent on mastering the social means of thought—language. Two aspects of Vygotsky's and Piaget's theories are similar. They both believe that there is an innate precondition or prerequisite for thought and language (speech) and that developmental stages of thought and speech grow from a prelinguistic period to the period of fully intelligible language. Vygotsky's conclusions about the functional and structural relationships between thought and language are:

1. In a child's biological development, thought and language have different roots.
2. In a child, it is possible to identify a prelinguistic stage in thought development and a preintellectual stage in language development.
3. Up to a certain point in time, the thought and language follow different, independent developmental lines.
4. At a certain time, these lines meet and thought becomes verbal and language becomes rational.

Thought and language merge in a child about the age of two. Then the child begins to acquire concepts and generalizations about the world. Vygotsky stressed the innately determined critical or sensitive periods when a child is most receptive to acquiring a particular generalization. On this, Vygotsky and Piaget only differ in their precise definitions of the developmental stages.

Vygotsky (1978) identified two levels of development. The first he called the *actual developmental level*. At this level, the child has a maturity resulting from completed developmental cycles. Mental age, as measured by standardized tests, is an example of an actual developmental level. The second level of development is represented by a period in which some children with an apparently similar level of development can solve problems of different levels of complexity and with different degrees of independence. He called this level of development the *zone of proximal development*. It represents a period between "the actual developmental level as determined by independent problem solving and the level of potential development as determined through problem solving under adult guidance or in collaboration with more capable peers" (p. 86).

These zones of proximal development are periods when a child's developmental process lags behind the learning process. Learning is directly related to the course of child development; yet, the two are not parallel or achieved equally. Vygotsky felt that each school subject has its own relationship to learning, which varies as the child goes from one stage to another.

Vygotsky did not agree with Piaget's explanation of an innate grammar preceding semantic understanding nor with his universal application of that theory. Vygotsky proposed that human communication presupposes a generalized approach to the world and that thought reflects a "conceptualized actuality." This actuality is seen as the basic characteristic of words. "Words play a central part not only in the development of thought but in the historical growth of consciousness as a whole. A word is a microcosm of human consciousness" (Vygotsky, 1962, p. 153). Vygotsky believed that a word acquires its meaning from the context in which it appears. Change the context and the meaning is changed. Also, a word in context means both more and less than the same word alone. It acquires new content, yet its meaning is limited by the context.

Vygotsky (1962) emphasized the role of society and culture in the development of thought and language. To him

> verbal thought is not an innate, natural form of behavior but is determined by a historical-cultural process and has specific properties and laws that cannot be found in the natural forms of thought and speech. . . . The development of verbal behavior will be governed essentially by the general laws of the historical development of human society. (p. 51)

The Development of Human Speech

The following discussion is about how children develop language's verbal and nonverbal features. These aspects of language are presented in an arbitrary order; yet, they are concomitant, codeveloping aspects of thinking and language (see Table 13–3).

Syntax

Speech acquisition begins when a baby imitates adult intonational patterns (see Table 13–3). This is then followed by a period in which single words appear. These words, although they have no direct tie to words found in a standard dictionary, are word approximations and relate symbols to objects. Children then show they understand words spoken to them. In addition, they use various intonational patterns, and it may be possible to distinguish the consistent use of declarative, emphatic, and question intonations in their utterances.

In the next stage of language development, children can combine two words to make a sentence. At first a child constructs a few of these sentences. Then, within a brief period, there is an effusion of them. These two-word sentences are not random combinations of words. They consist of two classes of words: pivot words and open-class words. The pivot words are the child's high frequency words—usually small and stable in number. They are words such as *on, more, big,* and *allgone,* and generally represent a quality or a process of something. The open class has a large and growing number of words representing attempts to name and classify the objects and events in the child's world. The pivot words may occupy the first or the second position in the sentence. They are easily recognized as those words with which many of the open words in the child's vocabulary can be joined. Examples of two-word sentences with the pivot word at the beginning are /Allgone milk./ /See Daddy./ /Big dog./. Two-word sentences with the pivot word at the end are /Baby down./ /Shoe on./ /Mommy off./.

The pivot constructions serve various functions in a child's speech. How-

TABLE 13–3
Language Development

Syntactic Phase	Semantic Phase	Nonverbal Phase
Birth	*Approximately 9–16 months*	*Birth*
Imitation of intonation	Sounds and meaning	Paralinguistics
Single-word sentences	*Approximately 16–24 months*	
Two- & three-word sentences	Grammar and dialogue	
Hierarchical constructions	*Approximately 24 months and on*	
Regularizations	Development of "scripts"	
Language transformations		
Approximately 10 years & on		*Approximately school-age*
Continued learning		Continued learning

ever, they soon begin to show a subject–predicate construction, change of quantity and quality, and negation.

Some two-word sentences seem to consist of only open-class words, but careful examination reveals the child's beginning awareness of the deep structure and surface structure features of language. For example, the utterance, /Mommy bottle/, might mean: /Mommy has the bottle./ /Mommy, give me the bottle./ or /Mommy, that is the bottle./

Determining the underlying meaning of the statement occurs through the context of the situation. In the previous example, the specific interpretation can be inferred if, when the child is told /Yes, I have the bottle/, the child cries. Observations of young children indicate that at different times, the same statement /Mommy bottle/ will produce different responses by the child's mother and different later behaviors by the child. The child, though demonstrating at least some understanding of adult syntactic and semantic structures, may not yet possess the capacity to produce more than two-word sentences.

After the child has begun to use two-word, pivot–open-class sentences, a stage of hierarchical constructions begins. The child takes the basic pivot–open sentences and begins to expand them by adding other syntactic features. The construction /More cookie/ might be expanded to /Want more cookie/ and then to /Want more cookie now/. In each case of expansion, the child is not just stringing words together but is creating a hierarchical pattern according to the grammatical structure of the language.

The child then enters a period of regularization. This period is also marked by deviations from adult speech, and constructions are created that are not usually found in the adult speech the child hears. For example, /came/ becomes /comed/, and /feet/ becomes /foots/. Most often the high frequency irregular forms are learned correctly and are then overregularized as the child learns generalizations in the language. The child continuously attempts to create order out of the language he or she hears.

The final stage is using language transformations. This is a highly complex phase of language acquisition, and researchers are just starting to show how children create transformations or basic sentences. Two early transformations made by young children are questions and negatives. When a child begins to form questions, the tendency is to invoke the question marker rule but not the subject-verb reversal rule. For instance, a child who is asked to create a question about what Mommy has in her hand will ask /What Mommy have in hand?/. It seems that children in this stage have a limited performance capacity that blocks the application of both transformations together.

By the time children are four years old, they have mastered basic grammatical structures. During the fifth and sixth years, children begin to control the inconsistencies of language, and by the end of the seventh year—roughly corresponding to the end of first grade—children have developed a grammar almost equivalent to that of adults, although by age ten some children are still struggling with complex structures. Lacking are the extensive vocabulary and the ability to manipulate the many grammatical transformations of adult speech.

Semantics

Along with learning the rules of word order, children develop the ability to "mean." As explained previously, children learn the semantic features of language when they begin using their language for communication purposes. There are three phases of semantic development. The first occurs between the ages of 9 and 16 months. The child, in interactions with adults and older children, makes sounds, the beginnings of words (although not necessarily using the first phonemes of the words), full words, and groups of words. These efforts are related to the general language function of

regulating behavior	/Bring book/
obtaining objects	/Want cookie/
instructing others for activities	/Play game/
questioning or curiosity resolution	/Want this/
personal statements	/Sleepy/
imaginative statements	/Choo-choo/

These statements are presented one at a time and may not be understood by everyone. They develop from interactions between the child and others in family activities, games, and excursions into the world. These functions are not lost but are retained and expanded in later phases of semantic development.

The second phase occurs between the ages of 16 and 24 months. It is sometimes called the stage of grammar and dialogue. In it, the child can deal with two or more meanings simultaneously and uses ever-increasing forms of syntax through extended conversations with others. In addition to the functions acquired in the first phase, the child adds three more:

learning and exchanging information	/I saw Grandma/ /That man hit the boy/
fulfilling practical or personal needs	/I can't tie this/ /Lift me up/
extending imaginative function, including pretense	/I see the bus coming/ (when there is no bus)

In this second phase the child combines functions to produce more complex meanings and expands syntax to signify meanings that are now comprehensible to almost all hearers. The child now uses language to obtain actions from others and to receive direct verbal responses to his or her statements. The child is both observer and participant in the communication process, using language in specific contexts and with specific intentions.

The third phase begins at about 24 months and continues throughout life. The child begins to distinguish between old and new information. This includes learning to use language for additional learning and learning to use language to act. During this phase the child develops the various "scripts" for behaving and speaking appropriately in different situations. As noted, the schemata underlying these scripts and the scripts themselves are developed as part of the total communication process, through communication with others in cultural and social settings.

Nonverbal Features

Equally important to the development of verbal language is the development of language's paralinguistic features. Wood (1981) and Lindfors (1980) have done much research on these paralinguistic features, and their findings are summarized here.

Voice manipulation, intonational features, body use, and space use are all learned with spoken language. The development of voice manipulations (pitch, pauses, loudness, tempo, and juncture) begin with the earliest production of language. These manipulations have not been set down into precise phases of development, however, nor have the nonverbal features of body language; yet, it is known that children by the age of two have acquired the body moves of gender. Children learn early in life to communicate with their facial expressions. The use of space in the oral language system has been studied extensively, and children seem to understand and use spacing behavior in a zone fashion. They seem to understand personal space early and move from intimate and personal space to social space. By the time they enter elementary school, they have established patterns of sex and ethnic background.

The importance of the nonverbal communication systems lies in children's ability to support or contradict a spoken message if conflicting messages are transmitted through the two systems. Children usually get these nonverbal features with the verbal; the two develop simultaneously, not in isolation. So children usually develop appropriate nonverbal "support systems" as they develop verbal scripts for various language functions.

Competence

The idea of competence has both theoretical and practical implications. To Chomsky, competence is the human capability of generating language. However, to other psycholinguists, competence refers to more than an innate sense of language. To them, competence is knowing how to use language as a tool in everyday situations (Vygotsky, 1978; Wood, 1981). It is the internalization of learning and is revealed as the child's independence in performance. It includes an individual's ability and skill to know the social/communication rules and to be able to act appropriately. These abilities and skills include cognitive and performance processes which function interdependently (Wiemann & Backlund, 1980). Therefore, children can be considered competent users of language if their language seems appropriate to the goals of the message, the participants, and the situation. It is usually the gross deviations from the generally recognized developmental patterns that are labeled either "immature" or "grown up."

IMPLICATIONS FOR EDUCATION

A few important implications of the research on the thinking process and the development of language presented in this chapter are mentioned here, and others have been cited throughout the text.

One important conclusion of Piaget's and Vygotsky's theories is that development affects learning. The way children learn will change as they mature. Their work shows that children's thinking is different from that of adults. Children's world views are not "wrong," but they are different.

In addition, some things cannot be taught to children in the usual sense. They must experience objects and activities to develop new cognitive structures. Children are constantly learning regardless of their activity, albeit not always what adults wish them to learn. School-age children are involved with their world, and even apparent daydreaming contains some aspects of learning.

The conclusions of Piaget, Vygotsky, Guilford, and the cognitive psychologists studying the structure of human memory have many parallel features. They all conceive of thinking as a process in which the information an individual receives from the world is systematically organized. The manner in which the information is catalogued and the strategies of the process seem to depend on prior experiences and prior information. Piaget theorized that the growing child develops an internalized view of the world. This may be another way of suggesting that the child has developed a strategy for encoding information into long-term memory.

The results of research based on Piagetian theory have some relevance to the practices of beginning reading instruction. Children in the later stages of the preoperational period—corresponding to the kindergarten and first-grade years—may not have developed "conservation." Such children are characterized by their inability to undo a task they have performed. They cannot deal with a slightly changed situation without thinking that it is a new situation. This implies that the use of a code-emphasis, rule-oriented phonics program in the beginning stages of reading is not consistent with the abilities of "nonconserving" children. In addition, Piaget's work points out the importance of curricula in which activities, including reading, are "carried out in social situations where children are working together, sharing information, and learning to take into account another person's point of view" (Raven & Salzer, 1971, p. 636).

In addition, it seems that the structure of language is

> designed to complement the ability of the human to piece together the meaning of a communication from a few isolated fragments. . . . The redundancy of the language . . . allows us to attend selectively to bits and pieces of a communication, to anticipate what will come next, and to look selectively for the key words and phrases that convey the basic meaning of the message. (Lindsay & Norman, 1977, p. 277)

When something has been learned, whether it is a mathematical concept, a grammatical rule, or the names of various objects, that information has been committed to a child's long-term memory. That which is transferred into long-term memory is under the control of the child. The control is not actually conscious; it may be a predisposition to gain other information and to transfer information from the sensory register through the short-term memory into the long-term memory.

Memory develops as a problem-solving process in which information is routinely analyzed to determine its consistency with past experience. The way in which a problem is solved may result from an interaction among

> the kind of information being analyzed and the form it is in;
> the way and place in which the information is presented;
> the language and thinking maturity of the individual;
> the plans for solving problems devised by the individual; and
> the knowledge the individual has about how he or she solves problems.

All these are acquired as part of the acculturation process and are what society calls "learning" and "knowledge."

In the classroom, the predisposition for learning can be facilitated by developing appropriate cognitive readiness. One procedure is to use **advance organizers,** which are questions or directions focusing on features of the information that should be retained. This allows the student to focus on the particular information to be learned, or an aspect of it. Most important, the teacher should help the student develop general advance organizers so that self-learning strategies can be developed. It is also wise to promote the use of rehearsal or practice. More rehearsal is needed for new or different information; old or additional information added to an already learned body of information needs much less rehearsal. A final procedure is to guide students in developing information-processing strategies. Since information is stored in long-term memory in deep structure form, students need training in processing information according to the nature of the information.

Different strategies are needed depending on

- the difficulty level of the information,
- the importance of the information to the individual,
- the interest of the information to the individual,
- the amount of information to be acquired, and
- the organization of the material (Kumar, 1971).

Teachers must be committed to understanding students and the content of instruction. The teacher should devise instruction procedures that allow the two to transact. And, the teacher must remember Vygotsky's (1978) premise that learning occurs "only when the child is interacting with people in his environment and in cooperation with his peers" (p. 90).

TRANSACTIVE/INTERACTIVE MODELS OF THE READING PROCESS

Since it is difficult to find a model of the reading process that is based on only one psychological school, it has become popular to classify models as bottom-up, top-down, or transactive/interactive. **Bottom-up** means that the model maker views reading as starting with some graphic input (print). These models show that reading begins with the synthesis of letters into words, words into sentences, and so on until a large enough unit of language is perceived. Then, as bottom-up theorists conclude, the reader understands what the author has written.

Top-down models show that reading begins with the reader's cognitive structures. In this view, the reader can understand what is on the page only if the ideas are already present in the reader's mind. Reading, from a top-down view, begins with the reader's prior understanding and proceeds to the reconstruction of the author's message. Whole words and entire sentences are the input—not individual letters.

The **transactive/interactive** model shows that reading draws from the top and the bottom simultaneously. In general, the transactivists/interactivists and the top-down proponents have more in common with each other than with the bottom-up proponents. The ideas presented in this text are consonant with the transactive/interactive and top-down points of view.

The three models depicting the transactive/interactive nature of reading are the *Goodman Model of Reading*, the *Rumelhart Interactive Model of Reading*, and the *Kintsch Model of Text Comprehension*. The Goodman model, presented first, has existed the longest and has generated much research to support it theoretically and to demonstrate its practicality in classroom applications. To some, the model is a top-down explanation. Here, however, it is presented as a transactive/interactive model because of its feedback, or recursive, aspects. Any model that shows reading is not a direct, linear application of skills is interactive. The Goodman model and the research supporting it have strongly influenced the ideas in this text about the teaching and assessment of reading.

The Rumelhart model is presented because of its growing impact on reading researchers and practitioners. It was developed from Rumelhart's investigations into the nature of schemata and memory.

The Kintsch model, also based on schema theory, explains the reading process through an analysis of how written discourse is constructed. The Rumelhart and Kintsch models underlie this text's ideas about the nature of comprehension.

Each model attempts to demonstrate what occurs for a proficient reader during silent reading. (Less-proficient readers are identified not so much by the quantitative count of errors but by the qualitative assessment of where the breakdown occurs in the reading process.) The models are multidimensional in that reading is not considered a single, linear application of skills. Taken together, these models provide a comprehensive view of the reading process.

The Goodman Model of the Reading Process

Goodman (1968; 1984) defines reading as a transaction between a published text and a reader. The transaction begins with the selection of graphic cues that signal meaning, much as listening is a process of selecting auditory cues for meaning. He proposes that the experienced reader can derive meaning directly from graphic cues without translating them into phonemic cues (see Figure 13–7).

A proficient reader does not use all the signals built into the writing system, just as a proficient listener does not use every facet of spoken language. The reader anticipates meaning and has it reconfirmed. The less often the reader's thoughts about the message have to change during reading and the fewer cues from the page he or she needs for arriving at the author's meaning, the more proficient the reader is in that reading situation (Goodman, 1967, 1968, 1969a, 1984; Ryan & Semmel, 1969).

Goodman distinguishes among the aspects of **decoding** (deriving meaning), **recoding** (translating letter patterns into sound), and **encoding** (oral reading). Decoding occurs only when the writer's meaning is analyzed and understood; in other words, decoding is when the reader knows the deep structure of the message as generated by the writer. Encoding can take place only when decoding has preceded it. Recoding is a procedure whereby only the surface structure of the message is perceived and changed into a different form. (In most other sources about the teaching of reading, the term *decoding* refers to the process of translating the printed symbol into sound, that is, word-attack procedures. Goodman prefers to use the term *decoding* in referring to the meaningful unlocking of a message.)

According to Goodman, the process of reading can be compared to information processing. Long-term memory holds learned responses that have become automatic or habitual. Medium memory holds learning and responses based on the particular reading act.[2] They are the "guesses" (predictions) and confirmations made during reading. Short-term memory holds immediate images and signals needed during reading.

Prior to an act of reading, the reader has three sets of information stored in long-term memory: (1) regulating procedures for the physical control of reading; (2) a language repertoire of spoken and written rules and cues; (3) acquired meanings and concepts.

At the onset of a reading act (the optical cycle), the regulating programs direct the reader's eyes to move and focus on the material. The reader selects printed language cues in and around the word, makes guesses, and stores them in short-term memory. Prior predictions from medium-term memory aid in the reader's selection of cues only after the initial instance of reading.

The reader uses the selected cues to form perceptual images (the perceptual cycle) and stores them in short-term memory. The perceptual cues formed

---

2. In the Goodman model, short-term and medium-term memory refer to the sensory register and short-term memory that were discussed in Chapter 3.

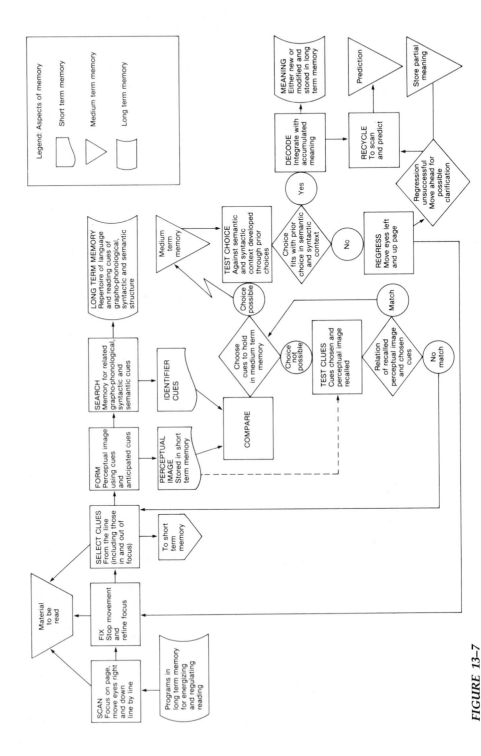

FIGURE 13-7
A Flow Chart of Goodman's Model of Reading

may be anticipatory rather than actual. The proficient reader does not use every cue available because then the act of reading would be slow and laborious. Some images formed, therefore, may be anticipations of actual cues that will be substantiated at a later time. The reader searches the language repertoire (the syntactic and semantic cycles) for known cues (grapheme–phoneme relationships, sentence structures, and meaning structures) that might be related to the present situation. When these cues are identified, they too are stored in the short-term memory.

The perceptual images and the identified language cues are then compared. The reader decides to hold these cues in medium-term memory by testing them to see if they fit with prior information (confirmed predictions and stored partial meanings). If they do fit, the message has been decoded. At this point the reader integrates meaning (deep structure) with other meanings, confirms predictions, and recycles the process.

There are two places in the process where a reader may decide the perceived cues do not fit and the message cannot be decoded. The first occurs after the perceptual image and the identified related language cues are compared. The reader recalls the perceptual image and the selected cues. If there is a match now, then the reader holds the cues in short-term memory and makes a second test.

The second decision is made when the cues are tested against the semantic and syntactic context developed through prior choices. If there still is no fit, the decision is made to regress and to seek the point of inconsistency. If the regression does not produce decoding, the partial meaning, if any, is stored in the medium-term memory. The reader moves on with the possibility that additional cues will lead to complete decoding of the message.

Goodman analyzed the responses of pupils reading orally and hypothesized the reasons for readers' deviations from the printed page. He does not call these deviations "errors" because the term implies something intrinsically bad or avoidable. He prefers to call them *miscues* because an analysis of them reveals the reader's use and misuse of available language cues. In addition, the miscue analysis reveals the process by which the reader utilizes the available cues to reconstruct the author's message. Chapter 10 contained a discussion of how an analysis of a reader's miscues is made and can be used in formulating an instructional program.

The Rumelhart Model of Reading

Rumelhart (1976) proposes an interactive model of reading to explain how a mature reader interacts with print. The model attempts to explain and illustrate the interactive aspects of the reading process more fully than other models do. The model is created on the plan of "parallel processing" in computer science. In parallel processing, more than one level of information can be acted on at any one time. That is, the information flow is not direct and linear; the information can be acted on by two or more types of processing, and the different

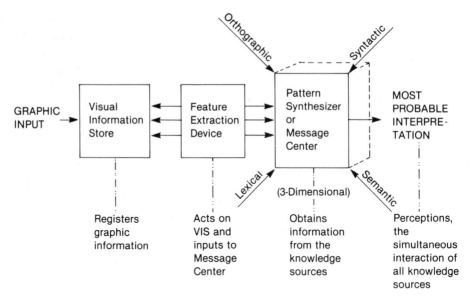

FIGURE 13–8
The Rumelhart Interactive Model of Reading

types of processing can interact with one another. Rumelhart was not the first to explain reading as an interactive process, but he was the first to introduce the idea of parallel processing to reading models.

According to Rumelhart, reading involves perceptual and cognitive processes in obtaining meaning from print. The purpose of reading is to produce meaning, and the meaning produced depends in part on the meanings already stored in the reader's schemata. Information is taken in from various sources, and these sources act together to produce meaning. Any one source can be primary at any one time, but utilizing information from one source often depends on utilizing information from the others (see Figure 13–8).

The model has six sources of information input. Each contains specialized knowledge about some aspect of the reading process. These sources of knowledge, stored as schemata, are (1) the semantic, (2) the syntactic, (3) the lexical, (4) the letter cluster, (5) the letter, and (6) the letter features. These are hierarchically arranged with the semantic level being the highest.

A reader can process information from a page by features of the individual letters (a bottom-up processing task) or by information from the semantic source about some general meaning category of the word(s) (a top-down processing task). For example, on seeing the words *the green house*, the reader might input this information by examining and analyzing

the individual letter features—the lines and curves that make up individual letter features such as in *h* and *o;*

clusters of those letters—*gr*, *ee*, or *ouse;*

the syntactic relationships—"noun phrase in the object position of a sentence";

the semantic relationships—"colored domicile" or "a place where someone lives".

A second important part of the model is the *message center* or *pattern synthesizer*. This center is a highly structured, global storage unit that examines, interrelates, and interprets the information received from any and all of the knowledge sources. Each source generates one or more hypotheses about the incoming information. The message center keeps track of all the hypotheses as well as their origins. With these the reader formulates the most probable interpretation of what is being read. The knowledge sources are used, in turn, to scan the message center for a hypothesis relevant to its sphere of knowledge. The reader evaluates this hypothesis in light of the information in the specialized domain.

During reading, the reader, using the knowledge source, confirms or disproves hypotheses; if disproved, they may be removed from the message center, or the reader's knowledge source may create a new hypothesis to alter or replace the old one. This process continues until a decision is made about the meaning of the information from the page. At the end of the process, the most probable hypothesis is considered to be the correct one.

The Rumelhart model is consistent with the information presented about the nature of language and the development of thinking. It demonstrates the importance of schemata in the reading process and the simultaneous interacting of information from both internal and external sources. Most important, it confirms what Goodman argued—that reading is not a precise, accuracy-driven activity or process. Rumelhart, however, seems to have presented his model as a compromise between pure bottom-up and top-down models, assuming that "pure" models truly exist. Although the model is still incomplete, it shows the need for an explanation of how semantic and syntactic information interact with graphophonemic information.

The weaknesses and limitations of the model can be traced in part from the direct link of Rumelhart's research to simulating the reading process through computer programming. He seems locked into hypothesizing about only that part of the reading process that can be programmed into a computer. In the computer technology field, parallel processing computers are not operational except for some use in game playing (for example, chess). The concept, then, is still theoretical. Rumelhart stresses information processing from two extremes—the top and the bottom. His model shows how semantic information (schemata) and letter information (features and clusters) are utilized. But it does not fully demonstrate how syntactic information is used (Diehl, 1978; Harste, 1978). These weaknesses can be attributed to Rumelhart's research being mostly in the areas of letter feature recognition and the development of schemata.

A Model of Text Comprehension

Kintsch (1979, 1980; Kintsch & van Dijk, 1978) explains the mental operations that occur during the reader's comprehension of a text and in the recall of information from that text. (Text is any written message and may be a passage in a fictional narrative or an expository, informational passage.) The model focuses on the inferences a reader makes in comprehending the text, and Kintsch assumes that the more inferences a text requires a reader to make, the harder it is to read. The purposes of the model are (1) to explain how a text is understood, and (2) to make predictions about the possible readability of a text by examining the number of "interactions" a reader might have with the text. These interactions are the inferences that require a search of the reader's schemata. The more searches required of the reader, the harder the text is to read (see Figure 13–9).

Kintsch's model grew from his analysis of printed texts. Understanding Kintsch's theory of the nature and structure of written messages, then, is the first step in understanding his model. According to Kintsch, a text's surface structure is interpreted as a group of statements or propositions. Propositions have several aspects: they (1) contain one or more arguments, (2) indicate a statement or event, (3) provide facts in relation to other propositions, and (4)

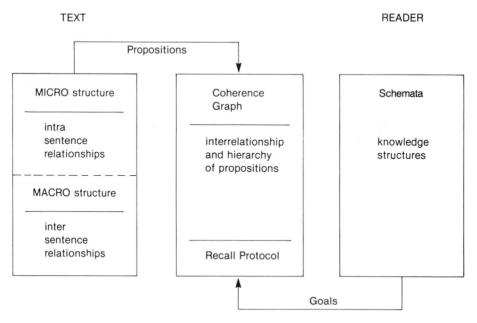

FIGURE 13–9
The Kintsch Model of Text Comprehension*

*A coherence graph, constructed for a text to show the structure and interrelationships of its features, is used to analyze the information comprehended by a reader.

qualify other propositions. The propositions, in turn, are organized according to different semantic relationships, some of which are explicit, others implicit.

The semantic structure of the text has two levels. One, the **microstructure,** represents the individual sentences and their intrasentence relationships—letters, syllables, words, and word order. The **macrostructure** of the text is more global in nature and represents intersentence information—the gist or main idea of the text, the familiarity of the text style and genre to the reader, the presentation of arguments or ideas new to the reader, and the text's placement on a narrative–expository scale. The ways in which a text is structured according to its macrorules are relative to the topic or theme of the text. These rules determine how the propositions are systematically arranged. In this model, information can be presented on more than one macrolevel and may be presented on several levels simultaneously. The microstructures—letters, words, sentences—are linked to form a coherent (connected and related) text. By processing these links, the reader can infer the macrostructure(s).

All texts are constructed to conform to certain schematic structures. These are typical ways in which an author develops a text, or are the rules governing the characteristics and conventions of writing. For example, a story conforms to certain rules depending on whether it is an adventure story, a mystery, or a comedy. The schematic structure is the logic in which propositions are placed. The macrostructure is the broader issue to which the text is addressed—love, triumph of humans over nature, retribution.

The second major aspect of the Kintsch model is the process of reading. Through a recall procedure, a reader's information processing is examined. This examination reveals the types of information understood in relation to the microstructures and macrostructures. To Kintsch, comprehension is a search of the reader's schemata—cognitive, informational, linguistic—in order to find a match with the proposition in the text. If there is a match, that is, if the text proposition is accepted, the process continues. If there is no match, the reader initiates a process of inferring. These inferences, which are searches of long-term memories, are time-consuming. The longer the search takes, the more difficult the reading task (or process) is, a situation more commonly referred to as "difficulty with comprehension."

The extensive time needed for the search can result from factors in the text or in the reader. For example, the microstructure can be so complex the reader cannot make a match. In this case, the reader has the schema for the information in some form other than that presented by the author: the text is written in a style and maturity of thought inappropriate for the reader, or the text may not be comprehended because the reader has no, or a partial or incorrect, schema for the information. In this case, the reader is not ready to read the material.

Through the construction of what Kintsch calls a *coherence graph*, the reader's recall of information is matched with how the information is structured in the text. The coherence graph shows the hierarchy of the interrelationships between the propositions (information) in the text and their pattern of interconnections; each text produces a unique graph structure.

The coherence graph illustrates the reader's schemata. By the type of information recalled, Kintsch examines what connections the reader makes and thereby gains a picture of the reader's comprehension strategies. When used in this way, the coherence graphs are known as **recall or summarization protocols.** They include the reader's direct remembrances and those reconstructed through inferring.

Kintsch assumes that text comprehension is always controlled by specific schemata, singly or in combination. They set the reader's goal(s) or purpose(s) for reading. There are different control schemata for different levels (specific or general) of comprehension. According to Kintsch's definition of reading, it is impossible to read for absolutely no purpose at all. The schema, which may be complete and detailed or incomplete and unpredictable, controls what features of the microstructures and macrostructures the reader attends to.

An example of a highly predictable text structure is a fairy tale; the actual story may be new, but the reader possesses a complete schema for fairy tales. The reading is easy because the story is predictable. But the reader may be forced into conflicting purposes when a controlling schema is imposed on him or her by a teacher or a situationally specific task. In this case, a reader may start to read a passage for pleasure only to encounter a detailed test after completing it. Or the reader may choose to read a text for purposes very different from those intended by the author. One well-known psychologist interprets fairy tales not for their plot, sequence of events, and unique language, but for their possible implications for ·interpreting children's behavior according to Freudian psychoanalytic principles. At other times, people may read highly structured texts without clear purposes or loosely structured texts with definite purposes.

Kintsch (1980) defines comprehension as learning, stating that comprehension is the "assimilation of a text into a particular knowledge structure, which through this process itself undergoes change. It is this change that is the learning" (p. 88). Important throughout his theory is the function of the reader's goals as set by the controlling schemata. Although Kintsch recognizes the importance of emotional interest during the reading of a text, his model focuses on what he calls its "cognitive interest." A text has cognitive interest because a unique pattern and structure of ideas and events exist. This interest is determined by an interaction of (1) how much the reader knows about the topic, (2) how uncertain the reader is about the text, and (3) how much sense the reader makes of the text. The last factor, a text's "postdictability," is the reader's attempts to explain how and why all the parts of the text (microstructures and macrostructures) fit together.

The three factors are another way of indicating that a reader must possess readiness for what is going to be or is being read. Without knowing the appropriate knowledge structures, a reader cannot think and learn. When the incoming information does not fit the existing expectations, the reader undergoes change. This change is learning, which occurs as information is added to and/or deleted from existing knowledge structures, both the permanent ones and those in working memory.

DISCUSSION QUESTIONS AND ACTIVITIES

1. What does the following statement by Miller (1973) mean to you?

   Not all physical features of speech are significant for vocal communication, and not all significant features of speech have a physical representation. (p. 10)

2. Observe a group of people in different situations—waiting in a line, eating in a restaurant, and so forth. What do you think are their attitudes and feelings? What gives you these impressions?

3. Collect a series of advertisements for some product. For example, collect ads for a particular car or television set. What message is directly stated in the written copy of the ads? What messages are implied in both the physical appearance of the ad and in the copy?

4. Examine a series of elementary or middle-school reading and language arts texts. What information does the series contain about the history and structure of the English language? How is it presented and what should the student do with the information?

5. A parent comes to you and says she has heard about the "linguistic" method of teaching reading. From the discussion, you realize she means a program that emphasizes the one-to-one correspondence between letters and sounds. She wants her child taught by this method. How will you answer her?

6. The following statement was made by Andreas Feininger (1966), a well-known and highly successful color photographer and author. In what way is his following statement substantiated by current research on the thinking process? In what way does his statement help to explain the reading and writing processes?

   [The phenomenon of color memory] of the eye–brain combine causes us to see color as we think it should look, not as it actually is.

7. Observe individual and small groups of children of different ages at play. For example, observe children of ages two, five, and eight. Note the language they use when playing alone or with other children. (If possible, tape record about five minutes of their playtime conversations.) How do the children use language in relating to their play objects? How do the children use language in relating to themselves or to other children?

FURTHER READING

Three journal articles that explain Piagetian principles and their application to reading instruction are

Cleland, C. J. (1980, October). Piagetian implications for reading models. *Reading World*, 20(1), 10–15.

Cleland, C. J. (1981, March). Learning to read: Piagetian perspectives for instruction. *Reading World*, 20(3), 223–224

Cleland, C. J. (1981, May). Piaget's legacy to reading. *Reading World, 20*(4), 287–288.

Those who wish to learn more about the history of the English language to understand current trends will find the following useful.

Meyers, L. M., & Hoffman, R. L. (1979). *Roots of modern English* (2nd ed.). Boston: Little, Brown.

Much that is now being written about nonverbal communication the teacher may already know intuitively. The following is a popular treatment of nonverbal communication and, unlike many other books on the subject, is not intended to be a "code" to use for interpreting someone's intentions through nonverbal behavior.

Davis, F. (1973). *Inside intuition: What we know about nonverbal communication.* New York: McGraw-Hill.

The following two books, although slightly more scholarly, are popular presentations of nonverbal communication. Their subjects are the unstated aspects of language.

Hall, E. T. (1959). *The silent language.* New York: Doubleday.
Hall, E. T. (1966). *The hidden dimension.* New York: Doubleday.

In the following popular book on the nature of language and communication, the author answers basic questions about what happens when people talk.

Farb, P. (1974). *Word play.* New York: Knopf.

Piaget's books are sometimes difficult for the neophyte to read. Nonetheless, every teacher should know his ideas. The following clearly delineate Piaget's theory and positions on education.

Elkind, D. (1975). *A sympathetic understanding of the child: Birth to sixteen.* Boston: Allyn & Bacon.
Elkind, D. (1976). *Child development and education: A Piagetian perspective.* New York: Oxford University Press.
Furth, H. G. (1970). *Piaget for teachers.* Englewood Cliffs, NJ: Prentice-Hall.

The following highly readable book on thinking explains the mental process that children undergo during learning.

Smith, F. (1975). *Comprehension and learning: A conceptual framework for teachers.* New York: Holt, Rinehart & Winston.

The following book contains explanations of different theoretical models of the reading process. Although highly technical, the book is an excellent reference.

Singer, H., & Ruddell, R. B. (Eds.). (1985). *Theoretical models and processes of reading* (3rd ed.). Newark, DE: International Reading Association.

References

Aiken, L. R., Jr. (1972). Language factors in learning mathematics. *Review of Educational Research, 42,* 359–385.

Albert, B., Jr. (1971). Purple marbles and little red hula hoops. *The Reading Teacher, 24,* 647–651.

Alexander, A. (1960). *Noise in the night.* Chicago: Rand McNally.

Alexander, C. F. (1980, February). Black English dialect and the classroom teacher. *The Reading Teacher, 33,* 571–577.

Allen, R. V. (1976). *Language experiences in communication.* Boston: Houghton Mifflin.

Allington, R., Stretzel, H., Shake, M., & Lamarche, S. (1986). What is remedial reading? A descriptive study. *Reading Research and Instruction, 26,* (1), 15–30.

Alvermann, D. E., Dillon, D. R., O'Brien, D. G., & Smith, L. C. (1985, October). The role of the textbook in discussion. *Journal of Reading, 29,* 50–57.

Ames, L. B. (1983). Learning disability: Truth or trap? *Annual Review of Learning Disabilities, 1,* 16–17.

Ames, L. B. (1968). Learning disability: The developmental point of view. In H. R. Myklebust (Ed.), *Progress in learning disabilities.* New York: Grune & Statton.

Amoriggi, H. D., & Gefteas, D. J. (1981). *Affective considerations in bilingual education: Problems and solutions.* Rosslyn, VA: National Clearinghouse for Bilingual Education. (ERIC Document Reproduction Services No. 261 535)

Anastasiow, N. (1979). *Oral language: Expression of thought.* Newark, DE: International Reading Association and ERIC Clearinghouse on Reading and Communication Skills.

Anders, P. L., & Bos, C. S. (1986). Semantic feature analysis: An interactive strategy for vocabulary development and text comprehension. *Journal of Reading, 29*(7), 610–616.

Anderson, B. V., & Barnitz, J. G. (1984, November). Cross-cultural schemata and reading comprehension instruction. *Journal of Reading, 28*(2), 102–108.

Anderson, K. F. (1985). The development of spelling ability and linguistic strategies. *The Reading Teacher, 39*(2), 140–147.

Anderson, R., Hiebert, E. H., Scott, J. A., & Wilkinson, I. A. G. (1985). *Becoming a nation of readers: The report of the Commission on Reading.* Newark, DE: International Reading Association.

Anderson, R. C., & Pearson, P. D. (1984). A schema-theoretic view of basic processes in reading comprehension. In P. D. Pearson (Ed.), *Handbook of reading research* (pp. 255–291). New York: Longman.

Andre, T. (1979). Does answering higher-level questions while reading facilitate productive learning? *Review of Educational Research, 49,* 280–318.

Applebee, A. N. (1984). Writing and reasoning. *Review of Educational Research, 54*(4), 577–596.

Armbruster, B. B. (1984). The problem of inconsiderate text. In G. G. Duffy, L. R. Roehler, & J. Mason (Eds.), *Comprehension instruction: Perspectives and suggestions* (pp. 202–217). New York: Longman.

Armbruster, B. B. (1985). *Characteristics of a considerate textbook.* Paper presented at the

Sixth Annual Conference on Reading Research conducted by the Center for the Study of Reading, University of Illinois, New Orleans.

Armentrout, W. A. (Ed.). (1970). *What should the purpose(s) of American education be? A collection of notable responses on the subject.* Dubuque, IA: Kendall/Hunt.

Au, K. H., & Mason, J. M. (1981). Social organizational factors in learning to read: The balance of rights hypothesis. *Reading Research Quarterly, 17,* 115–152.

Aulls, M. W. (1970). Context in reading: How it may be depicted. *Journal of Reading Behavior, 3,* 61–73.

Baker, L., & Brown, A. L. (1984). Metacognitive skills and reading. In P. D. Pearson (Ed.), *Handbook of reading research* (pp. 353–394). New York: Longman.

Balow, I. H., Farr, R., Hogan, T., & Prescot, G. (1979). *Manual for administering and interpreting the Metropolitan Achievement Test: Reading, intermediate level.* New York: Psychological Corporation.

Baratz, J. C. (1968). Linguistic and cultural factors in teaching reading to ghetto children. *Elementary English, 45,* 199–203.

Barnitz, J. G. (1980). Black English and other dialects: sociolinguistic implications. *The Reading Teacher, 33,* 770–786.

Barret, J. (1968). Relevancy of content to today's students. In H. Huus (Ed.), *Evaluating books for children and young people* (pp. 99–109). Newark, DE: International Reading Association.

Beattie, S. S., & Greco, D. (1980). *Ourselves and others, windows on our world.* Houghton Mifflin Social Studies. Boston: Houghton Mifflin.

Beck, I. L., & McKeown, M. G. (1981). Developing questions that promote comprehension: The story map. *Language Arts, 58,* 913–918.

Bell, W. (1974). Social science: The future as a missing variable. In A. Toffler (Ed.), *Learning for tomorrow: The role of future in education* (pp. 75–102). New York: Random House.

Bercari, J. (1975). Unpublished manuscript, Queens College, City University of New York, New York.

Berger, C. F., et al. (1979). *Houghton Mifflin science, level 6.* Boston: Houghton Mifflin.

Berry, M. F. (1980). *Teaching linguistically handicapped.* Englewood Cliffs, NJ: Prentice-Hall.

Black, J. K. (1980). Those "mistakes" tell us a lot. *Language Arts, 57,* 508–513.

Blanton, W. E. (1972). *Preschool reading instruction: A literature search, evaluation and interpretation.* Final Report. Washington, DC: National Center for Educational Communication/DHEW.

Blanton, W. E., Moorman, G. B., & Wood, K. D. (1986). A model of direct instruction applied to the basal skills lesson. *The Reading Teacher, 40*(3), 299–304.

Blitz, B. (1973). *The open classroom: Making it work.* Boston: Allyn & Bacon.

Bloom, B. S. (1969). Some theoretical issues relating to educational evaluation. In R. W. Tyler (Ed.), *Educational evaluation: New roles, new means.* Chicago: University of Chicago Press.

Bloome, D. (1983). Classroom reading instruction: A socio-communicative analysis of time on task. In J. A. Niles & L. A. Harris (Eds.), *Searches for meaning in reading/language processing and instruction* (pp. 275–281). Rochester, NY: Thirty-second Yearbook of the National Reading Conference.

Bloome, D. (1985). Reading as a social process. *Language Arts, 62,* 134–142.

Bloome, D., & Green, J. (1984). Directions in the sociolinguistic study of reading. In P. D. Pearson (Ed.), *Handbook on reading research* (pp. 395–421). New York: Longman.

Bormuth, J. R. (1968). The cloze readability procedure. In J. R. Bormuth (Ed.), *Readability in 1968* (pp. 40–47). Urbana, IL: National Conference on Research in English.

Bormuth, J. R. (1969a). An operational definition of comprehension instruction. In K. S. Goodman & J. T. Fleming (Eds.), *Psycholinguistics and the teaching of reading* (pp. 48–60). Newark, DE: International Reading Association.

Bormuth, J. R. (1969b). *Research on literal comprehension.* Paper presented at the Symposium on Application of Psycholinguistics to Key Problems in Reading, International Reading Association, Kansas City.

Bormuth, J. R. (1975). The cloze procedure. In W. D. Page (Ed.), *Help for the reading teacher: New directions in research* (pp. 60–90). Urbana, IL: National Conference on Research in English and ERIC Clearinghouse on Reading and Communication Skills.

Botel, M. (1985). Becoming a nation of readers: A review. *The Reading Teacher, 39,* 260–262.

Branson, M. S. (1980). *Around our world, windows on our world.* Houghton Mifflin Social Studies. Boston: Houghton Mifflin.

Brewer, A. C., Garland, N., & Notkin, J. J. (1972). *Elementary science: Learning by investigating.* Chicago: Rand McNally.

Britton, J., Burgess, T., Martin, N., McLeod, A., & Rosen, H. (1975). *The development of writing abilities.* Urbana, IL: National Council of Teachers of English.

Brown, A. L. (1981). Learning to learn: On training students to learn from texts. *Educational Researcher, 10,* 14–21.

Brown, R., & Bellugi, U. (1966). Three processes in the child's acquisition of syntax. In J. A. Emig, J. T. Gleming, & H. M. Popp (Eds.), *Language and learning* (pp. 3–23). New York: Harcourt Brace Jovanovich.

Brown, V., & Botel, M. (1972). *Dyslexia: Definition or treatment?* ERIC/CRIER Reading Review Series.

Bruland, R. A. (1974). Learnin' words: Evaluating vocabulary development efforts. *Journal of Reading, 18,* 212–214.

Bruner, J. S. (1966). *Toward a theory of instruction.* New York: Norton.

Bruner, J. S., Goodnow, J. J., & Austin, G. A. (1956). *A study of thinking.* New York: Wiley.

Bullock, Sir A. (1975). *A language for life.* A report of the Committee of Inquiry. London: Her Majesty's Stationery Office.

Burke, C. L. (1973). Preparing elementary teachers to teach reading. In K. S. Goodman (Ed.), *Miscue analysis: Applications to reading instruction* (pp. 15–29). Urbana, IL: National Council of Teachers of English and ERIC Clearinghouse on Reading and Communication Skills.

Burke, C. L. (1975). Oral reading analysis: A view of the reading process. In W. D. Page (Ed.), *Help for the reading teacher: New directions in research* (pp. 23–33). Urbana, IL: National Conference on Research in English and ERIC Clearinghouse on Reading and Communication Skills.

Burke, C. (1985). Parenting, teaching, and learning as a collaborative venture. *Language Arts, 62*(8), 836–843.

Burns, P. C., & Broman, B. L. (1983). *The language arts in childhood education* (5th ed.). Boston: Houghton Mifflin.

Burns, P. C., & Schell, L. M. (1975). Instructional strategies for teaching usage of context clues. *Reading World, 15,* 89–96.

Burrows, A. T., Monson, D. L., & Stauffer, R. G. (1972). *New horizons in the language arts.* New York: Harper & Row.

Byers, P., & Byers, H. (1972). Nonverbal communication and the education of children. In C. B. Cazden, V. P. John, & D. Hymes (Eds.), *Functions of language in the classroom* (pp. 3–31). New York: Teachers College Press, Columbia University.

Cambourne, B. (1981). Oral and written relationships: A reading perspective. In B. M. Kroll & R. J. Vann (Eds.), *Exploring speaking-writing relationships: Connections and contrasts* (pp. 82–98). Urbana, IL: National Council of Teachers of English.

Cannella, G. S. (1985). Providing exploration activities in beginning reading instruction. *The Reading Teacher, 39*(3), 284–289.

Carroll, J. B. (1966). Words, meanings, and concepts. In J. A. Emig, J. T. Fleming, & H. M. Popp, (Eds.), *Language and learning* (pp. 73–101). New York: Harcourt Brace Jovanovich.

Cassidy, J., & Vukelich, C. (1980). Do the gifted read early? *The Reading Teacher, 33,* 578–581.

Chambers, M. (1986, December 9). Ending bilingual schooling. *New York Times,* p. C1.

Chamot, A. U., & McKeon, D. (1984). ESL teaching methodologies. In *Educating the minority student: Classroom and administrative issues* (pp. 1–5). Rosslyn, VA: National Clearinghouse for Bilingual Education. (ERIC Document Reproduction No. ED 260 600)

Chamot, A. U., & Stewner-Manzanares, G. (1985a). *A summary of current literature on English as a second language,* Part C Research Agenda. Rosslyn, VA: National Clearinghouse for Bilingual Education. (ERIC Document Reproduction Services No. ED 261 539)

Chamot, A. U., & Stewner-Manzanares, G. (1985b). *A synthesis of current literature on English as a second language: Issues for educational policy,* Part C Research Agenda. Rosslyn, VA: National Clearinghouse for Bilingual Education. (ERIC Document Reproduction Services No. ED 261 537)

Chapman, L. J. (1983). *Reading development and cohesion.* London & Exeter, NH: Heinemann.

Chavez, L. (1987, January 29). Struggling to keep Spanish pure. *New York Times,* p. B1.

Ching, D. C. (1976). *Reading and the bilingual child.* Newark, DE: International Reading Association.

Chomsky, C. (1971). Write first, read later. *Childhood Education, 47,* 296–299.

Chomsky, C. (1973). Reading, writing, and phonology. In F. Smith (Ed.), *Psycholinguistics and reading.* New York: Holt, Rinehart & Winston.

Chomsky, C. (1979). Language and reading. In R. E. Shafer (Ed.), *Applied linguistics and reading.* Newark, DE: International Reading Association.

Chomsky, N. P. (1965). *Aspects of the theory of syntax.* Cambridge, MA: MIT.

Christapherson, S. L. (1974). *The effect of knowledge of discourse structures on reading recall.* Paper presented at the Annual Meeting of the American Educational Research Association, Chicago. (ERIC No. ED 090 531)

Church, M. (1974). Does visual perception training help beginning readers? *The Reading Teacher, 27,* 371–374.

Ciardi, J. (1959). *How does a poem mean?* Part Three of *An introduction to literature.* Boston: Houghton Mifflin.

Clay, M. M. (1975). *What dis I write?* Exeter, NH: Heinemann.

Clay, M. M. (1982). Learning and teaching writing: A development perspective. *Language Arts, 59,* 65–70.

Clay, M. M. (1986). Constructive processes: Talking, reading, writing, art, and craft. *The Reading Teacher, 39*(8), 764–770.

Cleland, C. J. (1981). Highlighting issues in children's literature through semantic webbing. *The Reading Teacher, 34,* 642–646.

Clifford, G. J. (1984). Buch and lesen: Historical perspectives on literacy and schooling. *Review of Educational Research, 54,* 472–500.

Cohen, E. G. (1972). Sociology and the classroom: Setting the conditions for teacher-student interaction. *Review of Educational Research, 42,* 441–452.

Cohn, M. (1981). Observations of learning to read and write naturally. *Language Arts, 58,* 549–555.

Collins, C. (1985). The power of expressive writing in reading comprehension. *Language Arts, 62,* 48–54.

Combs, A. W. (1958). Seeing is behaving. *Educational Leadership, 16,* 21–26.

Combs, A. W., & Snygg, D. (1959). *Individual behavior: A perceptual approach to behavior.* New York: Harper & Row.

Congreve, W. J., & Rinehart, G. J. (Eds.). (1972). *Flexibility in school programs.* Worthington, OH: Charles A. Jones.

Corman, C. (1975). Bibliotherapy—insight for the learning handicapped. *Language Arts, 52,* 935–937.

Cramer, R. L. (1970). Setting purposes and making predictions: Essential to critical reading. *Journal of Reading, 13,* 259–262, 300.

Cramer, R. L. (1971). Dialectology—a case for language experience. *The Reading Teacher, 25,* 33–39.

Crist, B. I. (1975). One capsule a week—a painless remedy for vocabulary ills. *Journal of Reading, 19,* 147–149.

Cullinan, B. E. (1971). *Literature for children: Its discipline and content.* Dubuque, IA: William C. Brown.

Cullinan, B. E. (1974). Teaching literature to children, 1966–1972. In H. A. Robinson & A. T. Burrows (Eds.), *Teacher effectiveness in elementary language arts: A progress report.* Urbana, IL: National Council on Research in English/ERIC–RCS.

Cummins, J. (1986). Bilingual education and anti-racist education. *Interracial Books for Children Bulletin, 17*(3–4), 9–12.

Darkatsh, M. (1974). Who should decide on a book's merit? *Elementary English, 51,* 352–354.

Davey, B. (1986). Using textbook activity guides to help students learn from textbooks. *Journal of Reading, 29*(6), 489–494.

Davis, O. L., et al. (1971). *Exploring the social sciences: Asking about the U.S.A. and its neighbors.* New York: American Book.

Deighton, L. C. (1959). *Vocabulary development in the classroom.* New York: Bureau of Publications, Teachers College, Columbia University.

Diehl, W. (1978). A critical summary of Rumelhart's interactive model of reading. In E. W. Diehl (Ed.), *Secondary reading: Theory and application* of the *Language and reading studies* series. Monographs of the 1978 Lily Conference on Secondary Reading, 1.

Dillingofski, M. S. (1979). Sociolinguistics and reading: A review of the literature. *The Reading Teacher, 33,* 307–312.

Donlan, D. (1975). What is decoding? *The Reading Teacher, 29,* 142–144.

Downing, J. (1975). What is decoding? *The Reading Teacher, 29,* 142–144.

Downing, J., & Oliver, P. (1973). The child's conception of a word. *Reading Research Quarterly, 9,* 568–582.

Downing, J., & Sceats, J. (1974). Should school dictionaries be banned? *Elementary English, 51,* 601–603.

Dryer, L. G., Futtersak, K. R., & Boehm, A. E. (1985). Sight words for the computer age: An essential word list. *The Reading Teacher, 39*(1), 12–15.

Duchastel, P. C., & Merrill, P. F. (1973). The effects of behavioral objectives on learning: A review of empirical studies. *Review of Educational Research, 43,* 53–69.

Duffy, G. G. (1983). Context variables in reading teacher effectiveness. In J. A. Niles & L. A. Harris (Eds.), *Searches for meaning in reading/language processing and instruction* (pp. 9–294). Rochester, NY: Thirty-second Yearbook of the National Reading Conference.

Duffy, G. G., & Roehler, L. R. (1987). Teaching reading skills as strategies. *The Reading Teacher, 40*(4), 414–418.

Duffy, G. G., Roehler, L. R., & Mason, J. (Eds.). (1984). *Comprehension instruction: Perspectives and suggestions.* New York: Longman.

Durkin, D. (1968). When should children begin to read? In H. M. Robinson (Ed.), *Innovation and change in reading instruction.* Chicago: University of Chicago Press.

Durkin, D. (1974). Phonics: Instruction that needs to be improved. *The Reading Teacher, 28,* 152–156.

Durkin, D. (1981). Reading comprehension instruction in five basal reader series. *Reading Research Quarterly, 14,* 515–544.

Durr, W. K., LePere, J. M., Pikulski, J. J., & Brown, R. H. (1983). *Spinners.* Houghton Mifflin Reading Program. Boston: Houghton Mifflin.

Eberwein, L. (1982). Do dialect speakers' miscues influence comprehension? *Reading World, 21,* 255–263.

ECLDC/IRA. (1986). Early childhood and literacy development committee of IRA. Joint statement on literacy development and pre-first grade. *The Reading Teacher, 39*(8), 819–821.

Edwards, P. A., & Simpson, L. (1986). Bibliotherapy: A strategy for communication between parents and their children. *Journal of Reading, 30*(2), 819–821.

Edwards, T. J. (1969). Learning problems in cultural deprivation. (pp. 435–448). In A. Beery, T. C. Barrett, & W. R. Powell (Eds.), *Elementary reading instruction—selected materials.* Boston: Allyn & Bacon.

Ehri, L. C., Barron, R. W., & Feldman, J. M. (1978). *The recognition of words.* Newark, DE: International Reading Association.

Elkind, D. (1974). *Children and adolescents: Interpretive essays on Jean Piaget* (2nd ed.). New York: Oxford University.

Elkind, D. (1976). Cognitive development in reading. In H. Singer & R. B. Ruddell (Eds.), *Theoretical models and processes of reading* (2nd ed.) (p. 331–340). Newark, DE: International Reading Association.

Emery, A. (1965). *A spy in old west point.* Chicago: Rand McNally.

Erikson, F. D. (1968). "F" gets you Honkey! A new look at black dialect and the school. *Elementary English, 45,* 495–499, 517.

Esposito, D. (1973). Homogeneous and heterogeneous ability grouping: Principal findings and implications for evaluating and diagnosing more effective educational environments. *Review of Educational Research, 43,* 163–179.

Fay, L., & Anderson, P. S. (1981). *The Rand McNally reading program, level 11: Twirling parallels* (Teacher's Edition). Chicago: Riverside.

Fay, L., Ross, R. R., & LaPray, M. (1981). *The Rand McNally reading program, level 6: Red rock ranch* (Teacher's Edition). Chicago: Riverside.

Feeley, J. T. (1983, March). Help for the reading teacher: Dealing with the limited English proficient (LEP) child in the elementary classroom. *The Reading Teacher, 36*(7), 650–655.

Feininger, A. (1966). *Successful color photography*. Englewood Cliffs, NJ: Prentice-Hall.

Fenwick, S. I. (1968). Selecting and evaluating materials for recreational reading. In S. L. Sebasta (Ed.), *Ivory, apes, and peacocks: The literature point of view* (pp. 32–44). Newark, DE: International Reading Association.

Fillmore, C. (1968). The case for case. In E. Buch & R. Harms (Eds.), *Universals in linguistic theory* (pp. 1–88). New York: Holt, Rinehart & Winston.

Fiske, E. B. (1985, November 10). The controversy over bilingual education in America's schools: One language or two? *New York Times*, Section 12, Educational Fall Survey, p. 1–2.

Fiske, E. B. (1981, November 12). Reading analysis is called lacking. *New York Times* p. A19.

Flood, J. (Ed.). (1984). *Understanding reading comprehension*. Newark, DE: International Reading Association.

Foerster, L. M. (1974a). Idiomagic! *Elementary English, 51*, 125–127.

Foerster, L. M. (1974b). Language experiences for dialectically different black learners. *Elementary English, 51*, 193–197.

Foerster, L. M. (1975a). Kindergarten—what can it be? *Elementary English, 52*, 81–83.

Foerster, L. M. (1975b). Teach children to read body language. *Elementary English, 52*, 440–442.

Frase, L. T. (1977). Purpose in reading. In J. T. Guthrie (Ed.), *Cognition, curriculum, and comprehension* (pp. 42–64). Newark, DE: International Reading Association.

Fredericks, A. D. (1986). Mental imagery activities to improve comprehension. *The Reading Teacher, 40*(1), 78–81.

Frezise, R. L. (1978). What about a reading program for the gifted? *The Reading Teacher, 31*, 742–747.

Furth, H. G. (1970). *Piaget for teachers*. Englewood Cliffs, NJ: Prentice-Hall.

Furth, H. G. (1975). *Piaget and knowledge: Theoretical foundations* (2nd ed.). Englewood Cliffs, NJ: Prentice-Hall.

Gagne, R. M., & White, R. T. (1978). Structure and learning outcomes. *Review of Educational Research, 48*, 187–222.

Gelb, L. (1975). *Developing an experiential reading program*. Unpublished manuscript, Queens College, City University of New York, New York.

Gentry, J. R. (1982). An analysis of developmental spelling in GNYS AT WRK. *The Reading Teacher, 36*(2), 192–199.

Geyer, J. J. P. (1972). Comprehensive and partial models related to the reading process. *Reading Research Quarterly, 7*, 541–587.

Gillespie-Silver, P. (1979). *Teaching reading to children with special needs: An ecological approach*. Columbus, OH: Merrill.

Gillet, J. W., & Gentry, J. R. (1983, January). Bridges between nonstandard and standard English with extensions of dictated stories. *The Reading Teacher, 36*(4), 360–364.

Gillham, B. (1986). Equal opportunity and the language of school subjects. In B. Gillham (Ed.), *The language of school subjects* (pp. 1–7). London: Heinemann.

Glass, G. G. (1965). The teaching of word analysis through perceptual conditioning. In J. Figurel (Ed.), *Reading and inquiry*. Newark, DE: International Reading Association.

Glass, G. G., & Burton, E. H. (1973). How do they decode? Verbalizations and observed behaviors of successful decoders. *Education, 94*, 58–64.

Gombrich, E. H. (1974). The visual image. In D. R. Olson (Ed.), *Media and symbols: The forms of expression, communication, and education*. Chicago: University of Chicago Press.

Gonzales, P. C. (1981, February). How to begin language instruction for non-English speaking students. *Language Arts, 58*(2), 175–180.

Goodlad, J. L. (1969, April 19). The schools vs. education. *Saturday Review*, pp. 59ff.

Goodman, K. S. (1967). Reading: A psycholinguistic guessing game. *Journal of the Reading Specialist, 6*, 126–135.

Goodman, K. S. (1968). The psycholinguistic nature of the reading process. In K. S. Goodman (Ed.), *The psycholinguistic nature of the reading process* (pp. 13–26). Detroit: Wayne State University.

Goodman, K. S. (1969a). Analysis of oral reading miscues: Applied psycholinguistics. *Reading Research Quarterly, 5*, 9–30.

Goodman, K. S. (1969b). A communicative theory of the reading curriculum. *Elementary English, 46*, 290–298.

Goodman, K. S. (1969c). Let's dump the uptight model in English. *Elementary School Journal, 70*, 1–13.

Goodman, K. S. (1972). Orthography in a theory of reading instruction. *Elementary English, 49*, 1254–1261.

Goodman, K. S. (1984). The process and practice of reading. In A. C. Purves & O. Niles (Eds.), *Becoming readers in a complex society* (pp. 79–114). Eighty-third Yearbook of the National Society for the Study of Education, Part I. Chicago: The University of Chicago.

Goodman, K. S. (1985). On becoming a nation of readers: Comments. *Reading Today, 3*(3), 11.

Goodman, K. S. (1986). Basal readers: A call for action. *Language Arts, 63*(4), 358–363.

Goodman, Y. M. (1981). Test review: Concepts about print test. *The Reading Teacher, 34*, 445–448.

Goodman, Y. M., & Burke, C. L. (1972). *Reading miscue inventory: Manual.* New York: MacMillan.

Gorman, A. H. (1974). *Teachers and learners: The interactive process of education.* (2nd ed.). Boston: Allyn & Bacon.

Graesser, A. C. (1981). *Prose comprehension: Beyond the word.* New York: Spinger-Verlag.

Gray, W. M. (1978). A comparison of Piagetian theory and criterion referenced measurement. *Review of Educational Research, 48*, 223–249.

Greaney, V. (1986). Parental influences on reading. *The Reading Teacher, 39*(8), 811–818.

Grimes, L. (1981). Learned helplessness and attribution theory: Redefining children's learning problems. *Learning Disability Quarterly, 4*, 91–100.

Grundin, H. U. (1985). A commission of selective readers: A critique of *Becoming a nation of readers. The Reading Teacher, 39*, 262–266.

Guilford, J. P. (1967). *The nature of human intelligence.* New York: McGraw-Hill.

Guilford, J. P., & Hoepfner, R. (1971). *The analysis of intelligence.* New York: McGraw-Hill.

Gumperz, J. J., & Hernandez-Chavez, E. (1972). Bilingualism, dialectalism, and classroom interaction. In C. B. Cazden, V. P. John, & D. Hymes, (Eds.), *Functions of language in the classroom* (pp. 84–108). New York: Teachers College Press, Columbia University.

Guthrie, J. T. (1978). Inventing to read. *The Reading Teacher, 31*, 964–966.

Guthrie, J. T. (1980). The 1970's comprehension research. *The Reading Teacher, 33*, 880–882.

Guthrie, J. T. (1983a). Orchestration of lessons. *The Reading Teacher, 37*, 204–206.

Guthrie, J. T. (1983b). Students' perceptions of teaching. *The Reading Teacher, 37*, 94–96.

Guthrie, J. T. (1984). Contexts for testing. *The Reading Teacher, 38*(1), 108–110.

Hacker, C. J. (1980). From schema theory to classroom practice. *Language Arts, 57*, 866–871.

Haggard, M. R. (1985, December). An interactive strategies approach to content reading. *Journal of Reading, 29,* 204–210.

Hall, M. A. (1978). *The language experience approach for teaching reading: A research perspective* (2nd ed.). Newark, DE: International Reading Association.

Hall, M. A. (1972). Linguistically speaking, why language experience? *The Reading Teacher, 25,* 328–331.

Hall, M. A. (1981). *Teaching reading as a language experience* (3rd ed.). Columbus, OH: Merrill.

Halliday, M. (1975). *Learning how to mean: Explorations in the development of language.* New York: Elsevier.

Halliday, M., & Hasan, R. (1976). *Cohesion in English.* London: Longman.

Hamilton, S. F. (1983, November). Socialization for learning: Insights from ecological research in classrooms. *The Reading Teacher, 37,* 150–156.

Harber, J. R. (1981). Learning disability research: How far have we progressed? *Learning Disability Quarterly, 4,* 372–381.

Harker, W. J. (1973a). *Classroom implications from models of comprehension.* Paper presented at the Annual Meeting of the International Reading Association, Denver. (ERIC No. ED 089 226)

Harker, W. J. (1973b). Teaching comprehension: A task analysis approach. *Journal of Reading, 16,* 379–382.

Harris, A. J. (1980). An overview of reading disabilities and learning disabilities in the U.S. *The Reading Teacher, 33,* 420–425.

Harris, A. J. (1983). How many kinds of reading disabilities are there? In G. M. Senf & J. K. Torgesen (Eds.), *Annual Review of Learning Disabilities, 1,* 50–54.

Harste, J. (1978). Instructional implications of Rumelhart's model. In W. Diehl (Ed.), *Secondary reading: Theory and application.* Monographs of the 1978 Lily Conference on Secondary Reading, 1.

Harste, J. C., & Mikulecky, L. J. (1984). The context of literacy in our society. In A. C. Purves & O. Niles (Eds.), *Becoming readers in a complex society* (pp. 47–78). Eighty-third Yearbook of the National Society for the Study of Education, Part I. Chicago: University of Chicago.

Harste, J. C., Woodward, V. A., & Burke, C. L. (1984). *Language stories & literacy lessons.* Portsmouth, NH: Heinemann.

Hartman, N. C. & Hartman, R. K. (1973). Perceptual handicap or reading disability? *The Reading Teacher, 26,* 684–695.

Havighurst, R. J. (1964). Characteristics and needs of students that affect learning. In H. A. Robinson (Ed.), *Meeting individual differences in reading* (pp. 7–16). Chicago: University of Chicago.

Hechinger, F. M. (1980, September 16). Improvement in reading linked to broad support for the basics. *New York Times,* p. C5.

Hechinger, F. M. (1985, March 5). Tackling the textbook issue. *The New York Times,* p. C5.

Heimlich, J. E., & Pittelman, S. D. (1986). *Semantic mapping: Classroom applications.* Newark, DE: International Reading Association.

Henderson, E. H. (1986). Understanding children's knowledge of written language. In D. B. Yaden, Jr. & S. Templeton (Eds.), *Metalinguistic awareness and beginning literacy: Conceptualizing what it means to read and write* (pp. 65–77). Portsmouth, NH: Heinemann.

Henderson, E. H., & Beers, J. W. (Eds.). (1980). *Development and cognitive aspects of learning to spell: A reflection of word knowledge.* Newark, DE: International Reading Association.

Hennings, D. G. (1982, November/December). A writing approach to reading comprehension—schema theory in action. *Language Arts, 59,* 8–18.

Henry, G. H. (1974). *Teaching reading as concept development: Emphasis on affective thinking.* Newark, DE: International Reading Association.

Henry, M. (1947). *Misty of Chincoteague.* Chicago: Rand McNally.

Herber, H. L., & Nelson, J. B. (1975). Questioning is not the answer. *Journal of Reading, 18,* 512–517.

Hidi, S., & Anderson, V. (1986). Producing written summaries: Task demands, cognitive operations, and implications for instruction. *Review of Educational Research, 56*(4), 473–493.

Higgins, J. E. (1970). *Beyond words: Mystical fancy in children's literature.* New York: Teachers College Press, Columbia University.

Hittleman, C. G. (1983). *Peer conference groups and teacher written comments as influences on revision during the composing process of fourth grade students.* Unpublished doctoral dissertation, Hofstra University.

Hittleman, D. R. (1973). Seeking a psycholinguistic definition of readability. *The Reading Teacher, 26,* 783–789.

Hittleman, D. R. (1978). Readability, readability formulas, and cloze: Selecting instructional materials. *Journal of Reading, 22,* 117–122.

Hittleman, D. R. (1980). Adaptive assessment for nonacademic secondary reading. In D. J. Sawyer (Ed.), *Disabled readers: Insights, assessment, instruction* (pp. 74–81). Newark, DE: International Reading Association.

Hittleman, D. R. (1982a). *Peering at peer conferencing: A look at students' collaborative efforts to improve their reading and writing.* Paper presented at annual convention, International Reading Association, Chicago.

Hittleman, D. R. (1982b). *Students' collaborative efforts to improve their reading and writing.* Paper presented at the Ninth World Congress on Reading, International Reading Association, Dublin, Ireland.

Hittleman, D. R. (1983). *Peer conferencing as an aid to reading comprehension.* Paper presented at the annual convention, International Reading Association, Anaheim, CA.

Hittleman, D. R. (1984a). *Developing reading comprehension through peer conferencing.* Paper presented at Fifth Eastern Regional Conference, International Reading Association, Baltimore, MD.

Hittleman, D. R. (1984b). *Peer interaction groups as an aid to reading comprehension.* Paper presented at the annual conference, New York State Reading Association, Kiamesha Lake, New York.

Hittleman, D. R., & Robinson, H. A. (1975). Readability of high school text passages before and after revision. *Journal of Reading Behavior, 7,* 265–282.

Holbrook, H. T. (1985). ERIC/RCS report: Teachers working with parents. *Language Arts, 62*(8), 897–901.

Holdaway, D. (1986). The visual face of experience and language: A metalinguistic excursion. In D. B. Yaden, Jr. & S. Templeton (Eds.), *Metalinguistic awareness and beginning literacy: Conceptualizing what it means to read and write* (pp. 13–19). Portsmouth, NH: Heinemann.

Holt, S. L., & Vacca, J. L. (1981). Reading with a sense of writer, writing with a sense of reader. *Language Arts, 58,* 937–941.

Horowitz, R. A. (1979). Psychological effects of the "open classroom". *Review of Educational Research, 49,* 71–86.

Horowitz, R. (1985a). Text patterns: Part I. *Journal of Reading, 28*(5), 448–454.

Horowitz, R. (1985b). Text patterns: Part II. *Journal of Reading, 28*(6), 534–542.

Horton, R. J. (1972). *The construct validity of cloze procedure: An exploratory factor analysis of cloze, paragraph reading, and structure-of-intellect tests.* Unpublished doctoral dissertation, Hofstra University.

Huck, C. (1968). Reading literature critically. In S. L. Sebasta (Ed.), *Ivory, apes, and peacocks: Literature the point of view* (pp. 45–51). Newark, DE: International Reading Association.

Huck, C. S., & Kuhn, D. Y. (1968). *Children's literature in the elementary school.* (2nd ed.). New York: Holt, Rinehart & Winston.

Hutchins, R. (1973). *Tonka, the cave boy.* Chicago: Rand McNally.

Huus, H. (1975). Approaches to the use of literature in the reading program. In B. S. Schulwitz (Ed.), *Teachers, tangibles, techniques: comprehension of content in reading* (pp. 140–149). Newark, DE: International Reading Association.

Iannaccone, L. (1984). Reviewing the reviews on literacy and reasoning: Some selected themes and references. *Review of Educational Research, 54,* 682–688.

Irwin, J. W. (1986a). *Teaching reading comprehension processes.* Englewood Cliffs, NJ: Prentice-Hall.

Irwin, J. W. (Ed.). (1986b). *Understanding and teaching cohesion comprehension.* Newark, DE: International Reading Association.

Jacobs, L. B. (1971). Humanism in teaching reading. *Phi Delta Kappa, 464–*467.

Jaggar, A. M., Carrara, D. H., & Weiss, S. E. (1986). Research currents: The influence of reading on children's narrative writing (and vice versa). *Language Arts, 63*(3), 292–300.

Jalongo, M. R., & Bromley, K. D. (1984, May). Developing linguistic competence through song picture books. *The Reading Teacher, 37*(9), 840–845.

Jenkins, E. C. (1973). Multi-ethnic literature: Promise and problems. *Elementary English, 50,* 693–699.

Jenkins, J. R., & Pany, D. (1981). Instructional variables in reading comprehension. In J. T. Guthrie (Ed.), *Comprehension and teaching: Research reviews* (pp. 163–202). Newark, DE: International Reading Association.

Johns, J. (1980). First graders' concepts about print. *Reading Research Quarterly, 15,* 529–549.

Johnson, B., Schneider, M., & German, D. (1983). The debate over learning disability vs. reading disability: A survey of practitioners' populations and remedial methods. *Learning Disability Quarterly, 6*(3), 258–264.

Johnson, D. D., & Baumann, J. F. (1984). Word identification. In P. D. Pearson (Ed.), *Handbook of reading research* (pp. 583–608). New York: Longman.

Johnson, D. D., & von Hoff Johnson, B. (1986). Highlighting vocabulary in inferential comprehension instruction. *Journal of Reading, 29* (7), 622–633.

Johnson, J. E. (1979). Back to basics? We've been there 150 years. *The Reading Teacher, 32,* 644–666.

Johnson, R. E. (1975). Meaning in complex learning. *Review of Educational Research, 45,* 425–459.

Johnston, P. H. (1984). Assessment in reading. In P. D. Pearson (Ed.), *Handbook of reading research* (pp. 147–184). New York: Longman.

Jones, J. P. (1972). *Intersensory transfer, perceptual sifting, modal preference and reading.* Newark, DE: International Reading Association.

Jones, M. B., & Pikulski, E. C. (1974). Cloze for the classroom. *Journal of Reading, 17,* 423–438.

Jongsma, E. A. (1980). *Cloze instruction research: A second look.* Newark, DE: International Reading Association.

Karlsen, B., Madden, R., & Gardner, E. F. (1976). *Manual for administering and interpreting the Stanford Diagnostic Reading Test, green level.* New York: Psychological Corporation.

Kavale, K., & Nye, C. (1981). Identification criteria for learning disabilities: A survey of the research literature. *Learning Disability Quarterly, 4,* 383–388.

Kean, J. M., & Personke, C. (1976). *The language arts: Teaching and learning in the elementary school.* New York: St. Martin's Press.

Kimmel, S., & MacGinitie, W. H. (1985). Helping students revise hypotheses while reading. *The Reading Teacher, 38*(8), 768–771.

King, F. et al. (1971). *The social studies and our country: Concepts in social science.* River Forest, IL: Laidlaw.

Kingston, A. J. (1969). Do the advantages of the ungraded schools outweigh the disadvantages? In N. B. Smith (Ed.), *Current issues in reading* (pp. 308–316). Newark, DE: International Reading Association.

Kintsch, W. (1979). On modeling comprehension. *Educational Psychologist, 14,* 3–14.

Kintsch, W. (1980). Learning from text, levels of comprehension, or: Why anyone would read a story anyway. *Poetics, 9,* 87–98.

Kintsch, W., & van Dijk, T. A. (1978). Toward a model of text comprehension and production. *Psychological Review, 85,* 363–394.

Koss, H. G. (1972). Relevancy and children's literature. *Elementary English, 49,* 991–992.

Kumar, V. D. (1971). The structures of human memory and some educational implications. *Review of Educational Research, 41,* 379–418.

Labov, W. (1966). Some sources of reading problems for Negro speakers of non-standard English. Unpublished paper, Columbia University. (ERIC ED 010 688)

Labuda, M. (Ed.). (1974). *Creative reading for gifted learners.* Newark, DE: International Reading Association.

Lacey, P. A., & Weil, P. E. (1975). Number-reading-language. *Language Arts, 52,* 776–782.

Ladevich, L. (1974). Determining literary quality in children's literature. *Elementary English, 51,* 983–986.

Lear, E. (1966). *The complete nonsense book.* New York: Dodd, Mead.

Lee, D., & Allen, R. V. (1963). *Learning to read through experience* (2nd ed.). New York: Appleton-Century-Crofts.

Lehr, F. (1981). Integrating reading and writing instruction. *The Reading Teacher, 43,* 958–961.

Lehr, F. (1986). Invented spelling and language development. *The Reading Teacher, 39*(5), 452–455.

Leigh, J. E. (1980). Whole language approaches: Premises and possibilities. *Learning Disability Quarterly, 3,* 62–69.

Lerner, J. W. (1985). *Children and learning disabilities: Theories, diagnosis, and teaching strategies* (4th ed.). Boston: Houghton Mifflin.

Linden, M., & Wittrock, M. C. (1981). The teaching of reading comprehension according to the model of generative learning. *Reading Research Quarterly, 14,* 44–57.

Lindfors, J. W. (1980). *Children's language and learning.* Englewood Cliffs, NJ: Prentice-Hall.

Lindsay, P. H., & Norman, D. A. (1977). *Human information processing: An introduction to psychology* (2nd ed.). New York: Academic Press.

Lipa, S. E. (1984). Reading disability: A new look at an old issue. In J. K. Torgesen & G. M. Senf (Eds.), *Annual Review of Learning Disabilities, 2,* 51–55.

Lipson, M., & Wixson, K. K. (1986). Reading disability research: An interactionist perspective. *Review of Educational Research, 56*(1), 111–136.

Lloyd, H. M. (1969). Progress in developmental reading for today's disadvantaged. In A. Beery, T. C. Barrett, & W. R. Powell (Eds.), *Elementary reading instruction—selected materials* (pp. 529–535). Boston: Allyn & Bacon.

Lohmann, I. (1968). Reactions to using language experience in beginning reading. In E. C. Vilscek (Ed.), *A decade of innovation: Approaches to beginning reading* (pp. 24–29). Newark, DE: International Reading Association.

Lucas, C., & Borders, D. (1987, Spring). Language diversity and classroom discourse. *American Educational Research Journal, 24*(2), 119–141.

Lundsteen, S. W. (1974a). Levels of meaning in reading. *The Reading Teacher, 28,* 268–272.

Lundsteen, S. W. (1974b). Questioning to develop creative problem solving. *Elementary English, 51,* 645–650.

Lundsteen, S. W. (1976). *Children learn to communicate: Language arts through creative problem solving.* Englewood Cliffs, NJ: Prentice-Hall.

Lutz, E. (1986). ERIC/RCS report: Invented spelling and spelling development. *Language Arts, 63*(7), 742–744.

Lynch, J. (1986). *Building the global dimension of the multicultural curriculum.* Paper presented at the conference of Swann and the Global Dimension in Education, Bristol, England. (ERIC Document Reproduction No. ED 272 520)

Lyons, K. (1984). Criterion referenced reading comprehension tests: New forms with old ghosts. *The Journal of Reading, 27,* 293–298.

MacGinitie, W. H. (1969). Evaluating readiness for learning to read: A critical review and evaluation of research. *Reading Research Quarterly, 4,* 396–410.

MacGinitie, W. H. (1973). What are we testing? In W. H. MacGinitie (Ed.), *Assessment problems in reading* (pp. 1–7). Newark, DE: International Reading Association.

Mackey, W. F. (1973). Language & acculturation. In R. R. Fox (Ed.), *Essays on teaching as a second language and as a second dialect* (pp. 8–22). Urbana, IL: National Council of Teachers of English.

Maeroff, G. I. (1981, September 6). Reading results give the schools a lift. *New York Times* p. A18.

Maffei, A. C. (1973). Reading analysis in mathematics. *Journal of Reading, 16,* 546–549.

Malmstrom, J. (1977). *Understanding language: A primer for the language arts teacher.* New York: St. Martin's.

Manzo, A. V. (1969). The ReQuest procedure. *Journal of Reading, 13*(2), 123–126, 163.

Manzo, A. V. (1985). Expansion modules for the ReQuest, CAT, GRP, and REAP reading/study procedures. *Journal of Reading, 28*(6), 498–502.

Manzo, A. V., & Sherk, J. K. (1971). Some generalizations and strategies for guiding vocabulary learning. *Journal of Reading Behavior, 4,* 78–89.

Marksheffel, N. D. (1969). Reading in the content areas: A framework for improvement. In H. A. Robinson & E. L. Thomas (Eds.), *Fusing reading skills and content* (pp. 127–135). Newark, DE: International Reading Association.

Marquardt, W. F. (1965). Linguistics and reading instruction: Contribution and implications. In H. A. Robinson (Ed.), *Developments in reading* (pp. 112–121). Chicago: University of Chicago.

Marshall, H. H. (1981). Open classrooms: Has the term outlived its usefulness? *Review of Educational Research, 51,* 181–192.

Mason, J. (1984a). Early reading from a developmental perspective. In P. D. Pearson (Ed.), *Handbook of reading research* (pp. 505–545). New York: Longman.

Mason, J. (1984b). Schema-theoretic view of the reading process as a basis for comprehension instruction. In G. G. Duffy, L. R. Roehler, & J. Mason (Eds.), *Comprehension instruction: Perspectives and suggestions* (pp. 26–38). New York: Longman.

Maya, A. Y. (1979). Write to read: Improving reading through creative writing. *The Reading Teacher, 32,* 813–817.

Mayer, J. E. (1975). Evaluating reading readiness: A reply. *Elementary English, 52,* 343–345.

McConnell, B. B. (1985). *Basic education for limited English proficient students: The BELEPS program, 1982–1985,* Final Report. Yakima, WA: Yakima School District Number 7. (ERIC Document Reproduction Services No. ED 272 356)

McCorduck, P. (1985). *The universal machine: Confessions of a technological optimist.* New York: McGraw-Hill.

McDonell, G. (1975). Relating language to early reading experiences. *The Reading Teacher, 28,* 438–444.

McKeown, M. G., Beck, I. L., Omanson, R. C., & Pople, M. T. (1985). Some effects of the nature and frequency of vocabulary instruction on the knowledge and use of words. *Reading Research Quarterly, 20*(5), 522–535.

McLuhan, M. (1964). *Understanding media.* New York: Signet.

Meeks, L. B., & Heit, P. (1984). Health: Focus on you, K–8. Columbus, OH: Merrill.

Meyen, E. L. (1981). Developing instructional units: For the regular and special teacher (3rd ed.). Dubuque, IA: William C. Brown.

Michaelis, J. O. (1972). *Social studies for children in a democracy: Recent trends and developments* (5th ed.). Englewood Cliffs, NJ: Prentice-Hall.

Mickish, V. (1974). Children's perceptions of written word boundaries. *Journal of Reading Behavior, 6,* 19–21.

Miller, G. (Ed.). (1973). *Communication, language, and meaning: Psychological perspectives.* New York: Basic Books.

Miller, J.W. (1974). Linguistics and comprehension. *Elementary English, 51,* 853–854, 857.

Mishler, E. G. (1972). Implication of teacher strategies for language and cognition: Observation in first grade classroom (pp. 267–298). In C. B. Cazden, V. P. Johns, & D. Hymes (Eds.), *Functions of language in the classroom.* New York: Teachers College Press, Columbia University.

Moe, A. J., & Irwin, J. W. (1986). Cohesion, coherence and comprehension. In J. W. Irwin (Ed.), *Understanding and teaching cohesion comprehension* (pp. 3–8). Newark, DE: International Reading Association.

Moffett, J. (1968). *Teaching the universe of discourse.* Boston: Houghton Mifflin.

Moffett, J., & Wagner, B. J. (1976). *Student centered language arts and reading K–13: A handbook for teachers* (2nd ed.). Boston: Houghton Mifflin.

Monteith, M. K. (1980). Black English, teacher attitudes, and reading. *Language Arts, 57,* 908–912.

Monteleone, T. F. (1974). The thing from Ennis Rock. In R. Elwood (Ed.), *More science fiction tales* (p. 93). Chicago: Rand McNally.

Morine, G., & Morine, H. (1973). Teaching. In J. L. Goodlad & H. G. Shane (Eds.), *The elementary school in the U.S.* (pp. 272–298). Seventy-second Yearbook of the National Society for the Study of Education. Chicago: University of Chicago.

Moustafa, M., & Penrose, J. (1985, March). Comprehensible input PLUS the language experience approach: Reading instruction for limited English speaking students. *The Reading Teacher, 38*(7), 640–647.

National Assessment of Educational Progress (NAEP). (1985). *The reading report card: Progress toward excellence in our schools.* Champaign, IL: University of Illinois.

National Assessment of Education Progress (NAEP). (1986). *The reading report card: Progress toward excellence in our schools. Trends in reading over four national assessments, 1971–1984.* Princeton, NJ: Educational Testing Service.

Nelson, G. L. (1987, February). Culture's role in reading comprehension: A schema theoretical approach. *Journal of Reading, 30*(5), 424–429.

Nelson-Herber, J. (1986). Expanding and refining vocabulary in content areas. *Journal of Reading, 29*(7), 626–633.

Neuman, S. B. (1980). Television: Its effect on reading and school achievement. *The Reading Teacher, 33,* 801–805.

New York Times. (1987, January 12). A teacher shops for science, p. A19.

New York Times. (1987, January 13). Dyslexia's cause reported found, p. C1.

Nieto, S. (1986). Equity in education: The case for bilingual education. *Interracial Books for Children Bulletin, 17,* 4–8.

Northcut, N., et al. (1975). *Adult functional competence.* Austin: Adult Performance Level Project, Industrial and Business Training Bureau, University of Texas.

Nuthall, G., & Snook, I. (1973). Contemporary models of training. In R. M. W. Travers (Ed.), *Second handbook of research on teaching* (pp. 47–76). Chicago: Rand McNally.

Oliver, M. E. (1970). Organizing for reading instruction. *Elementary School Journal, 71,* 97–104.

Olmo, B. G. (1975). Teaching students to ask questions. *Language Arts, 52,* 116–119.

Olsen, J. L., & Mealor, D. J. (1981). Learning disabilities identification: Do researchers have the answer? *Learning Disability Quarterly, 4,* 389–392.

Olson, D. R. (1981). Writing: The divorce of the author from the text. In B. M. Kroll & R. J. Vann (Eds.), *Exploring speaking-writing relationships: Connections and contrasts* (pp. 99–110). Urbana, IL: National Council of Teachers of English.

Ortony, A. (1984). Understanding figurative language. In D. R. Pearson, R. Barr, M. L. Kamil, & P. Masenthal (Eds.), *Handbook of reading research* (pp. 453–478). New York: Longman.

Padak, M. D. (1981). The Language and educational needs of children who speak Black English. *The Reading Teacher, 35,* 144–151.

Page, W. D. (1976). Pseudocues, supercues, and comprehension. *Reading World, 4,* 232–238.

Painter, H. (1975). Literature develops reading skills. In B. S. Schulwitz (Ed.), *Teachers, tangibles, techniques: Comprehension of content in reading* (pp. 150–157). Newark, DE: International Reading Association.

Palincsar, A. S. (1984). The quest for meaning from expository text: A teacher-guided journey. In G. G. Duffy, L. R. Roehler, & J. Mason (Eds.), *Comprehension instruction: Perspectives and suggestions* (pp. 251–264). New York: Longman.

Palincsar, A. S., & Brown, A. L. (1986). Interactive teaching to promote independent learning from text. *The Reading Teacher, 39*(8), 771–777.

Pauk, W. (1973). Two essential study skills for the community college student. *Reading World, 12,* 239–245.

Pearson, P. D. (1985). Changing the face of reading comprehension instruction. *The Reading Teacher, 38,* 724–738.

Pearson, P. D., & Johnson, D. D. (1978). *Teaching reading comprehension.* New York: Holt, Rinehart & Winston.

Pearson, P. D. & Tierney, R. J. (1984). On becoming a thoughtful reader: Learning to read like a writer. In A. C. Purves & O. Niles (Eds.), *Becoming readers in a complex society* (pp. 144–173). Eighty-third Yearbook of the National Society for the Study of Education, Part I. Chicago: The University of Chicago.

Pehrsson, R. (1975). *The OP–IN procedure.* Paper presented at the Preconvention Institute, Psycholinguistics and Reading Instruction, New York State Reading Association Annual Conference, Kiamisha Lake, New York.

Pehrsson, R. S. (1985). *The OP–IN procedure.* Unpublished manuscript. Pocatello, ID: Idaho State University.

Pehrsson, R. S., & Robinson, H. A. (1985). *The semantic organizer approach to writing and reading instruction.* Rockville, MD: Aspen Systems Corporation.

Pezdek, K. (1980). Arguments for a constructive approach to comprehension and memory. In J. Danks & K. Pezdek (Eds.), *Reading and understanding* (pp. 40–73). Newark, DE: International Reading Association.

Pikulski, J. J. (1974a). Assessment of the pre-reading skills: A review of frequently employed measures. *Reading World, 13,* 171–197.

Pikulski, J. J. (1974b). Criterion referenced measures for clinical evaluation. *Reading World, 14,* 116–128.

Pikulski, J. J. (1976). Review of *A language for life.* A report of the Committee of Inquiry, Sir Alan Bullock, Chr. London: Her Majesty's Stationery Office, 1975. *The Reading Teacher, 29,* 409–410.

Postman, N. (1973). The politics of reading. In R. Winkeljohan (Ed.), *The politics of reading: Point-counterpoint* (pp. 1–11). Newark, DE: International Reading Association/ ERIC-RCS.

Powers, A. (1981). Sharing a language experience library with the whole school. *The Reading Teacher, 34,* 892–895.

Randhawa, B. S., & Fu, L. L. W. (1973). Assessment and effect of some classroom environmental variables. *Review of Education Research, 43,* 303–321.

Ratekin, N., Simpson, M. L., Alvermann, D. E., & Dishner, E. K. (1985). Why teachers resist content reading instruction. *Journal of Reading, 25*(5), 432–437.

Raven, R., & Salzer, R. (1971). Piaget and reading instruction. *The Reading Teacher, 24,* 630–639.

Reed, L. (1976). Multi-ethnic literature and the elementary school curriculum. *Language Arts, 53,* 256–261.

Reed, S. (1985, November 10). Bilingualism: What the research shows. *New York Times,* Section 12, Education Fall Survey, pp. 48–49.

Reid, D. K. & Hresko, W. P. (1981). *A cognitive approach to learning disabilities.* New York: McGraw-Hill.

Reutzel, D. R. (1985). Story maps improve comprehension. *The Reading Teacher, 38*(4), 400–404.

Reutzel, D. R. (1986). The reading basal: A sentence combining composing book. *The Reading Teacher, 40*(2), 194–199.

Robinson, H. A. (1969). Reading in the total school curriculum. In J. A. Figurel (Ed.), *Reading and realism* (pp. 1–8). Newark, DE: International Reading Association.

Robinson, H. A. (1978). *Facilitating successful reading strategies.* Paper presented at the Annual Conference of the International Reading Association, Houston, TX.

Robinson, H. A. (1983). *Teaching reading, writing and study strategies: The content areas* (3rd ed.). Boston: Allyn & Bacon.

Robinson, H. M. (1975). Children's behavior while reading. In W. D. Page (Ed.), *Help for the reading teacher: New Directions in research* (pp. 9–22). Urbana, IL: National Conference on Research in English and ERIC Clearinghouse on Reading and Communication Skills.

Rohter, L. (1985, November 10). The politics of bilingualism. *New York Times,* Section 12, Education Fall Survey, pp. 3, 77.

Rohter, L. (1986, November 24). Two systems of bilingual education, but which is best? *New York Times,* p. B1.

Rosenblatt, L. M. (1978). *The reader, the text, the poem: The transactional theory of the literary work.* Carbondale, IL: Southern Illinois University.

Rosenshine, B., & Stevens, R. (1984). Classroom instruction in reading. In P. D. Pearson (Ed.), *Handbook of reading research* (pp. 745–798). New York: Longman.

Rude, R. T. (1973). Readiness tests: Implications for early childhood. *The Reading Teacher, 26,* 572–580.

Rumelhart, D. E. (1976). Toward an interactive model of reading. (Technical Report No. 56). San Diego: Center for Human Information Processing, University of California.

Rumelhart, D. E. (1981). Schemata: The building blocks of cognition. In J. T. Guthrie (Ed.), *Comprehension and reading* (pp. 3–26). Newark, DE: International Reading Association.

Rupley, W. H., & Robeck, C. (1978). Black dialect and reading achievement. *The Reading Teacher, 31,* 598–601.

Ryan, A. B., & Semmel, M. L. (1969). Reading as a constructive language process. *Reading Research Quarterly, 5,* 59–83.

Samuels, S. J., & Kamil, M. L. (1984). Models of the reading process. In P. D. Pearson (Ed.), *Handbook of reading research* (pp. 185–224). New York: Longman.

Santa, C. M., & Hayes, B. L. (Eds.). (1981). *Children's prose comprehension: Research and practice.* Newark, DE: International Reading Association.

Sapir, E. (1967). Communication. In J. P. DeCecco (Ed.), *The psychology of language, thought, and instruction* (pp. 75–78). New York: Holt, Rinehart & Winston.

Sargent, E. E., Huus, H. & Andreson, O. (1970). *How to read a book.* Newark, DE: International Reading Association.

Satz, P., and Sparrow, S. S. (1970). Specific developmental dyslexia: A theoretical formulation. In D. J. Bakker & P. Satz (Eds.), *Specific reading disability—advances in theory and method* (pp. 17–40). Rotterdam: University of Rotterdam.

Saville-Troike, M. R. (1973). TESOL: Methods of materials in early childhood education. In R. P. Fox (Ed.), *Essays on teaching English as a second dialect* (pp. 102–106). Urbana, IL: National Council of Teachers of English.

Sawyer, D. J. (1975). Readiness factors for reading: A different view. *The Reading Teacher, 28,* 620–624.

Schafer, J. C. (1981). The linguistic analysis of spoken and written texts. In B. M. Kroll & R. J. Vann (Eds.), *Exploring speaking-writing relationships: Connections and contrasts* (pp. 1–31). Urbana, IL: National Council of Teachers of English.

Schaff, A. (1973). *Language and cognition.* New York: McGraw-Hill.

Schatz, E. K., & Baldwin, R. S. (1986). Context clues are unreliable predictors of word meanings. *Reading Research Quarterly, 21*(4), 439–453.

Schmitt, E. (1985, November 10). The three teaching methods in bilingual classes. *New York Times,* Section 12, Educational Fall Survey, pp. 50–51.

Schwartz, J. I. (1975). A language experience approach to beginning reading. *Elementary English, 52,* 320–324.

Schwartz, J. I. (1982). Dialect interference in the attainment of literacy. *Journal of Reading, 25,* 440–446.

Schwartz, R. M., & Raphael, T. E. (1985). Concept of definition: A key to improving students' vocabulary. *The Reading Teacher, 39*(2), 198–205.

Searls, D. T., Mead, N. A., & Ward, B. (1985). The relationship of students' reading skills to TV watching, leisure time reading, and homework. *Journal of Reading, 29*(2), 158–162.

Shepard, L. A., & Smith, M. L. (1983). An evaluation of the identification of learning disabled students in Colorado. *Learning Disability Quarterly, 6*(2), 115–127.

Shepherd, D. L. (1969). Reading and science: Problems peculiar to the area. In H. A. Robinson & E. L. Thomas (Eds.), *Fusing reading skills and content* (pp. 151–161). Newark, DE: International Reading Association.

Shepherd, T., & Iles, L. B. (1976). What is bibliotherapy? *Language Arts, 53*, 569–571.

Shook, R. (1986). The two-brain theory: A critique. *English Education, 18*(3), 173–183.

Shoop, M. (1986). InQuest: A listening and reading comprehension strategy. *The Reading Teacher, 39*(7), 670–674.

Silva, A. D. (1987, May). *Bilingual learners and becoming a nation of readers.* Paper presented at the International Reading Association Convention, Anaheim, CA.

Simons, H. D. (1971). Reading comprehension: The need for a new perspective. *Reading Research Quarterly, 6*, 338–363.

Sinatra, R. C., Stahl-Gemake, J., & Berg, D. N. (1984). Improved reading comprehension of disabled readers through semantic mapping. *The Reading Teacher, 38*(1), 22–29.

Sleeter, C. E. (1986, September). Learning disabilities: The social construction of a special education category. *Exceptional Children, 53*, 46–54.

Sloan, G. D. (1985). *The child as critic: Teaching literature in the elementary school* (2nd ed.). New York: Teachers College Press, Columbia University.

Slobin, D. (1979). *Psycholinguistics* (2nd ed.). Glenview, IL: Scott Foresman.

Smith, C. R. (1985, November). Learning disabilities: Past and present. *Journal of Learning Disabilities, 18*(9), 517–523.

Smith, F. (1971). *Overloading the competent reader.* Paper presented at the National Council of Teachers of English Annual Conference, Las Vegas. (ERIC No. 085 674)

Smith, F. (1972). Phonology and orthography: Reading and writing. *Elementary English, 49*, 1075–1088.

Smith, F. (1975b). The role of prediction in reading. *Elementary English, 52*, 305–311.

Smith, F. (1975a). *Comprehension and learning.* New York: Holt, Rinehart & Winston.

Smith, F. (1978). *Understanding reading: A psycholinguistic analysis of reading and learning to read* (2nd ed.). New York: Holt, Rinehart & Winston.

Smith, F. (1982). *Writing and writer.* New York: Holt, Rinehart & Winston.

Smith, F. (1983). Reading like a writer. *Language Arts, 60*, 558–567.

Smith, J. A. (1972). *Adventures in communication: Language arts methods.* Boston: Allyn & Bacon.

Smith, N. B. (1960). Literature for space-age children. *Education Magazine*, 1–4.

Smith, N. B. (1964a). Patterns of writing in different subject areas: Part I. *Journal of Reading, 8*, 31–37.

Smith, N. B. (1964b). Patterns of writing in different subject areas: Part II. *Journal of Reading, 8*, 97–102.

Sorenson, N. L. (1985). Basal reading vocabulary instruction: A critique and suggestions. *The Reading Teacher, 39*(1), 80–85.

Spiegel, D. L., & Fitzgerald, J. (1986). Improving reading comprehension through instruction about story parts. *The Reading Teacher, 39*(7), 676–682.

Spiro, R. J., Bruce, B. C., & Brewer, W. F. (1980). *Theoretical issues in reading comprehension.* Hillsdale, NJ: Lawrence Erlbaum.

Spiro, R. J., & Myers, A. (1984). Individual differences and underlying cognitive processes in reading. In P. D. Pearson (Ed.), *Handbook of reading research* (pp. 471–501). New York: Longman.

Stahl, S. A., & Fairbanks, M. M. (1986). The effects of vocabulary instruction: A model-based meta-analysis. *Review of Educational Research, 56*(1), 72–110.

Stahl, S. A., & Vancil, S. J. (1986). Discussion is what makes semantic maps work in vocabulary instruction. *The Reading Teacher, 40*(1), 62–67.

Stauffer, R. G. (1971). The quest for maturity in reading. In C. Braun (Ed.), *Language, reading, and the communication process* (pp. 9–19). Newark, DE: International Reading Association.

Stauffer, R. G. (1975). *Directing the reading–thinking process*. New York: Harper & Row.

Stauffer, R. G., & Pikulski, J. J. (1974). A comparison and measure of oral language growth. *Elementary English, 51*, 1151–1155.

Stewart, W. A. (1966). Nonstandard speech patterns. *Baltimore Bulletin of Education, 52–66*.

Stipek, D. J., & Weisz, J. R. (1981). Perceived personal control and academic achievement. *Review of Educational Research, 51*, 101–138.

Stotsky, S. (1983). Research on reading/writing relationships: A synthesis and suggested directions. *Language Arts, 60* (5), 627–642.

Stotsky, S. (1984). Research on reading/writing relationships: A synthesis and suggested directions. In J. M. Jensen (Ed.), *Composing and comprehending* (pp. 7–22). Urbana, IL: National Conference on Research in English and ERIC Clearing House on Reading and Communication Skills.

Strahan, D., & Herlihy, J. G. (1985). A model for analyzing textbook content. *Journal of Reading, 25*(5), 438–447.

Strang, R. (1969). *Diagnostic teaching of reading* (2nd ed.). New York: McGraw-Hill.

Strange, M. (1980). Instructional implications of a conceptual theory of reading comprehension. *The Reading Teacher, 33*, 391–397.

Strickland, D. S. (1972). Black is beautiful, white is right. *Elementary English, 49*, 200–223.

Suhor, C. (1984). The role of print as a medium in our society. In A. C. Purves, & O. Niles, (Eds.), *Becoming readers in a complex society* (pp. 16–46). Eighty-third Yearbook of the National Society for the Study of Education, Part I. Chicago: University of Chicago.

Sund, R. B., Adams, D. K., Hackett, J. K., & Moyer, R. H. (1985). *Accent on science, K–6*. Columbus, OH: Merrill.

Syzuki, B. H. (1984). *Socioeconomic cultural pluralism: Its meaning for the future and education*. San Diego State University: California National Origin Desegregation Assistance (Lau) Center. (ERIC Document Reproduction No. 272 587)

Taylor, H. G., Satz, P., & Friel, J. (1979). Developmental dyslexia in relation to other childhood reading disorders: Significance and clinical utility. *Reading Research Quarterly, 15*, 84–101.

Terry, A. (1972). *Children's poetry preferences: A national survey of upper elementary grades*. Urbana, IL: National Council of Teachers of English.

Thomas, A. (1979). Learned helplessness and expectancy factors: Implications for research in learning disabilities. *Review of Educational Research, 49*, 208–221.

Thomas, K. F. (1985). Early reading as a social interaction process. *Language Arts, 62*(5), 469–475.

Thompson, S. J. (1986). Teaching metaphoric language: An instructional strategy. *Journal of Reading, 30*(2), 105–109.

Thompson, W. I. (1972). *At the edge of history: Speculations on the transformation of culture*. New York: Harper & Row.

Toothaker, R. (1974). Developing an action-packed vocabulary. *Elementary English, 51*, 861–897.

Torrence, E. P., & Myers, R. E. (1972). *Creative learning and Teaching*. New York: Dodd, Mead.

Unsworth, L. (1984). Meeting individual needs through flexible within-class grouping of pupils. *The Reading Teacher, 38*, 298–304.

Vilscek, E. C. (1968). What research has shown about the language experience program. In E. C. Vilscek (Ed.), *Decade of innovative approaches to beginning reading* (pp. 9–23). Newark, DE: International Reading Association.

Vogel, S. A., & McGrady, H. J. (1975). Recognition of melody patterns in good and poor readers. *Elementary English, 52,* 414–418.

Vygotsky, L. S. (1978). *Mind in society: The development of higher psychological processes.* M. Cole, V. John-Steiner, S. Scribner, & E. Souberman (Eds.). Cambridge, MA: Harvard University.

Vygotsky, L. S. (1962). *Thought and language.* (E. Hanfmann & G. Vakar, Trans.). Cambridge, MA: MIT with Wiley.

Wagner, S. R., & Wilde, J. (1973). Learning styles: Can we grease the cogs in cognition? *Proceedings of the Claremont Reading Conference,* 135–141.

Wardhaugh, R. (1977). *Introduction to linguistics* (2nd ed.). New York: McGraw-Hill.

Waugh, R. P., & Howell, K. W. (1975). Teaching modern syllabication. *The Reading Teacher, 29,* 20–25.

Wehmeyer, L. M. (1975). It must be right. . .I read it in the encyclopedia! *Language Arts, 52,* 841–842.

Weinstein, C. S. (1979). The physical environment of the school: A review of the research. *Review of Educational Research, 49,* 577–610.

Werner, L. M. (1987, January 15). Reagan bill asks flexibility in funds for bilingual education. *New York Times,* p. A18.

Wheat, T. (1974). Reading and the culturally diverse. *Elementary English, 51,* 251–256.

Wiemann, J. M., & Backlund, P. (1980). Current theory and research in communicative competence. *Review of Educational Research, 50,* 185–199.

Wiig, E. H., & Semmel, E. (1984). *Language assessment and intervention for the learning disabled* (2nd ed.). Columbus, OH: Merrill.

Williamson, L. E. (1974). *Teach concepts, not words.* Paper presented at the Annual Meeting of the Western College Reading Association, Oakland, CA. (ERIC No. ED 092 925)

Willig, A. C. (1985, Fall). A meta-analysis of selected studies on the effectiveness of bilingual education. *Review of Educational Research, 55*(3), 269–318.

Wilson, M. J. (1981). A review of recent research on the integration of reading and writing. *The Reading Teacher, 34,* 896–901.

Witty, P. A. (1971). *Reading for the gifted and the creative student.* Newark, DE: International Reading Association.

Wixson, K. K. (1986). Vocabulary instruction and children's comprehension of basal stories. *Reading Research Quarterly, 21*(3), 317–329.

Wong, B. Y. L. (1985). Self-questioning instructional research: A review. *Review of Educational Research, 55*(2), 227–268.

Wood, B. S. (1981). *Children and communication: Verbal and nonverbal language development* (2nd ed.). Englewood Cliffs, NJ: Prentice-Hall.

Wood, K. D. (1984). Probable passages: a writing strategy. *The Reading Teacher, 37*(6), 496–499.

Ysseldyke, J. E., et al. (1982). Declaring students eligible for learning disability services: Why bother with the data? *Learning Disability Quarterly, 5,* 37–44.

Zuck, L. V. (1974). Some questions about the teaching of syllabication rules. *The Reading Teacher, 27,* 583–588.

Author Index

Subject Index

The Author

Dan Hittleman is an Associate Professor of Educational and Community Programs in the School of Education, Queens College of the City University of New York. He teaches courses concerned with the teaching and learning of reading and writing, the evaluation of student learning, the interpretation and evaluation of research, and the adaptation of curricula for students in special education and regular learning environments. Dr. Hittleman is Chairperson of the International Reading Association's Print Media Award committee and serves as a member of several professional associations including the Special Education and Reading Committee of the New York State Reading Association. In addition to his text on developmental reading, Dan has co-authored two other texts: *Teaching Reading Comprehension: A Review of the Research*, to be published by the International Reading Association, and *Strategies for Reading*, published by Allyn and Bacon. He has also served as past president of the New York State Reading Association.